Sailing and Other Adventures on the Redneck Riviera

Gary William Gebhardt

Copyright © 2022

All Rights Reserved

Table of Contents

Dedication

To my family and friends that were part of many of these adventures and to my grandchildren. Elizabeth, Emma, Amelia, Macie, Zen and Samadhi.

Acknowledgments

Tom Prohaska, my business partner, friend and travelling companion on many of these adventures. Tom helped in many ways to write this book.

About the Author

This is a story that starts with the attack on Pearl Harbor a rude awakening of Gary's curiosity of what was going on in the world outside of his house. It put him on a course to seek information, knowledge, and adventure. This book covers some of the many adventures that he experienced during the next eight decades of his life.

Introduction

Everyone has a story to tell; this is the story of my grand adventure and what started me on it. We all have memories of good and bad times in our lives, but that's not what I'm talking about: what I'm driving at is what triggered the memorable moment in your life that put you on course of your grand adventure.

Mine started on the 8th of December, 1941, three days after my 5th birthday. I was sitting around the radio with my mom, Margaret, and my dad, Bill, listening to the evening news. Suddenly there was a news flash from our 32nd president, Franklin Delano Roosevelt, telling us that we were at war with Japan for their attack on Pearl Harbor. I could tell something terribly important was happening by the way my parents reacted; they were both motionless, staring at the radio. I believe it was the rude awakening that sparked my interests and curiosity and set me on my course. At school, geography and history became my favorite subjects.

The war was frightening for the grownups, but for us kids, it was a time of excitement and high adventure. Throughout the war, my classmates and I were fascinated with it and tried to keep up with what and where it was happening. It also had a big effect on our lives; at school, we had weekly air raid drills and war bond drives. At home, we had a victory garden in a vacant lot that I helped tend with my parents; everything was rationed, and there was not a lot of money around to spend.

I listened to the war news with my parents every night, and at school, my friends and I would talk about what we heard. I became intrigued with airplanes; I knew the names of all of them and built models of most of them. I was determined to be an aviator someday.

During the war years, my parents and their friends, Frank and Catherine Cooper, bought an old surplus WWI army tent to set it up somewhere on the Jersey shore. They found a trailer park just down Princeton Avenue from the Lauralton traffic circle, about 5 miles from Point Pleasant Beach. During our first weekend at the park, our dads pitched the tent and built onto it a small kitchen, then a short distance away in the woods a outhouse. The next weekend they drove in a well about ten feet from the tent where every morning, we kids, Frankie, Geraldine, and I would prime and pump-up water for the day.

For the duration of the war, our two families would spend the summers in that tent while our dads worked at their jobs in the city, coming down for the weekends when they could. Our moms kept us busy during the day, doing chores around the tent and, once in a while, sending us out to gather wild blueberries and raspberries in the nearby woods. The Johnson brothers' farm across the street not only supplied us with eggs for next to nothing; they also allowed us to pick all sorts of vegetables from their fields. Our mothers would put up these vegetables and berries in mason jars to eat during the winters.

Occasionally, our mothers would take us on the bus for the 5-mile ride to the Point Pleasant train station, the last stop on the Jersey Central Railroad. We would walk a mile carrying our beach gear to Jenkinson's Beach. We kids would have a blast playing at the beach getting tar on our feet that washed up from ships sunk by German U-boats. The U-boats, in turn, were being hunted by the blimps out of Lakehurst NAS. We could see them from the beach

patrolling up and down the coast. There was also a Coast Guard Station with a lookout tower on the beach by the Manasquan Inlet, where they kept an 83' cutter to patrol up and down the coast. It was a point of interest for us kids; we would walk down the beach to the station and talk to any Coast Guardsman that happened to be around. From there, we would climb onto the jetties to watch the fisherman and the boat traffic in the Inlet before heading back to Jenkinson's Beach.

After the war, my mother put her teaching degree from Princeton to work by buying from the Johnson brothers, their small country store on the corner of the trailer park: the same park where my parents kept the tent during the war. After a lot of work, she converted it into a nursery school.

During the transition, everyone worked; I worked in the store with my mom while my dad and Uncle Henry were busy adding on a couple of rooms to live in. Once the rooms were constructed and set up, my mom had a sale, selling all the equipment and merchandise. It took another week of setting up before she opened "Pinewood School" for business.

Money was scarce, and there was no such thing as sitting around doing nothing; if I couldn't find a job for weekends, my parents would find one for me. I worked on the farms around the area and eventually saved up enough money to buy a used 8ft canoe. I would carry it across the Johnsons' farm with my dog, Bugs, to the Metedeconk River to sail the canoe that I rigged up with a makeshift sail of old sheets. I dreamed of getting a real sailboat someday and 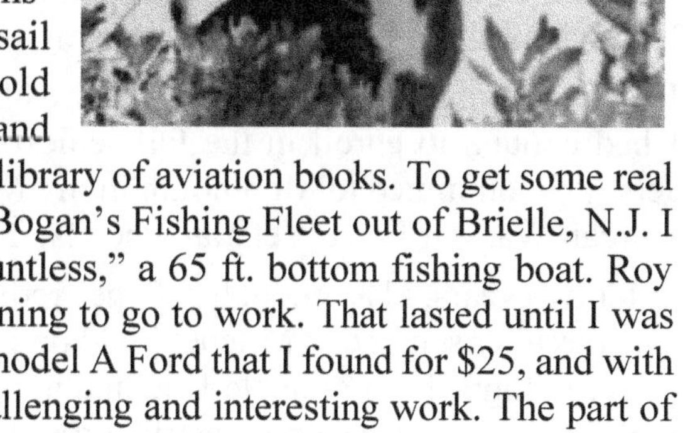 sailing to exotic ports of call; I added sea stories to my library of aviation books. To get some real sea time, I found a weekend and summer job with the Bogan's Fishing Fleet out of Brielle, N.J. I worked as a mate for Capt. Roy Skillman on the "Dauntless," a 65 ft. bottom fishing boat. Roy lived close by and would pick me up at five in the morning to go to work. That lasted until I was old enough to get a driver's license and bought a 1930 model A Ford that I found for $25, and with a little work, I got it running. Every day at sea was challenging and interesting work. The part of my job, besides cutting bait and selling drinks, was to solve any conflicts among the up to sixty or so fishermen on the boat. It was definitely a learning experience for me, and after a while, you get good at doing just that, solving problems.

Just before graduating high school, my parents bought an old boarding school in Lakewood, N.J., and opened up another school, "Lakewood School ". It was a big place with lots of rooms. I moved into one of the bedrooms upstairs and helped my dad, who now worked full time at the schools.

After graduating, my uncle Tony found me a job with "Horn Construction Company," where I worked as a rodman on the engineering team. The job site was in Harlem, building a bridge across the East River. My commute to work in the morning includes: catch the 5:25 a.m. train from Point Pleasant to Hoboken, catch the ferry across the Hudson River to Manhattan, take the subway to 122nd Street, then walk over to the job site on 3rd Avenue, arriving just before 8:00 a.m. At quitting time, I did the reverse back to Point Pleasant, all for $40 a week. After paying for the commute and giving some to my mom for the house, there wasn't much leftover. I was making more during the weekends on the boats.

Thankfully, after three months on the job, I got a raise. My uncle Tony and I were both sent to a job site building new storm drains at Idlewild Airport. He would pick me up every morning for the two-hour drive to Idlewild, later called JFK International Airport. That job lasted five months, and I was sent to a job rebuilding Hog Island Wharf in Philadelphia, and my uncle Tony was sent to a different job. I went looking to buy some reliable wheels to do the commute. I had just enough savings to buy a used 1952 M.G. T.D. It had a right-hand drive and was a blast to drive. I worked for Horn Construction during the week and the fishing boats on weekends. When the job ended at Hog Island Wharf, the boats became my full-time job.

I had ambitions of going to college; by using my meager saving plus a lot of help from my parents. I had enough to enroll in the fall semester at Monmouth Junior College in Long Branch, New Jersey. I commuted to Monmouth in my M.G. with my cousin and fellow student, Jacky Drone, a Korean War Air Force Veteran who also lived with us at the Lakewood School.

After two years, I had enough college credits to apply for the U.S. Air Force Aviation Cadet Corps. The recruiter sent me to Mitchel Field on Long Island for aptitude tests and a physical. On my way there, I stopped at my uncle Eric and aunt, Elfriede's house in Huntington, Long Island, for the night. Eric worked as an industrial artist for the Grumman Aircraft Company during the war. He was involved in the construction of the Grumman Hellcat and showed me some of his old industrial drawings of the Japanese Zero killer.

After three days of testing at Mitchel Field, I headed back home, stopping on the way to my uncle Eric's for the night. A few days later, I received a letter of acceptance and was sworn in. A few days later, I received orders to report to Lackland AFB, Texas, for preflight training. Before leaving town, I signed over the M.G. to my parents to enjoy while I was gone. They eventually sold it for me to my cousin, Jon Dugan.

It was the start of a sequence of events that would take me a long way from N.J and would eventually bring me to a barrier island on the Gulf Coast of Florida.

Years later, when I finally did step out onto the beautiful white sands of its beach to look out over the Gulf of Mexico and realized that maybe I could live my dream of getting a boat and sailing to those exotic ports of call. This barrier island was the kicking-off point from where many of my sailing and other adventures started. This area located along the Florida Gulf Coast between Pensacola and Panama City is known affectionately by locals and visitors alike as "The Redneck Riviera ".

This book is based on events as I remember them, with input from my friends and from the logbooks of the Windsong and Pele.

Chapter One: 1960 – 1971

The cadet corps was tough, with three months of preflight training at Lackland AFB in Texas and nine months of basic navigation training at Harlingen AFB, Texas, near Brownsville and the Mexican border. On August 5th, 1959, I graduated with my class, 59-14N, pinned on my silver navigator wings, and was commissioned a 2nd Lieutenant in the United States Air Force.

As soon as the ceremony was over, I was given orders sending me to Mather AFB, California, for six months of radar bombardier training. On completion of that training, I received orders to my first duty assignment, the 1st Tactical Reconnaissance Squadron at RAF Alconbury, England. But first, I had to get through a six-week survival training course at Stead AFB, Nevada, and three months of crew training in the Douglas RB-66 at Shaw AFB, South Carolina.

When I finally finished with all the training and was on my way to England, I had a week's leave en route to visit my parents in New Jersey. My mother made sure I was well-fed while I told them about my experiences in the Air Force. At the end of my leave on September 2nd, my parents drove me over to McGuire AFB, N. J. At McGuire, I was given orders as a courier officer for 2600lbs of classified material loaded in the cargo bay of the C-54 for the flight over to RAF Mildenhall in the U.K.

During the flight, we had an engine problem and diverted in the middle of the night to Keflavik Air Station, Iceland, for an engine change. Base security wasn't happy with me when I told them to post guards on the airplane while maintenance changed the engine. We finally arrived at Mildenhall on Friday, September 4th. After signing over the classified cargo, I boarded a bus for a wild ride in the fog to RAF Alconbury. Arriving alive, I signed in with the duty officer and checked into my room at the Bachelor Officers Quarters (BOQ).

Once settled into my room, I found my way to the Officer's Club (O-Club) just in time for happy hour, where I met most of the personnel of the 1st TRS and the 30th TRS, our sister squadron on the base. Apparently, they had not seen a second lieutenant in a long time. After too many stingers, they took me to the railway station in Huntingdon and put me on the train to London. Thankfully, they gave me the address of where to stay, the Columbia Club (U.S. Forces Europe Officers Club & BOQ), to sink or swim in London for the weekend.

Part of the clearing process at Alconbury was going to a weeklong international driver training course. As soon as I finished the course and received my International Driver's License. I walked over to the Base Exchange (B.X.) and bought a brand new white 1960 Austin-Healey bug-eyed Sprite. It was the only car they had available at the time. To get used to driving my new wheels on the wrong side of the road, I would burn up my monthly gas ration by familiarizing myself with

the local area. On my way back from these sorties, I would stop at the pub or the fish & chip shop in Little Stukeley, a village just out the main gate at Alconbury. I would buy a pint of bitters to get used to the currency, shot darts, and try to understand the way the English spoke English.

Being stationed in England was a great adventure for this young man from New Jersey and opened my eyes to the wonders of the world. Cambridge, a university town with the River Cam running through it, was just a short drive down the road from Alconbury. In Cambridge, there were plenty of pubs, students on bicycles, an art theater, punting on the Cam, Dorothy's Dancehall 'Dirty Dots,' and other points of interest. On Wednesday evenings, some of my squadron mates and I would load into an old Rolls Royce owned by Billy Graham (the Preacher) and drive there to dance and flirt with the ladies.

For the dependent children on RAF Alconbury, they had a DOD (Department of Defense) School where every August, a new crop of schoolteachers would arrive to teach. Most of these teachers were young women fresh out of college, and we (the bachelors) were waiting for them with open arms. We invited them to a welcoming cocktail party at the O-Club, followed by an excursion on the weekend to Cambridge to take the new arrivals punting on the Cam. We always had some sort of misadventure when they tried to use the punt, like falling into the river. Once our new teachers were settled into their housing off base, they would, in turn, invite us over to their parties. There was always some sort of romantic liaison formed during these events.

If I had a weekend off, I would take the train from Huntingdon Station to London's King's Cross Station, then take the underground to the Lancaster Gate stop that's close to the Colombia Club. The club was located just across the street from Hyde Park and Kensington Gardens. If I was lucky at happy hour, I would meet a beautiful English lady to take to dinner, the theater, and maybe for the rest of the weekend, she would show me around her city. London had plenty to offer with theaters, museums, good restaurants, plenty of pubs, and thousands of years of history. Wandering about on my exploratory walks around London. I would occasionally come across bombed-out areas from the war still under repair, mainly in the east end of London. On my way back from these walkabouts, I would stop at the Swan, a pub around the corner from the Colombia Club, for a pint and socializing.

From Alconbury, my squadron was tasked to fly to NATO airfields located all around Europe and North Africa. We were sent to these fields on temporary duty (TDY) that usually lasted around a

week or so, flying photo reconnaissance training missions. Since most of these airfields were located close to major cities, it afforded me the opportunity to explore, sample the local cuisine and absorb some of their cultures. During these TDY's over the years, I was able to observe some of these wonders; Paris, France [the city of light]; the bullfights and Flamingo dancers of Seville and Madrid, Spain; the markets of Marrakech, Morocco; the beer gardens of Berlin, during the construction of the wall just to mention a few.

In April '63 my mother, Margaret and my cousin, Judy on a two-week tour of Europe, stopped at Alconbury to pay me a visit for a few days. They stayed with Dick Wilson's wife, Sheila for a couple of days until Dick, and I returned from a mission.Sheila then had a dinner party for us before my mom and Judy went on to tour Italy, France, and Germany before flying back to the USA.

The squadron occasionally would make one of our planes available for a volunteer crew to go on a weekend cross-country training mission to any NATO airfield in Europe that could accommodate the B-66. Base Flight also had a couple of T-33s available to fly on weekends to any airfield within its flight range. This was a ticket to ride for me, and once I figured out where I wanted to go. I would round up a pilot from the squadron and talk him into going.

One of my favorite destinations in the T-bird (T-33) was the short hop across the channel to the Paris Airport-Le Bourget. Once in Paris, we enjoyed a weekend of hanging out at the sidewalk cafes along the Champs-Elysees to people-watch and maybe take in a show at one of the cabarets. There was always plenty to see and do in Paris.

My favorite weekend cross-country destination in the RB-66 was a Danish fighter training base near the town of Aalborg, Denmark, located near the tip of the Jutland Peninsular. Since Aalborg hardly ever had visitors, we were welcomed there with open arms.

Occasionally the squadron would send me to RAF Sculthorpe or Chambley AB in France to maintain my proficiency with the K-5 bomb-nav system on the BB-66, the bomber: a totally different nav system from what's on the RB-66, the reconnaissance version of the plane that I normally flew around in. Since we pulled alert in the bombers at Toul-Rosieres Air Base, France, I needed to know how to operate the navigation system. The planes on alert were loaded with an ECM (Electronic Counter Measure) cradle, and our mission was to provide ECM protection for the NATO strike force in the event we went to war.

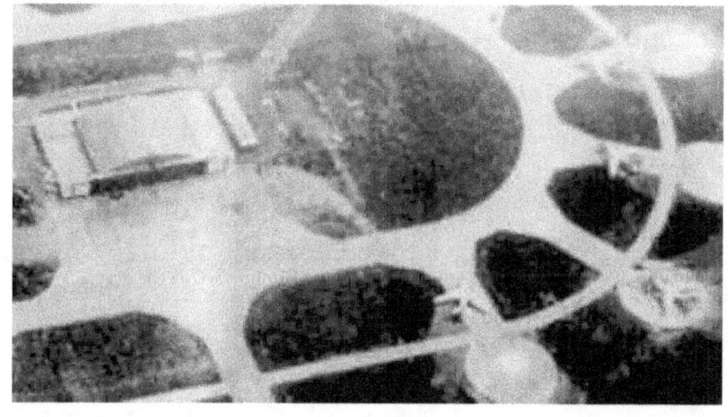

The cold war was tense during the 60s but really heated up in 1962 during the Cuban crisis. During the height of it, I was put on alert, and when I arrived at Toul-Rosieres Air Base, the airfield was loaded with airplanes. The Air National Guard and the Air Force Reserves had been activated, and their planes flown over to Europe and then put on alert. When I checked into our alert facility, I was handed a target folder and told to target study because the B-66 we were standing alert in was loaded with two one-megaton variable yield nukes. The whole crew was scared to death, waiting for the horn to blow. Thank God it did not happen.

I was allowed to go on leave a few times, but not during the holidays. They were reserved for the families; bachelors got what was left; it didn't matter to me. I was ready to go anytime they let me loose. Once I had accumulated two weeks of leave time, I would sign out on a Friday and, having no plans, would drive to the Columbia Club in London to think about where to go. On one occasion, during happy hour at the club, I ran into Gerry Terhune, a fellow graduate of cadet class 59-14N, was assigned to the 30th TRS, the other squadron on Alconbury. He had also just signed out on leave, and after a couple of cocktails, we decided to head to the continent.

After hanging around London for the weekend, we drove over to Dover in my bug-eyed Sprite and boarded the ferry to Calais. They say all roads lead to Paris, so we started driving, and sure enough, they do. During the night, as we drove, we could see the glow from the spotlights on the top of the Eifel Tower, a good sign that we were headed in the right direction. We arrived in Paris on the Champs-Elysees around 22:00, and by the time we found a place to stay, it was approaching midnight. After checking in at our hotel, we made our way to Le Halle, the market where there were some late-night restaurants. We arrived in time for something to eat, then joined the ongoing party that went on till dawn. We stayed in Paris for the rest of the week, then headed back to London. The fact that neither one of us could speak a word in French did not slow us down. We were always able to get our point across. I always have a grand old time in Paris, the city of lights.

During the following winter, while having a beer at the Alconbury officers club with Gerry, we found that we were both thinking about taking some leave. We had skied together at Squaw Valley, Nevada, while going through bomb school. After a couple of beers, we decided to go on a little trip to check out the slopes in Europe. The next day at the travel agent in the Base Exchange, we bought a two-week ski package to Zermatt, Switzerland.

Once signed out on leave, we made our way to the Columbia Club for the night. In the morning, we boarded the train that eventually took us to Brig, Switzerland, where we boarded a narrow-gauge, cog railroad to Zermatt. After checking in at the hotel and getting fitted with skies, it was time for cocktails, dinner, and a walk around the town to check the action.

From our hotel, it was just a short walk to the Gornergrat Bahn, another cog rail line that takes you up to the peak, where there's a hotel, "The Kumhotel Gornergrat," with its spectacular view of the Matterhorn and other peaks around the area. Our days in Zermatt started with an early breakfast, then the short walk over to catch the first train for the 40 min ride up to the Gornergrat and our first run down the mountain. As you ski down the mountain, you go through a short tunnel and a couple of picturesque small villages before arriving back in Zermatt, hopefully, in time for lunch. After lunch, we would catch the Gornergrat Bahn to make another run, followed by a little Après Ski at the hotel bar before dinner. After a leisurely dinner, we would go out on the town for an evening of playing with the Europeans that was pretty much our agenda for the rest of our stay in Zermatt.

 One of my more memorable times on leave was to Majorca, one of the Spanish Balearic Islands in the Mediterranean. One of my squadron mates, Larry Bockelman, and I rented a villa at Palma Nova Beach for two weeks through the travel agency in the B.X. The villa, located at the beach on the outskirts of Palma, the capital city of Majorca, came with two Vespa scooters. We caught our flight in London and landed around midnight at the Palma airport, and took a cab to the town. By the time we got there, everything was closed, except for a bar on the municipal pier. We stayed at the bar until closing, then lugged our bags down the pier to the massive Santa Maria Cathedral and sat on its steps, waiting for the town to wake up.

Shortly after sunrise, we found a café, had breakfast then contacted our agent. He informed us that our villa was not ready and had booked a room for us in town at the California Hotel for a couple of days. So far, this trip has been nothing but a comedy of errors. After a nap in our room, we went down to the bar and sat at a table to talk about our situation. While enjoying a beer, we noticed some girls at the bar being hassled by a couple of drunks. Damsel in distress! We went up to the bar and invited the girls over to our table for a drink: they accepted our invitation, and after a little grief at the bar from the drunks, they joined us. Things were beginning to pick up.

We stayed at the hotel for two days, giving us time to spend with our new friends before moving over to the villa. The three sisters were from Sweden, spoke English, and were on holiday staying at the hotel with their mother and younger brother. That evening, and for the rest of our stay in town, we took them out to a nightclub just down the street to talk and dance.

When it was ready, Larry and I drove the Vespas out to the villa and moved in, a beautiful place on the beach. In the morning, we drove our Vespas into town and picked up two of the sisters to take them for a day at the beach and show them our digs. After spending the day at the beach, they decided to stay. In the morning, the girls wanted us to go retrieve their sister staying at the hotel with her mother and brother, who was a couple of months pregnant. After breakfast, they called their sister, and I drove to Palma and picked her up at the California Hotel.

They stayed with us until the day before their flight back to Sweden; we called a cab to take them back to the hotel in Palma. When we got there, their mother invited us to join them for dinner at the hotel. At dinner, we anticipated being chewed out for kidnapping her daughters; but it was the sisters that caught the grief. Their mother was upset because they didn't tell her where they were going. Needless to say, we had a good time in Majorca.

Toward the end of my tour at Alconbury, I bought a green '63 MGB to ship back to the states. I cleared out of Alconbury on September 3rd, 1963. After another wild bus ride in the fog to RAF Mildenhall; I boarded a flight back to the states for my next duty assignment, the 18th Troop Carrier Squadron flying Lockheed C-130As at Sewart AFB, Tennessee. When we landed at McGuire AFB, N.J.,

my parents were there to meet two of my friends and me. She took us to the Lakewood School, where my parents had organized a welcome home party for us in the cellar party room.

Dick Wilson and his wife Sheila were there. They had rotated back to the states on the USS United States from Alconbury and had arrived earlier at the Port of New York. I spent an enjoyable week at the Lakewood school with my parents before reporting for duty at Sewart AFB.

Sewart AFB is located about 25 miles Southeast of Nashville near the small town of Smyrna. While clearing onto the base, I was informed that I could live off-base. The squadron's bachelors recommended the Sherwood Terrace Apartments in Nashville, where some of them lived; taking their recommendation, I rented a small one-bedroom apartment there.

When the MGB arrived in N.Y., my dad and my grandpa went over and picked it up for me. He and my mom then drove it out to Nashville for me and stayed on for a little visit.

Life at the apartments was interesting. On Friday, there was usually a pool party where the resident musicians would get together to entertain us with mostly country music and moonshine. Also living at the apartments were players in the local hockey team, the Dixie Flyers, who gave us tickets to the games. Added to this mix of neighbors to make life interesting and complicated where a group of American Airlines stewardesses.

There was a lot going on in Nashville, one of my friends was dating the secretary of the president of the local radio station, WSM. She supplied us with passes to some of the recording sessions held in bars on Printers Ally in downtown Nashville. I was really just getting to enjoy living in Nashville when, out of the blue, tragedy struck; our 35th president, John Fitzpatrick Kennedy, was assassinated on November 22nd, 1963, shocking the whole country.

My squadron, the 18th TCS, was a newly formed squadron and was just getting its airplanes and personnel. The airplanes were all hand-me-down old C-130A from squadrons that were getting new planes, and it was going to take a while for us to get combat-ready. As soon as the planes were ready to fly, we flew training missions around the country, hauling cargo and dropping paratroopers. After a few months, we were ready for our Operational Readiness Inspection (ORI) that we passed in September. A month later, in October of 1964, the 18th TCS was sent on a three-month deployment to Clark Field in the Philippians. After making refueling and crew rest stops in California, Hawaii, Wake Island, and Guam, we arrived in the Philippians.

It took us a couple of days to get everyone settled in, set up our squadron operations at Clark Field, and start flying missions. Within a week, my crew was sent TDY to Ton Son Nhut Air Base in Vietnam to fly supply missions to airfields around Vietnam in support of our advisors. We were housed in a contract hotel in downtown Saigon giving us the opportunity to check out the town. Walking around Saigon, you could see the French influence from when it was one of their colonies; lots of sidewalk cafes, wide boulevards, and good restaurants. Most of the residents were bilingual, speaking both French and Vietnamese. It was really a beautiful city.

Our crew was also sent TDY for two weeks to Don Mueang Airport, Bangkok, Thailand, in support of our airbases there. We stayed in a hotel in downtown Bangkok giving us plenty of time to explore the sights, sounds, food, and other treats of that exotic city. After three months, we completed our deployment and flew our planes back to the United States. We were only back at Sewart AFB for a short time when the squadron was moved in February 1965 to Lockbourne AFB, Columbus, Ohio.

Shortly after settling in at Lockbourne, the squadron was sent on a three-month TDY to Evreux-Fauville Air Base, France, in support of NATO. After arriving in France and during a break in my flying schedule, I took a train to Baden-Baden, Germany, and bought a 1965 blue V.W. Bug to drive while at Evreux. If I had a two or three-day break, I would drive somewhere, taking some of my squadron mates with me. I even had an opportunity to drive over to Paris for a long weekend. On another occasion, I drove to Deauville-Trouville on the coast to check out the casino. I shipped the V.W. back as a used car when the squadron returned to the states.

Within a month of our return to Ohio and Lockbourne AFB, I married my girlfriend Gail Kostalonsky, who was pregnant. She was one of the American Airline stewardesses that I had met at the Sherwood Terrace Apartments in Nashville. We rented a bigger apartment and tried to settle in being married. Later that month, we drove to Cleveland and picked up the V.W., our new family car, for Gail to drive around in. The flying schedule kept me busy and out of town, flying all over the country, away from my bride.

Gail gave birth to our baby boy, Michael William Gebhardt, at the Lockbourne AFB Hospital on November 25th, 1965. I wasn't in town long; shortly after Michael was born, I received orders for a three-year accompanied tour of duty to the 817th Troop Carrier Squadron at Naha Air Base, Okinawa, with a reporting date in January 1966.

For Christmas, just before I departed for Okinawa, my parents drove over to see their grandson. I gave them the MGB to drive back to N.J. for safekeeping when they left.

As soon as I signed in with my squadron at Naha, I went over to the housing office and signed up for base housing. I found out the list was long, and it would probably take a year and a half to get my family over to Okinawa. That was unacceptable. I needed to get my family over there fast, so I looked off-base to find a place for us to live. I needed wheels to do that, so I bought a used motorcycle and started looking.

While driving around on my first day looking, I came across a sign advertising a housing development called Kakazu Heights, about twenty minutes from Naha, and stopped to check it out. The conversation in the sales office was with the developer himself, who spoke very little English, making it difficult to communicate, but after a little tea and a little hot sake, we were beginning to understand each other. I thought I had a little leverage negotiating because it was a new project, and he hadn't made many sales. I told him, I was ready to buy, but I could not wait for three months for the house to be built. I needed a place to live in as soon as possible to get my wife and baby over to Okinawa. After about an hour of negotiating, we made a deal. I would pay him upfront, and he would supply a place rent-free for my family and me while he built our house. We drove up to Kakazu Heights to look at my lot, then drove over to show me the one-bedroom house that he had available out the back gate of Naha. I thought it was a sweet deal and signed the contract.

As soon as the housing office opened in the morning, I was there with the paperwork for the house he gave me. A couple of weeks later, they inspected the house, Gail received orders for her and Michael to fly over and join me.

Shortly after moving my stuff into the house, I was put on the flying schedule and was sent TDY to Vietnam for two weeks to fly in-country missions out of Saigon's Ton Son Nhut Air Base. Not long after my return to Naha, Gail and Michael arrived, just a month and a half after I reported for duty at the 817th TCS. Gail beat our V.W. there by two weeks. After

settling in our little house out the back gate, we went looking for and found a mama-son to hire and help Gail with our baby boy. The first couple of weeks were difficult. I think the fact that Gail had been a stewardess helped her cope with the stress of the move. Once we picked up our V.W. at the port, Gail could get around, making life a lot easier for her. My flying schedule had me out of town two weeks out of the month, mostly to Vietnam, with occasional trips to Thailand, Taiwan, Singapore, Japan, and South Korea. We only lived in our little house for a couple of months before moving into our new house on top of Kakazu Ridge, where we had a great view of the South China Sea.

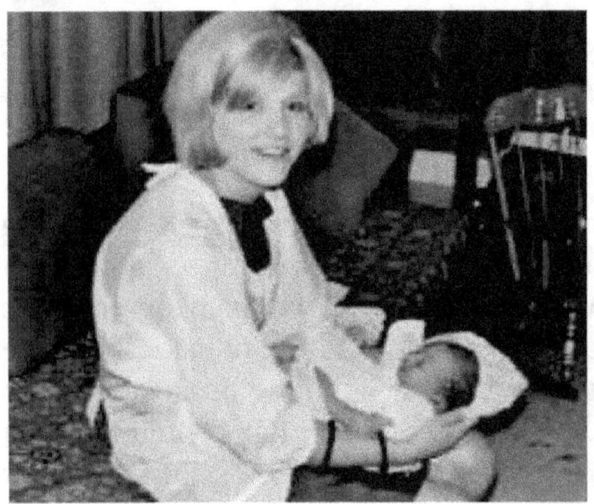

The ridge was part of the Japanese Suri defenses during the Second World War, and there were remnants like mortar and small arms ammunition that would surface occasionally.

Over the next few months, Kakazu Heights built up, and our neighborhood expanded with mostly military families that were stationed at Naha and Kadena AB. We were all about the same age with young kids about the same age. Gail and I added to the population with the birth of our second son, Jon Gary Gebhardt, on December 18th, 1966.

While their husbands were away TDY, the wives looked after each other and partied together as a regular rat pack. They all had mama-sons for their kids, sew girls to make their clothes, lawn boys, and occasionally even pony rides for the kids. All the military services had a base on Okinawa, including the CIA and FBI, all with their own B.X. and clubs. There was plenty to keep the wives busy while their husbands were down south fighting the war. Gail and I had plenty of parties with our neighbors on Kakazu Heights.

My crew was sent on a six-week Blind Bat mission to Ubon Air Base in Thailand to fly a night forward air control (FAC) missions on the Ho Chi Minh trail. It was an interesting mission, flying just above the small-arms fire, dropping flares to light up the target for the fighters to bomb.

During the three and a half years we were stationed in Okinawa, Gail and I were able to take leave a few times to visit some of the countries in Southeast Asia. Dependents could fly space available on military aircraft, and we took advantage of it. Leaving our kids with mama-son, we took trips to Bangkok, Taipei, Manila, Hawaii, Tokyo, and Hong Kong. Events began to unfold in late 1968, towards the end of my tour of duty on Okinawa. The war was winding down, and a reduction in force (RIF) was going on. I was informed that I had been passed over by the promotion board. The board would meet again in a year or two, and if I passed over again, I would be released from

active duty. My future in the Air Force did not look very promising. I started looking at my options for future employment. I found that in civilian life, there was not a lot available for ex-Air Force navigators. The airlines had started phasing out their navigators, but there were other options, the Air Force Reserves and the Air National Guard. They were just getting C-130s and would need instructors. Base housing on Naha became available in '68, and we moved into a duplex on base and sold the house on Kakazu Ridge. On base, our next-door neighbors were Madge and Jack Schofield, who had previously been our neighbors at Kakazu Heights.

I received orders for my next assignment, Forbes AFB, Topeka, Kansas. On June 15th, '69 we packed up and departed Okinawa on a flight that eventually took us to McGuire AFB, New Jersey, where I took some leave to visit our parents before reporting for duty at Forbes.

On arrival at my hometown, Point Pleasant, we rented a little cottage on the boardwalk at the beach to greet and entertain our family and friends that we had not seen for three and a half years. Especially, my parents and grandparents, Max (Pop) and Ida. The two weeks of having fun in the sun at the beach went by way too fast, and all of a sudden, it was time for me to head for Kansas.

When I shipped out for Okinawa, I left the MGB with my parents for safekeeping. They were having way too much fun taking care of it while I was gone. My dad had kept it in a good shape and enjoyed driving around town in it with my mom. Now that I was back, I was taking his toy away from him.

After an enjoyable couple of weeks of seeing all our friends and relatives, I loaded up the M.G. and started my drive to Forbes AFB, leaving Gail and the boys behind with family in N.J. They would fly out to Topeka, once I had us a place to live.

After signing in at Forbes AFB and being assigned a house in base housing, I had Gail and the boys fly out to their new home. A while later, we drove to Cleveland, Ohio, to pick up our '65 V.W. bug that was shipped from Okinawa. The last delay was our household goods from Okinawa, eventually delivered after a week or so, and the move was made.

Shortly after getting my family settled in at Forbes AFB, my squadron was sent on a three-month TDY to Rhein-Main AB in Frankfurt, Germany. Once the squadron completed the flight across the Atlantic and was in place at Rhein-Main, I started looking around for a way to get Gail over to Germany to maybe do a little touring around on my time off between missions. What I found was that Icelandic Air was offering cheap airfares, 98 dollars for the flight from N.Y. to Luxembourg and 103 dollars for a return flight. I gave Gail a call, and she ran out and bought the tickets for a flight to N.J., where she would leave the boys with my parents at their nursery school in Lakewood before catching her flight over the pond to Luxembourg.

In the meantime, while waiting for her to arrive in Luxembourg, I rented a room for us at a B&B close to Rhein-Main AB and went shopping for wheels. I bought a new V.W. Camper, and it just happened that I made the purchase on the last day before the German Mark was floated, at the old rate of 4 to 1 to the dollar. I thought that with two kids, the camper would make a good family vehicle and give Gail something to drive around while I was on a mission. Buying and driving the camper in Europe allowed us to ship it back tax-free when the TDY ended, just like I did with the V.W. bug in 1965.

I drove over in our new wheels on a typical dreary, cold overcast European day to meet Gail at the Luxembourg airport and drove back to Frankfurt in the rain. On our arrival at the B&B, I introduced Gail to our house frau, who told her the house rules. Our room was spotlessly clean, and the breakfast every morning was good and plentiful. My busy flying schedule hampered our exploration around the local area some, but I did get one long weekend off, and we headed for Paris.

After a long drive, we finally arrived at the tourist aid office on the Champs-Elysees just before they closed for the day. They found us a room at a small hotel nearby, and once we checked in at the hotel, they recommended a restaurant where we had a wonderful meal. Over the next two days, we went up the Eiffel Tower for lunch at the Le Jules Verne restaurant, climbed up the Arch de Triumph, and during the afternoon, people watched from one of the sidewalk cafés on the Champs-Elysees. At night we enjoyed some great French cuisine, danced at nightclubs, and closed out the nights at Le Halle for a midnight snack before retiring for the night.

After a wonderful weekend, we got a late start for the drive back to Germany; by nine in the evening, we were just entering Metz and needed to find a place to eat before everything closed. The café/restaurant we found was next to a movie theater and didn't look like much, but we were hungry. Once inside, I told the maître d' that we were there for dinner. He ushered us through the café to the dining room in the back. We were the only ones there and had a marvelous meal served by a charming waitress; we were having such a good time that by the time we were back on the road, it was well past midnight. Gail stayed on for about a month and then flew back to the states. She wasn't all that impressed with Germany or its people. Her loss, I found them to be fun-loving and friendly once you broke the ice. Plus, they brewed some really good beer.

After my return to Forbes AFB, Gail and I, with the boys, drove to New Jersey to pick up the V.W. While there, we stopped to visit my parents and my grandparents, Max and Ida, living with them at the Lakewood school. It just so happened that it was Max (Pop) and Ida's 50th wedding anniversary. Pop's first wife, Frieda, my dad's mother, died in the flu epidemic in 1918.

Shortly after returning to Forbes, I was notified that I had been passed over again for promotion and would be released from active duty with a separation date of September 3rd, 1971. I needed to find a job. I was still a reserve officer, so all I needed to do was find a National Guard or Air Force Reserve unit to work for.

I immediately got on the phone and started calling and was optimistic about finding one. It just so happened that at the time, the Air Force Reserves and Air National Guard units were just getting the older hand-me-down C-130s from the active-duty units. I was an instructor navigator, and these units needed instructors of all kinds to make the transition to the new bird. My preference in my job search was to find one in a warm climate. What I found during my search was that most of the established units were in the northern states, with relatively few in the south. However, with a bit of luck, I found a reserve unit that was just being activated, the 919 Tactical Airlift Wing. The 919th is located at Duke Field, an auxiliary field on the Eglin AFB reservation located near Fort Walton Beach on the Gulf Coast of Florida. I contacted the commander, and he hired me on the spot.

To prepare for my release from my active duty and to lighten the load for the move, we sold a lot of stuff. The first to go was the MGB; I sold it shortly after getting back from my deployment to Germany. Then just before we departed Kansas, I sold the blue 65 V.W. bugs that had been our wheels while on Okinawa. Before leaving Kansas, I made reservations at the Surfview Motel/Apartments in Fort Walton Beach.

We were all cleared out of Forbes and ready to start the drive on September 3rd. Our 69 V.W. Camper (nicknamed the War Wagon) was loaded up, and with a trailer full of more stuff, we headed for Florida. Two days later, we rolled into Fort Walton Beach, a small town located in the northwest panhandle of Florida between Pensacola and Panama City, on the Gulf of Mexico, and checked in at the Surfview Motel/Apartments.

The next day I drove out to meet my new commander. After driving for forty-five minutes, I turned off highway 85 onto the access road to Duke Field. There were no guards at the main gate and very few people walking around on the base and on the flight line; there were no airplanes. It looked to me like an old, abandoned airfield leftover from WW2. After finding the base operations building, I went in and introduced myself to my new boss, Colonel Don Haugen. There were five or six other people there; we were the initial cadre of personnel of the 919th.

Now that I had a part-time job in the reserves, my wife and I went looking for a place to live. We contacted a realtor, and after driving her crazy for a couple of weeks looking at houses, she informed us that the apartments we were staying in were up for sale. The asking price wasn't much more than the houses we were looking at. I talked about buying the place with my wife, and we made an offer. I thought we made a really low-ball offer and was surprised when the owners jumped at it. Maybe we offered too much. In any case, within a month, we closed on the place. So now, to add to my part-time job on the 919th, I had a full-time job in the apartment rental business; hopefully, the combination of incomes would be enough to live on.

The apartments that we just bought were located on the barrier island across the Santa Rosa Sound (called the Sound by locals) from Fort Walton Beach. To the east of the apartments, a quarter mile is the Brooks Bridge that connects the island to Fort Walton Beach. Further east, a couple of miles is the Destin Bridge that connects the island to Destin. The island parallels the coast all the way to Pensacola and is named Santa Rose Island in Santa Rosa County and Okaloosa Island in Okaloosa County. Heading west from the apartments for two miles, you come to the military gate for access to the part of the Island that Eglin AFB has and goes all the way to Navarre, about halfway to Pensacola Beach.

On the west end of the island, just passed Pensacola Beach, is Fort Pickens, named after Andrew Pickens, an American Revolutionary War hero. Constructed in 1834 and stayed in use until 1947, when it became part of The Gulf Islands National Seashore, administered by the National Park Service. There are two other forts; Fort McRea on the west side of Pensacola Pass, that's abandoned, and Fort Barrancas on the north side of the bay on Pensacola Naval Air Station, that's also run by the National Park Service.

There really was not much on our little section of Okaloosa Island, a few more small apartment

buildings, a gas station, and the Seagull Bar/Restaurant down by the Brooks Bridge. The one thing we did have was some of the most beautiful beaches in the world.

We moved into our new home, The Surfview Apartments, a four-year-old complex of eleven 600 sq. ft. two bedrooms apartments plus one 300 sq. ft. one-bedroom unit that must have been the office at one time. Also located on the property was a short, dilapidated dock and tied to it a half-submerged 16ft fiberglass boat with an old Evinrude 25 horse outboard attached to it. The place was definitely a fixer-upper. As soon as it was available, we moved into the apartment that was closest to the Sound and converted it into the office and our home. A little small for a family of four, but it was a small sacrifice to be able to live in paradise.

The Gulf of Mexico was just to the south of the apartments, three hundred yards or so with its beautiful quartz sand beach. This stretch of the gulf coast is unbelievable; the sand is so white that it reflects the sun's rays allowing you to walk barefooted on it without burning your feet even at high noon during the dog days of summer.

Only half of the apartments were occupied when we bought the place, it had been operating as a motel/apartment, and most of the tenants were short-term. My wife Gail wasn't too keen on cleaning rooms, so as soon as these units became vacant, we dropped the motel operation and only rented them out as furnished apartments on a year's lease.

I bought a used Honda 450 motorcycle to do the 45 minutes commute to Duke Field. Leaving the V.W. Camper (war wagon) for my wife to use. The 919th didn't have aircraft at the time, and I needed to stay current in the C-130 (herky bird). It turned out not to be a problem, and the 919th farmed me out on training weekends to other reserve and guard units to help train and qualify their navigators in their newly acquired old C-130s. These weekend trips helped me out a lot, I needed the extra income.

In February, I was sent on a mission as part of the five-man crew to pick up a C-130 in Germany for the 919th. I was delighted, in the reserves, you only get paid for the days you are on duty, and this mission would take at least a week and maybe longer to complete. We were flown commercially to Rhein-Main AB in Frankfurt, Germany, where we would pick up the C-130 to fly back across the pond.

Checking in at Rhein-Main AB, we were informed that our plane was out of commission for at least a couple of days with maintenance and would have to stay in Frankfurt since there was no housing available for us on base. Fine, the delay would give us a chance to learn some German while drinking beer with the frauleins. Being that I still had a valid international driver's license, I talked to the crew into renting a Mercedes. I always wanted to drive a Mercedes on the autobahn. In Frankfurt, we rented a couple of rooms in a small hotel on the Kaiserstrasse (main street) close to the Hauptbahnhof (the main train station) and went on a walkabout town.

While waiting for our plane to be fixed, we were instructed to drive over to Wiesbaden AB for a classified briefing on our mission. What we learned at the briefing was that the C-130 we were tasked to fly, had the cargo compartment modified to include a secure room that was loaded with classified equipment. We also learned that our mission's destination was now a remote airfield in Texas where the airplane would be de-modified before being turned over to the 919th. In addition, the plane would be required to have armed guards around it anywhere we stopped on our way to Texas.

After three days of drinking some really great beer, we were informed that our bird was ready to fly. To celebrate, we drove across the Rhine River to Sachsenhausen for a meal of schweinshaxe and sauerkraut washed down with some apffelwine. We were having such a good time that we stayed too late. After only a couple of hours of sleep, we turned in the Mercedes and called the base motor pool for transport to Base Operation to mission plan our flight across the pond.

The pilots and I worked up our flight plan. The first leg would be to Lajes Field in the Azores to refuel and remain overnight for crew rest. Then in the morning, on to Bermuda for more fuel and crew rest before finally flying on to Texas.

We were halfway through our flight to Lajes Field when we received a weather warning that the weather at the Azores had deteriorated to the point that we would have to divert to an alternate airfield. Looking over the charts, Torrejon AB, located just outside of Madrid, Spain, was suitable, within range, and had a good weather forecast for our ETA.

We called Torrejon and told them that we were on our way there and that we would need security for our plane; they weren't too happy about that. On landing at Torrejon AB, our flight engineer informed the pilot that we had a problem with one of the propellers and that it would require a prop change; the mission was going to take more time than anticipated. Over the next five days, while waiting for the new prop, we were having way too much fun trying to learn Spanish from the senoritas. We were there too long, and all of us were running out of cash and ready to get on with the mission.

We were finally airborne with our new prop and on course for an uneventful flight to Lajes field for fuel and crew rest. We made two more stops, Bermuda and Charleston AFB, South Carolina, where we landed in one piece after a bumpy flight. Getting some food and a good night's sleep, we were ready and eager for an early morning takeoff for the last leg of our flight to Texas. On landing at our destination, a small airport in the boondocks, we handed over the plane. After completing the transfer, we loaded up into a small eight-passenger twin-engine plane for a short flight to Dallas, where we caught a commercial flight back to Fort Walton Beach. Finally, the mission was complete after almost three weeks.

Back at the Surfview, all of our short-term renters were gone. Gail had succeeded in leasing out most of the units, leaving just a couple of vacant that she had all cleaned up and ready to go. I had plenty of projects around the apartments to take care of, and with the 919th farming me out on weekends, I was a busy man. We finally filled up the apartments with tenants, mostly from my reserve units or people associated with the military at Eglin AFB.

By September the 919th was finally starting to get airplanes and the personnel to fly them, and I was offered a two-year temporary civil service job as a GS-12 to train our new navigators. Everything was starting to come together, with my income from the apartments, my civil service job, and flying with the reserves during the week, I was making a living, and life was good.

Everything changed in October 1972; my wife Gail decided to divorce me. I hadn't realized she was so unhappy with me and our life together in paradise. I tried to convince her that we were building a good life and future on our little pile of sand, she was determined to bail out. I could not believe it, just as everything was starting to come together, she dropped the divorce bomb on me. I thought I could handle any situation. After all, the Air Force trained me to do just that, even a marriage. Well, maybe not a marriage, so things were not going as well as I thought.

She packed up my boys and moved to an apartment a couple of blocks away, and found a job as a cocktail waitress at one of the bars/restaurants on the island. Even though the boys were spending their weekends with me at the Surfview, I was pretty miserable. No one in my family's history had ever been divorced. I was brought up to believe that once you married, it was forever.

My parents had just retired earlier in the year, selling their two nursery school businesses in New Jersey. They bought their retirement home in DeBary, Florida, and had recently moved there from New Jersey. Once I told them I was getting a divorce, they came up to Fort Walton Beach to give me some moral support; conveniently, the apartment next to mine was empty at the time, so they moved in.

They were in Fort Walton Beach no more than two weeks before informing me that they had made an offer to buy a two-bedroom unit, number 142, at the El Matador, the first condominium complex to be built on Okaloosa Island, located just two miles down the road from the Surfview by the gate to Eglin's part of the island. They also had the option to buy a one-bedroom unit, number 325, for future construction. I thought it was a great buy and hoped the deal would go through and it would be a good thing to have them close by.

My sons were staying with me during their Thanksgiving break from school, giving their grandmother the opportunity to put on a great Thanksgiving feed for us at the Surfview. The boys stayed on through the weekend before going back to their mother. My parents closed on the El Matador a week later, just before my birthday on December 5th, which just so happened to be the day my divorce was final. Happy Birthday?

Gail also let me have the boys for Christmas. The festivities were held in my parent's new place at the El Matador. Their unit was located on the fourth floor and was all tricked out with new furniture and appliances. The boys had a good time running around the place and swimming in the heated pool. Mom cooked a turkey for Christmas Day with all the trimmings, it was a quiet celebration with just the boys and my parents. Mom and Dad stayed on in their condo to celebrate the New Year, then drove back to DeBary. Their visit with all their support and understanding helped me a lot to cope with all that was going down in my life at the time. In February '73, my ex moved out of the Fort Walton Beach area to live with her sister Ellen in West Palm Beach, Florida. That meant that I would only see Michael and Jon during their summer vacation.

1973

I missed my boys and to keep my mind off of it. I kept busy. I worked my day job at Duke, flew a lot at night and on weekends with the reserves, and worked on the apartments. It all helped, but I still miss my boys.

During the year, I made some improvements to the apartments. One of my first projects was to float and repair the sunken boat. I then rebuild the old Evinrude outboard on the floor of my apartment. The boat was reincarnated as the "Sinkeze" and designated to be the Surfview launch. As soon as the outboard was operational, my buddies and I started making runs in the Sinkeze to the clubs up and down the Sound. One of our favorite late-night watering holes was Bacons by the Sea, near Hurlbert Field, the place where Jimmy Doolittle planned his Tokyo Raid.

With the help of my friends, we rebuilt and lengthened the dock, put in a seawall, and dug up the cane break that ran along the shore of our beach. I also planted a few palm trees to make the place look like Florida and built two 8ft long picnic tables. The tables were a place where we could sit, look out over the Sound and have discussions, sometimes heated on what was going on in the world. Slowly I was easing back into the dating game and started enjoying life.

My parents drove up from DeBary to their condo at the El Matador to be with the boys when they flew in for the

summer. As a surprise, I bought a couple of Sunflower Styrofoam sailboats for them to learn how to sail in. The two Sunflowers were a real hit. They gradually turned into a fleet when some of my tenants bought them. We started having Sunday sailing regattas at the Surfview. The races would have a Le Mans start off the beach on a course around the intercostal buoys located in the Sound and back to the beach. It turned into quite the event with lots of fun and laughter being had by all. From the tables, we could sit and watch the fun. Life was becoming very enjoyable in paradise. The weekend regattas were becoming more competitive, and the summer was flying by fast. After, Michael and Jon flew back to their mother in West Palm Beach. My parents informed me before leaving that they would be back up at El Matador for Thanksgiving.

When they drove back up, they brought along my Aunt Dorothy and Aunt Helen to stay at their condo with them and join the festivities. On Thanksgiving Day at the Surfview, Dad and I set up the tables, and Mom roasted a turkey with all the trimmings for the feast. I invited some of my friends to join us. Thanksgiving turned out to be an enjoyable and memorable event that would be repeated almost every year.

On New Year's Eve, I loaded up some of my friends in the Sinkeze, the Surfview Launch, and cruised around, stopping at our favorite bars on the Sound. We ended up at the Seagull in time to bring in the New Year.

1974

Things were starting to come together at the 919[th,] and we finally received our full complement of airplanes from the active-duty units, and our personnel ranks were filled, mostly with local area reserve recruits. By putting in eight hours a day at my day job as a GS-12 at Duke Field and flying night low-level air-drop missions during the week as a reservist, plus a training weekend once a month, I was making ends meet. One of the advantages of flying on the Tuesday and Thursday night missions was that I would get back to town around 11 at night, just in time to strafe (check out) the bars on the way home. I also volunteered for any additional weekend cross-country missions for the extra pay and retirement points. I still had time on my hands and started to look for other things to do.

From the time I was in High School at Point Pleasant Beach, N.J, until I joined the Air Force, I worked on and off as a deckhand on the fishing boats out of Brielle, N.J. I contacted the fleet I worked for and asked them if they had kept a record of my sea time. To my surprise, they did and said they would send me a copy. I was even more surprised at how much time I had accumulated, 371 days. Checking with the Coast Guard, I found out that I had just enough sea time for a Coast Guard Captain's license. I bought a study guide, studied up, then drove over and took the test at the Coast Guard office in Mobile, Alabama.

With the license in my hand, I went looking for and found three other sailing enthusiasts that so happened to be my friends and tenants at the Surfview. We talked about forming a partnership for the purpose of buying a boat for fun and charter. It didn't take long for us to file the paperwork for a subchapter S limited corporation with Tom Prohaska as our president, who worked as a senior scientist for a contractor on Eglin AFB, for treasurer Bill Everett, a pharmacist and reservist, Bubba Bost (everyone in the south knows a Bubba) as a deckhand and a fellow reservist, myself as captain of the boat that we didn't own yet. All of us lived in Surfview and were either divorced or single. We ran the bars, partied together, and were now in the charter boat business; all we needed was a boat.

We found one, a fellow reservist in the 919th, David Krebs, had a 36' Kenner Skipjack, a shawl

draft centerboard bug-eyed ketch with an 8' dinghy for sale, and we bought it. The boat was named the Windsong, and we used its name for our subchapter S corporation, Windsong Charters Inc. We started taking people out on day charters on the Sound and Choctawhatchee Bay. Most of our cruises around the local area were with our friends, and we were definitely having fun with the boat. We sailed her as often as we could get a crew together, day or night, up and down the coast and the Sound. In the summer, when my boys and other kids were on board, I would put them to work as apprentice deckhands to learn how to work the boat.

In the spring of 1974, Hobie 16 catamarans started to make their appearance in the area. One of the first was acquired by one of my tenants at the Surfview. He heard that one had arrived at a dealership in Destin, so we drove over and took it out for a test hop. He bought it right then and there, and we took off to sail it back to the Surfview. On the way, we pitchpoled it, then learned

the hard way how to get it right side up again. It wasn't long before it seemed like everyone and his brother had one. Hobie regattas became a big deal on Choctawhatchee Bay. Before long, they started having races around the island, around the bay, and regional and even national races. Just about every weekend during the summer, there was a Hobie regatta somewhere in the local area, and there was always a shortage of crew.

In June, I picked up Michael and Jon at the airport to spend the summer with me at the Surfview. My parents had already driven up from DeBary to their condo in the El Matador to be around to enjoy with their grandsons. The summer was full of fun adventures for us and the boys, to do. The Sinkeze was running well enough to teach them how to waterski and sail in the Surfview Regattas on the weekends. The boys were also learning how to crew on the Hobie Cats.

During the year, building three at the El Matador was complete, and my parents exercised their option to buy their second unit, the one-bedroom unit number 325. After they closed on the deal Jack Brown, one of the pilots in the 919th living at the Surfview, became my parent's first tenant. Their investment was starting to pay off. Tom and I helped Jack move into his new digs. The hardest part of the move was getting the bar he bought in the Philippines up to the second floor of the building and into his apartment. Once we got it in place, we had to break it in.

While my sons were enjoying their summer at the Surfview, my ex moved to Fort Lee, New Jersey, with her parents near the George Washington Bridge. At summer's end, my dad and I drove the

boys to the airport for their flight to Newark and their new home. These prisoner exchanges were rough on everyone, especially my two sons. Unfortunately, over the last couple of years, their mother saw fit to move them around all over the place.

On August 22nd, Doug Spitler, one of my tenants who was also a pilot in the 919th, got married at the Surfview. He and his new wife Judy, a lovely woman from Melbourne, Australia. They had been hanging out together for a while, so the wedding was no big surprise. The celebration was a truly memorable event for the whole gang at the Surfview and many of our flying buddies from the 919th. It was our first wedding at the Surfview, and the party lasted well into the evening.

On September 3rd, I was promoted to major in the Air Force Reserves, and a short time later, my temporary civil service job that I held for two years ended. The result was that I had a big cut in

income. Fortunately, the profit margin from Surfview had increased, but my total income was down.

My parents drove up to their apartment at the El Matador from DeBary for Thanksgiving. To get ready for the feast at the Surfview, my dad helped me put the picnic tables together in the parking lot and cleaned up the area. Everyone at the Surfview was invited. Just bring some food to add to my mom's huge roasted turkey on the table. We gathered quite a crowd. Tom, Bill, my parents, my girlfriend Judy Bean, Bubba, and his parents, plus a few others that had no place to go. The feast turned out to be a great success lasting until late in the evening. Lots of conversation, wine, solving all the world's problems, we were all having way too much fun.

After Thanksgiving, my parents headed back to DeBary to prepare for the upcoming Christmas holidays. My mother decided to have Christmas dinner at their home in DeBary again that year, and there was no way I was going to be late for it. I started my drive early to make sure I didn't miss anything.

My mother, Margaret, was in her glory. She had ten people there for Christmas dinner; uncle Eric

and aunt Elfriede, uncle Eddy and aunt Vera, their son and my cousin, Kevin, aunt Helen, and uncle Henry and a couple from next door. They were all ready and eager to enjoy my mother's wonderful cooking. We all had a marvelous time and absolutely ate too much, especially Mom's special Christmas cakes. It was great to see and chat with my relatives again; the only ones missing were my boys.

I arrived back in Fort Walton Beach in time to join my Windsong partners in celebrating the New Year by doing a pub crawl of the local bars on the island.

1975

On January 3rd, 1975, Windsong Charters board members had a business meeting to discuss our financial status. Since we did not have much to talk about, the discussion eventually turned to taking the Windsong on a cruise somewhere. After much discussion, we all agreed on a cruise to the Bahamas. One big problem, my partners all worked steady jobs and could not take off the amount of time needed to sail to and from the islands, but they could take off for a week or two while the boat was in the Bahamas. All we needed to do was find a crew to help sail the Windsong to the islands.

Once we found a crew, we would be good to go, but in the meantime, we began planning for the trip. We started gathering maps and charts, a Bahamas guide, foul weather gear, a 20-man life raft that I borrowed, and everything else we thought we needed.

The plan was to wait for a northerner (cold front) to blow on through and then set sail on the backside of it. You would still have north winds of up to 20 to 25 knots to blow you onto the south, and after the first day, the wind would usually moderate to 10 to 15 knots and shift to the NE, then on to the E. This would give you about 3 to 5 days of a good wind to sail south before it returned to normal NE trade winds at 10 to 15 knots.

The middle of January brought a northerner, and we were ready to go. We loaded the last few things on board. Last but not least was my 20-man life raft and the dinghy. The volunteer crew, Don Elwell and Norm Muncie, both experienced sailors, loaded their gear; they were neighbors from the Anchorage Apartments next door.

The next morning on January 20th at 08:10, we were underway. The wind was out of the NW at 18, cold, but a nice sail down the Sound with the sails reefed down. We cleared Destin Pass at 10:00 and set a course of 120 degrees, everything was just honky dory. The Windsong was sailing on a broad reach and riding easy on the seas with a bone in her teeth. At 12:00, the wind shifted further north and freshened to around 20 knots, everything was going as planned, so I went below to get a Coors. Coors at the time was only available west of the Mississippi, and I had smuggled a few cases back on a reserve mission to Colorado. We brought the beer along as a sort of forbidden fruit. Everyone was in high spirits and enjoying the ride.

Then around 14:00, things started to happen. The cable that holds up the centerboard broke, allowing the centerboard to fall all the way down. It started bumping around in the centerboard trunk. We didn't think it was that serious a problem at first, the boat was still sailing well, and we found a point of sail where it wasn't banging around so much. We broke out the maps and charts to look at our options of where we could go to get repairs. The wind was out of the N around 20 knots, and Panama City was NE of our position, out of reach. We would try to make Port St Joe.

By 18:00, I realized we were not going to make it into St Joseph Sound and Port St Joe. We had to fall off and go around the shawls at Cape San Blast, then try to make it into either Apalachicola or Carabelle. Motor sailing with double-reefed sails, we made our way around the San Blas buoy at 23:00. We were miserable, in the middle of the night, enduring freezing cold, a howling 20 to 25 knots of wind, and high seas. That's when our situation went from bad to worse.

Midnight, the bewitching hour, Don fell while down below and laid open his lip. At about the same time, we started to take on water. I went down below and patched up Don's lip, then went looking for and located the leak around the centerboard trunk under the floorboards. We started sending out mayday calls on the C.B. radio, and the situation was getting serious. No answer to our distress calls. The bilge pump was keeping up with the leak, so we hauled down the sails and motored for the beach. Around 01:00, the bilge pump stopped working. The float switch failed, so I hot-wired the pump and got it back online. The leak was getting worse, the centerboard hinge pin was busting up the centerboard trunk. We tried to knock the pin through the centerboard, but no luck. By 02:40, water was pouring in, we tried stuffing everything we could lay our hands on into the leak. We were in deep kimchi.

We were still calling May Day on our worthless radio to no avail. At 04:00, with water a foot over the floorboards, we started bailing with buckets. The bow was getting low in the water when we sighted some lights on the horizon and shot off some flares, but no luck. At 05:00, the batteries shortened out by 05:30, we were taking on water in the engine room. We realized it was time to save our butts and abandon ship.

Up on deck, we unlashed the raft and dinghy at around 06:30, we launched the dinghy, then launched and inflated the 20-man raft. It looked like the Hilton. We started loading, and we put the sharp equipment that might puncture the raft in the dinghy and the rest in the raft; it was sort of a controlled bailout. We took with us the sextant, compass, food, water, clothing, flares, first aid kit, flashlight, a bottle of bourbon, and a case of Coors. All loaded, and while still tied up

alongside, we made a last pass through the boat for anything we missed.

At dawn, we boarded the raft, and with the dinghy in tow, we abandoned the Windsong. She sank at 07:50, bow first on an even keel just like the Titanic, into the deep six. I took a picture of her going down. I estimated our position at the time to be 10 miles south of St. George Island.

The wind had shifted around to NE at around 10 knots and the seas moderated. We were drifting to the SW headed for Mexico the hard way. At 08:20, we sighted an orange and white boat to the east of us. We fired off some flares, but no luck; they turned east and went out of sight. At 10:00, I changed the bandage on Don's lip, it was still bleeding, then took an inventory of what we had taken off the Windsong. We were all exhausted and pretty much all passed out. We were lucky to be alive.

We were adrift on a beautiful day in the Gulf of Mexico and not a thing in sight. Occasionally, we would see some gulls flying around and a few porpoises popping up to check us out. There was nothing else for me to do but have a beer and think of all the things I should have done and where I screwed up the most. After all, I was the captain and responsible for my crew and ship. After pondering my screw-ups for a while, I finally came to some conclusions. When the cable for

the centerboard broke, the right course of action should have been to head for the beach as fast as possible. I did not do that fast enough. In fact, if anything breaks that cannot be fixed on the spot, head for the beach or the closest port and make repairs. Mother Nature is way too unforgiving, and you must respect her awesome power. A situation at sea can get out of hand real fast, you must be aware of what is going on around you and your vessel, or you will pay the price. You live and learn if you survive.

In the afternoon, we had some peanut butter sandwiches, carrots, celery, and some juice. Right around 16:30, we spotted a boat to the east of us and headed our way. We fired off some flares, but by then, the sun was low to the west, and they probably couldn't see them. However, they kept coming heading directly toward us, spotted us, and picked us up. It was the "Janis Rowe," a shrimp boat operated by Capt. Orin Rowe and his son Langston. We were really lucky and happy to meet them, they even cooked up the steaks that we unloaded from the dinghy and raft that we pulled on board. Capt. Rowe said he never saw us until he was right upon us at a position 15mi South of

Cape San Blas. We had drifted about twelve miles SW from where the Windsong sank. I called Tom Prohaska, the president of Windsong Charter, he was not overjoyed. When the "Janis Rowe" dropped us off at the Panama City Pier, Tom was there waiting for us. Don, Norm, and I thanked Capt. Rowe and his son profusely for rescuing us. I had a lot of explaining to do on the drive back to Fort Walton Beach. Don got his lip sewed up; it took 12 stitches and would recover completely. That was the end of the Windsong, but not the end of Windsong Charters, Inc.

The day after our rescue, we contacted our insurance company and told them that their boat sank. Since I had photos that would be absolute proof of the Windsong sinking, under maritime law makes it a total loss, and the claim would be paid in full with no deductible. I told them that I had a pretty good position of where the Windsong sank. I had copied the Loran coordinates of where the "Janis Rowe" picked us up and the estimated position of where the Windsong sank.

When I took the 20-man raft in to get repacked and recharged, they told me that the CO2 bottle wasn't attached properly and were amazed that the raft inflated when I actuated it during our abandoned ship. It's a good thing to have a bit of luck.

Days later, while talking on the Surfview dock about the sinking of the Windsong with Skip Price, who I met at a New Year's Eve party shortly before we left on the Windsong's disastrous cruise. He was a professional diver that worked in the oil industry at oil patches all over the world, and after talking for a while, he put up an idea that we might be able to recover the Windsong. Since she sank in only 70 feet of water, it would be relatively easy to salvage. My partners were there as well, and we debated what our next move would be. If the boat was salvaged by the insurance company, they would give it back to us in lieu of paying off our claim. We could also offer to buy the salvage rights from them after they paid us off and salvage it ourselves. We did have a lot of stuff on the boat that would be nice to get back. We decided to introduce Skip to the insurance people and see what happened. A few days later, we had a meeting with the insurance people, they didn't seem very interested in any of our ideas, so I gave them a copy of the photos I took of the boat sinking.

Days later, I got a call from the insurance company stating that they wanted to hire Skip to go find the Windsong for them. He went to meet with them the next day to discuss what they had in mind. He came back saying they hired him and gave him some upfront money to hire a boat and go find her. Skip and I drove to Panama City, Mexico Beach, and Apalachicola looking for a boat to hire. We were pretty worn out by late afternoon and headed back to Panama City, where we spent the night. In the morning, we found a 50-foot sports fisherman available to hire for a two- or three-day trip.

A few days later, we were ready to depart on the search for the Windsong. Jack Brown, a fellow reservist, drinking buddy, and my parent's tenant at the El Matador, came along for the ride. We loaded up all our gear, steaks, beer, and diving equipment for an early departure from Panama City. It would take a couple of hours to run out to the spot where the "Janis Rowe" picked us up. The weather was beautiful, with calm seas and the temperature in the 70s, a perfect day for a cruise in the Gulf. We popped a couple of beers and settled in to enjoy the ride.

Around noon we arrived at the position where the "Janis Rowe" picked us up, then turned to a heading of NE and motored toward the position on my chart where I thought the Windsong sank. It took around an hour to get there, and I started scanning around with the boat's depth recorder and fish finder. We spotted something floating on the surface and went over and picked it up. To our surprise, it was one of the fenders off the Windsong. Well, that was easy; we found it right off the bat. No such luck. We scanned around for the rest of the day; nothing worth diving on. So, we anchored up for the night, had a few beers, then cooked up our steaks and had a wonderful dinner. After our meal, we enjoyed a beautiful sunset, chewed the fat for a while, and then turned in for the night.

After an enjoyable leisurely breakfast, we again started our search for the Windsong. During the search, we noticed that there was a lot of flying activity going on in the area, probably from Tyndal AFB, located just east of Panama City. Later on, in the early afternoon, we noticed a large parachute deploying pretty much over our heads. It turned out to be a target drone from Tyndal that splashed down about 100 yards from us. We motored over to check it out. It was painted orange and around 20 feet long, sort of like a large model airplane. On the tail, there was a sign that said that there was a $500 reward for its recovery. Skip saw the sign, grabbed a line, dove in, swam over, and tied it to its tail, to the chagrin of our captain, who wanted to leave it alone.

It wasn't 20 minutes before we saw a recovery boat charging over the horizon, looking for their drone.   On their arrival, we all kind of looked at each other for a while before the captain of the recovery boat grabbed a bull horn and asked us to let go of their drone. Skip asked them for a receipt, and after a little shuffling around, they gave us one, and we cast off the drone. We watched them go through the procedure of picking up the drone, then went back to searching for the Windsong.

We returned to Panama City around 1700 after an unsuccessful but interesting search. We thanked the captain of our search boat for an enjoyable cruise and headed back to Fort Walton Beach.

That pretty much ends the saga of the Windsong, except for notifying the insurance company that the search was unsuccessful. Skip went up and gave them the bad news the next day and asked if they wanted to spend any more money on the search, but they declined.   A short time later, they paid off Windsong Charters in full. We never saw the drone recovery reward; the owner of the boat must have received it.

My partners were not too happy about me sinking the Windsong, although the insurance payoff helped ease the pain. A short time later, Bubba are partner was hired by a reserve unit up north and would be departing the area in a couple of months. He sold out his share in Windsong Charters, Inc. to Jack Brown on the 14th of February '75. About this time, with the help of my friends, I added to the dock a few feet and built on it an enclosure for a refrigerator modified to hold a keg of beer and tap. Now with the addition of a couple of chairs and a bench, we had a little beer garden on the end of the dock.

My girlfriend Judy Bean moved out of the local area and took a job as a deckhand on an 85' yacht owned by Taylor Diving Company in New Orleans, the same company the Skip worked for. She invited me to come over and stay on the yacht for Mardi Gras. That sounded like a great idea to me, and when I mentioned it over a beer on the dock, Tom said he wanted to go. I called Judy and told her I would be there and that Tom wanted to come along. She had no problem with that since there was plenty of room on the boat.

We drove over to New Orleans on the Saturday before Fat Tuesday, and once we found the New Orleans Yacht Club where the boat was docked, I contacted Judy, who showed us aboard to stow our gear, then took us over to her boss's house to introduce us. He and his family were very hospitable, and after chatting with them for a while, he seemed to have no problem with Tom, and I was staying on the yacht for a couple of days. After leaving her boss's house, she took us over to meet his mistress at the house he had her set up in. Her name was Honey, and she was a very dynamic and energetic coonass (Cajun) woman who insisted on showing us around to some of her favorite haunts. On the way, she stopped to pick up her companion, a gay guy that her sugar daddy was okay with. She first took us to a gay bar to observe the craziness, then on to a jazz bar in Metairie, where we stayed till closing. By the time we got back to the boat, it was way past midnight, and you had to party hard to hang with the crowd in New Orleans.

Over the next couple of days, the three of us, Tom, Judy, and I, had the opportunity to watch many parades, enjoy some really great food, listen to some amazing New Orleans Jazz, drink way too much booze, and have way too much fun.

Back at the Surfview, Windsong Charters, Inc. was without a boat, so with our new partner, we went looking for another boat. We drove around the local area, checking out all the marinas for something that would suit our needs; we all agreed that we needed a bigger boat. We finally found

one near Pensacola, "Our Honey," an old wooden boat that needed a lot of fixing up, built in 1918 as a 60-foot gaff-rigged schooner at the Morton Johnson Boatyards in Bay Head, N.J. She originally served as a dory tender of the nets on the Jersey Banks. Its job was to sail up and down the coast with crews that would launch dories to help the fisherman that rowed out from the beach fill their surfboats with fish that they would row back to the beach. The boat was originally named the "Barbro," had a history of many owners, and was a survivor of many storms. In the 1946 hurricane that went ashore in West Palm Beach, she lost her foremast and was rebuilt as a double headsail sloop by stepping the mainmast where the foremast had been. It was later sold to a group of people from New York that used her for many years to sail the Bahamas and the Southeast coast of Florida. Damaged again in a storm that she encountered off Nassau, she was sold to a man named Wigle. This owner ran her on the rocks in Florida at Point Everglades, jumped in to push her off, and got his legs smashed in the process. A policeman observed what was going on and came to his aid and pretty much saved his life.

Wigle later died from his injuries, but not before selling the boat to a policeman named Smith at a low price in appreciation for his help. Smith renamed it "Our Honey" and sailed her up to Little Sabine Bay near Pensacola, where he was employed as the county sheriff. Windsong Charters, Inc. bought the boat from Smith on March 29, 1975.

On the morning of March 30th, the proud new owners boarded "Our Honey" with some adventurous friends, loaded our gear, and cast off from the dock at Little Sabine Bay. We hoisted the sails and headed down the Sound to Fort Walton Beach and the Surfview Apartments, where she would be docked. The trip was pretty much uneventful, except that we were a little anxious about making it under the Navarre Bridge. We made it and then had a pleasant lunch of shrimp, cheese, bread, and wine as we sailed east down the sound, tying up at the Surfview dock by early afternoon.

On May 26th, with the owners and friends on board, we took her for a little sail up the Sound. The boat had a Grey Marine gas engine that was a pile of rust that scared me to death. I thought that any minute would blow up; we have to replace it ASAP. The wind quit a mile up the Sound, so we tried to come about and head back to the Surfview dock. We ended up ramming a pine tree on the island in the process. Of course, the Grey Marine would not start and would never run again. We had to tow her home, first with the Sinkeze, which ran out of gas, then like the "Volga Boatmen" towed her home by hand.

Wow! That was a lot of fun.

During May, my parents drove up from DeBary, and a couple of days later, Dad and I picked up my boys at the airport for the summer.   They were just in time for the festival. Every year on the first weekend of June, there is a festival in Fort Walton Beach called "Billy Bowlegs," a reenactment of an invasion of the town by the famous pirate.

To take part in the event, we loaded up the boat with people, towed Our Honey out with the Sinkeze, and anchored up in the Sound, where we could observe all the activity that was going on. It turned into quite a day, a squall line blew on through and, causing the boats to drag anchor, it

turned into a tangled mess. We ended up losing one of our anchors while trying to reset it, the bitter end wasn't tied off. Luckily, we made it back to the dock in one piece. My kids just enjoyed the confusion immensely. They were having just a good old time at the Surfview with their dad and grandparents.

We decided on the 19th of June that the name "Our Honey" had to go, so we had a name on the boat contest. The name that won, submitted by Tom Prohaska, was "Pele ". He lived in Hawaii for a while and knew about Pele, the Hawaiian goddess of volcanoes that sort of went with the figurehead of a Hawaiian girl on the bow. I wanted to name it "Mary Ann Burns the Queen of All the Acrobats," but it was way too long.

On the 22nd of June, Bubba, our ex-partner in Windsong Charters, married Joyce. The ceremony was performed by Yvonne Miller on the Pele while she was tied up at the dock. A reception immediately followed in Norm Muncie's apartment at the Anchorage, the apartments next door. Norm, a fellow survivor of the Windsong sinking, put on a great reception for the newlyweds, and a good time was had by all.

Another wedding was performed on the 2nd of August by Yvonne on the Pele. Harry Tapper, one of my tenants, married Jackie. The reception followed immediately in the Surfview parking lot, with all the usual suspects. Tom Prohaska, Jack Brown, Bill Everett, Skip Price, Bill, and Marie Leibold and their sons Eric and Kevin, my parents Bill and Margaret, and my sons Michael and Jon, who were down for the summer, plus lots of other friends and neighbors.

Toward the end of August, with summer winding down, I had to send my boys back to N.J. and their mother.   My parents left shortly thereafter for their home in DeBary, Fl. I thanked them for coming up for the summer and helping with my kids. The boys really enjoyed the time with their grandparents, and I really enjoyed Mom's cooking and Dad's help around the Surfview.

A couple of weeks after their departure, we were under a hurricane warning. Hurricane Eloise was on the way to the Gulf Coast, and we were getting ready for it. She was forecast to come ashore to the East of us, putting us on the weaker side of the storm and could expect winds out of the NW and N. So we tied up the "Pele" in a way that hopefully she would withstand Eloise and battened down the hatches. As an afterthought, we tied one more line from the bow to a palm tree that was close to the Pele. After finishing all these preparations, Tom and I left the island to attend a hurricane party on the mainland.

Hurricane Eloise blew ashore with 130 mph winds in the early morning of 23 September to the west of Fort Walton Beach toward Pensacola, putting us on the stronger side of the storm. I woke up early to all the noise with the wind unexpectedly blowing in from the South. I found and woke up Tom, and we made our way back to the island, fearing what we would find. What we found

was that all the lines we tied the boat to the dock with had slid off the top of the pilings when the storm surge came ashore. The only line secured to the Pele was the line we tied to the palm tree. There she sat with her figurehead's breasts torn off and half full of water but still afloat with all the hatches blown away. She had road over the Sinkeze and pushed her to the bottom. Somehow the Surfview survived with just a couple of shingles blown away, so all in all, we survived Eloise's wrath pretty well.

During the next month or so, we were busy boys cleaning up the mess that washed up from Eloise. My first fix was repairing the roof on the Surfview and cleaning up the grounds. We salvaged a few pilings, lumber, and someone's deck that washed up on our beach. After removing the figurehead, we tied her to a palm tree (can't have a titless wonder on board), then pumped out the Pele, raised the Sinkeze, and even managed to get the old Evenrude outboard running again.

We eventually ran across a navy surplus Buda diesel engine that we bought to replace the rusted-out Grey Marine gas engine. On the morning of the 2nd of December, we towed the Pele over to the seawall at the Seagull Restaurant with the Sinkeze and dropped in the diesel. That was the last project before everyone took off for the holidays.

I drove down to DeBary to spend Christmas with my parents, just the three of us. Mom's cooking encouraged me to eat way too much during Christmas Dinner. I really had a great time, and I'm truly blessed to have such wonderful parents. I consider myself very lucky to be able to spend considerable time with them during the year. A few days after Christmas, I headed back to Ft. Walton for the New Year's Eve Party at the Hogs Breath Saloon, a new bar on the island to close out 1975.

1976

In March, the 919 TAW became the 919 SOW, and we started training our squadron, now called the 711th SOS, at Hurlburt Field in the C-130 gunship (Specter). I was on the crew that picked up our first gunship armed with two 40 mm cannons, a 20 mm Gatlin gun, plus two 7.62mm miniguns, all sticking out the left side of the airplane. From then on, we flew mainly night training missions on the Eglin ranges.

During the first couple of months of the year, my partners and I pretty much determined that the Buda diesel engine that we had just bought was worn out (no wonder it was so cheap). The head gasket leaked, causing water to get into the oil, overheating, low oil pressure, and numerous other problems. One consolation, however, was that it was a diesel and wasn't going to blow up. So, we dealt with it. We replaced the head gasket and ran it for the least amount of time possible. The engine problems didn't stop us in the least from sailing around the local area. Every opportunity was taken to round up a crew for a little cruise.

On one of these sails in June, we needed to determine how much mast clearance we had under the Brooks Bridge. Bill Everett volunteered to be hauled up the mast while we eased up to the bridge and measured how much clearance there was. What we found was that we had a 9-inch clearance when there were four planks showing on the bridge's fenders. With this knowledge, we felt much more comfortable about sailing under the bridge to get to Choctawhatchee Bay.

On the 22nd of June, we sailed the Pele over to the Spence Bros. Boatyard in Niceville to haul her out on their marine railway. Once the boat was out of the water, we could see that the hull below the waterline was being held together by a cement and chicken wire overlay, and it appeared to us that maybe the frames were rotted away. After fumbling around and making no progress, and since we really didn't know what we were doing, we hired the boatyard to make her seaworthy again. After a week of no visible progress by the boatyard, we cut out a few planks that we thought were rotten so that they couldn't launch her back in the water without repairs. They were upset with us but admitted that they were dragging their feet and gave us a contact of someone that could help us out. The contact was Leo Baer, an old shipwright who helped build wooden minesweepers in Canada during WW2. We contacted him, and he came over to the boatyard and looked over the Pele and agreed to take on the project and, in effect, saved the boat.

It was determined that since I could make time available during the week, I would be Leo's helper and gofer. On the weekends, my partners, friends, my kids (who were down for the summer), and any other volunteers were put to work. It was the beginning of the summer of hard slave labor. We decided not to mess with the cement below the waterline for the time being.

Under Leo's direction, the first project was to tear out the interior of the boat. Since the boat was ceilinged (planks on the inside as well as the outside of the frames), this had to be done to expose the frames. What we found once exposed was that ninety percent of the oak frames were rotted. The fix was to replace them one at a time with new laminated frames. This was a long-drawn-out process by first removing one frame and fasteners. Next, glue and nail quarter-inch thick cypress slats one on top of the other until this new frame was built up to the same dimensions as the old frame.

The weekends were a flurry of activity at the boatyard; whoever showed up was put to work down below working on the frames. During the week, Leo and I would drive out to Wilson's Sawmill on Hwy 90 West of Crestview, about an hour drive in my old 67 Chevy station wagon that we called "Jaws" for the teeth painted on its rusted hood by my uncle Eric, the artist. We loaded it up with rough cypress planks cut to Leo's specifications until Jaws bottomed out for the trip back to the boatyard. There we would cut the planks on their table saw into slates for the workers that showed up on the weekends. This went on for most of the summer. I put my kids to work, but my mom would only let me have them on the weekends. I thought they were having all kinds of fun, working down below, gluing and nailing new frames together. I guess. Mom wasn't much into child forced labor at a boatyard.

Since I did the driving, I would pick up Leo in Navarre and drive him home every day. A rainy day meant that we quit work at the boatyard early, and on the way home, Leo insisted on making some stops. He knew every bar and bartender between Niceville and his home in Navarre, and we had to stop at every one. We would have a beer, and he would tell me stories of his boatyard experiences. Leo was definitely a character and a fine craftsman that really knew his trade.

We also replaced any plank that showed rot and the rub rails with new bigger, sturdier ones. After working with Leo for a couple of months, I was beginning to learn a new trade, enough maybe to repair the Pele on my own in the future if need be. Leo amazed me with how he could fashion a plank for the hull that would fit perfectly out of a piece of rough lumber cut out of a log at the sawmill. Once we completed the frames and calked all the planks, we gave her a new blue paint job, and the Pele was ready to be launched back in the water.

We finally finished up and launched her on the 23 of August 76. We checked for leaks, then started up the Buda and motored the Pele back to our dock using a pipe wrench to steer and by calling throttle setting to the engine room; we hadn't installed the throttle linkage yet. We had reversed the steering gear in our newly built binnacle so that you stood behind the wheel instead of in front. We also swapped the old wheel for Skip's bigger and newer one, but unfortunately, we didn't have it yet. Skip, and the wheel was supposed to meet us on the bay in Bob Dryers' boat, the Independence. It did not happen, so we continued on, and without further incident, we made it to the Surfview dock. The Independence later joined us there with the wheel for the champagne welcoming at the Surfview dock.

The Pele still looked like a gutted grouper down below and needed a lot more work. Leo was still on the payroll and was kept busy working on the hatches, rails, and the bench's topsides. My partners and I worked on a design for the interior and decided to re-rig her as she was originally built, a schooner.

I found my old drafting board from college and went to work on making a scale drawing of the Pele. From this drawing, I extracted measurements to determine the height of the new foremast and the lengths of the cables for the standing rigging. Work went on in earnest; we built a worktable on the dock just a couple of steps away from the Pele, giving easy access for Leo and the rest of us to work on the boat.

On the 16th of October, we rented a crane to pull out the main mast and set it up on wooden horses in the parking lot of the Surfview, where we could work on it. While it was sitting there, we decided we needed to have more clearance on the bridge, so we chopped two feet off the mainmast. Leo was there supervising the whole operation, making sure we didn't screw it up while he was busy installing the new hatches, skylight, and stern bench.

It was a warm Thanksgiving Day in 1976. My parents drove up, and my mom roasted a turkey for the feast. We put the tables together in the parking lot for the feast, and around fourteen people

show up with food to add to the table. After filling our bellies with food and wine, we sat around and talked, and we all had an amazingly good time.

During December, we, with Leo's guidance, rebuilt the centerboard trunk as part of the dinette that could convert to a double bed and pulled all the ballast out, and pitched (tared) the bilges before replacing the ballast. Leo was busy down below, working on the quarter berth and the stateroom. I borrowed a lathe and started to turn out Dead Eyes for the new shrouds. From a machine shop, we had new chainplates manufactured. From the Lunenburg Foundry in Nova Scotia, we ordered a cast iron Fisherman stove and a Charlie Noble for its smokestack, plus hoops for the sails.

Later in December, I drove down to DeBary to be with my parents for Christmas. A neighbor, Dick Lefebvre, went with me. I dropped him off at his parents in Kissimmee on the way. At my parents, my aunt Helen was there with some of her famous pies and was told that she was in mourning. Her husband, my uncle Henry had recently died of skin cancer. It was good to be around family again, but uncle Henry's death did put a damper on the occasion and my mom's marvelous Christmas dinner. I hung around for a couple of days and then headed back to Fort Walton Beach, picking up Dick on the way.

My parents followed me back to the Surfview in time for the New Year and joined friends for the New Year's Party at the Hog's Breath Saloon to welcome in the New Year.

Once we installed the stove and the smokestack with the Charlie Noble on top, we fired it up, and it worked just fine. On a cold January afternoon, we fired it up and cooked up some dead eye stew. The Dead Eyes that I had just turned out on the lathe needed to be boiled in linseed oil to season them as a preservative. As they boiled away, we talked, drank some beer, and jokingly discovered that Tom was the only one with a real job. The rest of us were mostly part-time reservists. We fastened these newly seasoned Dead Eyes to the chainplates as the lower Dead Eyes for the mast's shrouds. Phil Mapp, a friend of ours from New Orleans, found us a spool of 5/8"stainless steel cable there at a good price. Once we got our hands on it, we went to work cutting, splicing, and

attaching the cables to the remaining upper Dead Eyes.

During the spring, we bought a pine pole that Leo picked out to shape into our new foremast from the Pensacola Pole Co. When it was delivered, we set it up on the wooden horses next to the main mast and started shaping it with a rented power planner, filling the parking lot with wood chips, under Leo's guidance, of course.

About this time, Gus showed up. Some of the local kids brought over a baby crow that they found lying in the road. I placed it in the Sago Palm Tree, located close to one of the picnic tables. We didn't know what to feed it, so we fed it what we had, minnows out of the fish tank, and whatever else it would eat. Gus became a fixture, squawking at us for keeping him awake with our late-night discussions at the picnic tables. During the day, we would put him on the workbench on the dock, where he had his beak in everything that was happening. Gus started hopping around enough to feed himself out of the fish tank and eventually started short flights around the parking lot. Gus would fly straight at you at eye level and expect you to put up your arm for him to land on. If you didn't, he would land on your head. This worked well around the Surfview, but when he expanded his range, he started freaking out of the neighborhood.

By early May, my parents drove up from DeBary to the apartment that I saved for them next door for the summer. Both their units at the El Matador were now being rented. When the boys got out of school, I made the airline reservations for their trip south. When they arrived, Dad and I went out to the airport to meet them. They seemed really happy to be back in paradise.

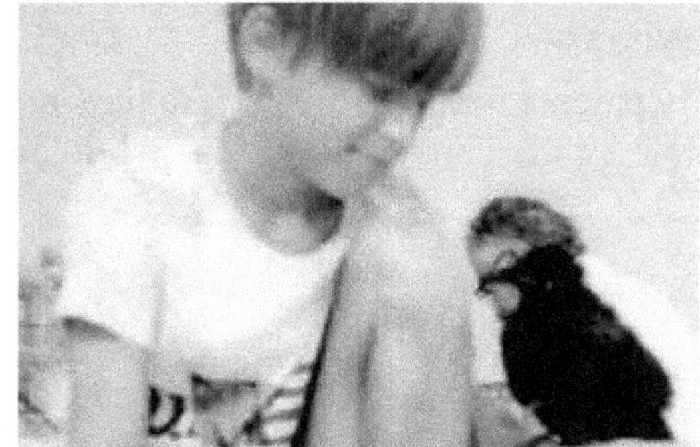

The boys had a blast with Gus, the crow. They seined up minnows for the fish tank to keep him well supplied with food and marveled at his antics. Gus was only around for a few months before he flew on; he will be remembered for how friendly, how curious, and how entertaining he was. Over the course of the summer, the boys were busy jet skiing, canoeing on the Blackwater River, Surfview regattas, sailing around the bay as crew on Hobie 16's, and sliding down the game. The boys had a blast with Gus, the crow. They seined up minnows for the fish tank to keep him well supplied with food and marveled at his antics. Gus was only around for a few months waterslide that our friend Skip Price had just built on the island. They were also pressed into some slave labor on the Pele.

By July, we had the new foremast shaped, seasoned with linseed oil, and ready to install with the main that was sitting next to it. With the standing rigging attached, we were ready for the big day. The crane arrived at 14:00 on 29 August 1977, and by 16:00, the Pele was successfully re-rigged as a schooner. Champagne flowed freely as we celebrated the event. The Pele was last a schooner in 1946. I was happy that my boys were there to witness the event since they had some skin in the game.

While we were setting the masts in place, a van showed up in the parking lot with one of my old tenants, Outlaw, a biker geologist that worked in the oil fields. He was lying down in the back of the van and looked really bad. He said he was dying from lung cancer and wanted his ashes spread from the Pele at sea off Panama City. His good friend, who was with him at the time, would make the arrangements when the time came. It kind of put a damper on all the excitement that was going on.

A couple of days later, the boys and I departed for the drive up to New Jersey so they could attend a youth camp in Canada that their mother set up for them. It was an interesting trip; we camped a couple of times in the War Wagon on our way north. One of the more interesting stops was at Kitty Hawk on the Carolina outer banks, it was deserted, and we had it all to ourselves to explore. We slowly and eventually made our way to Bricktown, New Jersey, where they now lived in time to leave for their camp in Canada.

After dropping the boys off, I drove up to Newport, RI, to check their maritime archives to do some research on the history of the Pele. On my arrival in town, there were all kinds of activities going on, and the America Cup teams were there getting ready to start racing on September 13th. At the same time, I was walking around on the docks observing all the activity and looking over the competing 12-meter sailboats. I somehow got invited aboard the "Australia" for a look around. Down below it was just a couple of bunks and a head (toilet) and a small galley. The one stand-out feature was that the hull was made of aluminum. I spent a couple of days there camped out in the War Wagon on the street near the docks while I did my research at the archives at the library and the Point Association; I found nothing.

From Newport, I drove to my old hometown, Point Pleasant, New Jersey, for a visit with some of my high school buddies. While in the neighborhood, I drove over to Bay Head, the next town south along Barnegat Bay, and visited the Morton Johnson Boatyard where the Pele was built in 1918, hoping to find out some of her history. I was looking for anything like maybe some construction drawings, but no such luck; they had no records dating that far back. The conclusion of my research was disappointing. The boat was built as a simple workboat and not built to last for any length of time.

My parents stayed on to help put on the Thanksgiving feast before heading back to DeBary. I couldn't put it on without my mom's cooking. Every year we have more attending the feast. We had close to 20 people, and the party lasted way into the night.

Waiting for Sabre Sails to finish making our new foresail didn't stop us from sailing the Pele around the bay with just a main and two headsails. To get underway, all we needed to do was round up a crew of friends.

On one of these occasions, on the 18th of December, while sailing the bay, Bob Dryer, on his Irwin 30, the Independence, pulled up on our lee to chat while sailing in formation with us. A short time later, a Ranger 23 pulled up on his lee. Bob realized that our leeway was putting the squeeze on him, so he sheeted in and sailed off. Shortly thereafter, the Ranger 23 on our lee was passing us amidships into the open area where our foresail would normally be. She caught an unobstructed wind gust causing the boat to head up in front of our bow. Once contact was made, she swung directly across our bow. The Pele's bowsprit chains road up to her starboard side amidships between her lifelines like a saw, healing her over and pushing her port rail under. At this point, I sheeted out the mainsail and started the engine to try and back off the boat. While this was happening, some of my crew boarded the boat, like a bunch of pirates, to help secure the backstay that broke from all the pressure on the rigging; that's when the Pele's engine quit. We had fouled the prop with a line. This was turning into a very interesting afternoon!

After untangling from the Ranger, we sailed around for a while before dropping the sails and anchoring up to free the prop. I asked for a volunteer, it was December and freezing cold, and I thought one of the young bucks on board would jump to the task. Bill Leibold, a professional diver, and a good friend, was on board. I asked him if he would give it a go. He said he only dives for money. No volunteers, so I had to do it. With my trusty, K-Bar knife clamped between my teeth, I jumped overboard and cut the prop free. Freezing, I climbed back on board and went down below where the fisherman stove was fired up to get warm. Then with the help of a couple of the ladies who massaged me back to life while I sipped on a hot toddy, it turned out not to be a bad afternoon after all!

On the 21st of December, Dad called and told me that Mom had a heart attack. I headed down to DeBary. She was in the hospital at Sanford, looking tired but in good spirits. The prognosis was that it was a minor attack and that she would be okay with medication. After they released her, I stayed on to help out. Christmas was pretty much a quiet, reminiscent and grateful occasion.

On my return to Fort Walton, work continued on the Pele's interior, and everything was pretty

much complete except for the fo'c'sle. Going from the fo'c'sle, the head (toilet) was on the starboard side, the galley on the port, dinette/bed on the starboard, the bench on the port, a quarter berth on the starboard, and the stateroom on the port. Even though the fo'c'sle wasn't completely finished, we now had a full set of sails and a boat we could maybe put to work in the charter business. We still had a problem with the Buda diesel that was continually plagued with engine overheating problems and putting out a lot of smoke. Friends that were mechanics worked on it but never could fix the problem. No matter, we were eager to get underway and try her out our new foresail.

1978

During January, the idea was floated that we needed to take a short shakedown cruise to test our confidence and proficiency in handling the Pele. We gathered up a crew that included Jack Brown and Skip Price, the guy with the waterslide who also supervised the search for the Windsong. He was now working in his new occupation as a captain on a supply boat in the oil patch. Bill and Marie Leibold (Bill had been Skip's dive tender and was now a diver in the oil fields), Lee Cooper, a pilot in my reserve unit, Mary Walton, a friend and nurse at the hospital, and Charlene Folly, a radiologist, my date for the weekend down and back cruise to Panama City.

We loaded on board wood and coal for the stove, some food, and a tapped keg of beer on the deck. We cast off from the Surfview dock at 08:00, hoisted up the sails, including our new foresail, and on a broad reach headed down the Sound to Choctawhatchee Bay bound for Panama City. We didn't have to worry about the beer getting warm up on deck, not with a cold NW wind and the temperature just above freezing. The stove was fired up and smoky down below, but it was keeping it nice and cozy, and with hot buttered rums all around, I had a happy crew.

On entering the canal (the Ditch) that connects Choctawhatchee Bay to Panama City West Bay and dropping the sails to motor down the canal to West Bay and on to Panama City, we arrived at 21:00, tied up at the Municipal Pier, and went to dinner at a local seafood restaurant, then on to bars to socialize with fellow rednecks. Everyone was feeling no pain when we returned to the boat later that night. Lee was cold; he didn't bring warm clothing, so he took the fire watch to keep the stove going. Charlene and I claimed the stateroom, Bill and Marie took the dinette/bed, Jack the quarter berth, and the rest crawled into the fo'c'sle. During the night, Lee fell asleep on fire watch

and fell over onto Bill and Marie; such fun.

The next morning, we cast off from the pier around 08:00 with a cold north wind blowing, and then it started to snow. We had plenty of cold beer on the deck, rum, and a warm stove down below, but it was still a cold cruise back to the Surfview. After we cleared the Ditch and

entered Choctawhatchee Bay, we hoisted the sails for what turned out to be a wonderful sail in the snow back to the Surfview, something we don't get much of in Florida. Our shakedown cruise was considered a success by all hands.

Tom's sister Jean and her husband Dwight owned a condo in Aspen, Colorado, and they offered to let Tom use it to go skiing. In turn, he invited some of his pals to go with him. We couldn't turn down an opportunity to ski Aspen and play with the rich and famous now, could we? Oh, yeah!

Jack, Tom, Bill, and I made a fast trip to Atlanta for the weekend to buy ski equipment and some ski clothes at a ski shop that was having a big end-of-season sale. I bought a pair of ski boots and a pair of Olin Mark IV skis, a ski jacket, gloves, and goggles to supplement my pair of Lederhosen nickers and knee socks that I bought years ago in Germany. The rest of the crew supplemented their old equipment with some new stuff.

In March, Tom, Jack, Bill Everett (one of the original owners of the Pele), and I loaded up the War Wagon and started our nonstop drive to Aspen. It would take thirty hours, including a stop halfway at a Mexican restaurant for some food in Amarillo, Texas. We drove in shifts, a driver would drive out a tank of gas for about four hours, then move to the co-driver seat, and that person would climb in the back and crawl into bed with the next driver to try and get some sleep.

Their condo at Aspen Square was located just across the street from Little Nell's bar/restaurant at the foot of Aspen Mountain; we would be located across the street, right in the thick of it. After checking in, we did a walkabout to check out the town. There were lots of restaurants, nightclubs, and bars; defiantly a party town. Of course, we were out late that night trying out some of the clubs to dance and chat up the ladies of Aspen.

Early the next morning, we were up bright and early to hit the slopes. We bought our ski passes when the lifts opened, and the lift lines were nice and short. We skied all day on Aspen Mountain (called Ajax by the locals), and for our last run of the day, we raced down Ruthie's Run to the bar at Little Nell's for a little Après ski with the crowd. All the characters at the bar were wearing the very latest in ski attire. We, on the other hand, were wearing what we could put together; after all, we were from the Redneck Riviera.

After a couple of hours at Nell's, we ran across the street to our condo to get rid of our ski gear, and once back on the street, we followed the crowd to Tippler's, the next bar down the road. We had an outrageous evening, too much to drink with not enough food and out way too late at night. But when the lifts opened in the morning, we were there ready to go, and so started another day of high adventure on the slopes in Aspen. Tom made a hit with the crowd by barfing in the lift line.

We all knew how to ski, but it's been a while, and you don't get a lot of snow in Florida to practice. We were slowly learning how to ski again and getting familiar with the different runs on the mountain. I found out that skiing in leather pants is not such a great idea because when you fall as I did the first couple of days, you tend to slide for a long way.

It did not take us long to slip into a daily routine, catch the first lift in the morning, ski all day, then catch the last lift to the top for a race down Ruthie's Run to Little Nell's for a little Après ski. Then after an hour or so of stomping around in our ski boots and chatting up the ladies, we head across the street to the condo and get ready for the evening. After getting something to eat, we'd get on the street and strafe the bars and nightclubs. That pretty much was our routine for the rest of our stay at Aspen.

One thing that Aspen was a-buzz about at the time was the killing of Spider Sabich, a pro skier who was a ski champion in 1971 and 1972. He was killed by gunshot by his lover Claudine Longet, a French actress, on March 2, 1976. She had been previously married to Andy William, the singer, but they divorced in 1975. She was eventually found guilty of criminal negligence and sentenced to serve 30 days in the county jail. On starting her sentence in Pitkin County Jail on 18 April 1977, she was allowed to repaint her cell, which she found drab and uninspiring, in lively primary colors. Don't you just love it!

After two weeks of hard-core skiing and being party animals, we took our last look at the beautiful mountains and the town of Aspen. We loaded up the War Wagon and hit the road for our thirty-hour drive to Florida. Once on the road, we had plenty of time to lick our wounds and elaborate on our adventures; it also gave us time to recover some.

After our return from skiing and over the next few months, we made numerous short sails in the Pele on the bay and the sound. Work on the interior of the Pele continued in the fo'c'sle. There was not much up there except for the anchor locker, so we would have to design and build some bunks there to finish the job. Plus, the never-ending job of making other small repairs and improvements.

Early in June, Dad and I picked up the boys at the airport for their summer in Paradise. When we arrived at the Surfview Apt, they peeled off their clothes. They had their bathing suits on underneath and jumped off the dock into the sound. During their stay, we sailed the local waters with the Pele every chance we could. We would load her up with friends and their kids and hoist up the sails and go.

On these pleasure cruises, the boys were usually my deck hands with Phil and Donna's kids, Chrissy and Derrick. They were learning how to handle and sail the Pele. These charters and pleasure sails were enjoyable, and my pirate crews usually had more fun than anyone.

Shortly after putting my boys on the plane back to New Jersey, we put the Pele back on the way at Spence Brothers Boatyard for her annual redo. Big pieces of the cement were still coming off the bottom during our sails on the bay and needed to be taken care of.

Once hauled out, we removed the loose pieces of cement from the bottom and refastened some planks, and sealed up permanently the hole in the centerboard trunk where the centerboard was a long time ago. The Pele was repainted and launched back into the water on the 25th of Aug.

 On 16 Sept '78, we cast off from the Surfview at 07:15 and headed for Panama City with the Sinkeze in tow on a quest to find the Windsong (another sort of half-assed attempt). Jack and Jan Norman were along as my crew, we were supposed to have more crew, but they chickened out. We sailed down the bay to the canal (the Ditch) and motored the rest of the way to Panama City, tying up at the Municipal Pier.

The next morning, the 17th, at 08:30, after taking on water and fuel, we started motoring in light wind for Apalachicola. Shortly before sunset, we arrived at Lake Wimico. Bob Dryer on Independence arrived shortly thereafter and rafted up with us for the night. Jan made a lovely dinner of coq au vin for the whole gang. We were the only ones anchored on the lake on a quite pitch-black moonless night with the stars on brilliant display. After dinner and the conversations lasted long into that beautiful night.

With an early departure the next morning, we arrived at the Apalachicola dock a little before noon and explored the town noted for harvesting the best oysters in the world, and stopped at the historic Gibson Inn for lunch; the Inn had been an officer's club during WW2. During the Civil War, Apalachicola was a big port for shipping cotton to the Confederacy. The cotton came down the river from Columbus, Georgia, for transshipment by blockade runners to Europe.

We fueled up on the morning of the 19th and sailed the bay with the Independence headed for

Horseshoe Cove on St George Island, where we anchored up a little after noon. Bob, on the Independence, headed back to Apalachicola to meet his wife, Carol. We spent another night there at anchor and then made a supply run in the morning to St George Yacht Basin in the Sinkeze. After stowing our supplies, we sailed to Dog Island to anchor and explored the island. Since we never went to look for the Windsong, the expedition to find it ended in failure.

The next morning, we sailed back to Apalachicola to meet up with the Independence for the trip back to Fort Walton Beach. We were back in Apalachicola by 16:00 and underway again by 17:00, bound for Lake Wimico. After spending another peaceful night on the lake, we were on our way toward Panama City. While motoring in quiet conditions at around 11:30, I heard a loud rumbling from the engine room, and we started to slow down. While we were still moving, I ran her aground on the south bank to investigate. What we found was that the propeller shaft coupling came apart. By rigging the Sinkeze as a yawl boat, we were able to push the Pele the rest of the way to Panama City Municipal Pier. By digging around in the bilge, I found the nuts and bolts and reassembled the coupling. A new crew arrived on the morning of 24 Sept: Tom, Jan, and Rita Margarita, my latest girlfriend.

On the sail back to the Surfview, the subject was raised that Halloween was a month away and that maybe we should have a party. After a lot of debate, it was agreed unanimously to have a Halloween costume party at the Surfview. The party was a huge success, most of the usual suspects were there, and almost everyone turned up in some sort of costume.

For Thanksgiving, I drove down to Marathon in the Florida Keys to meet my parents at my uncle Eric and aunt Elfriede's place in Little Venice, a sub-division on the island. They have a little one-bedroom house that Eric, being an artist, had added a second story to it for his studio. They have a nice setup on a canal that has a nice view of the Atlantic from his studio.

I drove back down to DeBary for Christmas with a passenger, Dick Lefebvre. I dropped him off on the way at his parents in Kissimmee and promised that I would pick him up on the way back.

Christmas that year was more of a Gebhardt family reunion, my parents Bill and Margaret, uncle Eric and aunt Elfriede, plus grandpa Pop, uncle Rudy, and aunt Claire, who drove down from New Jersey, only my sons Michael and Jon were missing. Not only did I get to feast on Mom's cooking, but I had the opportunity to renew family bonds. It was a fun time; my uncle Eric was always the life of the party, keeping us well entertained.

After my return from DeBary, one of the partners of Windsong Charter, Bill Everett, sold his holdings to the three remaining partners. I would now be treasurer of Windsong Charters and Captain of the Pele. We then adjourned the meeting and joined the Surfview crowd gathered at the Hog's Breath Saloon for the New Year's Eve celebration. The place was mobbed mostly by the people that we knew and who lived on the island.

1979

In early March of 1979, Tom arranged with his sister, Jean, for another two weeks stay for us at her condo in Aspen. Yahoo! Off on another ski adventure with the rich and famous celebrities of Aspen. Tom, Jack, and I departed in the War Wagon with a stop to pick up Phil Mapp, a friend and our contact in New Orleans. Twenty-four hours later, after a food stop at a Mexican restaurant in Amarillo, Texas, we arrived in Aspen at the Aspen Square condo and were eager to hit the slopes.

We knew the drill for Aspen Mountain (Ajax), be at the lift when they opened up in the morning, and ski all day. Make the last run of the day, a race down Ruthie's Run to Little Nell's for cocktails, then on to Tippler's to chat up and dance with the lovely ladies of Aspen.

About a week into our stay, we raced down to catch the last lift before it closed. I left the maniacs in the lift line and went over to the condo to get rid of my gear and clean up a bit before going to Little Nell's. To my surprise, when I opened the door, the place was full of people. I thought for sure that it must be Tom's brother Jon's crowd, who I had never met, so I introduced myself around. They were just about to throw me out when Tom showed up and saved the day and introduced me to his brother-in-law, Dwight.

That was the end of our free digs. We started packing our gear and moved out. We were lucky; even though the town was pretty much filled up, Dwight got on the phone and found us a condo to rent for our remaining week. Later on that evening, we met up with Dwight and hung out with him for a bit before continuing our mission of chatting and dancing up the ladies of Aspen.

Skiing at Aspen is a real treat for the enthusiast, we spent most of our stay skiing Ajax, but there are other ski areas around like Aspen Highland Ski Resort, Buttermilk, and Snowmass, to name a few, that offer other challenging runs.

After two weeks of running at full throttle, we were exhausted and ready for Florida. Licking our wounds, we started our drive home and back to my never-ending challenges of the Surfview and the Pele.

We finally solved Pele's engine overheating problem, oysters growing in the cooling system, but that was only part of the problem. We also had some sort of leak in the cooling system that allowed water to get into the oil. We changed the head gasket again, and all the other gaskets on the water jacket still leaked. My guess was that we might have a cracked block, but it still ran, so we would deal with it and just run it only when necessary.

My dad and I picked up the boys at the airport in June for their summer with us. They couldn't wait to jump off the dock into the Sound. Windsong Charters Inc. finally booked our first charters on the Pele. A couple of day sails around the bay during June and July with Tom and Jack as deckhands. I think they had a good time flirting with the women on board, plus making a couple of dollars. But most of the time, we loaded up the Pele with my parent, my kids, and friends to sail around the bay.

On the afternoon of 6 August, a thunderstorm swept over the Pele while tied up at the Surfview dock. Tom and I were working on the boat and had left the Pele with the sail cover off the main for a short trip to the hardware store. What we found on our return was a mess. The main boom had 6' broken off the end. The main sail had two panels torn. The boom gallows and the stern bench were busted up. A hard lesson learned, never leave the sail cover off at the dock or anytime you're not using the sails. After a couple of weeks of waiting to get the sails repaired at Sabre Sails and for Leo to repair the boom and the rest of the damage, we were finally back in business.

The summer was winding down, and I was getting ready to send my boys back up north when their mother called and asked if I would keep them until January. What a pleasant surprise! I agreed and ran over real quick to enroll them in school.

Hurricane Frederic made landfall just west of Pensacola on the Aug 12th with 130mph winds that pretty much tore up the gulf coast from Navarre to Mobile, Alabama. Being located about 80mi east of where Frederic went ashore, we escaped any serious damage.

Now that I had my sons living with me, I had to make some changes to my routine. My parents left and were back at their home in DeBary. No more Grandma's cooking and Grandpa helping to keep the boys in line. I broke out the cookbooks and put together a repertoire of meals and some sort of orderly routine for our lives.

The routine that I set up for the boys was pretty straightforward. During the week after school, we played a little cutthroat racquet ball, followed by dinner at 17:00, then homework, and to bed by 22:00. The exception was on Fridays when they cooked their own frozen pizza while their dad went to the Hog's Breath Saloon to drink beer with his buddies. After a week or two, we pretty much settled into the routine.

The local Hobie Cat fleet, sponsored by the Hog's Breath Saloon and others, was very active in the area and hosted the 1979 Hobie Nationals. My partners and I volunteered the Pele to be the committee boat. On the 24th - 26th of September, we would be anchored up by 08:00 in the bay, one mile north of the number one channel marker, until the racing was over for the day. Then from the 27th to the 29th, we would anchor up a ¼ mile off the beach in the gulf by the Ramada Inn in

Destin–a shuttle boat to take people back and forth to the beach, plus it kept us supplied with food and drink. The responsibility that the Pele's crew had was that once anchored up in the position, we were to keep out of the way of the race committee running the races. When the racing was over for the day, we would tie up at Marina Point Marina to spend the night and be ready to load the committee in the morning for that day's racing. After the last day of racing, there was the awards ceremony and banquet on Okaloosa Island. At the ceremony, there was lots of beer, conversations, and entertainment, and a good ol' time was had by all.

On the 21st of Oct, around eleven in the morning, we cast off from the Surfview dock, destination White Point for the Boggy Bayou Mullet Festival. Once we found a place on the west side of White Point to drop the anchor, Bob and Carol Dryer on their boat, the Independence came over and rafted up with us on the port side. They had on board with them Bill and Marie Leibold and their boys Keven and Eric. A short time later, Rick Sauter, on his boat, the Fair Lady, rafted up on the other side. For my crew on the Pele, I had my two boys, Michael and Jon, Phil and Donna, and their two kids, Chrissy and Derek and Skip Price, all ready and eager to invade the festival. The festival lasted all weekend with bands, all kinds of food, and dancing in the dirt till the wee hours of the morning. After three days of activity, everyone in our rat-pack was worn out, even the kids. One night during the festival, while my son Jon was rowing the dingy out to the Pele with Skip in the bow and me in the stern, we tried to change seats. The dingy sank. Jon thought we had lost the dingy and started swimming, then had a good laugh when he realized that Skip and I were standing in the shallow water.

Thanksgiving at the Surfview was getting to be a bigger event every year. My parents came up for it, and Mom roasted a turkey for us with all the trimmings. I supplied some of the wine. My son Jon got into some booze and chocolate-covered cherries, got sick, and didn't eat a lot of turkeys, too bad. Maybe he learned something.

For Christmas, I loaded up the boys in the War Wagon and drove down to DeBary for some more of Grandma's cooking. We picked up Dick Lefebvre on the way and dropped him off at his parents in Kissimmee. Arriving at my parents' house in DeBary, we were greeted by uncle Eric, aunt Elfriede, and aunt Helen, who were there to take part in the celebration. Mom put on a great feed that included a turkey with all the trimming, plus my favorite, her Christmas cakes. My parents

just loved having Michael and Jon for Christmas, and so did I.

On the drive back to Fort Walton, I gave the boys their first driving lesson in our standard shift VW Camper (War Wagon) on a long straight road with very little traffic through a national forest. They took turns driving while Dick, our captive passenger that we picked up in Kissimmee, was terrified. We arrived alive with no one getting hurt, so the driving lesson was a success.

My ex-wife called in January and wanted the boys back, and they, of course, wanted to stay at the beach. I told them that since I had agreed to the terms of the deal, I would have to keep my word and send them back. But, if they could talk their mother into letting them stay, they could stay. They tried, they called her, but she insisted that they should return to New Jersey, and I had to keep my word and send them back. On the way to the airport, I told them that while they were up north to talk it over and decide positively where they wanted to live. Then, when they come back in summer, tell me their decision and I will make it happen.

The next four months were pretty quiet, we only picked up a few charters for the Pele, and it looked like we were going to have a slow year. That meant that we had plenty of time for pleasure cruises on the bay and along the beautiful Gulf Coast of Florida. As soon as we could gather up a crew to go sailing, we went.

During June, we hauled the Pele again at Spence Bros in Niceville. During the year, occasionally, a chunk of the concrete and chicken wire on the bottom would come off. We sailed around with a hack saw, and when a piece came loose, we'd jump overboard and use it to cut the piece free. It needed to be fixed. We also needed to find out what was causing the leak in the engine water jacket.

We finally hauled out at Spence Bros. and, over the next two weeks, accomplished a lot except for the engine. We peeled the rest of the cement off the bottom, and under Leo's supervision, replaced the Starboard garboard strake (the plank next to the keel), refastened, and replaced other planks that needed replacing. We also added four inches to the keel. Jack's sister Donna and her husband Phil always seemed to show up from up north at the wrong time for a visit. Phil always ended up being recruited to work on the Pele as part of the slave labor gang. He turned out to be a good worker and had a lot of fun with his New York/Italian humor. Once repairs were completed, the hull was painted dark blue with a red lead bottom and looked beautiful. We launched her back into the drink on the 12th of June.

Summer was upon us, and the boys were out of school. My parents were in place and patiently waiting for their arrival. I sent the airline tickets up to New Jersey for the boy's trip south, but when my dad and I went to meet them at the airport, they were not on the plane. I called their mother to find out the reason. Her excuse was that she forgot to call me to tell me she didn't have

enough money for the cab fare to the airport. I sent her the cab fare and rescheduled the flight. She was just being a bitch, I guess. Dad and I went to meet their flight again, but still no kids. This time she wouldn't even answer the phone. I called my lawyer to rattle her cage for some immediate action since their summer vacation was running out fast. He threatened her with a lawsuit, it worked, and the boys finally arrived just in time for a mudbug boil (crawfish) at the Surfview with the whole gang.

I wasn't going to push the issue about their decision, but time was running out. They finally let me know that they really wanted to stay in paradise with their daddy. So now it was my move. I called up their mother and told her I was not sending them back to New Jersey. Needless to say, she was not happy.

When I told my lawyer what I did, he informed me that there was no way I could legally keep the kids, but he could slow things down by filing for a modification of custody. Since the divorce was granted in Okaloosa County, Florida, that's where and when the court hearing would have to take place. In the meantime, I would have to get them back in school and ease them back into the routine of living on the beach. The next few days were busy getting the boys registered for school and buying some go-to-school clothes.

Life was good until two weeks later when my ex showed up with her sister Ellen intending to take the boys back to New Jersey. The boys spotted her coming and skedaddled; one took off down the sound in one of our Sunflower sailboats, and the other ducked around the apartments with his surfboard and headed for the Gulf.

After the initial barrage of shouting at one another, where she accused me of pirating the boys away from her. We talked, and I told her that the boys wanted to stay with me in Florida. When the boys finally came back, I agreed to let Gail and her sister Ellen take the boys out to lunch, and they promised to bring them back. Before leaving, I gave the boys $10 each and briefed them to head for the woods across the street from the airport if they tried to kidnap them.

When they returned, we had another meeting that started off okay but soon went downhill and ended up in another shouting match. I finally had to throw her out. As they were leaving, Gail's sister Ellen got me aside and told me not to let her have the kids no matter what, and drove off. Whatever Ellen's reason, it gave me the confidence to persevere in my decision to press on in my quest to keep my boys. Who knows what the court will decide? My lawyer was not encouraging and kept telling me not to be overly optimistic; great!

About the same time, I was having all this drama with the boy's mother. On the 5th of September, I was informed by the 919th that I had completed 20 years of service as a reserve officer in the Air Force and was eligible to retire. This was good news, now I could spend more time with my boys if I get them. They needed their daddy to lean on them. Michael was turning 15 on the 25th of Nov, and Jon was turning 14 on the18th of Dec, both are know-it-all teenagers; no doubt I'm going to have my hands full.

Earlier in the year, Skip bought a sailboat, an Erwin 36', and brought it over to keep it at the Surfview dock, he named it "Silent Lady". He had just separated from his wife and moved onto the boat with his parrot "Precious". During October, while swapping sea stories with Skip, I had a brilliant idea! Why don't we take his boat and my boys on a short shakedown cruise to south Florida during their Christmas break from school? This would kill two birds with one stone, get Skip and I cruising, and give my sons some time before the mast. After many beers and a lot of talks, Skip agreed. I hit him at a weak moment, he was out of work, and his wife was hounding his ass; he needed to get out of town. From their house (The Castle), a big two-story concrete bunker, she could watch every move he made on his boat and around the Surfview.

I called my parents to give them a heads up on what was happening and asked if they would mind coming up and overseeing the operation of the Surfview. They were coming up for Thanksgiving, and being a businesswoman, my mom was happy to stay on and run the place till we got back

A northerner was blowing through during Thanksgiving, causing a change in venue for the usual Thanksgiving feast at the Surfview, and Skip suggested moving it over to Skippy's castle. All the usual suspects were there except my parents, who canceled out because of the weather. They came up a week later. The feast was a great success. All the kids, young and old, had a blast running around the castle, checking out all the rooms and up the spiral staircase, and out through a submarine hatch onto the roof.

After Thanksgiving, our excitement grew as we started planning for our upcoming cruise. We needed to decide how much food, beer, clothing, charts, and books we needed to stow on board. We topped off the fuel and water, and serviced the engine, sails, standing rigging, running rigging, and ground tackle. We loaded the dinghy along with my trusty 20-man life raft and secured them to the deck. Below decks, we stowed all the canned food, fresh food, beer and soda, and all of our personal gear. All we had to do now was wait for the boys' Christmas vacation. I did go to their school to give them a heads up that they might be late when school started up again.

The weather in December was beautiful, with the temperature in the high 70's during the days and in the 50's at night. The Thanksgiving northerner had already pushed through the area, and another one was in Canada, heading south. The trick is to wait for the front to pass, and then get on the backside of it, then let those 15 to 25-knot winds blow you south. The same plan we had for the Windsong in 1975 before I sank her.

My parents were up from DeBary, ready to operate the Surfview while we were gone on this little adventure. I pulled the boys out of school a couple of days before their Christmas vacation started, to their delight. We set sail early on my son Jon's birthday, December 18th. It was a beautiful day for sailing, and by midnight the first night, we passed by Cape San Blas, where I sank the Windsong four years earlier. The seas were running 3 to 5 feet, with wind around 20 knots out of the north. The Silent Lady was sailing well under a reefed down main, and full jib on a clear star filled night, sailing at a steady six to seven knots on a course to Sarasota. Michael and Jon, a little seasick, were stumbling around trying to find their sea legs and eventually fell asleep up forward in the V berths. Skip, and I were in hog heaven, having a few beers and telling lies. All is well.

Dawn, and what a great day to be sailing. The Silent Lady was charging through the seas on a broad reach, shrouds vibrating in the wind with a bone in her teeth. Not a thing on the horizon, the temperature in the mid '50s, a beautiful day, what more could one ask for. In the morning, the boys were on deck, ready to stand their watch, their spirits and complexions had improved, and their movements were not as awkward as they were yesterday. If the Silent Lady maintains her present speed, we should arrive in Sarasota the next day around noon.

Around two in the morning, we could see a glow from St. Petersburg on the horizon, and at dawn, the ships at anchor off Egmont Key waiting for the pilot into Tampa Bay. By one in the afternoon, we sailed through Sarasota New Pass, and by two, we were tied up at Marina Jack. Our first leg was completed in 2 ½ days, and now shore leave for all hands.

Marina Jack has all the facilities you need, and after a look around the dock at all the boats, the boys got started on the laundry detail. Skip and I refueled the Silent Lady and then headed for the lounge at Marina Jack for happy hour. After doing the laundry, the boys joined us for dinner. Over dinner, we talked over our next destination, Boca Grande, and maybe even further down Pine Island Sound, then back to the Silent Lady, anticipating an early departure in the morning.

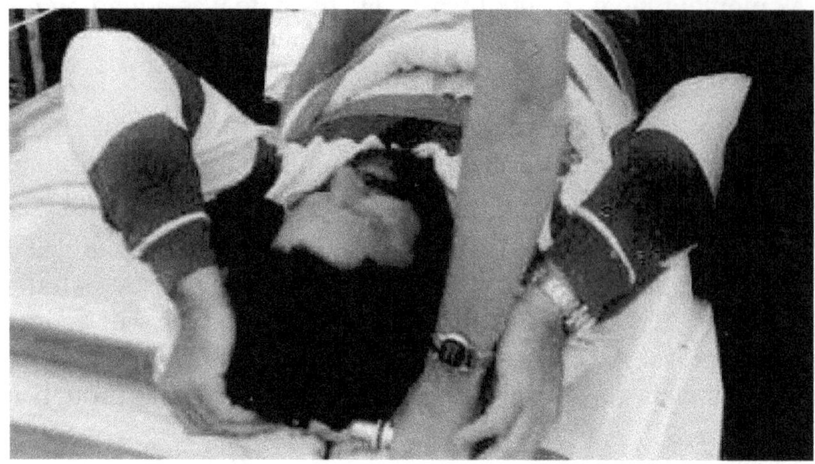

At two in the morning, I heard Skip moaning and groaning; his back was hurting him big time. I tried to help him get in a more comfortable position, but it didn't help him much. By eight, he was obviously in a lot of pain, and it being Sunday, there was no other choice except to call 911.

At first, it was just the rescue squad; they took one look around and decided there was no way that the three of us could get Skip out of the hatch and into their truck. They called in for a fire truck. Now we had ten firemen stomping all over the boat, we were starting to draw a crowd, but they finally wrestled Skip out of the boat. What a scene!

The boys and I followed the ambulance in a cab to the hospital, we feared for the worst. We waited for around an hour, with no word. Everyone was getting tired, so I sent the Boys back to the boat to clean up all the black marks on the deck from the fireman's boots and take a nap.

When I was finally able to talk to Skip and the doctor, his diagnosis was a pulled back muscle. He prescribed some painkillers and muscle relaxes and told Skip to lie down and take it easy and do nothing for a couple of days. Skip wanted out of there and back on his boat, and once I rounded up a wheelchair for Skip, I went out to find a big cab driver.

When I came back to get him, I could see in his eyes that he was still in pain. He was sitting in the wheelchair, supporting his weight with his arms. I asked him if he wanted to press on. He grunted a yes. The cabbie and I wheeled him out and started to load him into the cab, with the hospital security guard looking over our shoulder. The guard grabbed the wheelchair and told us the hospital would not let us borrow it. Without it, we knew it would be rough getting Skip down the dock and onto the boat.

On the way, we made a stop at a pharmacy to get his drugs. The muscle relaxer looked like little home plates, and the painkillers were blue. I got a bottle of water for Skip to take his pills and a beer for me.

The cab driver was cool, he acted as though he did this sort of thing day in and day out. He drove carefully to the dock, talking all the way, while Skip sprawled all over the back seat, moaning and groaning in pain. At the marina, the cabby and I slowly walked Skip down the dock. With the boy's help, we managed to get him on board and down below into his bunk; what a chore. The cab driver deserved and received a good tip.

That evening over dinner onboard the Silent Lady, we talked about what to do next. Skip was in because of the pain. I didn't think we could press on with the cruise. The boys and I could sail the Silent Lady back to Fort Walton, and Skip could have someone drive down and pick him up. Or, we could wait a few days and see what happens. We decided to wait. It looked as if our cruise was pretty much over.

Early next morning, Skip was up and seemed to be raring to go. He said he felt better, although his back was still sore. I asked him if he wanted to head back to Fort Walton or continue on, and he answered, "Let's go south." If he was up for it, so were we. We checked out of Marina Jack and cast off our lines, and by nine in the morning were motoring out New Pass into the Gulf of Mexico. Once clear of the pass, we set sail for Boca Grande, around six hours down the coast, hoping that Skip's back would hold out.

It turned out to be an easy sail. The wind had moderated to around ten to fifteen knots out of the northeast, which put us on a nice broad reach down the coast. Skip was lying in his bunk bitching at us, but by feeding him pain pills and beer, he was soon asleep and snoring up a storm.

After a really lovely peaceful sail, we eased into Boca Grande Pass, cutting the corner by the pier to the channel at about four in the afternoon, lowered the sails, and motored into Miller's Marina, bumping the bottom on the way, and tied up to their dock. Leaving Skip on the boat to rest, since his back was still giving him enough pain to make him a grouch, we were glad to get away from Captain Bligh for a while.

The boys and I went on a walkabout to check out Boca Grande. It has a neat old hotel and an abandoned rail line that runs through the middle of town that ends at a vacant loading pier at the southern tip of the island. The pier had been used in the 70's to load processed phosphates from the bone valley region onto waiting cargo ships. The waters in the pass are naturally deep and could accommodate ocean going ships. The site is now a park. The walk took around an hour, and we were hungry when we arrived back at the marina.

Our return to the marina office, a combination country store, ships store, and a hang out on the dock. Inside there were cats all over the place, candy jars on the counter next to the cigars, an old coke machine with bottled soda plus old, overstuffed chairs to sit in while you make up your mind to buy something. Outside on the porch, there were a couple of rocking chairs where we found Skip. Scattered around outside were the remnants of old boat yard machinery and rusted out old cars. This small town on Gasparilla Island was definitely old Florida. We got Skip moving and had a nice meal at the hotel before turning in for the night.

After a leisurely breakfast, we departed Miller's Marina and motored down Pine Island Sound for the six-mile run to Cayo Costa. The island, according to the chart, has a neat small cove just south of Cayo Costa State Park. We decided to anchor there for the night.

Working our way around the corner into the cove, we anchored up, and Skip put the turkey in the oven. The boys and I went ashore to explore the island, leaving Skip on the boat to cook. What we found were lots of mangroves, a few deserted, dilapidated buildings, and a garbage dump. During our exploring, another sailboat eased into our secret cove and anchored up. We all hustled back to the dinghy to row over for a hospitality check. On the way, we stopped to pick up Skip and a bottle of wine. The Boys noticed that in addition to a middle-aged couple, there were two teenage girls on board, so it took a while to get everyone moving for our hospitality check.

They welcomed us aboard and were friendly, eager to talk, their girls were ready to get off the boat, and the boys were only too happy to oblige. They loaded up the girls in the dinghy and headed to shore to show them around. Skip, and I offered our wine; they refused and offered us instead gin and tonic. During the ensuing conversation, we found out they were three days into a three-month cruise to the Bahamas on a new boat. This was their first cruise, and they were really excited about living their dream. Real nice people, they brought out hors d'oeuvre and refilled our glass. When they invited us to stay for a dinner of hot dogs and beans, we asked them if they might want to join us for a turkey dinner instead. The look of disbelief appeared on their faces, we had to take them aboard the Silent Lady to show them we were not kidding.

The galley on the Silent Lady has a gas four burner stove with an oven and a refrigeration system that even makes a few ice cubes. A real first-class galley and, so far, has worked perfectly. Dinner was a delightful affair, and maybe a little bit crowded for eight people. The wine flowed freely with the conversation. The teenagers, after dinner, took off in the dinghy and left us alone for a while. The wife raved on about our galley and insisted that at their next port, they were going to buy one. The husband did not look pleased about that idea but, of course, went along with her to keep peace in the family. Skip found and opened up a bottle of brandy to keep the conversation flowing. It did flow till late into the night.

By the time we got up in the morning, our friends had already departed, no doubt off to buy a stove. Michael and Jon told Skip and I that the girls were ready to jump ship. They missed their friends and the comforts of home. Come to think of it, they did look kind of sorrowful. I wish them all the luck in the world, they will definitely need it.

After a leisurely breakfast, we motored over to Cabbage Key, about five miles further south of where we spent the night. We tied up to the dock and looked the place over. The main building, built in the 20s, was a restaurant and lounge. The lounge has dollar bills, with boat names on them, stuck up all over the walls like a kind of neat wallpaper. The food in the restaurant is supposed to be good, although we did not stick around to taste it. Other than the main building, there are a few other houses and cottages for short-term rent. We did use their shower on the dock for a long leisurely shower before we left. Our total stay at Cabbage Key was just over two hours and all was well with the world, especially after a nice hot shower.

Sailing further down Pine Island Sound to Captiva Island, where we anchored up off the marine and took the dinghy ashore for a walkabout. We stopped at the Bubble Room for cocktails and something to eat. It's an interesting touristy place filled with all kinds of stuff to look at, and the food wasn't bad. Over dinner, we decided that our next intended destination would be the Dry Tortugas.

The next morning at seven, we weighed anchor, and once clear of Fort Myers Pass, we set our course for the Fort Jefferson – Dry Tortugas National Park. It's considered a rich man's national park because the only way to get there is either by boat or seaplane. It's located around sixty nautical miles due west of Key West and, according to our calculations, should take us around twenty-four hours to get there.

Weather conditions were perfect, a clear morning, the temperature of sixty degrees, and the wind coming offshore at around ten knots which should shift to northwest ten to fifteen once we get offshore. The forecast indicated that there was a cold front located up in the panhandle of Florida pushing south, expected to reach South Florida in thirty-six hours. It gave us twelve hours leeway to get comfortable in the Dry Tortugas before that Northerner caught us. The wind did shift around to the northwest at around eleven in the morning, but with a wind speed under ten knots. This gave us a boat speed of right around four knots, making our estimated time of arrival at the Dry Tortugas early afternoon the next day.

The boys were standing their watches during the day, two hours on and two hours off. Skip and I were doing our, five hours on and five hours off, during the night. It worked out better that way with either Skip or I awake while the boys were on watch as a precaution in the event of an unexpected situation arising.

During the night, the wind dropped to almost nothing, so I started up the diesel to continue on our course at around six knots. The seas were flat on a moonless star filled night. It's amazing how many shooting stars there are when you take the time to look. The wind finally came up on my watch at around two in the morning, just enough to ghost along at a couple of knots, so I killed the engine and enjoyed the peace and quiet.

Daybreak on another beautiful day, wind speeds up to ten to fifteen, and the Silent Lady was moving along smartly at five to six knots. The boys were up and took over the watches, and I was down for a nap. Skip's making his own concoction for breakfast that he calls sailor's delight, an omelet with everything handy thrown in. You do work up an appetite rocking and rolling along, especially tasty if somebody else cooks it.

At two in the afternoon, when we finally had the 49ft high marker northeast of the Dry Tortugas in sight. Working our way up the channel into the anchorage on the east side of the Fort, we picked a nice spot to anchor up. Not a minute too soon, a squall line from the approaching Northerner swept over us with all its wind and rain. It's a nice cozy feeling to be securely anchored in a safe harbor when it's blowing.

Looking around our little harbor in the morning, we had company. Three other boats had sought shelter during the night. One was a sports fisherman, another a powerboat that looked like a commercial fishing boat of some sort, and a sailboat of around thirty feet. We took the dinghy ashore to explore the fort and meet the three park rangers that work and live there. Since we were the only ones ashore visiting, they gave us an interesting talk on the fort's history and then pointed us in the right direction for a walking tour.

The fort is located in the Dry Tortugas National Park on Garden Key. Construction started in 1846, the largest masonry/brick structure in the western hemisphere consisting of 16 million bricks, but never completely finished. Dr. Samuel Mudd, a coconspirator in Lincoln's assassination, was imprisoned there from 1865 till he was pardoned in 1888.

That night, Christmas Eve, after a lovely dinner of leftovers, we exchanged gifts and settled in for the evening. The winds were still blowing in from the north, but the clouds were starting to break up, letting the stars peek through, all indications that the front was pushing on by us. We were all ready for a good night's sleep.

Christmas Day, and what a beautiful sunny morning, excitement abounds in anticipation of a day full of adventure. Our plan was to finish exploring the fort, then go back to the Silent Lady for lunch, then after lunch, pick up the anchor and motor over to Loggerhead Key to check out the lighthouse. Everything went according to plan, even better than planned.

On our arrival at Loggerhead Key, a Coast Guardsman invited us to tie up to their dock for the night. Everyone seemed really happy to have company, even the dog. There were three Coast Guardsmen on duty at the lighthouse. Their hospitality was great, they gave us water to fill up our tank, let us take showers at the lighthouse, and the dog took us on a tour of the island. That night they invited us to join them for Christmas Dinner of roast turkey with all the trimmings, and we supplied the wine. Everyone, including the dog, had a great time.

Sunrise and another beautiful morning with the temperature expected to reach into the mid 70's, and we were out in the dinghy looking for the sunken wreck that the Coast Guardsmen told us about. We found it in ten feet of water, easy surface diving, but the water was cold. There were lobsters all over the place, feeling real safe because you can't take any in a National Park. There were also lots of barracuda. The boys took one look at their jaws, constantly moving with all their teeth. They were out of the water and back in the dingy in a flash.

That evening we followed the Coast Guardsmen around in the lighthouse as they went through the procedure of turning on the light. Then followed them back to their quarters, where we helped finish off the rest of the leftovers for supper, sat around, chewed the fat, and watched TV. Everyone was getting tired, and they needed to get ready for their relief boat that was coming in the morning. We said goodbye to the lighthouse dog and our Coast Guard friends. Back on the boat, we moved her away from the dock and anchored up for the night, anticipating an early departure back to the anchorage at Fort Jefferson.

Back at the fort, we noticed only one boat anchored in the anchorage, a fishing boat. We anchored nearby and dinked over to visit. They were a lobster boat from Cuba and came to the fort to find refuge from the Northerner and then found out they had a problem with their engine. It looked as if they were going to be there for a few more days awaiting parts. Later on, we sent Jon over in the dinghy to barter for lobster with a six-pack of beer. He came back with a half dozen big lobster, not a bad trade. Our evening meal of broiled lobster, rice, and green peas washed down with a nice chardonnay was a gastronomic delight. After dinner, Skip found the eggnog that we couldn't find on Christmas Eve, so we celebrated this good fortune by consuming most of it while we contemplated the stars and the world political situation. A memorable evening and fitting since it was to be our last in the Dry Tortugas and Fort Jefferson.

Morning found the Silent Lady on a broad reach passing by Rebecca Shoal headed for Key West. Skip, and I are feeling a little green around the gills from all the eggnog, and the boys are showing us no mercy. They caught a barracuda and put it in a bucket in the cockpit about the same time we snagged a lobster pot. We luffed the sails, and Skip went overboard to free the rudder; and once again, we were underway. The barracuda was starting to smell, that's when Skip told my son Jon, who was sitting on the leeward side of the cockpit, to move. Jon hesitated and almost got himself barfed on. Skip damn near set me off to the boy's delight. The memory was still fresh in their minds of how merciless we were; when they were seasick, turnabout is fair play.

We made a fast passage to Key West, averaging over six knots. Once we spotted the sea buoy, we worked our way down Northwest Channel and anchored up around three in the afternoon just outside of the channel by marker #10. After cleaning up, we dinked ashore and walked over to Duval Street to introduce the boys to Sloppy Joe's. The town was crowded, to be expected during the holidays, with lots of noise with people moving around. But with a little luck, we found a table, ordered drinks, and settled in to watch the entertainment.

Sloppy Joe's had a country band on the bandstand with a female fiddle player. She was interesting because of the way her large breasts moved around as she played. The boys soon lost interest in this nonsense and left to go back to the boat. Skip, and I decided to have a few more beers to observe the situation and relax.

Hours later, we noticed that the wind appeared to be getting stronger. We decided to finish our beers and go back and check on the boat. As we walked down Duval Street, we noticed that the wind had picked up considerably while we were in Sloppy Joe's. The closer we got to the boat, the faster we walked. On arrival, we could see that the anchor had dragged, and the boat was on the rocks.

The Silent Lady was about ten feet from shore, surging in the waves and pounding on the rocks. The boys had the motor running and were trying to power off the rocks. Skip jumped on board, and I jumped into the water and tried to push the bow into the wind. People were appearing out of nowhere to give us a hand; well, most of it was verbal. But with their help and a lot of luck, we finally got her off the rocks, recovered the anchor, and retrieved our dinghy. We then motored across the channel to the lee of Tank Island and anchored up for the night, and finally settled down.

The boys had a tale to tell. When they left Sloppy Joe's, they dinked out to the boat. Once aboard, they went below to take a nap. Awakened by the boat bouncing on the bottom, they rushed on deck and found that they were on the rocks. Jon started the engine, and Mike called the Coast Guard on the VHF. The Coast Guard would not respond, saying that the boat was too close to shore. Mike then jumped ashore and rousted out the drunks that were living in beached derelict boats strung about the area. He then led them into the water to try and push the Silent Lady off the rocks. That's about the time Skip, and I arrived on the scene and managed to get her off the rocks and anchored. I thought the boys handled themselves really well during the crisis.

Morning turned out to be miserable, with wind and rain. We moved the Silent Lady over to the old submarine pens in what appeared to be an unused portion of the old Navy Base and tied her up, hopefully out of harm's way. Although there were some swells in the pens, the Silent Lady would be safe there. We located a person in charge who assured us the boat would be ok and allowed us to use the showers in the old Navy administration building. After a nice hot shower, we were off on shore leave to see some more of Key West. I gave the boys each twenty dollars and told them to meet us at Sloppy Joe's at around five for dinner. They took off in a flash like they were glad to get away from us, the nerve!

To keep out of the rain, Skip and I spent most of the day ducking in and out of shops and bars. Finally, we ended up at Rick's Bar, across the street from Sloppy Joe's, and settled in for some serious people-watching, friendly bartenders, and cold beer. It was turning into a lovely afternoon by observing the people walking by. You could spot the natives real easy by their dress and laid back attitude. Tourists like us stuck out like a sore thumb. The atmosphere of Key West gives you the feeling that you're out of the United States and in some banana republic somewhere.

The next couple of days were spent playing tourist. We visited Hemmingway's house and his cats, the lighthouse, the turtle crawl, and Mel Fisher's galleon, in addition to many bars and restaurants. There was good food in the restaurants, the waiters were all good, and many were obviously gay Caballeros. We also took in the sunset ceremony at Mallory Square, sort of like a carnival with a lot of street entertainers and hustlers. The boys bought a twenty-two-dollar bill from a guy dressed up as Uncle Sam; the sunsets were beautiful.

While we were at Mel Fisher's galleon, Skip asked Mel if he needed more divers. Mel told him that he always needed divers. Skip thought about it but decided against it. The trouble with the deal was that after you pay a fee to join the search, you work for nothing and share the wealth if any treasure is found. As it turned out, he should have joined up because in just a couple of years Mel would find the remains of the Spanish treasure ship Atocha on July 20th, 1985. His organization would successfully recover a load of gold artifacts and tons of silver ingots from the wreck.

For New Year's Eve, the boys and I were determined to stay up for the New Year. At midnight we ended up in Billy's Bar shooting pool, where we toasted the New Year with the rest of the crowd. After watching the action for a while, we headed back to the Silent Lady, our home. Skip was smarter than the rest of us, he left early.

The next morning the 1st of January 1981, at around eight in the morning, we sailed out of the sub pens and left Key West in our wake. Our next destination was just up the east coast to Marathon, where uncle Eric and aunt Elfriede lived.

By four in the afternoon, after an easy sail up the keys, we had Marathon in sight and were working our way into the anchorage at Boot Key. By five, we were anchored and launched the dinghy to go ashore and call Uncle Erick, no answer. While at the dock looking over the marina, we noticed some old cannons laying in the water a couple of feet off the dock.

The dock master told us they were salvaged from a wreck on Delta Shoal. We decided on the spot that we needed to explore Delta Shoal. After asking and getting directions to the shoal from people hanging around the dock and the restaurant. We were fired up to go treasure hunting, and after finishing our meal, I tried calling my aunt and uncle again and finally got to talk to them. I made arrangements to meet them at the Boot Key Marina dock the next evening at five. That would give us time to do Delta Shoal in the morning.

The next morning, bright and early, we were on our way to Delta Shoal, located only around five miles from Boot Key and about two miles SE of Sombrero Key, real easy to find. We anchored up on the shoal, and all jumped into the water to look for treasure. No treasure chests, just sand, and some nasty looking barracudas. Jon, when he saw the barracudas, was out of the water in a flash, deciding that he needed to man the dinghy as our chase boat. The only thing we found was some

old timbers that might have come off a ship, maybe. There were lots of lobster pots all over the place and a couple of Groupers hanging around. While in hot pursuit of a Grouper, I burst an eardrum, which put me in a tailspin. Talk about getting disorientated. That was the end of my diving for the rest of the trip.

Back at the dock, while waiting for my aunt and uncle, I talked with a couple on a sailboat that was on an extended cruise. I told them that I blew out my eardrum and would have to go find a doctor somewhere to get some antibiotics. They said they had plenty on board, and gave me a ten days supply, just what the doctor ordered.

Uncle Eric picked us up at around five in his old VW bus and drove us to his house on the Atlantic Ocean side of Marathon in the Little Venice subdivision, where aunt Elfriede was waiting for us, and Eric took us around to show their house, and dock, while Elfriede worked on dinner.

They live in a south Florida cement block building with jalousie windows. Eric added an upstairs studio/apartment to use in his work as a portrait artist. He has a nice setup, the studio had lots of windows for light and was full of paintings of all descriptions. There was also a deck on the East side of the studio with a view to the South overlooking the Atlantic, which was just beautiful.

Aunt Elfriede was a vegetarian and teetotaler, so dinner was mostly vegetables and no booze. The meal was all right for me, and I just overdosed on veggies. Skip, and the boys hardly eat at all. Too bad! After dinner, Eric mentioned that in the morning, we could bring the Silent Lady around and tie her up at his dock. Sounded like a good idea and would make it easy for us to get the boat ready for the trip back to the Redneck Riviera and would give them a little time on the Silent Lady sailing her over. Everyone agreed that it was a good idea.

In the morning, Eric had something to do, so he dropped us off at Boot Key Marina with Elfriede to guide us over the reef into their lagoon and dock. The two hour sail was easy, and Elfriede enjoyed every minute of it. She loves the outdoors and the sea and swims every morning, a major feat when you are in your seventies. She guided us over the reef to the channel into their lagoon. Once inside the lagoon, we turned around and tied up to their dock, where Eric was waiting to help us.

For the rest of the day and the next day, we were all busy preparing the Silent Lady for the trip

back. We were running out of time, and the boys had to be back to start school. Skip had to get back to go find a job. That left me, the only one that really did not have to get back since my parents were running the show at the Surfview for me.

After finally completing the job of provisioning the Silent Lady, we made our plan for the sail back home. A straight course to Destin Pass seemed like the quickest way back and would take an estimated three days. If the weather became unbearable, we could always divert and duck into any one of the passes up the West coast of Florida. So far, the weather has cooperated with us, but the real test lay ahead.

On the evening before we departed, we took my aunt and uncle out for dinner at one of the local restaurants. We really had a good time; Eric is quite a character and the life of the party and kept us well entertained with all his carrying on. I hope I'm that active and as much fun when I get to be his age.

In the morning, we were underway by seven in the morning. As we sailed under the seven-mile bridge going from the Atlantic to the Gulf of Mexico, Eric and Elfriede were on the bridge-waving goodbye. They stayed and watched us for a long time.

We set our course for Fort Myers, so much for a straight shot to Destin Pass. A cold front was pushing down from the North, so we figured to get into sheltered waters before it caught up with us. Our estimated time of arrival at Fort Myers was around seven the next morning. That's if we average around five knots. The wind was out of 290 degrees at fifteen knots, and we had the Silent Lady close hauled beating into the seas on a port tack holding a course of just under 330 degrees. The day dragged on, and the continual pounding into the seas was wearing us down, with any luck, the wind will die down at sundown.

By evening there was no letup in the wind or seas, and by ten that night, the wind started to clock around to the North. We tacked over to a starboard tack. I was happy with that since that should give us a lot of sea room passing by Cape Ramano. The wind speed picked up to around twenty-five knots. We reefed the main and furled down the jib, and settled in for a rough ride. I was still happy with our situation because there was no way we would get blown up on a lee shore on a starboard tack.

Never saw anything of Cape Ramano when we passed by it around midnight. The morning was overcast with rain, and twenty knots out of the North, we came about onto a port tack looking for land. We sighted land at around nine and finally made it through the pass at Fort Myers and around Bowditch Point, then down Matanzas Pass for about a mile to tied up at the marina just short of the bridge at Fort Myers Beach. By the time we had the Silent Lady all secured, it was noon, and the northerner was upon us. We were very thankful that we made it into a nice snug harbor.

Fort Myers Beach was pretty much deserted, and we had no trouble finding a place to eat. The restaurant we found was close to the dock, and the food was good. During lunch, we talked over our options. Since the weather was pretty rough, we decided that as soon as the northerner blew out, we would stay inside and sail up Pine Island Sound with a stop again for the night at Cabbage Key.

While having dinner in Fort Myers, we talked about the fact that on our sail from Marathon, our dead reckoning was off by about fifteen miles. We attributed this error to getting inaccurate readings off of our knot meter, caused maybe by the heavy seas that we were in, it was just a guess, but that's all we could think of. We figured that during the last 24 hours at sea, the last 15 hours were in over twenty knots of wind and big seas, and we came up with a correction for our knot meter. In the future, under the same circumstances, we will take a knot off of the indicated reading on the knot meter and use that speed to DR with. This was the first time that we had any problem with our navigation on the trip. Hopefully, this correction will help. The navigation equipment on the Silent Lady was limited to a knot meter, a compass, and a depth recorder. We used the information from this equipment to dead reckon our position. It all worked really well until now.

The northerner had blown on by, but it was a cold, dreary morning when we departed Fort Myers Beach and motored up Pine Island Sound. The trip was uneventful, arriving at Cabbage Key around two in the afternoon. Once tied up to their dock, we explored the island for a couple of hours and then used their shower to get ready for happy hour. At the bar, the boys tacked up the twenty-two-dollar bill that they had bought in Key West from Uncle Sam in Mallory Square during the sunset ceremony. They added it to all the other bills tacked to the wall, with our boat's name and date on it. After a few Pina Coladas and a lovely dinner, we retired to the Silent Lady for the evening.

In the morning, after a hearty breakfast, we motored out through Boca Grande Pass and hauling up the sails and beat our way up the west coast of Florida. The weather was overcast with a cold wind out of the northwest at fifteen gusts to twenty knots. The boys stood their watches in an uncomfortable wet sail up the coast. It was getting close to sundown as we approached Sarasota, and while we still had some daylight left, we decided to put in there for the night. We passed up Big Sarasota Pass and went for New Pass since we had entered through there on the way down. It was dusk by the time we got there, and after visually picking up the light on the sea buoy, we headed for the pass that was marked with channel markers on poles. We found them with our spotlight and lined up in the middle. On the way in, we ran aground and damned near broached. We yelled at the boys down below to get on their life jackets as we took a wave into the cockpit (pooped) that went right on down the open hatch. Skip fired up the engine and fire walled the throttle. We were pooped again by the next wave and then bumped two more times before we finally made it on in. The boys brought us up a couple of beers that we sucked down with shaking hands. Sarasota has lousy passes.

We tied up at Marina Jack and retired to the bar to talk over our near tragedy. Talking to some of the locals, we found out that New Pass was closed because it had shoaled over. We already found that out the hard way. Also found out that Big Sarasota Pass had big waves breaking all the way across it. I guess we lucked out since going that way would have been worse. The next day we motored up the Intercoastal waterway to Clearwater and found a fuel dock to tie up to for the night. After refueling, we stayed on the boat and cooked chicken with rice for dinner, and went to bed.

We cleared out the pass at Clearwater's North Channel into the Gulf of Mexico by 09:00 and set our course on a starboard reach for home. The weather seemed to have moderated a bit, and we had a beautiful day for a change with the sun shining, and it was even a little warmer. The good conditions didn't last long, the wind shifted further to the north, and the temperature dropped. By late afternoon we were beating into a twenty-knot headwind and taking on spray over the bow with every wave. We reefed down the main and pressed on into the night.

During my watch, at around one in the morning, I noticed that the boat was not responding to the helm. I woke up Skip and the boys, and we investigated. What we found was that the steering cables had slipped off the rudder yoke, the problem had to be fixed. We hove-to, and Skip, and I wormed our way into the very stern of the boat, wedged ourselves in, and wrestled the cables back onto the steering yoke. While we were down below, the boat was pitching and rolling all over the place. By the time we regained control of the situation, it was daybreak. What a night!

The morning brought us more wind, colder temperatures, and rain. Our dead reckoning position had us passing Cape San Blas during the night, we didn't see a thing. That's the good news, and the bad news was that we hadn't had a good navigation position since we left Clearwater. Everyone on board was cold, wet, tired, and miserable, and the fiasco during the night wore everyone out. Down below, everything is either wet or damp; this was turning into a survival situation.

The Silent Lady was sailing well, all reefed down with the main double reefed and the jib furled. The temperature kept dropping with the wind gusting up to 25 knots. Our DR position had us approaching Panama City, but there was no land in sight. Obviously, our navigation was a little off. It looks as if we are in for another miserable night.

By nine-thirty that evening, we finally could see some lights on the horizon to the North. We cranked up the diesel dropped the sails, and headed north toward the lights. They really looked

strange, since they were on the horizon, they appeared to be magnified, giving you the feeling that you were closer to shore than you really were. We approached the coast with caution, trying to spot some prominent landmark or buoy, and after what seemed like forever, we finally located the offshore structure south of Panama City. With a well-known position, at last, we set our course for the pass at Panama City and at 00:30 in the morning, clearing on through the pass. After finding a place to anchor out of the channel, a totally exhausted crew hit the sack.

Early in the morning, everyone was anxious to get underway. We decide to do the last leg up the Intercoastal Waterway, motoring all the way, turns for home as they say. The weather was clear but cold, no matter we were in fine spirits. After all, we survived.

Bob Dryer on the Independence was waiting for us when we entered Choctawhatchee Bay and escorted us to the Surfview for a welcoming champagne party. The date was January 13th, 1981, 28 days before the mast that was filled with adventures that Skip, my boys, and I will never forget.

Back to reality and back to school for the boys, for me, a subpoena to appear in the Okaloosa County Court House for the judge to decide who gets the boys. However, I was a little bit more optimistic about the outcome because of a conversation I had at a Pre-Christmas party with a lawyer just before we set sail on the Silent Lady. I mentioned to him what I did with my kids; he told me not to worry about it. So I asked him if he was familiar with my case, but he didn't answer, indicating to me that maybe something favorable was happening.

By the end of January 1981, I was definitely stressing out waiting for the court date. When it came, I was there in the Okaloosa County Court House on time with my lawyer, dressed in my best clothes. I looked around for my ex-wife, and the judge asked the county prosecutor where she was. He also didn't know. As it turned out, she never showed up, so by default, I was granted custody of the boys. Oh! Happy day, or was it? My boys, Michael and Jon, now have a permanent address and have some stability in their lives, living in paradise with their daddy, I hope.

Shortly after we returned from our adventure to Key West, Skip was hired back on as a diver and would be gone traveling all over the world for the oil industry. He left the Silent Lady in my care and use. Oh boy!

In early February, Tom and Jack started talking about going skiing, and once my parents agreed to take care of the boys and run the Surfview for me, I would be good to go. Since we had already skied Aspen, we were eager to try somewhere else. Tom's sister Jean had a cabin in Crested Butte, and he gave her a call about staying there for a week or so. She agreed to rent it to us for a week at a reduced rate starting on March 17th. Telluride was another ski area close to Crested Butte, where we booked a couple of rooms for our second week.

I told Mom and Dad, who were in the process of redecorating their apartment next door, about the ski trip, and they agreed to keep an eye on the boys and to keep everything running smoothly at the apartments.On March 15th Jack, Tom, and I started our thirty-hour drive in the War Wagon to Crested Butte, Colorado. We made our usual stop in Amarillo, Texas, for Mexican food on the way. After an uneventful drive and finally found the small town of Crested Butte, located in a box

canyon, and the cabin. We unloaded our gear and did a quick walkabout town. The first thing we came across was the Wooden Nickel Saloon. Of course, we had to check it out. It would be our watering hole for the week.

After a particularly good day of skiing on the slopes at Crested Butte and while doing happy hour at the saloon, we talked about the fact that there really wasn't much in the way of

nightlife going on. Thinking of something interesting to do, I mentioned that I had read about a bathhouse in a town called the Sunshine Paradise and asked the bartender about it. He knew all about it and gave me direction. It was just down the street at the end of the box canyon.

No one else was interested, so I left to go check it out. As I walked down the street following a woman and she ended up leading me to the Sunshine Paradise. Once inside the building, I paid a small fee at the counter and followed her into a room where she started taking off her clothes, so I took off my clothes too. Once we were both naked, I followed her into a large shower room. While standing there showering, she said that I looked familiar and thought that she had waited on me the night before at the restaurant where she worked. Once we got out of the shower, we got into a large hot tub where we just chatted away. After a while, she jumped out of the hot tub into the cold plunge located just next to the hot tub and left to get dressed and go to work.

Once back at the Wooden Nickel, I couldn't' wait to give the report on my recon mission to the Sunshine Paradise and to tell them what I learned from talking to the girl in the hot tub. What I learned was that during the ski season, the only cheap rooms available for the seasonal workers didn't have bathing facilities, so they all used the Sunshine Paradise. Everyone was now enthusiastic about going, the next day was our last at Crested Butte, and after a full day of skiing, we adjourned to the Wooden Nickel for happy hour. By the time we left the Wooden Nickel and walked down to the Sunshine Paradise with our toothbrushes. We were too late; the crowd had come and gone.

The next morning, we were on our way to Telluride, another small old mining town in a box canyon. The skiing here was noted more for their cross-country trails than their downhill runs. Like Crested Butte, there was not much nightlife. After a week of fun skiing on their few downhill runs, we hit the road for Florida.

Back at Surfview, my parents had everything under control. They told me that my son Jon had his membership in the Boy Scouts transferred to a local troop in Fort Walton Beach and was working towards becoming an Eagle Scout. Jon's brother Michael was busy competing in all the local Windsurfing events, so there was definitely plenty going on in the neighborhood to keep them busy.

Jon informed me that he was competing in the around the Island race as a crew on a Prindle 16'catamaran. The race is a big deal annual event that draws sailors from all over Northwest Florida. It's a 120nm overnight race that starts in Choctawhatchee Bay and goes out Destin Pass to the Gulf of Mexico, then west along the coast to Pensacola through the pass there. Then down the sound to the finish in Choctawhatchee Bay. It's an ordeal that usually takes a full 24 hours to complete.

On the day of the race, the weather was overcast with a light wind, and it turned out to be slow going. The race took well over 24 hours, and my son and his friend Phil Moss did well. They finished third in their class.

Skip was spending his time between jobs living on the Silent Lady tied up at the Surfview dock, studying for and getting his captain's license. During the summer, he occasionally orchestrated big shrimp or crawfish boils on the dock to feed the crowd at the Surfview.

On the 8th of May, we sailed the Pele over to be hauled at the boat yard in Destin Harbor. We were there for three days for a quick check of the bottom for rot and a paint job, Red lead bottom, white boot top, and blue-black hull. With the help of Phil DiDonato, Jack's brother-in-law, the Pele looked really pretty when we launched her.

On the 16th of May, we anchored up off of buoy #10 in the bay as the committee boat for the Hog's Breath Regatta. It's a two-day regatta that ends with an award ceremony and pig roast on the Island.

Dick Lefebvre was the pig cooker-upper and prepared a great feed for the banquet. This is an annual event that's open to all the sailors from around Northwest Florida and a great opportunity to get together to party on down.

On the 13th of June, we sailed the Pele up the sound to Jay Scherf's dock in Mary Esther, the next town west of Fort Walton Beach, for his wedding to Mary Walton. The wedding and reception took place in the back yard of his big old house on the north side of the Sound. There was plenty of champagne, good food and a lot of conversation with good friends. Later on, we motored down the Sound to continue the party at the Seagull.

On the 9th of October, Phil DiDonato and I departed for a weekend cruise on the Pele. We sailed down the coast to Panama City, then motored through the pass to the treasure ship, a local tourist attraction, and picked up his wife Donna, who drove over to meet us with the kids. Once we had everyone on board, we motored over to the north side of Shell Island, where we rafted up with Skip on the anchored Silent Lady. We now had a full crew, Donna and Phil, with their kids Chrissy and Derek, plus my boys Michael and Jon.

The next morning, we enjoyed a marvelous breakfast of eggs and sausage prepared by Phil and Jon. After breakfast, Jon and Derek set off in the dinghy with their tents to explore Shell Island. They were back on board in time for lunch; they found out that there were a lot of snakes on Shell Island. In the afternoon, we motored over to the treasure ship's fuel dock and refueled while Donna drove over to the Panama City Seafood Festival with the kids. Apparently, it was not much of a festival. They were back a short time later and decided to head back to Fort Walton Beach. After dinner on board, they offloaded their seabags, said their goodbye's and started the drive back home. After they left, Phil and I sailed the Pele over to raft up with the Silent Lady for an enjoyable evening chewing the fat over a couple of beers with Skip. The next morning with an early departure, we sailed out the pass and had a nice sail up the coast to Destin Pass. We arrived at the Surfview dock a little after one in the afternoon. Ending a fun filled weekend cruise where a good time was had by all.

On the 24th of October, the Pele was the committee boat for the Prindle Fleet 53 regatta. We cast off from the Surfview dock early and anchored the Pele in the bay at 10:30 to wait for the racing committee to arrive and get ready for the first race scheduled to start at noon. They brought with them plenty of food and beer for themselves and the crew of the Pele. After two days of racing, we anchored the Pele close to the beach next to Deckhands Marine, where the awards ceremony and party took place, always a fun event for all hands.

Not long after recovering from the regatta, it was time for the annual Thanksgiving feast. Every year the crowd gets bigger and better. Mom and Dad were there to supervise the activities that lasted until late in the evening. The next day we all went on an after-Thanksgiving cruise on the bay.

Christmas followed shortly thereafter at the Surfview for a nice quiet Christmas Dinner with my parents and kids. My parents informed me at dinner that since they were spending most of their time at the Surfview, they were thinking about what to do with their house in DeBary. I suggested they sell the place and move up to their apartment at the Surfview to be with their grandkids. They were not ready to do that yet, my mother's two sisters, Helen and Dorothy, live close by in DeBary.

Chapter Four: 1982 - 1984

In January, Jack, Tom, and I started talking about our annual ski trip, and I talked to my parents about staying on to take care of the boys and the apartments for two weeks while I played in the snow. They were okay with it, and so were the boys, anticipating grandma's cooking.

Colorado was having a bad winter for skiing with not much snow on the mountains. By February, we had to make a decision and started looking for an alternative. We searched around and finally found a good cheap package deal for four to Austria for in around $500 a piece that included a round-trip flight out of JFK on Icelandic Air to Luxembourg and a van to drive to Austria. The package also included ski passes and B&B's at Kitzbuhel for five days, then another five days at St. Anton. It also included a night, coming and going at a hotel in Luxembourg, which is not a bad deal. We needed another person, so we contacted Phil Mapp, our skiing buddy from New Orleans, who was good to go, and we signed up.

On the 2nd of March, we hit the road in the War Wagon for JFK International Airport in N.Y., with a stop at Baltimore harbor to eat some crab; we arrived at JFK in the early afternoon of the 27th for our overnight flight to Luxembourg. Checking in with Icelandic Air, we were informed that the plane had a maintenance problem and was delayed. They gave us rooms at the airport hotel, and after checking in, we adjourned to the bar.

Scoping out the clientele at the bar, we spotted a beautiful blonde and went over to talk her up. Found out she was on our flight, so I started buying her cocktails. A couple of hours later, she appeared to be stone sober, I had to quit and go to bed. *Icelandic girls can put it away.*

Not two hours later, they called the flight, and I was feeling terrible. I kept my mouth shut, and luckily, they let me board the plane. The flight stopped at Keflavik, Iceland, to refuel. In the terminal, I bought a sweater, I was so hungover and couldn't wait to get back on the plane and try to sleep.

After our arrival in Luxembourg, Jack, Tom, and Phil went after the luggage; my duty was to get the van. I found where to pick it up and got in line. I almost made it to the head of the line before I felt sick and got out of line to find a toilet. After barfing up my guts, I got back in line and almost made it to the counter before I had to barf again. Back in line again, Jack came looking for me, and I told him my sad story. He took my place in line and signed for the van. Finally, after clearing out of the terminal, we drove over to the hotel, where I found a bed and passed out.

The next morning, we were on the road to Kitzbuhel in lousy overcast weather with a lot of black ice the road. Along the way, we passed a wreck site that had pieces of Mercedes all over the road. Shortly thereafter, Jack lost control of the van on some black ice and did a 360, and somehow came to a stop without hitting anything. Jack was shook, so I took over as driver. After all, I was supposed to be the driver on this adventure in the first place.

We arrived in Kitzbuhel a little after 19:00 and found that our contact's office was closed for the night. We had his name, so we asked around in some of the local bars and got his address. Finding the address, we knocked on his door. He answered in his underwear and let us into a small room where his girlfriend was lying in bed with the sheets pulled up to her neck. After filling out the required paperwork and giving us our Kitzbuhel ski passes, we left him with a totally embarrassed girlfriend to go find our B&B.

A short time later, we checked in with the housefrau of our B&B. She gave us a briefing on the rules of the house, showing us how to get into the cellar where we were to remove our boots and

don slippers to walk around. She then showed us our rooms, I was to share a bed with Phil, and Jack and Tom would share a bed in the other room. Breakfast was served for two hours, starting at 7:00 in the dining room. There would also be a packed lunch available to take with us up the mountain.

We were up early for a wonderful breakfast in the dining room, which gave us an opportunity to chat with our fellow B&Bers. One friendly couple was from Luxembourg and seemed to be interested in our experiences traveling in Luxembourg. They gave us lots of information about the city's history and their contact info. We promised to contact them in Luxembourg on our way back to the states.

With breakfast over, we grabbed our lunches and headed off to find the lifts. The slopes at Kitzbuhel are long runs compared to Colorado's steep, narrow runs and were lots of fun to ski. The trails were not marked very well, and the ski patrol was about nonexistent. Getting used to skiing with the Europeans is another story. They were rude in the lift lines, pushing, shoving, and stomping all over our skis. It didn't take us long to get with the program and start pushing and shoving back. We did find out that our ski package was actually part of a tour group that had bussed down from Sweden.

That evening after dinner, while checking out the bars, we happened to meet one of the instructors from our group. She told us where to meet up with her and the rest of the group the next morning. We showed up right on time, expecting a big crowd, but no such thing, just two instructors and us. We skied with them until we broke for lunch. We asked them why no one showed up. They told us that they were either too hungover to ski or already at the bars. In Sweden, the laws are really tough on drinking, so they sign up for tours like this to tie one on.

After five days of great skiing at Kitzbuhel, we started on the short drive to St Anton and got hung up in a traffic jam, making our arrival too late to get in some time on the slopes. Once checked in at our B&B in St Anton, we headed out to do a walkabout town and found a place to eat and drink.

The next morning after a good night's sleep and a hearty breakfast at the B&B, we were ready for the mountain. It was not a pretty day, overcast with snow flurries, but we pressed on up the mountain. After all, we were there to ski. During the early afternoon, weather conditions deteriorated to a total white out. We slowly skied our way down the mountain, and to our surprise, we found ourselves in a different town on the other side of the mountain. Looking around, we found a bar/restaurant to celebrate our survival with other survivors. We were having such a good time with these people they invited us to come back to party with them later on in the evening. That sounded like a good idea to us, and after finding a bus, we headed back to St. Anton.

Jack decided to stay in St Anton that left Tom, Phil and I to drive over the mountain to find and join the party. We found it all right but stayed too long. On the drive back to St. Anton in the middle of the night on a two-lane dark winding road going over the top of the mountain, we ran out of fuel in the freezing ass cold, we were defiantly in deep kimchi. Getting out of the van to

assess the situation, we had stopped near the crest of the mountain on a sharp curve. We needed to move the van, so we pushed it over the crest, and with a little luck, we could coast to a place where we could pull off the road. Low and behold, once over the crest, we coasted all the way down the mountain into St Anton and ended up rolling into a bar parking lot near our B&B. It was not skill and cunning that saved our butts. It was just plain dumb luck.

The following afternoon at happy hour, while celebrating our survival of the previous night and while drinking hexenfires (a flammable cocktail) with some of the Swedes in our group, one of them inadvertently set himself on fire that we quickly extinguished. These events would lead one to believe that skiing trips were dangerous, which is not true if you're invisible and bulletproof.

Another couple joined our ski group, auto workers on strike from Detroit, a white guy, and his black girlfriend. They were sociable and were a lot of fun, and the woman was a real hit with the Austrian kids and everyone else. The kids would come up to her and try to rub the black off of her skin; she took it all in stride and thought it was hilarious. She couldn't ski worth a darn but was game to try. She entered our group's slalom race, screaming all the way straight down the slope. She won an honorary award for courage.

The morning of the 12th of March, we departed St Anton and started the long drive to Luxembourg, arriving around three in the afternoon. After checking in at our hotel, we turned in the van and called our friends that we had met in Kitzbuhel to arrange a meeting for dinner. Dinner was a fun

event, they enjoyed all of our misadventures at St Anton, and we enjoyed theirs of past skiing trips around Europe. After thanking them for a wonderful evening, we called it a night to get some rest before our early flight in the morning.

Once through the delay of clearing Customs and Immigration at Kennedy International, the long drive to Fort Walton Beach was thankfully uneventful. All in all, our skiing adventure in Europe was most enjoyable.

On the 29th of April 1982, we were safely back in Florida, and it wouldn't take us long to slip back into living in the Redneck Riviera. My parents had everything under control at the Surfview and even had some inquiries to charter the Pele.

In early May, My Uncle Rudy, Aunt Clare, and Pop drove down from N.J. for a visit, and we took them out for a sail. It was great to see them again. Pop was pushing 100.

On the 20th of May, we sailed the Pele over to Joe's bayou for its annual bottom job. It was a nice easy haul out this time, we had her launched back in the drink four days later looking real good in her new paint job.

Windsong Charters, Inc. volunteered the Pele to be the committee boat for the Hog's Breath Hobie 16 Regatta. Early on the 22nd of May, we loaded up the committee of twelve members, 20 cases of Miller Lite, and 20 sub sandwiches at Deckhands Marina. The rest of the day was spent watching the races, drinking beer, eating the sandwiches, and harassing the committee. After the last race of the day, we would sail the committee back to the marina, clean up the boat and secure her to the dock for the night. That was our routine for the next couple of days of racing.

After all the races were concluded on the 24th, we anchored the Pele a 100yrds off the beach next to the marina for the awards ceremony and banquet. The party that everyone enjoyed went on late into the evening.

On the 29th of May, while on a charter on the bay, we ran across the Billy Bowlegs invasion fleet and joined up. We stayed with them for a while as they invaded Fort Walton Beach for the start of the annual festival. The Billy Bowlegs Festival occurs on the first weekend in June when hundreds of boats congregate in the sound right in front of The Surfview. There was plenty of entertainment watching all the craziness from our beach, where we had a crowd of friends and neighbors to watch the invasion.

On the 24th of June, the boys and I loaded into the war wagon and drove to my parents' house in

DeBary to help them celebrate their 50th wedding anniversary. Once we arrived, we went to work helping set up for the party to be held the next day at their house. The afternoon of the party, Michael and Jon were put to work as bartenders, giving them an opportunity to meet some of their relatives that they had never met before. My parents and I were busy socializing with their old friends and our relatives, many of whom I hadn't seen in years. It was a wonderful celebration of their life together.

Once back at the Surfview, we didn't have a lot of time to recuperate. My parents celebrated their anniversary again on July 9th with all their friends in Fort Walton. They rented the Fiesta Room for the party at the El Matador, where they have their condo. The boys had so much fun being bartenders at the last party in DeBary that they volunteered to do it again. This party turned into a big event, and the whole gang was there when they shooed us out of the Fiesta Room. The party moved to Surfview.

In October, we sailed the Pele with Phil DiDonato, his family, and my boys, towing the Sinkeze, up to Pensacola Beach for the weekend. On our arrival, we rafted up with Skip in the Silent Lady, Rick in the Fair Lady, and one of my tenants Van Richards sloop the Fire Escape in the sound off of Flounders restaurant for dinner and an evening ashore. The next morning, we sailed further up the Sound and anchored up in the cove by Fort McRea, just west of Pensacola Pass. All the kids went ashore to explore the remains of the fort, one long dark tunnel. A couple of them went into the tunnel, including my son Jon. I went in after them and spooked them. We all had a good laugh when they came running out screaming. For the divers in the crowd, we sailed out the pass in the Silent Lady to dive on the remains of the battleship Massachusetts. There was not much left of the old battlewagon, but it was a fun, easy, shallow dive. The next morning after an early start, we sailed down the coast back to the Surfview by way of Destin Pass. Everyone agreed it was a fun filled couple of days.

So far, Windsong Charters, Inc. was having a pretty good year with 19 charters that helped to pay for some of the expenses of maintaining an old (1918) wooden sailboat.

It was time for our annual Thanksgiving celebration feast for the residents and guests of the Surfview. The tables in the parking lot were loaded up with plenty of food and wine. It was a beautiful day temperature in the 70's, perfect conditions for the feast. We had a group of around twenty tenants and friends in attendance, and as usual, the whole operation was overseen by my mom. The feast was followed up with lots of conversations that went on until late into the evening.

My son Michael turned 17 on the 25th of Nov, so now we had a new driver on the streets. I told him that he could now drive to school in (Jaws) our old 67 Chev station wagon with shark teeth painted on its rusted-out hood by my Uncle Eric, the artist. He declined the offer saying he would be too embarrassed to show up at the high school with it and would continue to take the bus, his loss. When I was seventeen, I would have been overjoyed to be able to drive anything with wheels to school.

Being that my sons and I have our birthdays all within two weeks of each other, my parents decided to give us an all-in-one birthday party in their apartment next door. During the party, they told me that they were leaving to drive out to visit my cousin Gloria and her family in Denver, Colorado, for Christmas and that the boys and I were also invited to attend. I told them that we would follow up as soon as possible. It would give our new driver some time on the road with his daddy looking over his shoulder.

As soon as school let out for their Christmas break, we hit the road for Denver with maybe a side trip to do some skiing. Steve Dowell, one of our friends from Ft. Walton, was in Breckenridge

working in a T-shirt shop for the ski season. He offered, if we could break away, to put us up for a night in the condo, he was sharing with Mark Rush, an airbrush artist, also from Ft. Walton. My parents had given me their old 72-green Plymouth station wagon (Green Hornet), and with our new driver (Michael) and I at the wheel, we would drive nonstop.

The road trip was a long and thankfully uneventful thirty-hour drive. We arrived alive at my cousins, three days before Christmas, my parents were there, and we had a nice little reunion. The next morning the boys and I headed up the mountain, about an hour and a half drive to Breckenridge for a day on the mountain and maybe spending the night at Steve's. As we pulled into Breckenridge, I stopped at a gas station to refuel. After taking on fuel, the car would not start. After much debate, it was determined that the timing chain had jumped a couple of teeth on the timing gear. Finally, after many phone calls, I found a mechanic that would take on the job, telling me that he had no idea how long it would take to get parts for the fix.

We finally spotted Steve and flagged him down, he was driving a cab. He drove us to the condo and gave us the key. It turned out to be an exterior bedroom with a double bed and bath attached to the condo unit that was occupied by others. It was going to be really crowded with five of us sleeping there. We still had time for a half day of skiing, so we rented skis, bought lift tickets, and took the lift up the mountain. On our first run, Michael took off, and we didn't see him the rest of the afternoon. Jon stayed with his daddy and skied the rest of the afternoon, getting familiar with some of the different runs

When the lifts closed and we couldn't find Michael, I started to get worried, and just as I was heading for the ski patrol to report him missing, here he came walking up the road looking miserable. What a sad story, on that first run he wanted virgin snow skied out of bounds, and got lost. He finally worked his way down the mountain to a road where he hitched a ride to town. Suffering from a little altitude sickness and totally exhausted, he was one miserable puppy. If he was looking for sympathy from me, he was barking up the wrong tree; I was thankful that he was alive, but somehow, I couldn't feel sorry for him, and maybe he learned something. We headed back to the condo and called my cousin to give her a heads up that we would not be there for Christmas.

Accommodations that night were interesting; Steve's roomy, Mark, stayed over with his girlfriends while Steve and I shared the bed with the boys sleeping on the floor, real cozy. In the morning, I talked to the woman living in the condo. She took pity on our situation and agreed to let me use her kitchen and let the boys sleep in her living room.

In the morning, it started snowing as I enrolled the boys in ski school, then I took the lift up the mountain for some enjoyable skiing alone. I skied over to meet up with the boys after their morning lesson for lunch on the mountain. During lunch, they told me all about their lesson and that Jon had the instructor sign him off for his BSA ski merit badge. During lunch, I lectured them on the importance of staying together, and if they didn't, I would pull their pass. They were both eager to get back on the slopes to try out what they had learned. I skied with them for a while before going down the mountain to talk with the women who saved our butts. I found her at the condo and offered to cook Christmas dinner for everyone, and she was delighted. I figured it was the least I could do as payback for her kindness. I went shopping for the bird and groceries and luckily found what I needed, plus a couple of bottles of wine.

On Christmas Day, we woke up in the morning with a blizzard blowing, and even the lifts were closed down due to high winds. Our benefactor left for work, and the boys took off with Steve to go play in the blizzard, leaving me with the place to myself to enjoy the peace and quiet while I prepared the meal. The turkey and the trimmings turned out to be one of my better efforts. At the table that evening was our hostess (I can't remember her name), her boyfriend, Steve, my two sons, and myself. We all had a wonderful time and were up late celebrating the holy event as the blizzard raged on through the night.

The next morning, we awoke to a beautiful sunshiny morning with Breckenridge covered in a new blanket of snow. We were out early, waiting for the lifts to be dug out and back in operation. While we waited, Steve brought out his homemade ski board to play around with. I just couldn't get the hang of it. The boys and Steve were getting pretty good at it. Maybe the fact that the three of them were skateboarders helped them out.

Over the next three days, we tried skiing many different ski runs, getting in lots of amazing skiing. Michael and Jon were now skiing on the more challenging runs with their daddy. They were now staying close as we raced down the slopes. Back at the condo, I knew we had to be wearing out our welcome even though the woman wasn't really pushing for us to leave. After we were done skiing on the third day, I finally got a call from the mechanic working on The Green Hornet. It was repaired and ready to roll. I made my way over to the garage and paid him off. Santa was definitely good to him. On the morning of the 28th, we cranked up the Green Hornet, thanked our hostess, and Steve then drove down the mountain to my cousins in Denver. By the time we got there, my parents had already departed the day before on their way back to Florida. We spent the night at my cousins, telling them all about our Breckenridge adventure. In the morning, we started the drive back to Florida, and thirty hours later, driving none stop, we arrived back home at the Surfview just in time for New Year's.

1983

After surviving the New Year's Eve party at the Hog's Breath Saloon, things quieted down for a while as we geared up for the upcoming activities of Spring. I had plenty to do like giving the Surfview a new coat of paint, cleaning up the landscaping, replacing rotted planks on the dock, and the never-ending work on the Pele.

On April 2nd, Jack Brown, the vice president of Windsong Charters, married Linda, giving us another occasion to party on down. They had a nice ceremony with a small group of family and friends, followed by a small reception in their apartment at the El Matador. Shortly after the wedding, Jack moved into Linda's house in Niceville, and Joe Brown, his father, took over the apartment at the El Matador that Jack had been renting from my parents.

Later on, in April, Steve Dowell, our man in Breckenridge, showed up at the Surfview with his girlfriend, whom he met on the mountain, and rented an apartment at the Surfview. The ski season was over, and he was in need of a job.

Skip was now divorced, living on his boat, the Silent Lady tied up at the Surfview Dock with Precious, his parrot. His ex-wife got the car and half his house (the castle) in the divorce settlement. In order for Skip to get to his job in Morgan City, Louisiana as a Captain on a crew boat in the oil patch, he was temporarily carpooling it. Since Steve Dowell had a car and was looking for a job, Skip offered him a job as a deckhand on his boat.

After making one trip to Louisiana and back, they decided that Steve's car didn't have enough room for all their gear. I had the old War Wagon with lots of room, so after some lengthy negotiation by the beer keg on the dock, we agreed to swap cars, problem solved. My 69' VW camper (War Wagon) was starting to rust out, and Steve's 72' VW Rabbit was newer but had been ridden hard. We figured it was pretty much an even swap.

On the 27th of April, my grandpa (Pop) had his 100th birthday and Marlboro, N.J., where he lived with his son Rudy and his wife Claire, who threw a party for him. The whole town turned out, and Pop had a great time dancing with the ladies.

On the 29 of April, we sailed the Pele up to the dock at Jay Sherf's house in Mary Esther on the sound for his annual weekend feast that he calls the "Rights of Spring Hog Roast" that we try not to miss. It's a feast of huge proportions that always has plenty of great food and drink. The party gives you an opportunity to rub elbows with some movers and shakers in town. Jay puts on two big parties a year, the hog roast and Halloween, and both are always big events and lots of fun.

Summer in paradise had arrived, and when not competing in the sailing regattas, the boys were occasionally put to work crewing on the Pele; they were having way too much fun.

May 7[th,] we dry-docked the Pele at the A&W Boatyard in Destin harbor for her annual bottom and paint job. After a week of manual labor by my partners, friends, and I, plus any slave labor we could round up, we completed the task. We launched her on the 12th of May with a new propeller shaft, zincs, cutlass bearing, and black paint job. We were back in business, just in time to be the committee boat for the two-day Hog's Breath Regatta on the 21st.

My son Michael graduated high school in June and aspiring to go to the 84' Olympics in California and was busy competing in windsurfing events around the country.

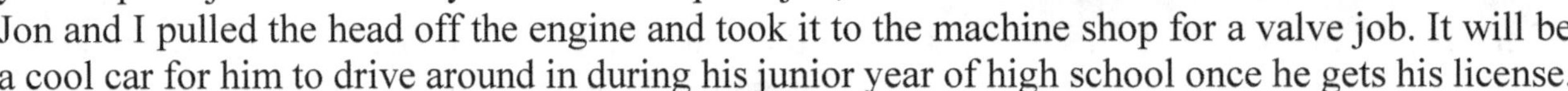

Jon, who was about to get his driver's license in Dec, was fired up to drive anything. He was inspired to help me strip the VW Rabbit inside and out and give it a new yellow paint job in the backyard. After the paint job, Jon and I pulled the head off the engine and took it to the machine shop for a valve job. It will be a cool car for him to drive around in during his junior year of high school once he gets his license.

We had a pretty good charter season; we did 17 charters between March and Sept and actually made some money for Windsong Charters, Inc.

Thanksgiving 1983 turned into another wonderful feast for everyone at the Surfview. Around twenty participants this year, Mom made sure everyone was well fed and having a good ol' time.

The day after Thanksgiving, with a crew of survivors, we sailed up the sound to Pensacola in the company of the Silent Lady and the Fair Lady. After tying up at the Pensacola pier, we headed directly for Trader John's, the most notorious bar in Pensacola. It's sort of a titty bar and the unofficial museum of Naval aviation, loaded with all kinds of naval memorabilia hanging and stacked all over the place. Trader, the proprietor, had left-over turkey from his thanksgiving dinner and fed us starving swabs; needless to say, a good time was had by all hands.

One other noteworthy incident happened on the 11th of Dec. At around five in the morning, a waterspout or squall hit the Pele while tied to the dock and tore her up. The mainsail was pretty much destroyed, a broken boom, boom gallows, and stern bench busted up. This time the mainsail was beyond repair and had to be replaced with a new one from Saber Sails. We took the boom to Navarre and hired Leo Baer to repair it. He estimated that he would have it repaired by the 28th. That pretty much put the Pele out of action for the rest of the year.

A family Christmas was held at grandma's next door, followed by a New Year's Eve '84 party held in the Fiesta Room at the El Matador. One of our friends rented the place for the occasion. It turned into a memorable event with a lot of our friends, families, and acquaintances there.

1984

On the 9th of February, we picked up the new main sail for the Pele from Saber Sails – the repaired main boom from Leo. The rest of the damage was repaired over the next couple of days, and the Pele was again ready for sea. Ten days later, we took the Pele on a shakedown cruise around the bay. The new mainsail set beautifully, and the other repairs checked out okay; the Pele was defiantly back in action.

On March 12, 1984, my grandfather Emil Max Gebhardt (Pop) died; he was one month short of his 101st birthday. He emigrated from Germany in 1914 and found a job working in a hosiery mill. He eventually brought his wife Ida, daughter Dora and his sons William and Eric over on the 19th of December 1916, shortly before we entered the First World War. On his 100th birthday, the whole town of Marlboro, N.J., turned out to celebrate the birthday of their oldest resident.

My grandfather's death put a damper on the things for a while. However, I'm thankful that he did get to spend a good amount of time with his great-grandsons, giving them an opportunity to get to know him and appreciate his wisdom.

In early April, I received a call from Marie Leibold wanting to know if I would like to drive down to Key West with her; Bill, her husband, needed a crew to help sail their boat "Yankee" back to Fort Walton Beach.

Bill and Marie are good friends, so I eagerly accepted the invitation. Bill had sailed the Yankee down to Key West, something he had wanted to do for a long time. While serving in the U.S. Navy, he was stationed at Key West in submarines a long time ago. An interesting note is that Bill's dad also served as a submariner in WW2 on the Tang; submarines run in the family.

Bill's job as a diver in the oil fields keeps him traveling around the world and keeps him out of town for weeks and months at a time. When at home, he's busy catching up with honey dues and home maintenance. Whatever is left, he spends messing with his boat, the "Yankee", a 38-foot Morgan sloop. Bill's dad had originally bought her and kept her at Bill's dock. It was not long before Bill bought her from him; now, she's his pride and joy. He keeps her well maintained, and she looks beautiful. We usually see Bill and Marie sailing locally around the Choctawhatchee Bay and on short trips up and down the coast.

Bill finally had the opportunity to make the trip to Key West. He had with him his diving partner Paul McLin and Phil DiDonato as crew. They set sail for Key West, but the trip took a lot more time than they had planned, leaving little time to explore the pleasures of Key West. After just a couple of days and out of time, Paul's wife was about to have a baby, and Phil had to get back to his day job.

Marie picked me up, and an additional crew member, my girlfriend Belinda, "The Viking Princess". She's a nurse, and I love nurses. Three drivers would make the twelve-hour drive to the Keys a lot easier. After an uneventful drive, we found Bill and his crew on Duvall Street at "Rick's", our favorite bar in Key West. After a couple of beers, we drove over to the Yankee that was tied up in one of the sub pens at what used to be the Navy submarine base where Bill had been stationed and had a crew change. We loaded our gear on board, and after Paul and Phil loaded their gear in the car, they started driving back to FWB. After getting everything squared away on the Yankee, we walked back to "Rick's Bar" to hear from Bill about the sail down and what was going on in Key West.

At Rick's, the bartender informed us that all food and drinks were on him. Bill had taken him out for a sail on the Yankee, and ever since, Bill got a lot of freebies. The story is that on the sail, the bartender had brought along his pistol that he had never fired before to try it out. When they were far enough offshore, Bill told him he could try out his pistol. They were in the cockpit at the stern of the boat, and as he fiddled around loading up the pistol, it accidentally went off, luckily missing everyone. The round went through the deck and bounced off the refrigeration compressor beneath the deck, putting a dent in it but no other damage. That's why the free food and booze at Rick's.

After playing around Key West for a day provisioning the Yankee, we adjourned to Rick's to plan our route back to Fort Walton Beach. After a few beers, we decided to go by way of Fort Jefferson. I assured the crew that the fort would be well worth a visit. In 1980 I was there with Skip and my boys on the Silent Lady and had a good ol' time.

We departed the sub pens at Key West after an early breakfast at Rick's and enjoyed a lovely sail down the keys to Garden Key and Fort Jefferson. We arrive at the anchorage by the fort in time to celebrate happy hour on the Yankee. Fort Jefferson was one of the shore defense forts built along our entire shoreline after the war of 1812 with England. Located on Garden Key, the next to the last key in the Florida Keys. The only way to visit this national park is by boat or seaplane, and it is quite a sight, a huge brick structure located in what seems like the middle of the ocean.

After a couple of days of touring around the fort and partying with some of the other boaters anchored up by the fort, we sailed over to spend the day at Longboat Key and the lighthouse. Not much had changed since my last trip. There were different coast guardsmen on lighthouse duty, with the friendly dogs welcoming us ashore. We had a great time talking with the coast guardsmen and playing around with the dogs that took us on a tour of the island.

After a while, we sailed back to the anchorage by the fort and anchored up near a fifty-foot sports fishing boat and asked them about their catch. They had a good haul of dolphins, red snapper, and grouper. After talking with them for a while, they invited us over for cocktail hour and to dine with them on the catch. The party was a lot of fun and went on until the late evening.

We finally put our act together in the morning to get underway to our next destination, Fort Myers. It turned out to be an overnight motor directly into the wind and seas, and the closer we got to Fort

Myers, the nastier the weather got. When we finally arrived, we anchored up in the lee of the SE corner of Sanibel Island and spent a bouncy night on the hook.

Next morning, it was still blowing out of the north when we got underway, motoring up Pine Island Sound to Cabbage Key, where around midafternoon, we anchored up. Once ashore, we walked around the island until happy hour, followed by a nice meal at the restaurant. We hung around for an after-dinner drink, then took the dinghy back to the Yankee and spent a nice comfortable night on the hook.

The plan in the morning was to head out Boca Grande Pass and pick up a direct course to Apalachicola. It didn't happen, and we ended up motoring up the coast to Tampa Bay, where we spent the night anchored up in the lee of Egmont Key. Next morning, with the wind still on our nose, we continued motoring up the coast to Tarpon Springs, where we tied up to the town's wharf. Since we arrived in the early afternoon, we had time to check out the area and all the tourist shops.

We also watched a sponge diving demonstration with a diver using the old hard hat diving gear; Tarpon Springs used to be a big area for sponges. Later on, we had a great dinner at a Greek restaurant on the wharf.

The early departure next morning found us motoring across the big bend toward Apalachicola, the wind had moderated a little, but it was still an uncomfortable ride. Finally, by late afternoon we passed through Government Cut into Apalachicola Bay, headed for the dock by Caroline's, then walked over to the Gibson Inn in time for happy hour. For supper, we walked up the street to an Oyster bar and had some great Apalachicola oysters on the half shell, followed by a wonderful seafood dinner.

For the rest of the trip, we motor/sailed up the Intercoastal Waterway to Fort Walton by way of Lake Wimico and Panama City. One incident of interest along the route back was that we ran aground, and try as we might, we could not get the Yankee off the mud. We tried wiggling, backing, and careening, and it only put us deeper in the sticky, smelly mud. We had to swallow our pride and call the Coast Guard for help. When they arrived, they conducted a thorough inspection of the boat, documents, and safety gear and then took our names and date of birth; that's when I found out I was dating young stuff. The rest of the trip back to Fort Walton was uneventful. Key West was a fun short little cruise that was packed with high adventure, Belinda and I thanked

Bill and Marie for inviting us along.

Back at the Surfview, the summer was turning into a busy one. On the 5th of May, the Pele again was the committee boat for the Around the Island Race, and my son Jon was crew for Phil Foss, one of my tenants, on a Hobie 16. They finished in third place and received a trophy at the awards ceremony.

Then on the 10th, we sailed the Pele up to Jay Scherf's Rights of Spring Pig Roast at his place on the sound. The annual event at his big house on the sound in Mary Esther is a celebration that goes on for days that will take you days to recover from.

Toward the end of June, my oldest son Michael was flying out to Los Angeles as the training partner for Scott Steel. Scott, who had beat out Michael at the Windsurfing Olympic Trials earlier in the year, had asked Michael to train with him for the 84' games being held in L.A. starting on July 28, 1984

Windsong Charters was having another successful season. We picked up quite a few charters, mostly four-hour sails around the bay, a couple of birthdays, and a wedding.

In early August, the friend of Outlaw's, who contacted us earlier about a burial at sea, called and asked if the Pele was still up for charter, and I told him we were still in business. He informed me that Outlaw had passed away. A short time later, we got the call from the executor of his estate and scheduled a burial at sea for the 21st.

On the 20th of June, we sailed the Pele to Panama City to be in a position to pick up Outlaw's funeral party. The next morning, with the funeral party on board, we sailed out the pass and positioned the Pele off of Powell Street for the ceremony. The spreading of his remains was performed by a priest and was a very solemn moment. After the ceremony and a short sail along the coast, we disembarked the funeral party. Afterward, it was a short sail over to the marina by the No Name Lounge, where we tied up for the night and walked over to the lounge to tip a couple for Outlaw.

In late August, my son Michael returned from Los Angeles. Scott Steele won a silver medal at the games, and Michael was now all fired up and determined to go to the next Olympic Games in 1988 to be held in South Korea. Since Michael almost beat Scott in the trials for the '84 games, Michael thought he could maybe beat him at the trials next time around.

Not long after Michael returned from the games, he informed me that he was moving to Fort Pierce, Florida, with his girlfriend, Edithe. She's a lovely French Canadian from St. Anicet, a small town across the river from Montreal. Over the next couple of days, they loaded up his stuff into the Plymouth station wagon (Green Hornet) and hit the road headed south.

On the 4th of July, we loaded up the Pele with our friends and sailed over to Boggy Bayou in Niceville, where we rafted up with a couple of other sailboats to watch the fireworks.

It was time to take the Pele on her annual trip to the A&W Boatyard. On the 25th, we sailed her over and had her hauled out with their boat lift. After a quick bottom and paint job, we launched her again on the 4th of August, looking really pretty.

While on a charter for a day sail in the gulf on the 11th of August, we blew out our foresail, it was in pretty sad shape, to begin with, and the twenty-knot wind was too much for it. Once back at the dock, we stripped both the foresail and the main for a trip to Sabre Sails for a new foresail and to put another set of reef points in the main. For the next couple of weeks, we had to contend ourselves with motoring up and down the sound and around the bay.

We picked up our sails from Sabre Sails on the 24th, just in time for a charter on the 25th. The Pele was back in action. She was sailing better than ever for the remainder of what was left of the charter season and the beginning of just sailing with our friends around the Redneck Riviera.

In October of 1984, Skip, who had been working as a captain on a crew boat in the Gulf of Mexico oil patch with his deckhand Steve, was in-between jobs. Steve had just broken up with his girlfriend, his true love that he brought back with him from Colorado. Apparently, being unhappy with her situation packed up her stuff and headed back to the mountains for the upcoming ski season.

While talking on the dock by the beer keg, both Skip and Steve indicated that they were ready to get out of town for a little adventure and thinking of maybe doing the Bahamas and maybe even going as far as the Lesser Antilles. Hurricane season was winding down, with Josephine headed up the east coast, hopefully being the last one for the year. I volunteered to go with them; you can always use another hand.

I checked with my parents to see if once again they were game to come up, run the apartments and watch over my youngest son Jon while I was gone. They were only too eager to do it.

We started preparing for our departure. The next couple of weeks were busy gathering and stowing charts, cruising guides, provisioning up the Silent Lady with food and beer, loading onboard the dingy and the 20-man life raft. Finally, we were ready to go.

On the 14th of October, we cast off from the Surfview dock, underway for our first port of call, Tampa. The weather was pretty nasty in the Gulf. There were elephants on the horizon, so we stayed inside, motoring down the intercoastal to Lake Wimico, where we anchored up in a beautiful moonless star-filled night. It's amazing how bright the stars are. You could almost read a book by their light. We departed early in the morning, heading down the intercoastal waterway and Apalachicola River to Apalachicola, hoping to get there in time for happy hour at the Gibson Inn. A beautiful place that was used as an officer's BOQ during WW2 that has a great roomy bar and a big veranda with rocking chairs where you can think, rock and drink.

We decided to stay on another day for the weather to calm down, giving us the opportunity to fill our bellies with Apalachicola oysters and do the tour of the Inn. The weather conditions were getting worse, not better; a tropical depression had developed about 100mi west of Apalachicola, giving us strong winds and seas out of the south. We decided in the morning to sail down Apalachicola Bay in the calmer seas, then up the Carrabelle River, where we tied up to the Pirates Cove Restaurant for the night. In the morning, after breakfast at the restaurant, we cast off and headed south. The wind and seas had laid down a little. A day later, we were in Tarpon Springs, where we tied up to the municipal wharf for the night.

Next morning, we motor sailed down the coast to Egmont Key and into Tampa Bay, where we anchored up in the St Pete North Yacht Basin and dinked ashore. The Bounty replica that was built for the movie was tied up to the municipal pier. We went aboard and did the tour; they sailed it around the world, showing it off. There was also a boat show going on in the South Basin, so for the rest of the day and the next, we looked at boats and harassed the girls in the Central Ave bars.

We sailed out of Tampa Bay in the morning for an uneventful sail down the intercoastal to Sarasota. We called ahead to the Marina Jack for a spot to tie up for the night, arriving there in time for happy hour. Sarasota is where Skip screwed up his back four years ago on our sail to Key West with my boys.

In the morning, after refueling, we motored out Big Sarasota Pass, a little bit tricky since it was shawled over quite a bit. Once clear of the pass, we had a nice easy sail down the coast to Pine Island Sound, clearing the pass at Boca Grande in the late afternoon. Once inside the pass, we tried to but couldn't find a place to anchor near Miller's Marina, so we nosed up the bayou a little way and found a place where we tied off to the mangroves near the Pink Elephant Restaurant. After securing the boat, we took the dinghy ashore and went on a short walk around town before dinner.

Boca Grande changed quite a bit since 1980 when we sailed here with my boys – lots of new construction and people; it kind of lost the feel and appeal of old Florida. It was no longer a sleepy little old town on the Florida West Coast.

Next morning, with an early departure, found us motor sailing down Pine Island Sound to Fort Myers, where Pine Island Sound connects up with the Caloosahatchee River that's part of the Okeechobee Waterway. That evening just short of the I-75 Bridge we anchored up for the night; from here on, we are headed into new territory.

After two days of motoring up the river with a short stop on the way at La Belle, where the river changes its name to the Okeechobee Waterway, we tied up at the Moore Haven municipal dock. Once ashore, we wandered around town for a couple of hours, eventually returning to the boat for dinner. After an early morning departure through the Moore Haven Lock, we continued motoring down the canal. Later in the afternoon, we anchored up in the canal for the evening. By shining the spotlight around during evening cocktails, you could see the beady red eyes of the alligators watching for one of us to fall overboard. Pretty spooky!

We pulled the anchor at dawn and entered Lake Okeechobee and actually had an opportunity to haul up the sails for a while before entering the locks at Port Mayaca. Now comes the tricky part, getting under the RR Bridge there. How much clearance required for getting under the bridge (we needed around 50') depended on the height of the lake. We worried about it and had all kinds of schemes on how to heal the boat over and give us more clearance. In the end, we made it under by a hair on the first attempt. With a sigh of relief, we continued motoring to the Sailor's Return Restaurant in Stuart and tied up at the dock in time for happy hour and dinner at the restaurant.

Next morning, we motored over to join up with the intercoastal waterway and headed south. By early afternoon we found a cove to anchor up in near Jupiter with a grocery store nearby to re-provision. In the morning, we continued motoring down the Intercoastal to Palm Beach, where we anchored up for the night near Peanut Island.

On the morning of 11 Nov, we motored over to Sailfish Marina, a designated U.S. Customs reporting station, where you check-in and out of the U.S. We spent most of the day getting all the paperwork squared away and getting the boat refueled. Just after sunset, we cast off and set sail for our first port of call in the Bahamas, West End on Grand Bahama Island.

The theory is that you want to leave after sunset for the 10-hour sail to West End to arrive in early morning daylight, flying your yellow quarantine flag from the spreader to clear customs and immigration for entry into the Bahamas at the Jack Tar Marina. You want to get there early, so you have plenty of time to find your way onto the Little Bahama Bank in good daylight. It all sounds reasonable except for one thing – you're sailing perpendicular to all the heavy shipping going up and down the coast at night. They are steaming along at around 15kts, and you're doing around 5kt, and you really have to be on the ball to maneuver out of the way if you see one closing in on you.

Dodging the ship traffic kept us on our toes, and at daybreak, we could see land on the horizon. Around 08:00 on the 12th, we tied up to the dock at the Jack Tar Marina in West End, Grand Bahama Island. Skip went up to the Customs and Immigration office with our passports to clear in and get the cruising permit that allows you to cruise the Bahamas for a year.

We were number three in line, and it seemed to take forever, but just before noon, the official came out with Skip to inspect us and the boat and issued us our cruising permit. We then hauled down the yellow quarantine flag from our starboard spreader and replaced it with the Bahama courtesy flag; now, we were good to go.

Once we found Indian Cay Rock, the entrance to the channel over the reef onto the Banks, we were on our way to Mangrove Cay. We anchored up in the lee of the cay with two other boats around 16:00 in the afternoon in time for happy hour on the Silent Lady and to plan our next destination.

By dawn, we were already underway for our next port of call, Green Turtle Cay, with a stop for the night somewhere along the way. By five in the afternoon of the 13th, we were anchored up on the banks in around 10ft of water near a coral head to snorkel around for an hour or so, looking for dinner. We found a couple of conches, and Steve speared a nice grouper.

While cooking up, our catch Skip discovered he had left our passports at the Jack Tar Customs office. Skip contacted Jack Tar on the VHF radio and arranged for them to send our passports on over to Green Turtle Custom Office. The incident gave Steve and me an excuse to give our captain a bunch of grief and would cost him a few rounds.

After a short sail to Green Turtle and working our way up the channel, we tied up to the marina's dock. We spent the day doing the laundry, cleaning up and refueling the Silent Lady, and looking around the marina. The Green Turtle Club has a nice bar, and while chatting up the clientele, we heard some horror stories about sailing out Whale Cay Channel. The advice is, if you see large waves rolling in, don't attempt it.

 The deal with this channel is that you have to get by Whale Cay shallows to get to Treasure Island and Marsh Harbour. There's Don't Rock Passage on the banks, but it's shallow and navigable only by shallow-draft boats. The Silent Lady draws 4 1/2feet, so we had a choice, get by these shallows by going out Whale Cay Channel, sail around Whale Cay, and back on the banks by way of Loggerhead Channel. Or risk going aground by taking Don't Rock Passage over the shallows. It's not really a passage at all; you just visually pick your way across by having someone on the bow guiding you to the darkest blue water ahead that's supposedly 4 to 5ft deep.

Our passports arrived on the mail boat late in the afternoon. At dinner, we planned to be on our way early in the morning and decide then what course we would take.

After a great breakfast at the Club on the 14th, we cast off on our way for parts unknown, towing our dinghy on a ten-foot painter on a beautiful Bahama morning. We decided to wait until we could look over the channel before deciding how to get around Whale Cay.

There wasn't a cloud in the sky and a steady 10 -15 kt wind from the NE. Approaching Whale Cay Channel, it looked pretty calm with maybe 2-4ft seas rolling in from the deep and didn't look like that big a deal, so we went for it. We had Steve on the bow hanging onto the bow stay, looking for shallows and coral heads. The closer we got, the bigger the waves. Halfway through, a monster wave crested and broke right over us. It swept us from stem to stern; with all the hatches open, everything down below got soaked, but we made it through. Steve was still hanging on at the bow stay, he actually took a picture of the wave, but our dinghy broke loose and was gone. Searching around with the binoculars, there she was, just bobbing up and down on the inside. You have to have a dinghy, it's your transport, like your car. We had no choice. We turned around and went back in to pick her up.

Going back through the channel onto the banks was pretty much uneventful, thank God! Once we recovered our dinghy and with Steve on the bow guiding us, we worked our way down Don't Rock Passage and on to Marsh Harbour; we had enough of Whale Cay Channel. By early afternoon we were safely anchored near The Conch Inn Marina in Marsh Harbour on Great Abaco Island. Headed for shore in our dingy, we tied up to the dinghy dock at the Conch Crawl Sunset Patio in time for cocktails to celebrate our survival. Later on, we had an excellent meal at Mangoes, next door. Life is good.

In the morning, we picked our next destination, Hope Town on Elbow Cay. While en route, we decided to do a little cruise through the harbor at Man of War Cay. On entering the harbor, we made a turn to port to cruise the North Harbor. Looking around, we could see the pretty good-sized Edwin's Boatyard, the Aubury's Ferry Dock, and what looked like a government dock. On the way out, we peeked into the South Harbor, where the anchorage is located, to look around, then went on to Hope Town.

The 120ft Elbow Cay Light at Hope Town that guides the way can be seen a long way out. We anchored up near the Hope Town Harbour Lodge, then jumped into our dingy to go over and climb the lighthouse, a must-do in Hope Town. From the top, there's a spectacular view of the beautifully picturesque town with all the colorfully painted houses. After a dinghy ride across the harbor to the town's dinghy dock, we did a little walking tour of the town before dinner at the Club Soleil. We made an early arrival back to the Silent Lady for a good night's sleep before our departure in the morning.

November 16th, we were underway at dawn and motored the mile or so down Elbow Cay to White Sound Harbour, tied up stern-to at the Abaco Inn's dock for a nice leisurely breakfast. After a little walkabout, we were back on board the Silent lady to continue our cruise down the Abaco's by slowly working our way down the banks to a small cay called Little Harbour.

We arrived in the early afternoon and anchored up around 50ft off of a little sandy beach. On the beach is a small shack with a big sign that says Pete's Pub, so far so good unfortunately, no one was in sight to sell us a beer. A man eventually showed up and sold us a beer. While talking to him, we found out a little about Little Harbour's history.

In the 1960's Randolph Johnson, a sculptor from the NE somewhere showed up at the island in an old schooner with his family and homesteaded it. Apparently, they all lived in a cave on the island while they built a house and eventually a foundry. Mr. Johnson's family is famous in the Bahamas. His bronze busts are on display in Nassau and the US. His wife is famous for her ceramics, and his son Pete for his large sculptures of dauphins, sea animals, and gold jewelry. They have a shop/studio and give tours of the foundry. Unfortunately for us, it was closed during our stay. All in all, we had a pleasant stay on Mr. Johnson's private island.

On the 17th, we set sail in the afternoon from Little Harbour for an overnight sail to Nassau on New Providence. Six hours later, we rounded Hole in the Wall Lighthouse and said goodbye to the Abaco's. Our next check point will be Paradise Island Light at the west end of Nassau Harbour.

We started to see the light around an hour before sunrise, and just before entering the harbor at dawn, we contacted Nassau Harbour Control for permission to enter the harbor. Searching around, we finally found a pretty good place to anchor about half a mile west of Potters Cay Bridge on the Paradise Island side of Nassau Harbour near Club Med, where we checked in with customs.

Taking the dinghy over to the Nassau side, we tied up at a dinghy dock and started exploring. We went strolling through the shops in downtown Nassau and found a friendly café for lunch. After lunch, we continued our stroll, heading toward the bridge. On the way, we came across Randolph Johnson's bronze bust sculptures, permanently on display in a square near the center of town.

 Our next stop was under the bridge to re-provision. The vendors there sell all kinds of fish, conch, lobsters, and all sorts of fruits and vegetables. At one of the kiosks, we noticed a woman pulling the meat out of a conch. We had tried for a good two hours trying to get the meat out of the two we had, but with no success, we finally gave up and threw them back in. We asked her (Geraldine) to show us how to do it. After our lesson, we were now fired up and ready to give it a go as soon as we found some victims. Before leaving, Geraldine talked us into buying a conch mallet from her to tenderize the conch. Once back on the Silent Lady, we tallied our load of goodies: four bottles of Cruzan Rum, a real bargain at 90 cents a bottle, a bunch of plantains at $1.80, conch mallet at $8.00, plus the usual groceries and two cases of beer. We were all set and raring to go as soon as the sun came up in the morning.

On November 19th, after making a stop at the fuel dock to take on fuel, water, ice, and a departure call to Nassau Harbour Control, we were underway for Eleuthera Island. Sailing East out of Nassau

Harbour into Montagu Bay, then over to the east end of Paradise Island, we took up a heading for the cut between Salt Cay and Rose Island Rocks. It was an easy sail from there to Spanish Wells, located on the eastern end of St. George's Cay, and followed the channel into the harbor where we anchored up in the east end just south of town. After getting the boat squared away, we took the dingy ashore to do a little walkabout. The place is well populated and supports a well-established tourist and sport fishing industry. We had no problem finding a bar/restaurant for cocktails and dinner.

After breakfast on the Silent Lady in the morning, we hauled up the anchor and set sail for Dunmore Town. By following the Devils Backbone, a five-mile stretch of shallow jagged-edge reef across the north end of Eleuthera that led us to a bay, then four miles down the bay to Dunmore Town. Once we arrived and found a place to anchor, we headed ashore, tying up our dingy to Government Dock for a walkabout town. Most of the small shops that we checked out were located in close proximity to the dock, where we also found a small café for lunch. After lunch, we wandered around town for a little while longer, then headed back to Spanish Wells, getting back in time for cocktails and dinner at one of the town's fine restaurants.

In the morning, we got underway to continue our cruise down Eleuthera Island to Hatchett Bay. But to get there, we would have to pass through Current Cut, located an hour and a half down the coast on the North end of Current Island. Sure enough, we ran aground on the rocks while making our way down the twisting channel. After a lot of maneuvering and cursing, we finally got free. Once clear of the cut, we anchored and inspected the bilge, hull, screw, shaft, and rudder for damage. We found that the keel was scarred up; other than that, no real damage. While checking out the bottom, we noticed some conch crawling around, so we loaded our victims into our conch bag. With a shot of rum and a sigh of relief, we headed for Hatchett Bay.

While en route, the fun began, trying to get the meat out of two of our conchs. Geraldine said you have to cut a hole in the shell near the point and cut the meat there. Then you can pull the conch out of its shell. It's not as easy as it sounds; we screwed around with it for what seemed like an hour before we got the first one out. It's slimy and hard to hang on to; the second one was a lot easier. We cut the guts and the hard sole on the foot off, then washed the meat in seawater to get the slime off, then soaked the meat for around a half-hour. Then we beat it up with the mallet, cut it up into pieces, put the meat in a bowl with lime juice and a cut-up red pepper, and let it sit for a quarter hour. Walla! Ceviche for lunch. The remaining live conch we put in the bag to hang overboard.

Four hours later, just before sunset, we were in Hatchett Bay, tied up at the Hatchett Bay Yacht Club. As we disembarked from the Silent Lady, we had a little shooter of rum to celebrate our survival. At the club, we didn't stay long; we just had a meal and called it a night. We were all exhausted.

We sailed out of Hatchett Bay in the morning on the 21st for the five-hour sail down the coast to Governor's Harbour. This leg of the cruise turned out to be a piece of cake, a beautiful day with a nice 10-15kt wind on a broad reach almost all the way. On the way, we had fried plantains and eggs for breakfast and fried conch for lunch, just a great day.

In the early afternoon, we anchored up in Governor's Harbour and spent the rest of the afternoon snorkeling around, looking for some victims to eat. We didn't have much luck, just one conch that we put in our conch bag with the only other occupant. We took shore leave to walk around town, go grocery shopping, and find a place for dinner. We found the Buccaneer Inn, where after cocktails, we had a great lobster dinner, something we hadn't been able to catch ourselves.

After a short sail in the morning down the coast to Cape Eleuthera, we anchored up a short distance off the beach for the night. While snorkeling around the area, we found a couple of shovel-nosed lobster plus a couple of conches. Wow! We are becoming real hunters of the deep. The catch supplied us with a nice Thanksgiving Day meal of lobster, conch fritters, peas, and rice.

The morning found the Silent Lady en route to the Exuma Cays, around a five-hour sail, and arrived early afternoon in the vicinity of Allen's Cays. By carefully finding our way through Highborne Cut back onto the banks, we eventually found a spot with good holding at the South end of Highborne Cay. We spent an hour snorkeling around, checking out the area for victims finding none. Back on board, while having a little rum and enjoying a beautiful Bahamian sunset, we contemplated our next destination. Looking over our chart, we decided to just sail down the banks until midafternoon and find a place to anchor for the night. We were slowly acquiring a laid-back Bahamian attitude.

On the 24th of November, after an uneventful sail down the Exuma's, and in the afternoon and came across Staniel Cay. We decided to stop, made our way up the channel, and anchored up off of the Happy People Marina. We climbed aboard our dinghy and, once ashore, headed for the bar for happy hour. Inside we encountered the crews of the other boats anchored up in the harbor. We had a grand ol' time swapping sea stories until late into the evening.

Exploring Staniel Cay in the morning, we found out that a scene in the James Bond movie Thunderball was filmed there in what they now call Thunderball Cave. Of course, we had to check it out after a short dinghy trip over to a tiny cay and underwater tunnel to a cave with a hole in the top where in the movie, they hauled James Bond out with a helicopter. We all swam into it and looked around. It looked a lot smaller than the movie.

 Later on, we moved over to the Happy People Marina dock to take on water and fuel. We were met by a couple on a cabin cruiser tied up ahead of us on the dock. He was a software engineer living on the boat with his wife and their three-year-old daughter. After chatting them up for a while, they invited us to dine with them on their boat. We brought over some wine and had a lovely evening with them. In the morning while in the process of casting off, their daughter brought us over a couple of drawings she made just for us, really sweet of her.

By mid-morning, we had worked our way out of Rock Cut and into Exuma Sound, heading SE for a destination undecided. The weather had deteriorated, becoming overcast with a wind velocity of 20kts the seas of 3 to 5 feet. The Silent Lady was sailing well under a reefed main and a furled-down jib. By late in the afternoon, we had Cat Island in sight, and in the approaching dusk, we worked our way up Hawks Nest Creek and anchored with another boat that was anchored further up the creek.

An hour or so later, we received a call on the VHF with an invitation for both crews for Thanksgiving leftovers from the people in a big house on the low hill by a short airstrip. We dinked over to the dock where we met the two guys from the other sailboat and hoofed up the hill to the house.

We were greeted by the caretaker and staff of the Hawks Nest Club, which was closed at the time. They had tons of food and drink, and we ate our fill. There was plenty of conversation until late into the evening when we thanked our hosts for their hospitality and made our way down the hill to the Silent Lady for a good night's sleep with a full belly.

With an early departure on the 26th, we headed out of Hawks Nest Creek and picked up a heading of SE in 4 to 6 ft seas and wind out of the NE at 20 to 25 kts. Under shortened sails, we were making 6 to 7kts, under overcast skies in light rain, really moving right along.

By early afternoon we had rain and 6 to 8 ft seas. The wind had increased to 30 to 35 kts blowing out of the North. We started looking for a place to hide; it was becoming obvious we were sailing into some sort of storm. Our dead reckoning position had us between the Crooked Islands and Samana Cay. The accuracy of our DR position was getting less reliable by the minute, and with the low visibility conditions we were running out of options.

After weighing all options, our decision was to run to the SE for the open sea instead of trying a risky approach to the Crooked Islands to the south of us or Samana Cay to the north.

Around four in the afternoon, we noticed a military-looking boat on our stern. We called them on the VHF, and they gave us a position from their Satellite Navigation System. We compared it to our DR position; it was 5 miles off ours. Using their position, we headed south toward the Plana Cays.

At nightfall, sailing before the wind with only a furled down jib on a southerly heading with winds now 30kts gusts to 40kts with monster cresting waves on our stern. Taking turns at the wheel, working our butts off, trying to keep from broaching. In total darkness and in howling conditions, we DR to a point beyond the westerly end of West Plana Cay, then turned due east, heading for a point south of East Cay.

A short time later, the seas moderated, and the wind died down a little indicating to us that we were now in the lee of the Cay. Once we reached our turn point South of E. Plana, we started the engine, hauled in the jib, and picked up a heading of North. In total darkness, we motored on watching our depth gage, and when it suddenly marked up to 15 ft, we shined our spotlight ahead and could see land 50 ft ahead. It was four in the morning when we dropped the hook, and with the anchor set, we had a shot of rum to celebrate our survival we were all totally exhausted.

Late morning on the 28th of November, after a good breakfast of bacon, eggs (our last), and fried plantains, we went on deck to survey the area. To the north, a beautiful white sandy uninhabited beach as far as you could see.

The rest of the morning was occupied by beachcombing and snorkeling around our anchorage, looking for victims. We did find one conch and a huge ship anchor 50yds to the east of where we anchored. The rest of the day was spent cleaning up the Silent Lady, turning the conch into ceviche, and doing nothing.

We weighed anchor early the next morning and set sail for Mayaguana, our last stop in the Bahamas; the estimated time en route was a little over six hours at 6 kts. The wind had moderated overnight and was now a steady 20kts out of the North under overcast skies. That put us on a nice reach to Mayaguana, making right around 6 kts.

After sailing for around five hours, we sighted Mayaguana, and a few hours later, we found our way over the reef into Abraham's Bay, located on the south side of the island. We anchored up near the village, tied up our dinghy to the town dock, and started looking around. The villagers were really friendly and showed us around their town; they probably didn't get many visitors to this far-out island. We picked up some groceries and headed back to the boat to get ready for an early morning departure

Dawn found us underway, our destination a British Crown Colony, the Turks and Caicos Islands. With a morning breeze of 15 to 20kts from the NE, giving us a pleasant sail until the wind started to clock around to the E. From there on, it was motor sailing. An hour before sunset, we worked our way up Sand Bore Channel to anchor up on Providenciales off of Gussy Point.

Once ashore, after we had our breakfast on board the Silent Lady, we went looking for the customs office. We ended up spending most of the day walking down a dirt road into town to find it. After clearing in, we found a pleasant café in town for lunch followed by a little walkabout before we started our trek back to our anchorage.

Next morning, we departed early for an easy sail to South Caicos Island. We anchored up just north of Government Pier, dinked ashore for happy hour and maybe a nice restaurant for dinner. We found a bar for happy hour close to the pier, where we tied up our dinghy, and after getting a couple of beers, we noticed that the clientele was intently looking us over. It started to become uncomfortable, so we packed up and left. We decided to have dinner on the boat. We just couldn't understand why it seemed so unfriendly there when the rest of the Islands were.

The next morning, as soon as customs opened, we were there to check out of the Turks and Caicos. We asked the customs officials as we were checking out why Grand Turk didn't appear to be as friendly as other Islands we've been to, they had no explanation, and we wasted no time setting sail. Once clear of Dove Cay and the coral heads, we picked up an SSE heading down the Turks Island Passage, picking up the NE trades bound for Puerto Plata in the Dominican Republic (DR).

In the early afternoon of 3 Dec, land ho, we could see Mount Isabela de Torres that rises just behind Puerta Plata on the horizon. About an hour out, we called up the port captain for permission to enter and requested customs and immigration. They instructed us to Mediterranean moor to the Municipal pier and to stay on our boat to await customs.

Entering the harbor, we passed between the remains of a large shipwreck just west of the channel. On the east side was Fort San Felipe on an outcropping with a couple of cannons. Once inside, we located the pier, and after a couple of attempts, we finally set the anchor in the mud. Once the anchor was set, we backed down on it between two other boats and tied it up to the pier to complete the Mediterranean Moor. There was a substantial surge rolling into the harbor, so it was going to be pretty tricky getting on and off the boat. By late afternoon customs finally showed up, and after giving the Silent Lady a thorough search, they cleared us in.

Exploring Puerto Plata, we stumbled across an antique-looking hotel restaurant near the pier, had a cocktail there, and decided to stay for dinner. The women that ran the place came over and joined us. We had a good meal and conversation and learned a little history of the town. Skip hit it off with her and rented a room; I guess he got lucky. After dinner, Steve and I wandered around town for a while, then headed back to the Silent Lady. Sure enough, there was a surge rolling into the harbor, making getting on the boat without busting your butt a challenge.

In the morning, we wandered over to the hotel for breakfast. Skip wasn't around, so we ordered up and had the proprietor call his room. After she brought breakfast, she then joined us for a chat and recommended that we hire a guide to show us around that sounded good to Steve and me. When Skip finally showed up, we talked it over and decided to do it. An hour or so later, we were rolling down the dirt roads on mopeds, following a young teenage local. It was an interesting tour driving around town in probably the biggest town we've been in since Nassau. It seems like on every vacant lot; there were kids playing baseball. We stopped for lunch at a small café on the outskirts of town before heading over to check out the old cannons at Fort San Felipe, then headed back to the hotel for cocktails and dinner.

That evening after dinner at the hotel, we wandered around town and found a really friendly bar called "Poopies". The owner, a retired black cop from Chicago with one leg, he got shot on duty, and they had to amputate it. He ended up in the DR and married a local woman, and opened a bar that was actually a bar/whore house. That's why the girls were so friendly! Anyway, we had a fun time kibitzing the girls and talking it up with the owner and his wife. By the time we headed back, it had started to rain. We had intentions of checking out in the morning but decided, then and there, to stay another day, hoping the weather would clear.

By the time we finished breakfast at the hotel, and even though the weather had moderated, we decided to stay another day, my birthday. It turned out to be a good day to wander around Puerta Plata. In the afternoon, we stopped at a bar/café for some lunch. The owner was from the states and had just opened for business a couple of months earlier. He was probably in his late 20s; he chatted with us enthusiastically about his plans and expectations for his venture. We wished him the best of luck.

As soon as customs opened on the morning of December 6th, we cleared out of Puerta Plata. Once clear of the harbor, we picked up an ESE course toward Puerto Rico straight into a 15 to 20-knot headwind with 3ft seas. We motored into the wind all day, not making a lot of progress. The seas and wind finally laid down a little around sundown. The morning found us near the twin capes of Cape Carbon at the eastern end of the DR. We had enough pounding into the wind and seas and decided to look for a port of call. Samana was close, just around the corner from Cape Carbon and up Samana Bay a few miles.

The capes have high cliffs that you can hear the seas beating against for miles. Skip had the helm as we rounded the capes early in the morning. Steve and I were down below preparing breakfast. As I headed topside with a cup of coffee for Skip, and as soon as I hit the deck, I knew something was not right. I heard the pounding of waves on the cliffs off both sides of the boat. Skip had rounded the first of the twin capes and was charging downwind between them, thinking he was sailing down Samana Bay. The morning haze hid the fact that he was headed down a dead end.

After beating our way out of the trap, we rounded the other cape and had an easy sail down the bay to Samana. We called the harbor master for permission to enter and were instructed to tie up at the Municipal Pier for customs. The customs official met us at the pier. We explained to him that we had just departed Puerta Plata en route to Puerto Rico and diverted to Samana for the weather. He called over to Puerta Plata and confirmed our story. He did a quick look around, and since we had never really left the DR he informed us that we could hang around a couple of days and to just inform the harbor master when we set sail for Puerto Rico.

We spent most of the day topping up with fuel and water, just relaxing on the boat and talking to other yachties' on the dock. We listened to some horror stories about crossing the Mona Passage, the notoriously rough passage between the DR and Puerto Rico. But the big story around the dock was that a cruise ship recently ran aground in the fog on Isla de Mona, a small island in the middle of the passage. Anticipating the worst, early on the morning of Dec 8th, we headed out into Mona Passage for the 1 ½ day sail to San Juan.

Sure enough, choppy seas and a 15-knot headwind forced us to motor all the way, bouncing around and taking on a lot of spray. One good thing was the sun finally broke through in the afternoon and by nightfall, the wind dropped some. We stopped taking on spray, but neither one of us got much sleep, keeping alert and looking out for ship traffic going up and down, Mona Passage. By morning we sighted the NW corner of Puerto Rico on the horizon, and two hours later, we rounded the corner and headed up the north coast of the island toward San Juan.

By early afternoon we had the San Felipe del Morro Fortress at the entrance to San Juan Harbor in sight. After getting clearance from Port Authorities, we called US Customs/Immigration and then contacted the Club Nautico de San Juan [the yacht club] for a mooring. By the time we found and hooked up to our mooring buoy, it was time to hit the bar at the yacht club for a cocktail and some food.

Next day was spent touring around San Juan and the old fort and found a comfortable café for lunch in the old town. We slowly made our way back to the Silent Lady for an early turn for an early departure in the morning. A good plan, but we stopped in the club on the way and ended up chatting it up with other sailors at the bar until late in the evening.

We finally did get underway around 09:00 the next morning. Our intention was to make it to Charlotte Amalie in the US Virgin Islands (USVI) by happy hour. No way, we only made it as far as Isla Cayo Luis Pena, a small cay off the west coast of Isla de Culebra. We anchored up off the lee of the island and were getting ready to dive in and catch some dinner, and I went down below to go to the head. Where I could hear a power boat approaching and then a commotion on deck. When I came out of the head, there were two guys pointing guns at me with two more topside covering Skip and Steve. The DEA had boarded our boat like a bunch of pirates. They thought I had gone down below to get a weapon and were ready to do battle. Their boat was unmarked and wore no uniforms. After showing us their credentials, they started searching the Silent Lady for drugs. After they finished searching, they told us to enjoy our cruise, boarded their boat, and headed back toward Puerto Rico. The whole episode was really scary, and after talking it over, we decided to report the incident on our arrival in the USVI. Later after a little rum, we settled down for some spaghetti, snapper, and more rum for dinner.

December 11th, in the early afternoon, we entered Charlotte Amalie harbor and contacted the harbor master for a mooring buoy at the anchorage. Once ashore in the harbor master's office, Skip got on the phone to US Customs and complained about us getting boarded by the DEA. It didn't do much good, but it made us feel better. Once finished with the harbor master, we went over to The Bridge, the bar of choice for the cruising crowd in Charlotte Amalie. We had a fun evening of listening to all the sailing adventures, telling a few of our own, and flirting with the women.

For the next couple of days, we just hung around the harbor, cleaning up and resupplying the boat. Skip's daughter Chrissy, and my son Jon were flying in to join us on their Christmas break from school, so we needed to lay on some extra food. We did take time to sail over to Red Hook Harbor, on the east end of the island, to visit friends of ours, Chuck and Lindsey from Fort Walton Beach. They have been living on their boat in the VI for the last year or so. Chuck, a real craftsman, has a boat repair business there, and Lindsey makes Chuck's life worth living. We anchored up and

spent the rest of the day and evening talking about and updating them on happenings in FWB.

We sailed over to the airport early on the 22nd and anchored up in Lindbergh Bay. Steve stayed on anchor watch while Skip and I took the dinghy ashore and walked over to the terminal to meet our kids. Chrissy and Jon arrived in one piece and were at baggage claim, where we found them.

Once back on board the boat, we sailed back to our mooring at Charlotte Amalie. Just enough time for them to get reacquainted with the boat, stow their gear and try to figure out how we were all going to fit on the Silent Lady. Once we had the boat hooked up to our mooring, we went ashore and showed them around town, followed by some bar food at The Bridge. By the time we got back to the boat, we were all ready for the sack.

Christmas Eve turned into a grand festive event for the five of us. Skip prepared a marvelous Christmas turkey dinner on board with all the trimmings. After dinner, we brought out the charts and started planning what islands we wanted to see before the kids flew out on the 29th.

Sunrise Christmas Day, we slipped our mooring and set sail for St. John, USVI, an Island that is mostly a national park and not much else. After four hours of sailing, we made our way to the anchorage off of Wharfside Village in Cruz Bay. After checking out the area, we ended up at the Parrot Club for a very enjoyable evening of cocktails followed by a tasty meal. Jon and Chrissy updated us on the happenings in Fort Walton and a good time was had by all hands.

The morning of the 26th found us underway off the South shore of St John. Around noon as we were passing Coral Bay on the southeastern shore of St John, we noticed a sailboat wrecked on the rocks at Red Point. We decided to investigate and anchored up close by. She looked to be an old wooden 49 or 50 ft yawl, the name on her stern was Sandavore. We clambered aboard the dinghy and boarded her looking for something to salvage. We found two big beautiful bronze winches that took us a couple of hours to get loose. Looking down below for more booty, we could see that she was pretty well flooded, picked over, and too torn up to mess with. All-in-all, our salvage operation tally was the two bronze winches and a couple of other small bronze fittings, not a bad day's haul for a bunch of amateurs. We found out later that the Sandavore was the sailboat in Alan Alda's movie the Four Seasons. She was a 49 ft yawl, designed and built out of teak from Burma by Uffa Fax in 1952 at his boat yard in the Solent for Lord Runciman, who had supposedly hosted a weekend outing on her for Queen Elizabeth II and Bonnie Prince Charlie.

By early afternoon we were anchored up off the marina in the inner harbor of Road Town, Tortola, British Virgin Islands (BVI). We headed ashore to clear customs and told them about the boat on

the rocks. They knew about it but didn't seem very interested. After all, the wreck was in the USVI, not the BVI, so much for doing our civic duty. We wandered around town for a while, then settled in at Charlie's Bar/Restaurant for food and drinks. After hashing over our experiences of the day, we headed back to the Silent Lady for the night and looked over our charts for our next destination: The Baths at Virgin Gorda, BVI.

After a hearty breakfast of a Sailors Delight omelet, ala, Skippy, we were underway for the three-hour sail to Virgin Gorda. The Baths, which are located just north of Devil's Bay on the southwest coast, are famous for their beautiful white sandy beaches and large granite boulders that form caves and pools, a really cool place. We anchored up close to the beach in the crowd of boats and went ashore to check it out. It was a beautiful day, and the beach was crowded, especially around the Poor Man's Bar, the only watering hole on the beach.

After a day of sun and fun at the beach, we motored up the coast to Spanish Town and picked up a mooring in the Virgin Gorda Yacht Harbour. It was shore leave for all hands, so we piled into the dinghy and headed for shore. After doing a tour of the town, we eventually ended up at the yacht club for a nice leisurely dinner before heading back to the Silent Lady for the night.

A storm had us bouncing around on our mooring all night. By morning, the storm had blown on through, and the weather had calmed down. After having a big breakfast ashore at the yacht club and a short walk around town, we headed back to the Silent Lady, ready to go. Once back on board, we dropped our mooring and set sail, taking advantage of a 15kt NE breeze that put us on a broad reach making for a nice easy sail back to Charlotte Amalie. As we sailed by Red Point, we looked for the wreck of Sandavore there was nothing left but bits and pieces of wreckage floating around the rocks, last night's storm did a job on her.

By early evening we were anchored up in Lindberg Bay by the airport, anticipating a nice quiet evening aboard while Jon and Chrissy packed up their gear. It was then that Steve told us that he was jumping ship to chase after the girl that dumped him in FWB. The farewell party lasted well into the night.

After bon voyaging everyone at the airport, Skip and I sailed the Silent Lady back to Charlotte Amalie, picked up a mooring, and retired to The Bridge for a couple of beers. Later that night, one of our sailing buddies from FWB, Rick Sauter, called telling us that he was in the area. Skip invited him to stay on board; we had an empty bunk.

On the 30th of December, while Skip and I were hanging out at The Bridge, we got wind of a New Year's Eve party at Foxy's in the BVI and decided we needed to be there. Later that evening, Rick showed up at The Bridge with his sea bag, and we had a couple of beers to catch up on happenings in FWB. During dinner, we told Rick that we were setting sail in the morning for Foxy's Tamarind Bar on Jost Van Dyke, BVI. Famous for their notoriously outrageous New Year's Eve party, we had to be there.

We slipped our mooring relatively early for the six-hour sail to Great Harbor, Jost Van Dyke. On the way, Skippy cooked up his famous Sailors Delight for breakfast. It was a beautiful morning to be sailing in the Caribbean. Our destination, Jost Van Dyke, a small island (1 mi by 3mi) 4miles ENE from Tortola. On arrival, we found that Great Harbor is not all that big, about 1500' by 2000' and chock full of boats anchored up all over the place. We maneuvered around and finally found a spot to drop our hook. Within ten minutes, vendors were coming alongside, trying to sell us stuff. One girl, in particular, was selling jewelry, and from her insinuations, that's not all she was selling.

There was too much going on at the beach to play around with her. After we locked up the boat, we headed ashore in the dingy to partake in the ongoing activities.

The crowd was mostly

milling around talking until nightfall when the band showed up at Foxy's, and the fun began. There was dancing with the ladies, lots of conversation and fooling around. The New Year's Eve party lasted into the wee hours of the morning; we were definitely enjoying ourselves. When the party started winding down, I couldn't find Skip or Rick, so I stayed on the beach talking to the girl of my dreams. When the sun woke me in the morning, the girl of my dreams was gone.

The dawn broke on a new year, and after a refreshing swim, I made my 1985 new year's resolution not to drink, or was it to not drink as much. As soon as Foxy's opened for breakfast, I was there starving. Eventually, Skip and Rick showed up, and we recounted our adventures of the evening. Rick and I decided to walk off our hangovers by climbing the hill in the center of the island, a dumb idea!

By the time we got to the top of the hill, I had a pounding headache. We looked around for a little while, enjoying the view of the harbor and the boats. A lot of them were already weighing anchor and heading out of Great Harbour. We stumbled down the hill back to the beach, and that's when Rick noticed that he had lost his gold Rolex somewhere on the way down. Great, back up the hill, and we got lucky about halfway up, we found it.

After a day of licking our wounds on Jost Van Dyke, we were on our way back to Charlotte Amalie. On the way, Skip brought up the idea of taking a sail down to St. Croix, USVI. Looking at the

charts, it would be a 7- or 8-hour sail south out of Charlotte Amalie, and decided to go check it out.

On the morning of January 4th, we made an early departure for Frederiksted, St Croix USVI. The sail was uneventful, with favorable NE trade winds putting us on a nice broad reach, making a good 6kts, on a beautiful sun shining day. By midafternoon we were anchored by the Frederiksted Municipal Pier. There was a lot of activity going on getting ready for the Three King's Day parade that was happening the next day, Saturday the 5th. The parade is the culmination of the Crucian Christmas Festival that's already been going on for a month.

The next morning the festival started at 10 a.m. on Kings St, and we were there in place. They

started out by passing out little rum punch samples on the street. I guess to warm up the crowd. So much for my new year's resolution! A short time later, the steel drum bands arrived on flatbed trucks bouncing up and down to the beat of the music, and people were dancing in the streets. We were out there with them. By sundown, the parade ended, but the bands kept playing, and like the Pied Piper, Rick and I were in the crowd dancing to the music, following the band as they headed up the hill out of town.

The crowd eventually started to thin out, and all of a sudden, the music stopped, and everyone disappeared. It became spooky; there wasn't a sole in sight as we started walking down back down the hill. We eventually came across a bar with people in it on the outskirts of town and stopped for a beer. By 10 p.m. we were back in town and hailed Skip on the Silent Lady to come and rescue us.

We stayed another day in Frederiksted to tour around town and look over Fort Frederik, then sailed back to Charlotte Amalie on the 7th of January. Rick flew back to the states a day or so later.

That left Skip and me on the Silent Lady, running out of money and a long way from Fort Walton Beach and home. It's been quite an adventure so far, and it looks like The Virgin Islands were as far as we were going to get in the Caribbean, and we started planning our sail back to FWB. The first leg would be to Puerto Plata, a two or three-day sail from Charlotte Amalie.

We departed on January 10th and got as far as Culebra, where we anchored up for the night at about the same place we anchored on the way to Charlotte Amalie. There was enough daylight left for us to snorkel up dinner, a small snapper, shovel-nosed lobster, and a couple of conchs. After a nice enjoyable dinner, we talked over different route options for our sail back to Florida and the good old United States. We turned in early, anticipating an early departure in the morning.

We were underway early for Puerto Plata in the Dominican Republic, our port of call to refuel and resupply. Picking up the SE trade winds that put us on a comfortable beam reach on a beautiful Caribbean day, life is good. Early afternoon found us coasting by El Morro, The old Spanish Fort at the entrance of San Juan Harbor, Puerto Rico. The rest of the sail down the coast was uneventful. By four in the morning of the 12th, we started our crossing of the dreaded Mona Passage. Twelve hours later, after an uneventful crossing, we had the Dominican Republic in sight, and by four that evening, we were cruising on by Cape Carbon and Cape Samana, the twin capes.

By late afternoon of the 13th, after an uneventful sail down the coast of the Dominican Republic, we contacted the port authority at Puerto Plata, requesting customs/immigration and permission to enter. On entering the harbor, we noticed something new, a large sailboat with three masts, either bark or brigantine, tied up on the very south end of the harbor. We figured we needed to go check it out in the morning. By happy hour we were Mediterranean Moored to the pier and talking to the customs officials. Shortly thereafter, we were at Poopies having a beer celebrating the successful completion of the first leg of our journey.

In the morning, after a leisurely breakfast on the Silent Lady, we took the dinghy over to check out the boat that we had decided was rigged as a bark, square sails on the foremast, and mainmast and fore and aft sails on the mizzen. As we approached, we noticed the standing rigging was in pretty bad shape. The boat, in general, looked in need of a lot of work. We estimated the length at over 150' long with a beam of around 35'. We were hailed from the boat as we approached, and when we started asking questions about the boat, he invited us aboard. Once on board, we found out that he was her caretaker/manager and that it had been towed in shortly after we left Puerto Plata in December. The owners were trying to set it up as a casino boat, and in the meantime, it was being used as a party boat on Fridays and weekends. We learned from the caretaker that the boat was constructed of reinforced concrete in Canada as an ice breaker during the WWII. Sometime after the war, it was decommissioned and used as a breakwater somewhere on the Canadian coastline. It was later pumped out, rigged as a bark, and eventually ended up in Puerto Plata. That's all he could tell us. We talked him into letting us climb up on the rigging. Skip was interested in checking out the rigging since he was having a 63' schooner built back in Florida. As we were leaving, we promised to come back later to check out the happy hour scene and went back to resupplying the Silent Lady with fuel, water, and food. Weather permitting, we will be ready to depart Puerto Plata as soon as possible in the morning.

Happy hour that evening at the party boat was interesting, with plenty of a local brand of beer, and they were cooking up hot dogs and hamburgers. They drew a crowd of around twenty people, and we just had a good ol' time talking it up and dancing with the locals. We hung around until the crowd started to thin out, then headed back to the Silent Lady.

We departed early in the morning of the 16th for our second leg back to Florida, a two or three-day sail to our next port of call, Matthew Town on Great Inagua Islands, Bahamas. After two days at sea, just before sunset, we sighted the 132' high East Hill on Great Inagua on the horizon. The major industry of Great Inagua is salt, and Morton Salt has large salt evaporation pens all over the island. The salt pens produce and export a million tons of salt a year. There's a 102' pile of salt on the south side of the island that you can see approaching from the south a long way off.

Early on the morning of the 19th, we anchored up off the municipal pier at Matthews Town. By late morning we were in the customs and Immigration office showing them our cruising permit for the Bahamas, then went on a walkabout town.

During our walk, we found a café to have lunch and talked about the third leg of our sail back to Florida. The choices were sailing the Old Bahama Channel to Key West or sailing up the Bahamas to Palm Beach. Either way, it would take four and a half to five days with no stops along the route. We decided to sail the route up the Bahamas since it offered a lot of places on the way to refuel or hide if the weather turned bad.

We departed early in the morning, occasionally running the engine as we sailed for a couple of hours to charge the batteries. The day's sail was uneventful until just before sunset. When we tried to start the engine to charge the batteries again, it would not crank. Battery voltage and starter cable connections were all ok. We found that the only way we could start the engine was to take a screwdriver and cross the cable connections to bypass the starter solenoid.

Over cocktails, we talked over our options. We could live with it by crawling down to the engine with a screwdriver every time we needed to start the engine or stop somewhere. We decided to find a calm and comfortable place to stop and take our time to troubleshoot the problem. After all, we were not in that big of a hurry.

We decided on George Town in the Great Exuma Islands as our port of call, with its well-protected anchorage in Elizabeth Harbour. Our estimated time en route was a two or two-and-a-half-day sail from our present position.

Around midnight we passed to the west of Castle Rock, the island on the Southwest corner of the Crooked Islands. By noon we had the South end of Long Island in sight, and for the rest of the day, we sailed up its East Coast. During the night, around 03:00 on the 22nd, we rounded Cape Santa Maria on the north end of Long Island and set our course for Elizabeth Harbour East entrance to the Great Exumas and George Town, the southernmost cruising headquarters for yachtsmen visiting the Bahamas.

Six hours later, we were anchored up in Elizabeth Harbour a hundred feet in front of the Peace and Plenty Hotel, a large pink building next door to the government administration building. While Skip dinked ashore to the dinghy dock to check in at the government house with our cruising permit, I was down in the engine compartment troubleshooting our problem with the starter. It was pretty obvious that the problem was the connection between the ignition switch and the starter solenoid. It should be an easy fix, all we had to do was a little rewiring, but of course, I couldn't find any wire aboard. By the time Skip returned to the boat and we were getting squared away to go back ashore for wire, the shops were closed for the day. So, we adjourned to the bar at the Piece and Plenty for cocktails. After having a delicious meal of Bahamian cuisine, the band started to play, it was dance night, and we just had to stay to dance with the ladies.

Next morning, after an interesting evening ashore, I attempted to find the break in the wire to the starter solenoid. While Skip went ashore to do laundry and with a little bit of luck, I found the break around five inches up from the solenoid and spliced it up. We are back in business! After cleaning up, we upped anchor and motored around the corner of Regatta Point to top up on fuel, water, and some ice at the fuel dock in Kidd Cove (supposedly one of Captain Kidd's favorite anchorages). The evening's find was the Two Turtle Inn with a friendly happy hour crowd of fellow cruisers with a lot of conversation. Later on, over dinner, Skip and I agreed that stopping at George Town was definitely an enjoyable choice for repairs.

Departed George Town early next morning, the 24th of January, and sailed out Elizabeth Harbour toward our next destination Staniel Cay, by way of Galliot Cut. We cleared Galliot Cut by two in the afternoon, then motor sailed up the inside passage, spotting Harvey Cay Light in the late afternoon. After rounding the light, we picked up the channel on into Staniel Cay. By sunset, we were tied up at the Happy People Marina Dock and headed for happy hour at the bar. Not much was going on. After a couple of beers, we walked over to the Yacht Club to have one of our favorite meals, grouper peas and rice. By sunrise the next morning, we were underway, bound for Nassau.

We got as far as Allen's Cay, where we anchored up and went looking for dinner and caught a big black spider crab that would make a marvelous dinner with rice and rum; life is good. Allen's Cay is overrun with iguanas, we went ashore to check it out. Once ashore, they started to arrive, first one or two, then twenty or more. We decided that they could keep their island and went back to the boat to cook up our crab for dinner.

Next morning the 26th, after a leisurely breakfast of fried plantains and eggs, we headed for Nassau, about a five-hour sail on the banks. It was pretty much uneventful except for crossing the middle ground, where you have to keep a sharp lookout for coral heads.

By early afternoon we were calling Nassau Harbour Control for permission to enter the harbor and anchored where we anchored the last time we were there in November, just west of the Potters Cay Bridge. Later on, we took the dinghy over to Hurricane Hole Marina dinghy dock to look at all the big yachts and wander around the island.

In the morning, we motored over to Nassau Yacht Haven to refuel and went grocery shopping in the market under the bridge, buying plantains, eggs, fish, beer, and more rum for the two-day sail to West Palm Beach.

Finally, we got underway and rounded Paradise Island Light at around four in the afternoon and headed up Northwest Providence Channel toward the Great Stirrup Light. Twelve hours later, around four in the morning of the 28th, after keeping out of the way of big ships headed for Nassau, we passed the lighthouse and set our course for Fort Lauderdale by way of Great Isaac Light. Just before sunset, we had the Great Isaac Light in sight. Now the fun begins, dodging all the ship traffic sailing up and down the Gulf Stream during the night.

The crossing was interesting, with quite a bit of traffic that kept us on our toes, especially when we got closer to the Florida coast. After a sleepless night, at daybreak on the 29th of January, we could see the Florida coastline on the horizon.

By early morning the Silent Lady was tied up at Pier 66, Fort Lauderdale, and while I was taking on fuel and water, Skip was in with customs checking us back into the good old USA. It didn't take long to clear in, and we were soon underway motoring up the intercostal waterway, heading for the Okeechobee waterway and back to the gulf coast. After a few hours of motoring, we anchored up for the night in a little cove off the south side of the waterway.

Early next morning, we were underway, and after seven hours of motoring up the intercoastal, we anchored up just south of Delray Beach to spend the night. Both of us were pretty beat, and after a little food and a little rum, we were down for the night.

Early in the morning of the 31st, after a good night's sleep, we went ashore grocery shopping before getting underway to continue motoring up the intercoastal waterway. Around four in the afternoon, we were in Stuart, Florida, waiting for the bridge to open when we spotted someone on the bridge waving at us. Using the binoculars to check it out, low and behold, it was Steve.

Once under the bridge, we tied up at the Sailor's Return. Steve was waiting and helped us tie up, eager to hear of our adventures. Once settled in at the bar I called my son Michael in Fort Pierce, just up the road to come join the party. We had a grand old time telling stories, Michael with his stories of the LA 84' Olympics, Steve looking for his girlfriend in Colorado, and our adventures in the Caribbean.

The Olympics were defiantly an experience for my son Michael. Scott Steel won the silver medal for the USA, in Windsurfing at the 84' L.A. Olympics. Michael, who was there with him, was now fired up to go after a medal of his own at the next games to be held in Korea in 1988.

After jumping ship at Charlotte Amalie in December, Steve headed back to Breckenridge, Colorado, to chase down his girlfriend. He found her all right, but she had already moved on, no problem, it was ski season, and there was a lot going on. A short time later, Steve's uncle offered him a job managing his apartment complex in West Palm Beach. That's how Steve happened to be in Florida on the bridge, whereby chance, he spotted the Silent Lady waiting for it to open.

On February 1st, we were back underway, headed for the dreaded Port Mayaca railroad bridge, and four hours later, we were at the bridge. It looked like the water level was lower than the last time we went under it, so we just eased on through with no problem. An hour later we were anchored up for the night by the Port Mayaca Locks. Early next morning, we were through the lock and heading out across Lake Okeechobee, and by nightfall, we were through the Moore Haven Locks and tied up at Moore Haven. After topping off our fuel and water, we did a walk around town, eventually ending up at the Silent Lady for some spaghetti.

In the morning, we started the long cruise on the waterway and headed for Fort Meyers. By noon we were passing by La Belle, where the waterway's name changes to the Caloosahatchee River. By nightfall, we were near Olga, where we anchored up in the river for the night.

The early morning of February 4th, the weather deteriorated rapidly, with a cold front blowing on through that delayed our departure a little. We finally got underway by around 10:00 after the squall line passed. The rest of the day, we motored into a 15-knot headwind going by Fort Myers and up Pine Island Sound to Cabbage Key, where we tied up for the night and had something to eat at their restaurant.

By morning the winds had shifted further to the North at around 15 kts without a cloud in the sky. We passed through Boca Grande Pass at around 08:00, and by sundown, we made our way through Big Sarasota Pass and tied up to the Marina Jack in Sarasota. It had been a long eight-hour motor into a direct headwind up the West coast of Florida. There was not much going on at the Marina Jack Bar, so after a couple of beers and some food, we turned in for the night.

During a leisurely breakfast at the Marina Jack on the morning of the 7th, we contemplated our next course of action. We considered taking a direct course to Fort Walton, about a three-day sail, or Apalachicola, a two-day sail. Unfortunately the weather was against us. The wind was blowing out of the North at close to 20kts, putting our course out of a point of sail. We cast off to continue our long motor up the intercoastal to Tampa Bay and into the Gulf of Mexico at around 10:30. Our plan was to motor up the coast until we picked up a favorable wind to sail on home with.

Twenty-four hours or so later, we were working our way past Alligator Reef into Cedar Key to making a quick refueling stop. We tied up to the city dock a little after noon, only to find out there was no fuel available at the dock. After buggy lugging fuel in a five-gallon can from a nearby gas station that took a while, we decided to call it a day and spent the night.

Cedar Key is a small old Florida hideout with real friendly people, the area at one time was a source for cedar in Faber pencils. After a walkabout town, we settled in at a Bar Restaurant close to the dock for cocktails and dinner.

By morning the wind had shifted toward the Northeast, allowing us to hoist the sails and set a course for home. The wind stayed steady between ten and twenty knots out of the Northeast, making for an easy two-day sail back to Fort Walton Beach. We cleared Destin pass around noon on the 11th of February, and by early afternoon, we were tied up to the Surfview dock, mission complete!

There was a welcoming committee waiting for us when we tied up that turned into quite a party. While I was out sailing around, my mom had everything under control at the apartments. Doc kept the grass mowed, and there were no vacancies. She does a better job of running a business than I ever will.

After resting up for a couple of days, I went back to work at the Surfview and on the Pele. The Buda diesel was putting out lots of smoke, so we decided to pull the head off of it and take it to a machine shop for a valve job. By April 6th, we had the head back, torqued down onto the block, and motoring around the bay on a shakedown cruise. The Buda still smoked but not as much, it had seen better days, and we needed to start thinking about replacing it.

Skip had a nice big ship's wheel that I wanted to replace the smaller one that we swapped for earlier. We did another swap, his wheel for the bronze winch that was my part of the booty from the Sandavore. Skip needed it to add to the one he had for his new boat being built at Warships Shipyard in Panama City.

After a lot of effort and perseverance, my son, Jon, achieved his goal of becoming a BSA Eagle Scout in a ceremony at his troop on the 10th of May 1985. Then shortly thereafter, on the 5th of June, he graduated high school, and we had a graduation party for him at the Surfview. He didn't have time to rest on his laurels. His grandparents and I applied for and received a Pell Grant for him and enrolled Jon in the summer session at Florida State University in Tallahassee, Florida. When the semester started, I drove him to FSU in my truck with his bicycle in the back and dropped him off at the dorm; Jon-boy was on his way.

Over the next couple of days, I emptied out the boys' room at the Surfview and turned it into my office with a big old wooden desk that I bought for $50 at Eglin AFB surplus sales.

My boys were now on the great adventure to seek their own destiny,

and I now have an empty nest. Jon was a little homesick and hitched a ride back to Fort Walton a couple of times, but that was the last we saw of him for a while. He was definitely getting into the swing of things at college. On one of his visits home, he mentioned that he was thinking about signing up for Air Force ROTC. I advised him not to do it unless they could get him a pilot slot, and a semester later, they found him one.

On May 25th, the Pele left the dock to be the committee boat for another weekend-long Hog's Breath Regatta. They had a big turnout for the races, with people coming from all over the country to compete. These regattas are always a lot of fun.

One notable charter on the Pele that summer was the wedding of Eric Partin and Darlene Matuska on the 7th of July. With the bride's party on board the Pele on a rainy day, we sailed out into the bay and anchored up by the Coast Guard Station near Destin Pass. A short time later, the wedding guests' boat arrived and rafted up with us in the hard rain; pretty soon, the groom arrived on his sailboat. Miraculously the rain stopped, and once the wedding ceremony was completed, the bride and groom sailed away on his boat. Ten minutes later, it started to rain, no one minded, the champagne was flowing freely, and everyone was having a jolly good time.

On October 5, 1985, we heard that the La Vie Dansante, an Irwin 63' ketch, was being commissioned at Jim Tucker's boat yard and that the new owner was looking for a crew to deliver it to St Croix in the Virgin Islands. Skip Price and I went over to look it over and to talk to Tucker about the job. We went aboard to check out what kind of gear it had onboard. It had lots of goodies, a generator, air conditioning, TV, DVD, washer and dryer, three staterooms, two heads with showers, plus one small bathtub.

For navigation equipment, it had radar, autopilot with a second station down below by the radar, a satellite navigation system, and a VHF radio. The only thing it didn't have was a HF radio. We learned from our last trip that you need one for keeping track of the weather. She had all the safety equipment, plus a nice 8' dinghy on davits hanging off the stern.

Skip's job as captain on a supply boat in the oil patch in the gulf had ended, and he was available to take on the job. I was ready for a little adventure since my kids were gone and the charter season was about over. I mentioned to my parents about maybe I would be gone delivering a boat and if they wouldn't mind taking care of the place for a couple of weeks. They agreed that running a business is what Mom loves to do and Dad enjoys taking care of the maintenance around the Surfview, so I was good to go.

At the Hog's Breath Saloon, over a couple of beers with Tom Stewart, I mentioned that Skip and I were thinking about doing a delivery to the islands. Tom, also out of a job, was willing, able, and wanted to come along. It sounded good to me; you can always use another hand. After talking it over with Skip, we contacted Tucker that we had a crew that was available to do the delivery. Skip would be the Captain, Tom, and I deckhands. Jim contacted the owners who were in town and came over to meet with us. After some negotiating, the owner eventually agreed to put in a HF receiver and hired us to do the delivery.

When the commissioning of the La Vie Dansante was complete, we loaded our sea bags aboard on the 21st, provisioned the boat, and set sail. Our original course would take us down the coast and around Key West, then east through the Old Bahama Channel to St Croix, with maybe a stop somewhere along the way to re-provision.

While sailing down the west coast of Florida, we found a few things that didn't work, like the jibs roller furling, leaking hatches, and an inoperable generator. The Irwin boat yard where the boat was built is located in Clearwater along our route down the west coast of Florida. We decided to stop there and get these problems fixed. Three days later, on the 24th, we tied up at the Irwin dock, and once we explained the problems we were having with the boat, they assured us that they would fix us up.

After a couple of days of sitting tied up to the Irwin dock, it became obvious that they were dragging their feet with the repairs. They assured us again that we were on their list and would get to us as soon as possible.

On October 26th, low pressure in the Gulf of Mexico developed into Tropical Storm Juan. By the 28th, Juan became a hurricane, and we were feeling the effects in Clearwater with heavy squall lines blowing through as it passed well offshore. No work was being done at the boatyard, so while we waited, we hung out in the local bars, spending money and flirting with the local girls. On October 29th, Juan went ashore near Morgan City, Louisiana, and our weather conditions improved.

While waiting for repairs, we were living on the La Vie Dansante at the Irwin dock. Tom called an old girlfriend who came over to visit for a couple of days, and they took over the captain's room to the chagrin of Skip. The day after she left, the yard finally fixed the generator and the leaking hatches. We eagerly departed the Irwin yard on November 1st after having had too much shore leave, having too much fun, and about to run out of money. It was time to leave!

After having an enjoyable overnight sail to Key West, where we anchored up late in the afternoon, dinked ashore and walked over to Rick's Bar. After a couple of beers, we decided to sail up the east coast of Florida to get the roller furling repaired by the manufacturer in Ft Lauderdale.

We departed early in the morning for the sail up the Gulf Stream. On the way to Fort Lauderdale, we gave them a call, and when we arrived, a representative met us at the dock. While waiting around for the fix, we ran into our old sailing buddy, Rick Sauter, and his friend Fred. Over a beer or two, it was decided that since our new planned route would take us through the Bahamas, they could join us at least to the islands; after all, extra hands are always welcome.

Before heading for the Bahamas, we called the owner of the boat and told him what we were up to. We figured he should be appreciative of all the repairs we had done on the La Vie Dansante for him and not rush us. He wanted us to sail nonstop to St Croix; fat chance, we would get his boat to him as soon as possible, but we were also on an adventure and not in that big of a hurry.

With the roller furling repaired on November 9th, we cleared out of Fort Lauderdale late in the afternoon with a jolly crew to make the overnight crossing of the Gulf Stream. Crossing the Gulf Stream with radar was a lot easier, and by morning we had the Great Isaac Lighthouse, the entrance to the Bahamas Northwest Providence Channel, in sight. Twelve hours later, we were by Great Stirrup Light, heading down the channel to Nassau on New Providence Island, Bahama.

As we approached Nassau on the morning of Nov 11th, we called harbor control for permission to enter Nassau Harbour and anchored in about the same spot we anchored the Silent Lady the last time we were there. Once we were squared away, we launched the dingy for the trip ashore to clear customs/immigration and get our cruising permit for the Bahamas.

During the rest of the day, we were re-provisioning the La Vie Dansante and took a side trip to Paradise Island to look around. The resort had a big casino and beautiful shops and surroundings; it was way too fancy for us, so we went back to cruising around the harbor in our dinghy, looking at boats. We ended up in Nassau town that evening at a nice restaurant for cocktails and dinner.

We finally got underway in the morning and sailed out of Nassau Harbour through the narrows and Hanover Sound to Northeast Providence Channel and finally into the deep waters of Exuma Sound. Once in deep water, we encountered gusty winds of up to thirty knots with 3-to-6-foot seas. We were sailing on a reach, making 6 to 7 kts under reefed down sails. We were feeling the effects of a tropical wave that had formed east of Puerto Rico. At around 16:00, Fred was feeling woozy and suggested that we needed to duck in somewhere and wait to see what the weather was going to do.

At the time, we happened to be just off the coast of Staniel Cay in the central Exumas. Fred told us that he would buy dinner if we stopped; he was adamant about getting in where it was nice and calm and was looking a little green around the gills. We called the Spaniel Cay Yacht Club and made a 19:00 dinner reservation for five of grouper, peas, and rice.

To get there, we had to go through Big Rock Cut, a narrow pass through the rocks, and it was going to be tricky with the wind and seas pushing us from behind. As we headed in toward the shoreline that looked like a solid line of rocks, we were soon in breaking seas and committed before finally making out the opening in the rocks and surfing through. Once through the pass, you had to make a hard turn to port, or you would end up on the rocks. We survived, tied up at the Happy People Marina, and went to the bar for drinks to celebrate. Shortly after our success, we noticed that an 85-foot motor yacht had just made it in through Big Rock Cut and was tying up at the yacht club.

An hour or two later, we walked on over to the Staniel Cay Yacht Club for our dinner reservation. To our surprise, we found that the crew off the motor yacht was eating our meal. They were very apologetic, and we had a good laugh while we waited a little longer for our food. After our meal, the owner of the yacht invited us and a woman who was dining alone over to his yacht for cocktails.

On the yacht, we heard their horror story about their passage through Big Rock Cut. They damn near put it on the rocks coming through the cut, and once through, when they made the hard turn to port, the boat healed over, tearing loose some of the furniture and unstowed gear. Over drinks, the woman that was off a 21-foot sailboat told us her story. She was a recent graduate from nursing school and was celebrating the event by sailing to the islands with her boyfriend. He lasted as far as Nassau, and from there, she decided to keep going, a whole new definition of a traveling nurse. The evening turned out to be a great little party with a lot of interesting stories and laughs. Tom ended up spending the night with the nurse; we found him in the morning standing on the bow of her boat, looking for a way ashore.

Staniel Cay has, besides the two marinas, a short runway, several small shops, some tourist cabins, a clinic, a church, and friendly people.

While cooling our heels and waiting for what is now Hurricane Fabien to blow by, we were getting calls from an anxious owner who wanted his boat. Unfortunately for him, there was another tropical depression on the way that would no doubt slow us down. Rick and Fred had enough; they jumped ship and flew out on the 13th to Nassau, where they caught a twin-engine seaplane to Fort Lauderdale. It was a scary flight. On takeoff, the plane lost an engine and had to make an emergency landing in Nassau Harbour.

While waiting for better weather conditions, we monitored with the La Vie Dansante's HF radio the movements of Fabien and the tropical depression that had formed behind Fabien. From conversations with the locals, we learned that there was a way we could sail down the Exumas on the banks in relatively calm waters. We talked it over and decided to use that information to press on toward St. Croix since Fabien was blowing on by, even though we wouldn't be in protected waters for long.

Early on November 14th, we started sailing on the banks down the Exumas while keeping a close eye on the direction of the new tropical depression. That evening we sailed off the Bahama Banks between Hawksbill Rocks and Jew Fish Cay, leaving the Exumas behind, and sailed into rough seas.

The next morning November 15th, the weather report warned that the tropical depression had intensified while northeast of Puerto Rico into Tropical Storm Kate. Twenty-four hours later, Kate would intensify into a hurricane that was headed straight for us. By then, we were already looking for a place to hide.

The Crooked Islands were close, so we headed for them. The islands look like a big horseshoe, about 15 miles across with a reef across the open end with around 12 feet of water on the inside. Around noon on November 16th, we worked our way over the reef and into the horseshoe. We called on the VHF for directions to a secure anchorage, the answer was that a storm was coming, and they were taking down their antenna.

To ride out hurricane Kate, we anchored up about 1/2 mile from the beach on the east side of the horseshoe in ten feet of water and put out all three anchors, two on line and one on chain. Then stripped off the sails and stowed all loose gear, and by the time we finished, the weather was deteriorating fast; Kate was a fast mover.

Around 17:00 that afternoon, we heard a call on the VHF from a 50-foot ketch called the "Passion" out of Great Inagua, getting beat up down by Castle Rock on the SE corner of the Crooked Islands, wanting to know what was going on with the weather. We called and told them Kate was coming and to try to make it inside to where we were hanging out. By then, the wind was up to 50kts and gusting higher. Two hours later, it was blowing over 70kts. They called and gave us their next of kin, saying they were not going to make it. We tried to relay a May Day to the Coast Guard for them. Unfortunately, we couldn't use our HF radio since it was a receiver only. We tried calling Passion on The VHF again, but with no answer, and we would have no further contact with "Passion".

During the night, with the wind gusting over 100kts, we would take turns checking the bungees on the anchor lines and chain. To do that, you had to put on a snorkel and mask because of the amount of spray that was flying around and crawl up the deck to the bow. The boat was sailing around on the anchors and putting a lot of strain on the bow cleats. We made a plan that if we broke loose from our anchors, we would start up the engine and try to beach her before we were blown over the reef into deep water. While sitting around in our life jackets and shorts, Tom changed into his jeans and sneakers, saying they might protect him if he had to crawl over the reef. Good idea, Skip and I followed suit and quickly put on ours.

At dawn, there were a few squall lines, with winds gusting to around 40kt, and by early afternoon the weather was rapidly moderating; Kate was still in a hurry! We tried again to contact Passion, then the Coast Guard with no luck, but we did make contact with another boat anchored up west of us by Albert Town, one of the few towns on the islands. We told them of our communication with Passion. They had an old AM radio on board with a longer range than VHF and would try to relay our information to the Coast Guard.

By late afternoon, we had the sails bent back on and all the anchors hauled in, except for the one on chain. We had the La Vie Dansante cleaned up and ready for sea by nightfall. We relaxed with a little happy hour and some food and thanked our lucky stars that we survived and would get some sleep for a change.

We were underway early the next morning, November 18th. While sailing out of the Crooked Islands, we heard on the VHF the Coast Guard or the US Navy talking to a helicopter that was in the process of rescue. We tried to call and tell them about the Passion, no answer. A short time later, we overheard the helicopter's VHF transmission that they had picked up two people off the sailboat Passion. We knew that one of the crew was a native of Great Inagua Island from the next of kin information they gave us earlier. The Island wasn't far out of our way, so we decided to sail there and tell them what we knew about the fate of the Passion.

In the early afternoon of November 19th, the high pyramid of salt by Norton Salt's evaporation pens on the south end of the Inagua came into view as you approached the island. After anchoring off of the commissioner's office in Mathews Town and dinked ashore to relayed to the officials there what we knew of the Passion. After telling the story, it didn't take long for the family of the survivor to show up, and we told them what we knew of the Passion and the rescue operation. They thanked us for the information and gave us a cake. We did a little walkabout town for an hour or so, then hauled up the anchor for the three-day sail to Puerto Plata in the Dominican Republic.

Late in the morning of November 22nd, we spotted on the horizon the top of Mount Isabela de Torres, which rises to 2600'right behind Puerta Plata. Closer in, we called the port captain to request customs and permission to enter the harbor. They directed us to tie up to the pier for customs, where they came aboard, took our weapons, inspected the boat then told us where to anchor. We put out two anchors in opposite directions to try and keep us in one spot. After launching the dinghy, we headed back over to the pier for shore leave.

The big Bark that we climbed all over on our last trip was gone. It's now aground and abandoned on the Silver Banks, a huge reef north of the DR; it broke loose while it was undertow to a new location.

Our first stop on our walkabout was Poopies Bar, the friendly bar that we found a year earlier on our last trip to the DR. The proprietors, the retired Chicago cop, and his wife remembered us; we had a good chat with them and their girls. From there, we walked over to the old hotel by the pier for a meal, then back to the boat. Skip's friend from last year who managed the hotel had left the area.

The next morning, after going ashore to clear customs and getting our weapons back, we tried to pull our anchors out of the mud. In the process, the shackle that connected the chain to the anchor gave way leaving the anchor in the mud. We ended up hiring local boys to dive for it, I don't know how they found it in the mud, but they did. We finally got underway at around 09:00 on November 24th for the three-day sail to San Juan, Puerto Rico. It was still blowing out of the WNW, but the wind and rain squalls were on our stern, so we were able to sail most of the way with the jib and a reefed main.

On November 27, under moderate conditions and full sail, we sailed under the guns of Castillo San Felipe del Morro, the old Spanish fort at the entrance to Bahia de San Juan. We then headed up the east end of the harbor to pick up a mooring at the yacht club. Being eager for some shore leave and as soon as we secured the boat, we dinked over to the harbor master's office and customs. Once that was done, we made our way to the yacht club. At the club, we found it inhabited by a bunch of our friends from Ft Walton Beach. It just so happened that there was a Thanksgiving Hobie Regatta going on; what a coincidence! We were there just in time for their Thanksgiving banquet, an outrageous get-together that lasted late into the evening. In the morning, hungover and full of good food from the banquet, we decided to hang out for a couple of days and cheer on our friends that were racing in the regatta.

On the morning of December 1st, I awoke at 05:00, a little woozy from the farewell party and thinking of the ten-hour sail to Charlotte Amalie. If we could leave before 06:00, we could get there in daylight, around 16:00, in time for happy hour at the Bridge. Tom was also awake, so we started up the engine, cast off from our mooring, and cleared by El Morro, the old fort, before dawn. Sea conditions were 2-4 foot seas with winds near 25kts from the NW. We hauled up the sails, reefed them down, and were merrily bouncing along off the north coast of Puerto Rico on a reach toward Charlotte Amalie.

Skip arrived on deck around 08:00 and volunteered to cook breakfast. Shortly thereafter, we found out we had a stowaway. Jerry Dormany, the owner of the Hog's Breath Saloon in Ft Walton Beach and one of the sponsors of the regatta, had come aboard to check out the boat sometime during the evening and passed out. He eventually appeared on deck, feeling a little woozy to find that San Juan had been left in our wake. At the time, we were sailing off the north shore of Puerto Rico in and out of rain squalls in bouncy conditions. A short time later, we were able to duck into the lee of the islands west of Culebra, where there were calmer conditions that lasted for the rest of the run to Charlotte Amalie.

We arrived around 16:30 and picked up a yacht club mooring, and prepared to go ashore. Tom was in charge of launching the dinghy, but he seemed to be having a hard and appeared to be totally incapable of doing it. Jerry had brought some pot on board with him, and the two of them smoked some of it and were both higher than a kite. Skip, and I gave them some crap about it, then found out the brownies we had just eaten before boarding the dingy were laced with pot, great!

We were all in place at the Bridge a little after 17:00. I love it when a plan comes together. The bar was mobbed with people, but we eventually found some chairs, and I was soon in a deep conversation with a woman sitting opposite me. About that time, the pot kicked in, and all concentration went out the window. I was pretty much a blithering idiot. Tom was in worse shape; he was standing outside the toilet and totally paranoid about going in to take a leak. Our operation at the Bridge was a total failure. I don't know why people use it; booze is bad enough, but that shit turns you into an idiot.

On December 3rd, we slipped our mooring and set sail for St Croix. Jerry stayed with us for the final leg of the delivery. It turned out to be a great day to sail, arriving at Frederiksted in the early afternoon. The owner was waiting for us at the dock to take possession of his boat. He paid us off and gave us our airline tickets for our flight back to Fort Walton, ending another interesting adventure.

We had a couple of days before our flight to take in the sights of Frederiksted, and Jerry decided to hang out in St Croix before flying out. Skip, Tom, and I boarded our flight to the Redneck Riviera and arrived back just in time for the Christmas Holidays.

It was good to be back at the Surfview; time for a little R&R before getting back to work maintaining the Surfview and the Pele. While I was out of town, my mom organized and oversaw the annual Thanksgiving feast at the Surfview and really likes doing that kind of stuff. My sons Michael and Jon were back in town for Christmas, and Grandma's good cooking, it just was great to have them home again. They are busy boys, Jon's a college man, and Michael is pursuing the '88 Olympics.

December 27th was our last charter of the year, the wedding of Mark Baggs and Terry. They said their vows on deck before a small wedding party while we sailed the bay in a light breeze on a beautiful afternoon in the Redneck Riviera.

My sons hung around for the New Year's Eve celebration at the Hog's Breath Saloon, then took off; Jon went back to FSU, and Michael drove back down to Fort Pierce.

1986

The Pele was back in action with our first charter of the year on the 19th of January for a sail around the bay; it would be the last one for a while. The next would be after we dry-docked the boat on March 22nd at A&W Boatyard in Destin Harbor. Two days out of the boatyard, we were chartered to sail to Pensacola and back, the beginning of a busy charter season; we had a total of 24 for the year.

On May 24th, Windsong Charters volunteered to be the committee boat for the three-day Hog's Breath Regatta with Ike Espe, an old flying buddy from the Alconbury onboard, followed by the

Honest Jon Regatta on the 31st. Both of these events were a lot of fun, the committees are always entertaining, and they bring on board plenty of food and drink. The banquets at the end of the competition give all the participants a chance to mingle and party on down and give us plenty of publicity.

My son Michael beat out his competitors at the Windsurfing competition at Pensacola for the honor of representing the United States at Ted Turner's 1986 Goodwill Games in the USSR. The sailing events were held in July at Tallinn, Estonia, where he finished second behind a Russian for the silver medal. On his return from the games on the ferry to Helsinki, he acquired the Russian ensign off the ferry's stern post, not too smart; if they caught him, he would probably still be working at hard labor in a Siberian salt mine. He gave it to his brother to hang up in his frat house at FSU.

The annual Around the Island Race was coming up and Windsong Charters volunteered to be the committee boat. On September 19th, we sailed the Pele over on an overcast morning with a light wind out of the NE to the Cinco Bayou Bridge to anchor and dink ashore for the skippers' meeting. After the meeting, we sailed over to the Seagull and tied up for the night. On the 20th, we sailed over and anchored near buoy #8 to set up the start line for the 07:30 start of the race. After the start, we sailed back to the Surfview, where we hung out until around 17:00, then sailed over near the Elks Club to anchor and set up the finish line. The first finish at 18:40 was a Tornado crewed by the Hill Brothers; they finished way ahead of the rest of the fleet. The awards banquet the next day was a big event for sailors who came from all over the southeast.

On the 3rd of October, we sailed the Pele over to Destin Harbor with a crew of friends and tied up to the Kelly Docks for a weekend at the Destin Seafood Festival. We all had a good old time at the festival before finally sailing back to Surfview on the 5th of October.

The Air Force Thunderbirds were scheduled to put on a show at Eglin AFB on the 25th of Oct, so we sailed the Pele over to and anchored off the end of the runway at Eglin. The spot where we anchored would put us in a great position to watch the show; unfortunately, the weather deteriorated, and the show was canceled.

Skip's steel schooner was finally complete, and he was now living on it. He sold his old boat and was ready to sail his new boat, Silent Lady II, to the U S Virgin Islands and set up a charter business. All he needed was a crew, Bill Leibold and I volunteered to help him sail to the Islands, but he still needed a full-time deckhand to go with him. My parents were next door and willing to take care of the Surfview for a couple of weeks it would take us to sail on this boondoggle to the USVI.

The new Silent Lady II, a steel 63' topsail schooner, had captain's quarters in the stern, two

staterooms, two heads with showers, a crew's quarter in the fo'c'sle up forward, and on the stern davits a big Zodiac dinghy with an outboard motor. For navigation equipment, it had an autopilot with a second station down below at the navigation table, radar, Sat Nav plus VHF, and HF radios. Below decks, all the woodwork was finished in cherry wood. Also, put to use were the two bronze winches we had salvaged two years earlier off the wreck of the Sandavore in the Virgin Islands; he had them mounted up forward to trim the Jib.

Throughout October, Skip was busy putting the finishing touches on his boat and interviewing locals to hire on as a deckhand; he was looking for someone to take with him and to work for him in the USVI.

Finally, on the 12th of November, we set sail on the Silent Lady II on a beautiful morning with a full-time crew, Lamar, and two extra hands, Bill Leibold and me. We set our course for our first port of call, Key West, on our journey to Charlotte Amalie in the United States Virgin Islands.

The three-to-four-day sail to Key West would give us plenty of time to learn how to sail the Silent Lady II. I had plenty of experience sailing a schooner; the only thing a little bit different on the Silent Lady II was the top sail. After playing around with it for a while, we found that it was only effective for sailing on a broad reach or running before the wind.

Three and a half days later, on the 15th, we entered Northwest Channel to Key West, where we tied up the Silent Lady II to the Singleton Dock. Once we topped off our fuel and water, we walked over to Rick's Bar for a beer, where we talked over our next port of call. After a lot of talk, Skip decided on taking the Gulf Stream up to the Northwest Providence Channel to Nassau in the Bahamas. He was against taking the shorter route by way of the Old Bahama Channel because it would take us too close to Cuba for his liking.

We checked out with US Customs in Key West on the morning of the 16th and set sail on a course up the Gulf Stream to Great Isaac Light, the entrance to the Northwest Providence Channel, then on down the channel passed Great Stirrup Light to Nassau on New Providence, Bahamas. Just before noon on the 18th, we spotted the water tower on the west end of Paradise Island, a landmark by the entrance to Nassau Harbour; closer in, we called Nassau Harbour Control for permission to enter. On getting our clearance, we called Nassau Yacht Haven for a mooring. On the way to our mooring, we passed by cruise ships tied up at the Prince George Wharf; they must have just begun stopping at Nassau. Once tied to our mooring buoy, we took the dinghy ashore to clear in with customs and obtain our cruising permit.

Once all the paperwork was finished, we did a little grocery shopping and had lunch at a café near the docks. Later on, we took our dinghy up the canal to the lagoon on Paradise Islands to check out the hotel and casino. We didn't stay long and dinked over to Nassau for a little walkabout town. We ended up in a bar restaurant in downtown Nassau for cocktails and dinner. We noticed that there was not much going on in town anymore; all the action was on Paradise Island.

In the morning, we slipped our mooring and moved over to top off at the fuel dock, then did a little shopping, loading up on plantains, lemons, eggs, bacon, and more before departing the east end of Nassau Harbour. Once passed Paradise Island, we made a left turn over the narrows, then followed Hanover Sound to Northeast Providence Channel, passing Rose Island and across the banks to the deep waters of Exuma Sound.

By early afternoon the next day, while sailing down Exuma Sound abeam Great Rock Cut, Skip decided to make a stop at Staniel Cay. After navigating through the cut, always a thrill, we anchored near other boats off the Happy People Marina. Half an hour later, we were ashore at the marina bar conversing with the people off the boats. We were having a good old time talking it up and swapping sea stories. Skip was in hot pursuit of one of the girls, decided to have a cocktail party on the Silent Lady II, and invited the whole crowd at the bar, around ten people.

With an hour's head start before our guests would arrive, we loaded into our dinghy, including Skip's new friend, and headed for the boat. Once aboard, we started getting things ready while Skip showed her the captain's stateroom. When our guests arrived in their dinghies, we served them cocktails and gave them a tour of the boat. Everyone had a good time telling stories, except the boyfriend of the girl that Skip borrowed; he took off with her shortly after he came on board. The party was a lot of fun, and when the last of our guests departed in their dinghies, we cleaned up the boat preparing for an early departure in the morning.

The next morning's sun rose on a beautiful Bahamian day with a crew that was eager to get underway to our next port of call. One big problem was our dinghy was gone; either we didn't secure it properly, or sometime after the party, someone cast it loose in the night. Like maybe the cuckold boyfriend of the girl Skip was messing with and was seeking revenge. We reported the dingy missing to the Bahama Air Sea Rescue Association (BASRA) and then sailed around the rest of the day searching for it, with no success. We did notice that the boat with the girl that Skip was messing with had departed during the night. During the happy hour that afternoon at the Happy People Marina, everyone had a theory about what happened to our dinghy. All we knew for sure was that it came loose during the night and if the outgoing tide took it out Big Rock Cut, it was now long gone, floating around in Exuma Sound somewhere.

The next morning, November 22nd, we weighed anchor and sailed the banks toward Harvey's Cay to continue our search for the dinghy. We continued searching a while before giving up and sailed off the banks at Guana Cay South back out to Exuma Sound. Once in deep waters, we set a course for Puerto Plata in the Dominican Republic, an estimated four-day sail. After motor sailing with just the mainsail for ten hours, beating into the 15 to 20kt trade wind from the east, we sailed between Cape Santa Maria and Conception Island and entered the Atlantic Ocean. Eighteen hours later, we had Samana Cays in sight, the island that the National Geographic Society claimed that

Columbus first made landfall in the Americas on October 12th, 1492; we decided to stop and check it out.

We approached the island from the south and picked our way over the reef finding a decent place to anchor close to the beach since we didn't have a dinghy anymore. We swam ashore and split up to explore the island. What we discovered was a couple of dilapidated fishing shacks, a small corn field, some coconuts, and not much else, no artifacts from Christopher's visit. On the beach, Bill and Lamar did find some footprints, so maybe the place was visited by fisherman; no one came out to say hello. Snorkeling around the boat, we found a few conchs for our conch bag and speared some fish, and with corn from the island and rice; we had an enjoyable dinner, all washed down with a few fingers of rum.

In the morning, we worked our way back over the reef, and once in deep water, we continued motor sailing into the trade winds on course for the Dominican Republic. During the day, we processed a couple of the conch and made a batch of ceviche for a leisurely lunch on a nice sunshiny day on the Atlantic Ocean. Our course would take us down the Mayaguana Passage between the Plana Cays and Mayaguana, steering south of West Caicos of the Turks and Caicos Islands, then a straight shot to Puerto Plata.

This course put us on a more favorable point of sail, allowing us to use all our sails except for the top sail, and after five and a half hours, we passed north of Plana Cays and entered Mayaguana Passage. During the night, we sailed down the passage around the southwest corner of Mayaguana, and before noon on the 25th, we had West Caicos Island in sight. This was the most southwest Island of the Turks and Caicos Island, a British Crown Colony. We needed to hunt up dinner, so that afternoon, we made our way onto the Caicos Banks just north of West Sand Spit around 5 miles southwest of Grand Turk Island and anchored up on the bank next to a big coral head teaming with life.

After snorkeling around for an hour or so, I climbed back on board with my catch, a nice snapper, and a shovelnose lobster. I was the first one back on board and noticed a small boat approaching from the direction of Grand Turk Island and Cockburn Town, where we felt unwelcome two years earlier. As he came closer, I strapped on my S&W 357 Magnum and slung on my 12-gage Winchester pump. He stopped about 30' from us and yelled over, asking if I wanted to buy some fish. After I declined his offer, he headed back to town. We had a good laugh over the incident as we prepared our bountiful catch for dinner.

On the morning of the 26th, after a hearty breakfast on Skip's Sailors Delight, made with the last of our eggs, bacon, and plantains, we finally got underway. Finding our way off the Caicos Bank and onto the Turks Island Passage at around 11:00, we took up a heading of 175 degrees for the twenty-hour sail to Puerto Plata in the Dominican Republic.

At dawn on the 27th, Thanksgiving Day, we had Mount Isabela de Torres in sight, and a couple of hours later, we could see the channel markers for the channel into Puerto Plata Harbour. We called the Port Captain, who directed us to tie up to the pier and await customs. Once we were Mediterranean Moored to the pier, we noticed that the 21' sailboat next to us looked familiar. Sure enough, it was the nurse we ran into at Staniel Cay two years earlier. She didn't talk much; she was in a hurry to take a turkey to the local bakery to roast for her and her new boyfriend. Looking around the harbor while waiting for customs, we noticed a ship that looked like an old Liberty Ship tied up to the commercial dock, something we will have to check out while we're in port.

After a couple of hours, customs finally showed up and searched the boat, collected our weapons, and cleared us in. Our first stop was Poopies' to visit with the cop from Chicago and his wife and play with the girls. Later on, while doing a little walkabout town, we stopped by to check up on the guy that we met from the states two years earlier, that was opening up a bar/whore house. We found the bar, it was still in business, but his mother and sister were running the place he had died in a motorcycle accident earlier in the year. We ended up at the old hotel by the pier for cocktails and thanksgiving dinner.

In the morning, after an early breakfast at the hotel, Bill and I decided to go check out what we thought was an old Liberty Ship. After a short walk over to the commercial dock, we could see that they were letting people aboard, so we got in line. Once onboard, we found that it was a Liberty ship and bible boat that was spreading the gospel. After checking out their religious books and stuff in the store located in one of the cargo holds, we were on our way down the gangway when we were stopped by one of the crew telling us that the captain wanted to see us in his quarters. He wanted to congratulate us on the way we Mediterranean Moored to the pier on our arrival and somehow picked us out of the crowd as we boarded his ship. He had an interesting story to tell of all his travels around the world, then offered to take us on a tour of the ship. The tour took quite a while, and he seemed really happy to show off the old ship, Bill, and I had a lot of questions for him. Later on in the afternoon, we took the cable car up Mount Isabela de Torres for a great view of the town and harbor and briefed the rest of the crew about our Liberty Ship adventure that they slept through.

As soon as customs opened in the morning of the 29th, we cleared out of Puerto Plata, they gave us our weapons back, and we started our two-and-a-half-day sail to Charlotte Amalie, USVI. Late in the morning of December 1st, while sailing east along the north coast of Puerto Rico, we sailed by El Morro (the old Spanish fort that guarded the entrance to San Juan Harbor), and around four in the afternoon, we were near Isla De Culebra where we anchored up for the night.

The next morning after a leisurely breakfast, we weighed anchor and began the four-to-five-hour sail to Charlotte Amalie. By early afternoon while maneuvering in the West Gregerie Channel toward Charlotte Amalie, with Skip at the helm, we ran into a channel marker putting a big dent on the starboard side of the bow, the Silent Lady II was no longer a virgin. The incident gave us lots to harass Skip about at the Bridge Bar that afternoon during happy hour as we talked over the adventures of the last couple of weeks.

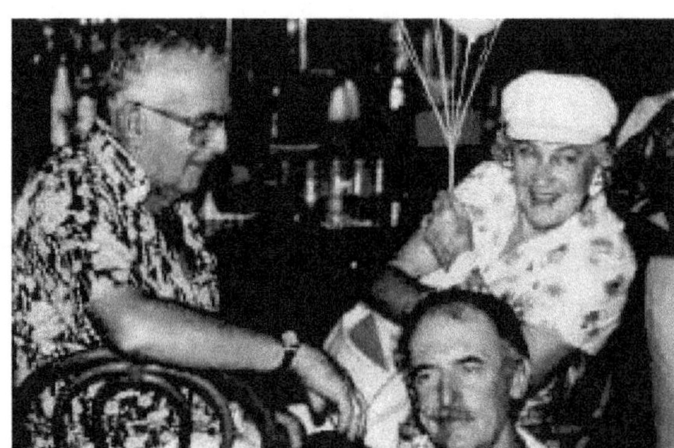

The next morning, Dec 3rd, Bill and I packed our sea bag and wished Skip good luck on his new venture, and took a cab to the airport for our flight back to Fort Walton Beach.

I arrived back at the Surfview just in time for my birthday on December 5th; my parents gave me a little party for me at the Hog's Breath Saloon with a lot of my friends, which continued on until late into the evening.

I drove down to DeBary to have Christmas with my parents. My aunt Helen, Uncle Rudy, and aunt Claire were also there to enjoy my mother's cooking. We were not disappointed. Christmas dinner with my parents and relative is always informative, listening to their many stories. It was a very Merry Christmas.

I drove back up to Fort Walton to celebrate New Year's Eve at Pandora's, a favorite bar/restaurant on the island; the whole gang was there, all the movers and shakers, to welcome in the New Year.

1987

During February and March, we sailed the Pele around the local area with our friends. On one of these trips around the bay on the 14th of March, the generator on the Buda stopped working. We headed back to the dock, and by 15:00, we had the generator removed and in the shop for a rebuild before they closed for the day. A couple of days later, we were back in business with a rebuilt generator just in time for our first charter of the year, a half day around the bay. The engine in the Pele was definitely on its last legs and had to be replaced; we have had nothing but problems with it since we installed it in 1980. We finally made the decision to start looking around for a reliable engine to replace it.

On the 8th of April, we sailed into Destin Harbor to haul the Pele at the Harbor Boatyard for its annual bottom job. While working on the boat, we let it be known that we were in the market for a new or used diesel engine. The next day we were contacted by a person that had an engine and found that it didn't have enough horsepower for his boat and wanted to sell it. We negotiated with him and ended up buying the engine, a brand new Westerbeke 4-154 diesel that came with a new propeller shaft and screw (propeller).

It was a busy two weeks at the boatyard; luckily, we had a lot of volunteer labor. The old Buda diesel was pulled out of the boat, new engine mounts were made, and the Westerbeke installed on them with a new cutlass bearing for the shaft; the screw (propeller) was in the shop to get re-pitched. While the work with the engine was going on, work on the hull was progressing. During the inspection of the hull, we found four planks with rot that we removed and were processing new ones to replace them with. Another problem was the ballast in the bilge (iron railroad rail couplings) that had turned into a mass of rust and had to be replaced with something else. We solved that problem by removing the ballast and tar that we sealed the bilge with it in 1976 and replacing it all with cement ballast that we poured into the bilge. Once the new planks were in place and caulked, the painting began, black above the waterline and red lead below a white boot top. She looked really pretty when we launched her.

On the 9th of April, we were back in action with a day charter around the bay and another half-day charter on the 14th. Our new engine worked perfectly; it's nice to know you have an engine that will start when you need it. We put in a lot more ballast than we took out, and it made a difference. The Pele was more of a straight-up sailor now. She didn't heal over as much in a strong wind making it feel a lot more stable and a lot easier to move around on deck.

Windsong Charters volunteered to be the committee boat again for the Hog's Breath Regatta, and on the morning of the 24[th,] the Pele was anchored in Choctawhatchee Bay 2 miles off of Black Point, ready for the start. We enjoyed two days of perfect weather and a fun regatta race committee that brought with them plenty of food and drink; the crew of the Pele had a good old time.

On the weekend following the regatta, we invited the friends that helped us at the boatyard for a shakedown cruise to Pensacola Beach. Only Rick Sauter showed up (even though he didn't help at the boatyard), so just the two of us set sail heading west up the sound and, after an uneventful cruise, arrived at Pensacola Beach at around 17:00, where we tied up to the Quietwater Bay Pier for the night. Once ashore, we headed for Flounder's Chowder House for dinner and later across the street to the Sandshaker Lounge for bushwhackers (their specialty cocktail).

In the morning, a little bit hung over, we cast off and sailed into Pensacola Bay, then out the pass into the Gulf of Mexico. With moderate seas and 20 to 25kts of wind out of the north, we sailed up the coast to Mobile, Alabama, under full sail speeding along at around 8-9 knots, really fast for the old boat. Late in the afternoon, we cleared the pass into Mobile Bay and anchored up behind Alabama Point for the night. So far, the shakedown cruise has shown that the engine is reliable and that the extra ballast helped make the Pele feel more stable in high winds.

Next morning, we started sailing east down the intercoastal and headed for home. What the shakedown successfully showed was that the Pele was definitely seaworthy enough and that the engine, sails, and rigging were reliable in heavy wind/sea conditions. The cement ballast also did a good job sealing up the bilges that leaked, not a drop.

We got as far as Perdido Key, where after taking a little-known channel around Ono Island, we tied up at a short, dilapidated dock across the street from the Florabama Lounge. The lounge was a mostly outdoor bar on the beach at the state line between Florida and Alabama. It's noted for having some serious party action with live music from local bands, plenty of beer, and food. Rick and I took the opportunity to dance with the ladies and rub elbows with fellow rednecks; we stayed until closing.

With a late start in the morning and only running aground once finding our way out around Ono Island, we were on our way down the intercoastal. We only made it as far as Little Sabine Bay on Pensacola Beach, having sailed about 30 miles. We tied up to a pilling behind the Sandshaker and waded ashore for some food, then back to the boat, we were partied out.

Early in the morning, we were underway, heading east down the intercoastal on a reach under full sail in a 10 kt breeze out of the north. Just before we arrived at Navarre, the wind shifted to the east, and we dropped sail and motored on into Navarre beach, where we anchored up off of Juana's Pagodas for lunch. After having lunch with the owners Mary and her sister Juana (their parents must have been pot-smoking hippies), we continued our uneventful cruise down the sound arriving at the Surfview dock just before nightfall on the 29th. For Rick and me, the Pele's shakedown cruise turned into an interesting four-day adventure.

During the charter season, we had 26 charters, including one wedding and one bachelor party giving us enough cash flow to keep Windsong Charters in business. We also sailed the Pele on 15 pleasure cruises, including two to Pensacola and one to Panama City. The old Pele was kept pretty busy.

My son Michael was doing a lot of traveling around competing in windsurfing regattas and qualified to compete in the 87 Pan American Games in Indianapolis. His brother Jon whom we

haven't seen much of since he started at FSU and got over being homesick two years ago. He took my advice and held up, signing up for Air Force ROTC until they finally secured a pilot training slot for him, he was having fun at ROTC summer boot camp. His grades were good, and he seems to be enjoying the challenges of college life; my boys are doing alright.

The Pan American Games started on the 7th of Aug, and Michael was there as a member of the United States Sailing Team in windsurfing. He had a good series of races in Lake Michigan and beat out the competition for the Gold Medal. When the games ended, Michael came back from Indianapolis all fired up and confident of achieving his goal of competing in the 1988 Olympic Games in Korea.

My Aunt Elfriede died in October. A vegetarian, animal lover, swimmer, and a lover of life will be missed. My mom talked my uncle Eric into driving up to Fort Walton Beach from his home in Marathon to come to join us for the Thanksgiving celebration at the Surfview. We had the usual group of around twenty people, plus or minus a couple. Everyone enjoyed the beautiful day; I think it helped uncle Eric to be around people.

On the 10th of December, Tom Prohaska, president of Windsong Charters, married Donna Mansfield. The ceremony and reception with a small group of family and friends was held in his condo on the Island. I'm the last partner in Windsong Charters that's not married; I'm looking and enjoying the vetting process.

Things quieted down after Tom's wedding, although we did take the Pele on a weekend pleasure cruise to the No Name Lounge at the foot of the Hathaway Bridge in Panama City. Christmas followed a short time later at my parent's apartment next door to me at the Surfview. Jon made it back again from FSU for the holidays; he was not going to miss Grandma's cooking if he could help it.

The El Matador party room was rented for the New Year's Eve party, and the whole gang attended. It was a blast. Everyone I ever knew from around Fort Walton Beach was there to bring in the New Year.

Chapter Six: 1988 - 1990

The year started off slow for Windsong Charters; we didn't pick up our first charter until the 16th of January, a two-day sail to Pensacola and back. This was followed by a couple of local charters in February. Things started to pick up in March with a sail around the bay for Tom's brother Jon's bachelor party on the 11th of March. It was an interesting sail. They hired some strippers and a bartender (pro bono) for the occasion. A couple of days later, on the 13[th,] Jon and Celeste were married on the Pele.

We sailed the Pele over for its annual haul out at the A & W Boatyard in Destin Harbor on the 5th of May, anticipating an easy time of it. In fact, it was an easy haul out, just a quick inspection of the hull for rot and new zinc for the propeller shaft and rudder. On the 9[th,] we had her launched back into the water with a new coat of paint ready for action.

Soon after we picked up a couple of charters, Windsong Charters volunteered the Pele to be the committee boat for the Hog's Breath Regatta on the 21st of May. The regatta lasted two days, followed by an awards banquet. These events are always a lot of fun, and by being on the committee boat, you're right in the middle of all the action and good public relations for our business.

After a busy couple of weeks of charters, it was decided it was time for a little R&R. So, on the 15th of June, we set sail for Pensacola and points west. We didn't get far; we ended up anchoring by Juana's Pagoda in Navarre. Continuing our sail in the morning, our next port of call was Quietwater Bay, Pensacola, for another night of mayhem. The next day we made it as far as Perdido Key, Alabama, which was as far west as we would go, and tied up at Gulf Gate Marina. In the morning, we started on our sail back to Fort Walton Beach and decided on the way to make a stop at the Florabama Lounge. After working our way around Ono Island to the dilapidated dock across the street from the Florabama Lounge. We Mediterranean Moored to the dock and were ready for shore leave. At the Florabama, we enjoyed an evening of debauchery with fellow rednecks. The rest of the sail was anticlimactic as we slowly sailed our way down the Sound back to the Surfview dock.

On July 5[th,] the sailing trials for the Games of the 1988 XXIV Olympiad at Seoul, Korea, were being held in Newport, Rhode Island and Michael was one of the forty-five competitors. The regatta lasted eleven days in the tightly contested competition, but Michael persevered and won the honor of representing the United States in the Sailing Mixed Windsurfing Event to be held at the Olympics Pusan venue. At the awards ceremony, Michael picked Scott Steele, who came in third, as his training partner to go to Korea with him. After all, turnabouts are fair play. Scott chose Michael as his training partner at the Games of the 1984 XXIII Olympiad in Los Angeles.

With the news of Michael's victory, and since American Olympic Athletes don't get much in the way of state funding, we started planning to have a big fundraiser at the Surfview. My uncle Eric even drove up from the Florida Keys to take part in the activities. We ordered T-shirts and hats for the fundraiser, and Mom started planning the hors d'oeuvres while Dad and I went to work cleaning up the Surfview.

About the same time all this was going on, I was contacted by AT&T, one of the sponsors of the Olympics, with an offer I could not refuse. For the parent of a competing U.S. athlete, they would pay for transportation and accommodations in Korea to watch their child compete at the games. What a deal. I accepted the offer and was contacted shortly thereafter by a travel agent who told me to expect a packet in the mail with my travel instructions and reservations.

Michael was back in Fort Walton by the end of July, ready to go to work fundraising. The T-shirts & hats were printed and available for us to sell at the meetings, interviews, and talks that we scheduled for him with local clubs and media. We picked the weekend of August 10th, shortly before he was due to leave with the sailing team for Korea.

The day of the event turned out to be a beautiful sunshiny day in paradise, and we were ready to party. Mom had a ton of hors d'oeuvres ready to go, Eric had his easel all set up, and a fresh keg of beer was loaded in the frig on the dock; all systems were go. People started to arrive around 11:00, but things really got going with the arrival of the media truck at noon. Mom was busy supervising food. I was the parking lot attendant/dock master/bartender, Jon was pushing T-shirts,

and Dad was the overall boss. Eric was busy painting portraits for contributions and was a big hit. People were coming to see their home-grown Olympian, and he was defiantly drawing a crowd. Michael was the star and spent most of the day talking the talk. During the afternoon, we ran out of beer and had to run to the Hog's Breath for another keg. By the time the last person departed, we were all exhausted and relaxing under the stars in the parking lot finishing off the last of the beer.

The fundraiser was a great success, and we did raise enough revenue to keep our Olympian going for a while. Michael drove out two days later to Fort Pierce in the old white Chevy station wagon that his grandpa gave him; he wrecked the last hand-me-down, the 72' green Plymouth station wagon that we called the Green Hornet.

After all the excitement, it was back to normal operations, running the Surfview and chartering out The Pele. We had plenty of -shirts left to sell, and we made them available on the Pele during charters. The Pele was kept busy during the remainder of August and the beginning of September, doing quite a few charters and selling shirts for our Olympian. I was getting excited about the Olympics and was ready to hit the road. Finally, on the 15th of September, I boarded a flight out of Fort Walton Beach, destination Korea.

I arrived in Pusan, Korea, in the early afternoon of September 16th and checked into my hotel. Michael was in Seoul for the opening ceremony for the Games of the XXIV Olympiad at the Seoul Olympic Stadium on the 17th. When Michael returned from Seoul, he showed me around the sailing

venue, where I received a security briefing and a security badge to get into the venue. I also signed up for the spectator boat. The regatta wasn't scheduled to start until the 20th, giving Michael and me an opportunity to check out Pusan. Scott Steele, his training partner, joined us as we wandered around looking at the sights and sampled the local cuisine.

On the day of the first race, I went through security to enter the venue with no problems. I then went over to board the spectator boat and found out that I didn't make the list. They handed me back the form I filled out that had Sept 21, the second day of racing, written across it with a marker pen. Security then informed me that you only get to ride on the spectator boat once. Well, I didn't come all this way to watch my son compete in just one race. I had to think of something! I found another blank form, went back to the hotel, borrowed a black marker pen, and used their copying machine to run off five more boarding passes.

On the second day of racing, I used my pass to get on the spectator boat. On the third day of racing, I boarded the boat using my fake boarding pass, and it worked like a champ; nobody batted an eye. My passes worked for all four of the remaining races. I figured security would eventually question me as to why of all the spectators, I was the only one getting on board every day; luckily for me, they never did.

The weather during the regatta was pretty miserable, mostly overcast, raining off and on, and cold. Michael was consistently finishing near the top of the pack. On the first four days of racing, he finished 4th, 1st, AC, and 11th; the AC was his throw-out. On the fifth day, the weather was terrible, with 25kts of wind, heavy seas, and miserably cold. There were only around twenty people that boarded the spectator boat. The crew wanted to abort, but we talked them into taking us out. A third of the people on the boat got seasick, including some of the crew. Only 19 of the 43 competing in the race completed the race, where Michael finished 5th. On the last two days of the regatta, Michael finished 8th and 4th in weather conditions that weren't much better.

At the end of the last day of racing, the officials tallied up the points and awarded the medals.

Bruce Kendall of New Zealand-Gold, Jan Boersma of Netherlands Antilles-Silver, and Michael Gebhardt of the USA-Bronze. That night Michael, Scott, and I went out on the town and did a little celebrating

On the 3rd of October, the day after the closing ceremony in Seoul, I boarded a flight back to Florida.

The Olympics are really the greatest sports and athletic competition on earth; the ancient Greeks had a good idea!

I was back at the Surfview a couple of days ahead of Michael, enough time to organize a little welcome home party for him. On his arrival, there was a crowd waiting; everyone wanted to see his bronze medal. The local media was there for an interview of their local Olympian; even the mayor showed up and gave him the keys to the city. Michael stayed in town long enough to join his brother Jon over from FSU to help us celebrate their grandpa's 80th birthday before driving down to Fort Pierce,

The next couple of months were anticlimactic, and I went back to work. We only picked up a few charters for the Pele to sail around the bay. But we did get to load up the Pele with a crew of friends for a weekend sail to Pensacola Beach on the 11th of November to see the Blue Angels.

Arriving at Pensacola Beach, we Mediterranean Moored to the Quietwater Beach pier. Going ashore that evening, we went to our favorite haunts, Flounders for food and the Sandshaker's for cocktails, mainly bushwhackers'. In the morning, we sailed over to and anchored off the Pensacola Light House to watch the Blue Angels perform. Their demonstration of precision formation flying is hard to beat. After the show, we sailed over to Little Sabine Bay, where we nosed into the beach and spent the night before sailing back to Fort Walton Beach in the morning.

Then all of a sudden, it was time to prepare for the annual Thanksgiving feed at the Surfview. We had the usual group of around twenty old friends and people living at the Surfview that brought their favorite dish to the table. The only thing unusual this year was that in addition to my mom's

turkey, one of our guests brought over a deep fryer and fried a turkey. Both were consumed by the hungry crowd along with most of the rest of the fare. Mom and Dad love these large get together, and so do I. There's always plenty of conversation, and later in the evening, after the crowd thins out, sitting around solving all the world's problems is always enjoyable.

Jon came home from FSU for Christmas. Mom and Dad put on a little Christmas party in their apartment for us and some of our close friends. A nice quiet affair was followed by a sail on the Pele on the bay. New Year's followed and was celebrated in the usual manner at the Hog's Breath Saloon until the bar closed, and they threw us out.

The year started off slow around Surfview; everyone was winding down from the holidays. I stayed busy catching up on maintenance around the apartments and on the Pele. We did get a crew together for a two-day sortie to Pensacola Beach. Setting sail on the 14th of January for an easy cold sail to Quitwater Beach. After tying up to their dock, we went over to visit our favorite restaurant, Flounders, for food, followed by a walk across the street to the Sandshaker for cocktails. Then after an early wake-up in the morning, we hoisted sails for a pleasant sail back to the Surfview.

On the 3rd of February, my son Michael called and informed me that he with the rest of the U.S Olympic Sailing Team were being flown up to Washington DC for a meeting and photo shoot with President George H.W. Bush at the white house. During the shoot, he actually had an opportunity to talk with the President and his wife, Barbara, the first lady.

On April 29th Jon graduated from FSU, and we had a little party for him in the Surfview parking lot for family and friends. His mother and grandma Mary came down from New Jersey to be there for Jon. I haven't seen my ex since the divorce, she hadn't changed much, and we really didn't have much to say to each other. Everyone had a good time. Jon showed his mother and grandma around before they left to continue on to South Florida.

Jon headed back to FSU for the summer semester. Since he didn't sign up for ROTC until his sophomore year,

he would have to put in another year to finish his commitment to the Air Force ROTC program. The extra year would give him the opportunity to work toward a higher degree.

Windsong Charters Inc. was having a pretty slow season, with just 11 charters and a bachelor party. Since we had no charters scheduled, we again volunteered the Pele to be the committee boat for the Hog's Breath Regatta on the 20th of May. We picked up the committee at Deckhands Marina and then anchored off of Black Point to start the regatta; just then, it started pouring down rain, and the races were canceled. The next day it was still raining, and they canceled the regatta.

During June and July, we picked up a few more charters, but we mostly just cruised the Pele around the local area with our friends.

On the 25th of August, we took the Pele over to the A & W Boatyard in Destin Harbor to haul her out. The charter season was pretty much over, and we didn't make

a lot of money, but we did make enough to pay for most of the expenses.

It turned out to be a long stay at the boatyard. We found some rot in the stern that had to be removed and rebuilt, and we also needed to rebuild the steering gear and rudder. We were getting better at it and did all the woodworking repairs ourselves. Leo would be proud. The steering and rudder repairs were done at a machine shop to our specs. On the 13th of September, we finally finished all the repairs, and with a new paint job, we launched her. On the shakedown sail back to the Surfview, all our repairs checked out okay.

Just in time, we picked up five more charters and a bachelor party in October before going on a little pleasure cruise to watch the Blue Angles perform in Pensacola. We left a day early on the 10th of November to make a side trip to the Florabama Lounge on the state line before the air show. On the way there, we were stopped for a safety inspection by the Coast Guard. They boarded us for the inspection and did a thorough job of it even though they were hindered by everyone on board being in high spirits, having a good time, and getting in their way.

The inspection slowed us down enough so that by the time we were attempting to find our way around Ono Island at night, we ran aground! It took us another hour to get unstuck and to Mediterranean Moor to the dilapidated dock across the street from the Florabama. It was worth it. The Florabama was a jumping place when we arrived. Lots of people, bar food, beer, and a redneck band; what else would you want?

By 13:00 the next day, we were anchored by the Pensacola Lighthouse in place and waiting for the scheduled start of the Blue Angles aerobatic flying demonstration team at 14:00. They put on a great show as usual. At the conclusion of their performance, we hauled up the anchor and started our sail back to Fort Walton Beach. We made it as far as Little Sabine Bay in Pensacola Beach, where at dusk, we nosed onto the beach behind the Sandshaker Lounge to spend a night on the town.

The sail back to Fort Walton Beach in the morning was slow and quiet. Everyone was licking their wounds and not saying much.

While I was working on the Pele at the boatyard, I noticed that my heart was skipping beats, so I made an appointment with my mom's cardiologist and had it checked out. After getting a heart echocardiogram, he diagnosed me as having mitral valve prolapse. He didn't seem to be concerned and scheduled me for an appointment in a year for another scan. I learned to ignore the skipped beats. Later on, I found a book by Lewis Grizzard about his ordeal with mitral valve prolapse. He painted a grim picture of what I had in store.

I then came across an article in the local paper about Dr. Cosgrove at the Cleveland Clinic, who had a procedure to repair mitral valve prolapse. The article stated that as soon as the echocardiogram detected an enlargement of the heart's left ventricle, you only had a couple of months to get it repaired. It also had the contact numbers for the Cleveland Clinic. I put the article under the class on my desk.

Windsong Charters had a pretty good season and ended up with sixteen charters, not bad considering we got off to a slow start. During the summer, we sailed around on the Pele a lot more than we took her out on charter. My partner's participation in these day and weekend boondoggles dropped off since they got married. Only once in a while would they bring their wives with them when the Pele was a committee boat for a regatta.

The Thanksgiving feast at the Surfview had its usual crowd of around twenty hardy souls on a beautiful sunny day. My Uncle Eric drove up from the Florida Keys to partake in the holidays with us. The party lasted until way after the sun went down. I had an empty apartment where Eric set up a studio and, for the next couple of days, did portraits of the ladies.

Not much happened during the beginning of December, leading up to a quiet family gathering for Christmas over at my parents' apartment at the Surfview.

We all celebrated the New Year at the Hog's Breath Saloon.

1990

The year1990 started off slow for Windsong Charters. We didn't pick up our first charter until April 14th. But the Pele wasn't idle for long; on the 10th of March, we took her on a seven-day sail to Fort McRae in Pensacola with stops along the way at Juana's Pagoda in Navarre and Little Sabine Bay in Pensacola Beach.

Jay Scherf chartered the Pele for his daughter's wedding on the 28th of April. We picked up the wedding party at his dock in Mary Easter and sailed up the sound to channel marker 51 and anchored. Two other sailboats rafted up with us for the ceremony. Later we all sailed over to Jay's

for the reception. Jay always puts on a great party, and his daughter's reception was one of his better efforts; it seemed like the whole town was there.

My parents and I drove over to FSU in Tallahassee on the 15th of May for my son Jon's commissioning, where I swore him in as a second lieutenant in the Air Force Reserves. He stayed on in Tallahassee with his girlfriend Maura waiting for orders. While waiting, he found a part-time job and took some computer courses at FSU.

Summer was in full swing with the Hog's Breath Regatta on May 19th, followed by the Billy Bowlegs Pirate Festival on the first weekend in June. For Billy Bowlegs, we had a crowd of partiers at the Surfview to watch the pirate's invasion of Fort Walton Beach. Also joining the party were two big white geese that had been hanging around the Surfview for a couple of months. It's a lot of fun watching all the craziness going on. The party at the Surfview went on till late in the evening. In the morning, I was up early to clean up the mess when I discovered L.T., one of my tenants, sleeping under a palm tree cuddled up with one of the geese; I wish I had taken a picture. His wife threw him out of their apartment after the party for being obnoxiously drunk.

The Pele was chartered for a bachelor party for one of Michael's friends, Jack Springfellow, on June 7th. Followed by a couple of charters later in the month, then on the 25th, we took a sail around the bay with a stop at a restaurant for my parent's 58th wedding anniversary. On the 30th, we finished off the month with a charter for a wedding. We picked up the wedding party at the Seagull Restaurant and sailed over to Garners Bayou, and anchored for the ceremony. After the vows were taken, we dropped them off at the Fort Walton Beach Yacht Club for the reception.

On the 4th of July, we sailed the Pele over to Destin and rafted up with Bill and Marie on the Yankee to watch the fireworks. The harbor was crowded, and we were not disappointed as Destin put on a pretty spectacular and lengthy fireworks display that ended just before midnight. On the way back, Bill ran aground in the Yankee, and after a lot of harassment from the crew of the Pele, we tossed him a line and pulled them off into deeper water.

It was time for a little pleasure cruise, so I rounded up a crew, my girlfriend Nancy (fancy Nancy), Tom Prohaska, Jack and Linda Brown, Tom Stewart, and Mary Scherf for a sail down the coast to Port St Joe for the beginning of scallop season. Scalloping is something we hadn't done before and could be interesting. Besides, I like eating scallops.

That was the original plan, and then my crew started dropping out. When we cast off from the dock on the 8th, I had three deckhands, Nancy, Tom, and Tom Stewart; we had the Pele all to ourselves. The rest of the crew would meet us later in Port St Joe or Apalachicola. With an early start around 07:30 and after a stop at Pop's Fuel Dock for fuel and ice, we headed for Destin Pass, clearing the sea buoy at 09:00. In a dead calm, we motored down the coast toward Panama City. The wind finally came up around noon, allowing us to hoist the sails and enjoy an easy sail to Panama City.

Once through the pass, we anchored off of St Andrews Park, just inside the pass for the night. We had dinner on board, and during cocktails, we decided to make a stop the next day on the way to Port St Joseph to explore Crooked Island. It's one of the Barrier Islands along the gulf coast that's just a couple of miles down the coast from Tyndall AFB. This is also an area from where they launch drones out to the military ranges in the Gulf of Mexico for pilots to practice air-to-air combat by shooting them down.

We weighed anchor early for the short sail to Crooked Island. Three hours later, around noon, we approached the unmarked pass cautiously to find our way through into St Andrews Sound, where we anchored in the cove just to the west of the pass and close to the beach. We weren't there long before an Air Force boat came over and warned us that they were about to start launching drones and that we could either stay where we were or pick up and leave; we opted to stay and watch the show.

We were just sitting in our deck chairs under the awning on a beautiful summer afternoon by an uninhabited island, enjoying the ambiance of the place, and decided to stay another day. We didn't see much of the drone launches, smoke trails just to the east headed out into the gulf. Later on in the afternoon, the Air Force boat came by and told us there were no more launches scheduled and we could move around.

We were on the beach early to do some serious beach combing. After a day of looking over jetsam and flotsam and finding no pieces o' eight, we retired to the Pele for an early happy hour under the awning. Nancy prepared dinner for us, followed by after-dinner cocktails and a lot of conversation late into the star-filled night.

Early morning of the 11th found us slowly maneuvering our way out through the pass to continue our sail to Port St Joe. By early afternoon we entered St Joseph Bay and anchored up at the anchorage in Eagle Harbor, where we spent the night.

We were up early in the morning, eager to try our hand at scalloping. After a hearty breakfast, we sailed south down the bay and anchored ½ mile SE of Blacks Island (a small island in the middle of the south end of the bay) to start diving for scallops. After a few hours of diving and finding only a few, we figured we were looking in the wrong spot. By then, the weather started deteriorating with thunderstorms moving into the area. We headed back to Eagle Harbor but couldn't find a good spot to anchor, so we motored over to and up the canal that connects Port St Joe to the intercoastal waterway (the ditch) and on to Lake Wimico where we anchored for the night. During dinner, we decided to sail to Apalachicola in the morning.

In the morning, after a three-hour sail on the intercoastal, we were tied up by noon at the Apalachicola Public Dock. We contacted Jack in Fort Walton so they could meet us there for happy hour. Jack arrived with Linda and Mary, and after loading their seabags on board, we all walked over to the Gibson Inn for happy hour. Once settled at the Inn, we briefed them on our little adventure at Crooked Island that they missed.

We took the next day off to tour around historic Apalachicola, once a major southern seaport during the civil war for the confederacy. It's where cotton was shipped down the Chattahoochee and Apalachicola Rivers on steamboats to be loaded onto ships running the blockade to Europe. Now it's a sleepy old Florida town with an oyster and tourist industry. Besides some great seafood restaurants, there's an old-time drug store with a soda fountain, and we all had an ice cream soda. After completing our walkabout town, we ended up at the Gibson Inn to plan our next course of action. We decided to sail around Apalachicola Bay for a day, then go back to Port St Joe to give another go at scalloping

On the morning of the 15th, we finally left the dock around noon and sailed over to St. George Island, where we anchored and went ashore to look around. Not much to see, just some summer houses on the beach, so we didn't stay long and sailed back to Apalachicola, where we tied up to the city dock.

In the morning, Tom Stuart and Mary jumped ship to drive Jack's car back to Fort Walton Beach, and the rest of us set sail for Port St. Joe. We sailed back up the intercoastal and the canal to St. Joseph Bay, then south down the bay past Blacks Island to the very south end of the bay in an area called Lighthouse Bayou, where we anchored close by the Apalachicola Lighthouse at 15:00.

This time we didn't dive for the scallops. We just waded around on the flats feeling for the little buggers with our toes and picking them up. We noticed as we were setting our anchor a little girl wadding in less than knee-deep water with a small bucket picking up scallops. An hour and a half

later, we had 91 scallops and quit for the day. That night while at anchor by the lighthouse, we consumed them during dinner with quite a bit of wine, celebrating our catch.

Next morning, after a breakfast of "Pele Scramble", a scallop omelet a'la Nancy, we were back wading around on the flats in hot pursuit of scallops. By noon we had our limit of 254, but we needed to get moving, thunderstorms were moving into the area, and we needed to find a more secure place to anchor. Once underway, we slowly worked our way out of Lighthouse Bayou into the deeper waters toward the north end of St Joseph Bay, eventually finding a place to anchor in Eagle Harbor for the night. The storms raged as we dined on scallopini fettuccine washed down with a little Chardonnay.

Next morning the 19th of July, we departed Eagle Harbor on our journey back to Fort Walton Beach. We thought we could sail up the coast the whole way, but the weather wasn't cooperating. We still had storms with strong winds out of the northwest giving headwinds for our course back. We took the easy way by heading over to and motored up the ditch to Panama City. We anchored by the No Name Bar at the foot of the Hathaway Bridge for the night, and after dinner on board, we dinked over to the No Name.

In the morning, we continued the trip via the ditch back to Fort Walton Beach. We did get a fairly early start in the morning, and after four hours, we exited the ditch into Choctawhatchee Bay. A couple of hours later, we were near Destin and decided that we should spend the night there. By the time we had our anchor set in Destin Harbor, it was time for dinner. Since everyone had their fill of scallops, we piled into the dingy and headed for Harbor Docks Restaurant to dine on something else.

After a leisurely breakfast ashore in the morning of the 21st, we departed Destin Harbor and sailed the bay, and after a short stop at Pop's Fuel Dock, we were back tied up to the Surfview dock, mission complete.

During the months of August and September, we only picked up a few charters; the season was winding down. This gave us the opportunity to take a few weekend sails to Navarre and Pensacola with our friends. On one of these boondoggles, I noticed that our foremast had some rot, but I couldn't tell how extensive it was. I brought it to the attention of my partners for us to figure out what to do about it. We decided to wait until our regular annual visit to the boatyard to pull out the mast and make the needed repairs.

In October, my parents drove down to Debary, their tenant there had moved out, and they wanted to get it ready to rent again. They stayed for about a week turning it around and meeting with a rental agent. By the time they returned, I had all the monthly maintenance done, and with time on my hands, I was ready for a little adventure.

I walked down the Island a couple of blocks to visit Bill Leibold, who was busy working on his boat, the Yankee. He had just installed an autopilot and GPS navigation system, and he was chomping at the bit to take her on a shakedown cruise. That sounded like a good idea to me, and I told him I was available if he needed a crew.

A couple of days later, the Yankee was headed out Destin Pass on a broad reach on a direct course for Key West. The trade winds were actually blowing out of the northeast for a change at 15 to 20 kts. The GPS worked great, but the autopilot was turning the boat the wrong way. After a little wiring adjustment, it worked just fine. We only sighted one boat on the three-and-a-half-day sail to Key West, a tug pulling a barge. They must have been lonely because they called us on the VHF to chat.

Once thru the Northwest Channel into Key West, we made our way over to the old navy subbase where Bill had been stationed and tied up in one of the sub pens. The man in charge of the place let us use the bathroom and showers in what had been the navy administration building. After getting cleaned up, we walked over to our favorite bar in Key West, Rick's, for a beer.

At Rick's, we talked about where to go next. We could sail back to Fort Walton Beach or maybe sail on to the Bahamas. An easy decision, Bahamas it is, and Bill called up his wife Marie with the news. After some convincing, she agreed to meet us in Nassau. I called my girlfriend Nancy (fancy Nancy) about our plan and to get in touch with Marie to make travel arrangements if she wanted to participate. We also called our sailing buddy Rick Sauter, who was working at the time in Fort Lauderdale, to see if he wanted to go. He said he would come down to do part of the sail up the coast with us as far as Fort Lauderdale.

The rest of the day we spent provisioning the Yankee. At around four in the afternoon, Rick showed up with Steve Dowell, and we headed for Rick's. Steve was still managing his uncle's apartment complex in West Palm Beach and drove Rick down. He stayed the night to help us enjoy an evening in Key West before driving back to West Palm.

The next morning found us in the Gulf Stream sailing up the Florida Keys to Fort Lauderdale, where we tied up late in the afternoon at Pier Sixty-Six Marina for the night. We spent the evening walking around, definitely a more intense town than Key West, and eventually found a restaurant for dinner.

The next day after checking out with customs Bill and I finally got underway just after nightfall to cross the Gulf Stream. The ship traffic was heavy, keeping us on our toes, but it was a clear night, making maneuvering around the traffic a little easier. At the morning's dawn, we spotted the Great Isaac Light at the entrance to the Bahamas Northwest Providence Channel. We decided to stop at the small Island located 1km SSE of the light to catch lunch and explore the Island. There was nothing to see on the island, and we didn't catch anything. We hauled up the anchor and picked up our course to Nassau, the same course we took when Bill and I crewed the Silent Lady for Skip in 1986. After passing Great Stirrup Light, we were on our final leg to Nassau, arriving a little after noon. Once cleared into the harbor by Nassau Harbour Control, we made our way to the fuel dock at Nassau Yacht Haven to take on fuel and ice. Bill walked over to customs to clear in and get a cruising permit, and after picking up a mooring buoy, we dinked ashore for shore leave.

Marie and Nancy flew in the next day, ready for a little adventure. Once we had them settled on board the Yankee, Bill and I showed them around Nassau town, then took them in the dinghy over to the Atlantis Hotel and Casino on Paradise Island.

By morning everyone was raring to go, and after waiting for the sun to get high enough for us to see the coral heads in Montagu Bay and the Yellow Bank, we departed Nassau Harbour. Our destination, one of our favorites, was Staniel Cay, with a stop overnight at Allan's Cay to look at the lizards and maybe snorkel up some dinner. No luck; we dined on spaghetti.

With an early start in the morning and after a pleasant sail on the Bahama Banks, we made our way through the channel to Staniel Cay, tying up at the Happy People Marina. Our planning was good, arriving there in time for happy hour. Later on, we walked over to the Yacht Club to dine on some lobster.

After a late breakfast in the morning on the Yankee, we loaded into the dinghy to show Marie and Nancy Thunderball Cave. After a couple of hours of snorkeling there and on other small cays in the area, we headed back to the marina. In the afternoon, we walked around the village, ending up at the Yacht Club for dinner.

Late the next morning, we started our overnight sail on the banks to Nassau so Marie and Nancy could catch a flight back to the states. Our timing was good, and after a pleasant passage, the morning sun was high enough in clear skies for us to see the coral heads on our approach to Nassau Harbour. We were there early enough to give the girls plenty of time to catch their flight. Bill and I hung around Nassau, preparing for our journey back to Florida by taking on fuel, ice, food, rum, and beer. Once we got that all taken care of, we went over and anchored up by Paradise Island for the night and took the dinghy over to the casino to look around and shoot some craps.

With an early start in the morning, we sailed out of Nassau Harbour, heading for the good old USA. Our planned route would take the Bahamas Northwest Providence Channel out the same way we came in, cross the Gulf Stream, and clear customs at West Palm Beach. It was a good plan, but we only got as far as a small cay short of Great Stirrup Light.

Late in the afternoon, we spotted the cay off our starboard side and decided to check it out and maybe snorkel up some dinner. We maneuvered in close to the cay, anchoring in 10 ft of water. Bill caught a couple of shovel-nosed lobster, and I speared a grouper and an ugly black spider crab with legs around 2 ft long that I brought up and threw into the dinghy with Bill, freaking him out. We had a great meal that night on lobster, crab, grouper, peas, and rice washed down with a little rum.

A day later, after crossing the Gulf Stream in daylight for a change, we entered the USA at the Palm Beach Inlet. After checking in with customs at the Sailfish Marine, we continued up the intercoastal until dark, when we anchored up for the night.

Continuing our journey the next day, we traveled the intercoastal to Stewart, Florida, where we spent the night. The next day we followed the St Lucie River, then the St Lucie Canal to the Port Mayaca Locks onto Lake Okeechobee. After crossing the lake, we entered the Caloosahatchee Canal through the Locks at Clewiston and followed the canal where we anchored at sunset.

Motoring west the next day along the canal past LaBelle, where the canal turns into a river, we continued on until Fort Myers and Pine Island Sound, following it north to Cabbage Key, where we tied up for the night. We had a great evening meal there, followed by a good night's sleep.

Bright and early In the morning, we were ready to start the two-day sail direct to Destin and Fort Walton Beach. The weather was calm, so we motor-sailed up the coast to Clearwater, where we needed to make a stop and take on more fuel. We stayed tied up to the fuel dock and walked around finding a restaurant for dinner, and called it a night.

We departed Clearwater early in calm seas using the diesel engine. During the one-and-a-half-day

crossing of the Gulf of Mexico, we ran across quite a few turtles, big manta rays, and porpoise. Once through Destin Pass and the sound, we reached our destination, Bill's dock at his house on the Island. Bill's little shakedown cruise lasted about a month.

We were back in time for Thanksgiving at the Surfview; we had a bigger crowd than usual, around thirty people. My uncle Eric came up from the keys, and Jon brought over his girlfriend Maura from Tallahassee to join in on the feast. We had to set up extra tables to handle the crowd. It was definitely one of our better Thanksgivings.

We definitely needed to do something about the rot in the Pele's foremast. We found out that Jim Tucker had a new travel lift at his boatyard across the sound that was capable of hauling the Pele.

On the 7th of December, we moved the Pele over to the boatyard and pulled the foremast out, and set it up on wooden horses. We then took the Pele back to the Surfview; this would give me time to work on the mast before we hauled the Pele for her annual bottom job. For the next ten days or so, I was busy cutting out all the rot I could find with a skill saw, then shaped, glued, and clamped in pieces of pine to fill the voids.

On the 20th, we brought the Pele back over to Tucker's and hauled her out. While I gave the finishing touches to the foremast, my partners started on the hull. A day or two later, Jerry Dormany, the owner of the Hog's Breath, showed up at the boatyard with his good friend Senator John McCain and his wife Cindy to look over the Pele. We all got to chat with them during their short visit.

My sons Michael and Jon with his girlfriend Maura showed up to be with us for Christmas at the Surfview. My boys are now in their mid-twenties and well on their separate pursuits in

life. Jon was hanging around Tallahassee with his girlfriend awaiting orders from the Air Force, and Michael was in hot pursuit of an Olympic gold medal. Grandma cooked up a grand Christmas dinner with all the trimmings. It was nice having them around; who knows when we can all get together again.

Work continued on the Pele through the New Year; it was slow going, and most of our volunteer help were busy with the holidays. We did take a break to go to the New Year's party at the Hog's Breath with all of our friends.

Shortly after New Year, our insurance company informed us that they were not going to renew our hull and liability insurance because of their new policy of not insuring wooden boats. We searched all over, even Lloyds of London, but could not find an insurer. For all practical purposes, not

having insurance pretty much puts us out of the charter business. We still can have fun on the old Pele, so planning started for taking the Pele on a cruise to the Bahamas, hopefully before the start of hurricane season.

We finally launched the Pele on the 14th of January and re-stepped the foremast before motoring back to the Surfview. Over the next week or so, we were busy rigging the foresail to the foremast hoops and adjusting the shrouds with the lanyards on the deadeyes. By the end of the month, the Pele was ready for sea.

In February, my son Jon finally received his orders from the USAF to report for pilot training at Williams AFB, Arizona. Jon stopped by to say goodbye to us at the Surfview on his way west. His girlfriend Maura would eventually join him at Williams.

Over the next couple of months, we put the finishing touches on the Pele and started to seriously plan for our cruise. There was the same problem we had when we were planning the Bahama cruise on the Windsong. No one could take off for a month or more from their job but could fly out to meet us in the Bahamas. My girlfriend Nancy (Fancy Nancy), a schoolteacher in Alabama, would be available when school lets her out for summer vacation in May. I just needed a couple of hands to help me sail the Pele to the islands.

By early May, I had a deckhand lined up, Reggie Dean. Nancy found him in Alexander City, where she teaches school. He would help me sail the Pele as far as West Palm Beach. Once there, Steve Dowell arranged for us to tie up at his uncle's dock, where I would wait for more crew. Things were coming together, and we got busy getting the Pele ready. We loaded on the 20-man life raft, a Coleman Camp Stove to cook on (it fit just perfect on top of the Fisherman coal stove), two extra five-gallon fuel cans, and a can of gasoline for the Coleman, plus spare parts for the diesel and outboard.

The big plan was for Reggie to drive to FWB to help me sail the Pele to West Palm Beach. Then, when school lets out, Nancy would drive down to join me at Steve Dowell's uncle's dock. Reggie would then drive her car back to FWB, pick up his car, and drive back to Alabama. From West Palm Beach, Steve, Nancy, and I would then sail the Pele over to the Marsh Harbour in the Abacos. From Marsh Harbour, Steve could fly back to Florida, leaving Nancy and me to wait for Tom and Jack to fly in and join us with whoever they bring along. Nancy and I would be left to sail the Pele back to Fort Walton Beach.

On the 21st of May, Reggie and I cast off from the dock at the Surfview in the rain and motored into Choctawhatchee Bay and a 15 kt headwind. We made it as far as the 331 bridge at the east end of the bay, where we anchored up east of the bridge for the night. It was a miserable night bouncing around on the hook.

Next morning, we had the anchor up and were underway early. The wind was still blowing out the SE at 15kts. For the rest of the day, we motored down the ditch to Panama City. We anchored on the east side of the Hathaway Bridge by the No Name Bar and dinked ashore. Then walked a short distance to J.Michael's Restaurant for some food and drink. After having a good meal there, we stopped at the No Name on the way back for a couple of beers before calling it a night.

We were underway early on a rainy morning and headed for Apalachicola. After an uneventful motor down the intercoastal, we arrived at Apalachicola in the afternoon at around 18:00. Then nosed the Pele into the city's public boat basin, looking for a place inside to tie up. There wasn't any room inside, and in the process of turning around, the Pele gave a little kiss to an old 24' Chris Craft motorboat knocking off its antenna. Once I found a place to tie up, I went looking for the owner of the Chris Craft. I posted a note on the boat and, by inquiring around the dock, found out that a middle-aged couple lived aboard the boat. An hour later, they came walking down the dock, apparently from a bar; they were both drunk. I told them what happened, and we went aboard their boat to examine the damage. After a little negotiating on the cost of repair, they settled for $75. With the cash in hand, they immediately headed for the liquor store.

The weather deteriorated during the night, with rain squalls with high winds, we weren't going anywhere for a while. While I was nosing around down below, I found a small leak around the King Post, giving me something to do and re-calking it. Over the next couple of days, waiting on the weather, Reggie and I pretty much saw everything to see and do in Apalachicola.

Finally, on the 28th of May, the weather broke, giving us some good sailing conditions. After refueling at the municipal dock, we finally took the sail covers off and set sail. We sailed across Apalachicola Bay and then into the Gulf of Mexico through Dog Island Pass at 16:30, setting a course for Clearwater, Florida. Around midnight the wind died. So, we started up the diesel and motored on toward Clearwater. Ten hours later, we had the Clearwater Sea Buoy in sight, and by 21:00, we were anchored up inside by the causeway bridge for the night.

In the morning, after a good night's sleep, we motored over to the fuel dock to refuel. Then at noon, we sailed out the pass. We were having a nice sail down the coast until we were overrun by a thunderstorm; we hauled down the sails and started the engine that only a short time later started to overheat. We were abeam Egmont Key and maneuvered around to the lee of the key where we anchored. The usual culprit of an engine overheating is the water pump impellor, and once I took it apart and replaced it with one of the spares, we were good to go. It was already nightfall, so we decided to spend the night there on the hook.

Next morning, we hauled up the anchor and set sail to continue our sail down the coast, only to haul the sails down again when the wind quit, so we started the engine to motor down Sarasota Bay and out New Pass, then on down the coast to Boca Grande. Once through the pass there, we continued down Pine Island Sound to channel marker #60 near Cabbage Key, dropped the anchor, and dinked ashore just in time for cocktails and steaks at the Inn.

On the 1st of June, the beginning of hurricane season and we were underway heading down Pine Island Sound to Fort Myers Yacht Basin, where we stopped to refuel. We topped off the fuel and headed up the Caloosahatchee River to Lake Okeechobee. On the way, we anchored just short of Moore Haven for the night. What a miserable night the mosquitoes ate us alive. None of our insect repellants worked.

We were through the Moore Haven lock by eight in the morning and across the lake and through the lock at Port Mayaca at a little after noon. After making it under the dreaded railroad bridge, we followed the St Lucie canal and river to Stewart, where we tied up at the dock at the Sailor's Return Restaurant in time for happy hour.

After a great breakfast at the Sailor's Return in the morning, we continued our journey on the intercostal to West Palm Beach, where at 16:30, we tied up at Steve's uncle's dock. Phase one of the plan was now complete. The next day, the 4th of June, Nancy drove down to join us. She arrived late in the afternoon in time for us (Steve, Nancy, Reggie, and I) to go out to dinner. At dinner that evening, Nancy informed me that Jack wasn't going to make it and that Tom was going to bring his brother Jon along to meet us at Marsh Harbour. The original plan was still intact.

The next morning after thanking Reggie for his help, he headed north in Nancy's car while Steve, Nancy, and I started to provision the Pele for our crossing over to West End on Grand Bahama. Over the next couple of days, I changed the oil and filter for the diesel, refueled the Pele plus three fuel cans, one with fuel for the outboard, another with diesel fuel, and the last with gasoline for the Coleman Camp Stove, and restocked our spare parts supply. Nancy had brought down with her a small refrigerator from Alabama to deliver to Fred's (a friend) place on Treasure Cay in the Grand Abaco's, an island close to Marsh Harbour.

I called customs on the afternoon of the 7th of June to inform them that we were headed for the Bahamas. We were ready to go, and by 17:00hrs were sailing out the Palm Beach Inlet on a course for West End on Grand Bahama Island, Bahama.

It was an easy crossing in calm seas and not a lot of ship traffic, and by 03:00, we were anchored off of Settlement Point, West End, waiting for the sun to rise to make our way onto the banks at Indian Cay Rocks. From there, we sailed to Great Sale Cay by way of Mangrove Cay, where in the late afternoon, we anchored. The cay is uninhabited, so we loaded into the dinghy and went ashore to look around for treasure. On the way back to the Pele after our unsuccessful search, we snorkeled around for dinner: no luck. We settled for spaghetti that we cooked up on the Coleman and turned in early; it had been a long day.

After a good night's sleep, we awakened to a 20-kt. wind out of the northeast. We hauled up the anchor and started motoring into the headwind. By early afternoon we made it as far as Carter Cay, another beautiful uninhabited cay where we anchored. Over the next day and a half, we explored the cay and spent a lot of time snorkeling up our dinner, a good-sized grupper.

On the morning of the 11th, we departed Carter Cay for our next destination: Allen-Pensacola, another uninhabited cay along the way. What we found on our exploration of the island were some old, abandoned buildings and not much else; we ended up spending the night.

After an early departure in the morning, we sailed over to Treasure Cay to deliver Fred's refrigerator, we called him before we left, and he was waiting on the beach when we arrived. We anchored close to the beach and unloaded the refrigerator into the dinghy, and just like a bunch of smugglers brought the contraband to the beach. After helping Fred carry it up to his cottage, we sat around for a while drinking beer, our payoff. From there, we motored over to Green Turtle Cay, where we tied up to Government Wharf to clear customs and get our cruising permit, then moved the Pele over to the anchorage where we anchored and took the dinghy ashore for shore leave. We did a walkabout town, bought some supplies (rum), and eventually ended up at the Green Turtle Inn at their Club. A neat old place where cruising sailors congregate for cocktails and conversation; we had plenty of both before dinner, then headed back to the Pele for the night.

In the morning, Steve used the VHF radio to call a friend from Destin, Florida, Charles Morgan, the owner of Harbor Docks Restaurant there, who has a house on Great Guana Cay. Steve made contact with him, and during the conversation, Charles invited us to stop for a visit and gave Steve directions to where his house was and where we could anchor. We took Don't Rock Passage over the shallows to get by Whale Cay on the way to Great Guana Cay. Steve and I had sailed the passage seven years earlier on the Silent Lady when we about lost our dinghy attempting to sail around Whale Cay. I was a little apprehensive, but the seas were calm, and it was no problem navigating the passage with Steve on the bow looking for shallow water and coral heads. Once clear of the shallows, we followed the directions to the anchorage, and once securely anchored, we dinked ashore to meet our host.

We met Charles on the beach. He showed us around and introduced us to his local Bahamian caretaker, that watched over the place when he was gone. The caretaker had just returned from catching dinner and was in the process of unloading his catch of fish, crab, conch, and lobster. Being curious, I asked him where he caught the lobster. He told me that there was a shipwreck on the other side of the cay full of them and gave me landmarks to find it. Charles invited us to stay for dinner and to feast on the catch, and it was delicious. After dinner, we had some drinks, and he filled us in on the latest goings on in Destin and Fort Walton Beach before we returned to the Pele for the night; it had been a very enjoyable evening.

Upped anchor early for the short two-hour sail to Marsh Harbour, where we tied up to the fuel dock to refuel before anchoring up in the anchorage. That night we had dinner at the Conch Inn. Steve was flying back to Florida in the morning, so we celebrated our successful passage to Marsh Harbour.

On the morning of the 15th, Steve flew out, and a short time later, Tom Prohaska, president of Windsong Charters, and his brother Jon flew in. After loading their gear on board, we went on a walkabout town and later had dinner at the Colors by the Sea Restaurant, located close to the anchorage. During dinner, we talked over some of the places of interest that we could visit while they were here.

We sailed out of Marsh Harbour just before noon and took Don't Rock Passage with Tom on the bow looking for coral heads and shallows before sailing over to the anchorage at Green Turtle Cay.

By the time we anchored and dinked ashore, it was about time to go to the club and catch the end of happy hour. The chatter around the crowded bar was all about the upcoming 4th of July regatta, a big annual event for the island. During dinner, we decided to sail over to Hope Town with a stop on the way off the NW coast of Great Guana Cay to look for the wreck with all the lobster.

In the morning, after a leisurely breakfast at the Inn, we sailed out the channel and around Whale Cay to Great Guana Cay and anchored a little after noon, where there was supposed to be the wreck full of lobster. We all jumped in with our snorkeling gear expecting to see a shipwreck, but no such luck. After swimming around for what seemed like hours, we saw nothing but uneven sand and some small coral heads. Since we didn't catch anything, we had spaghetti and rum for dinner.

The next day at around noon, we hauled up the sails and set a course for Hope Town on Elbow Cay with an estimated time en route of five hours. We could see the Elbow Cay Lighthouse from a long way out and called Hope Town for a mooring. Once on the mooring, we loaded into the dinghy for shore leave. It was already early evening and getting dark, and we didn't have a lot of time to look around on our way to the Hope Town Inn for dinner

In the morning, we dinked over to the lighthouse and climbed the stairs to the top for a spectacular view of Hope Town. Around noon we cast off our mooring and sailed down Cherokee Sound to Little Harbour, where Randolph Johnson, the sculpture, has his foundry. Three hours later, we anchored close to the beach by Pete's Pub, the tiny shack on the beach that hadn't changed since the last time I was there years ago. There was no one around, so we walked over to the foundry's gift shop that was closed, but when they heard us, they opened up. They took us on a little tour and showed us how they forged bronze dauphins and other sea animals by using the disappearing wax method. With their help, Nancy forged a dauphin. She was delighted and bought it, along with a copy of Johnson's book. We were back onboard the Pele in time for cocktails and dinner by sunset.

In the morning, we sailed back up Cherokee Sound to White Sound, which led us to a small anchorage by the Abaco Inn. Its location is in an out-of-the-way place noted for its quiet, picturesque beauty and food. We were in place at their bar for happy hour and stayed for dinner, which was excellent. Next morning after a hearty breakfast at the inn, we sailed back to Cherokee Sound and followed it on over to Man O' War Cay, where we picked up a mooring and dinked ashore for a short walkabout. We were back on board by 15:00 and motored back to Hope Town, where we spent the night on a mooring.

On the morning of the 22^{nd,} we sailed back to Marsh Harbour to the fuel dock to refuel before anchoring in the anchorage. We had the whole afternoon ashore, where Tom and Jon were busy checking all the shops since it was their last day in the Bahamas. We later convened at the Conch Inn for cocktails and dinner.

Shortly after Tom and his brother Jon departed for the airport, it started to rain. For the next two days, the Pele stayed tied to the mooring buoy in the rain while Nancy and I cleaned up the boat, found a laundromat for our laundry, and did some maintenance on both the diesel and outboard. We actually enjoyed just hanging around; we did a little shopping to provision the boat, but most of the time, we just sat under the Pele's awning watching the rain.

Finally, on the 26th, the sun rose on a beautiful clear Bahama morning. Casting off from the mooring, we set course for Great Guana Cay to search again for the shipwreck full of lobsters. We were anchored and in the water hunting by noon at the site, this time with scuba gear. It all still

looked the same, but on closer inspection of the lumpy sand bottom, we found that it was the steel hull plates of the wreck covered with sand. The lobsters were hiding under the plates, and just as Nancy and I grabbed two good-sized lobsters for our bags, four big blacktip sharks showed up cruising around looking for something to eat. We stayed motionless for what seemed like forever before they swam away. That was enough for the day. We had plenty enough lobster for dinner. Later in the day, we moved the Pele around to the south side of the cay and anchored for the night, where it was calm. With the anchor set, we lounged in deck chairs, enjoying some wine and deciding how we were going to prepare our lobsters for a sunset dinner on the deck. We stayed on the hook for another day, using the dinghy to explore and snorkel around Great Guana Cay.

On the 28th, we departed Great Guana Cay and motored around Whale Cay and took the channel over to the anchorage by New Plymouth on Green Turtle Cay, where we anchored. Over the next couple of days, we explored with our dinghy; No Name Cay, Pelican Cay, Crab Cay and Manjack Cay. Then on the 4th of July, we watched the start of the Green Turtle Regatta and, when it was over, dinked over to the after-race party at Bluff House Beach that lasted until way late into the night.

The next morning at 09:15 on the 5th, we started our sail back to Florida, and by late afternoon, we were anchoring at Allen's/Pensacola Cay. While I was on the bow setting the anchor, Nancy jumped in with her snorkel gear, looking for dinner. Almost immediately, a barracuda struck at her wristwatch; unhurt, she was back on deck in a flash. I put out a line and caught the barracuda, but after a while, we decided it was too big to eat, so I threw it back in. We were anchored in 10 feet of beautifully clear water, and as we watched the barracuda sink to the bottom, about a five-foot shark attacked it and then hung around the Pele waiting for more; we decided to stay on board and eat spaghetti. When we threw our dinner scraps overboard, the shark was there waiting to gobble them up. The next day after sailing with a nice 15kt wind out of the NE for eight hours, we were by Great Sale Cay where we anchored just before being overtaken by a rainstorm. Mother nature was giving us an opportunity to get a freshwater shower, so we went up forward to the bow and took advantage of it by scrubbing each other down. The rain didn't last long, but it was long enough to do the job.

When we got up in the morning, there was another sailboat anchored near us named "Katrina's Bunny", and when they saw us getting ready to leave, they called us on the VHF and asked where we were headed. I told them we were bound for West Palm Beach; that's where they were headed, but they were having engine problems and wanted us to keep an eye on them crossing the Gulf Stream. I told them to meet us at West End, where we were going to anchor for the night.

At 06:00hrs in the morning of the 8th of July, we set sail and, keeping Katrina's Bunny in sight, we left the Bahamas in our wake. The crossing was uneventful, arriving at West Palm and the fuel dock at 17:30 to refuel and clear customs. We said goodbye to Katrina's Bunny and motored over to Steve's Uncle's dock for the night. Steve came over to meet us at the dock and took us out for dinner, where we bent his ear with our adventures after he left us at Marsh Harbour.

We stayed at the dock a couple of days partying with Steve and finally started up the intercoastal on the morning of the 13th, headed for the Sailor's Return Restaurant in Stuart, Florida. We tied up at their dock in time for dinner.

After a real early start in the morning, we motored down the St. Lucie River toward the Port Mayaca Locks and Lake Okeechobee. We made it as far as just west of Indiantown, where we anchored for the night.

Underway again in the morning to refuel in Port Mayaca and making it under the railroad bridge, we went through the lock into the lake. Once we entered the lake, we were engulfed in a cloud of blind mosquitoes that didn't sting but got in your nose, ears, eyes and mouth. Nancy hid down below for the 20 minutes it took to finally get clear of them. Other than that, the trip across the lake and the waterway across Florida was uneventful. A day and a half later, during the midafternoon of the 17th, we were anchoring in Pine Island Sound by Timmy's Nook, Captiva Island, on the west coast of Florida.

With a late start in the morning, we didn't make a lot of progress, only made it as far as channel marker # 60 by Cabbage Key, where we anchored for the night. We took the dinghy in for a nice leisurely dinner in the restaurant at the Cabbage Key Inn before heading back to the Pele for the night.

After a good night's sleep, we sailed out Boca Grande Pass and up the coast to Sarasota Bay by way of Big Sarasota Pass and were anchored up by Marina Jack by midafternoon. Once ashore, Nancy called her brother, who invited us to stay over at his place, where we hung out with him, his wife and their dog Gator for a couple of days.

By early morning on the 22nd, we were on our way motoring up the intercostal to Clearwater, arriving in the afternoon at the fuel dock where we topped off our fuel. We stayed at the marina that night and went out and found a nice restaurant for dinner before turning in early to get a good night's sleep for our two-day sail back to Fort Walton Beach.

In the morning, I checked the marine weather on the VHF; their forecast for the Florida big bend area of the Gulf of Mexico was calm seas with light and variable winds for the next couple of days. It looked like we would be running the diesel all the way. We were on our way and cleared out Clearwater Pass at 07:10, destination Fort Walton Beach.

It was an uneventful crossing until the afternoon when it started to cloud over, and the wind started up out of the NW in the direction we were headed. By nightfall, the wind had increased to 15kts, and it started to rain, and by midnight it was blowing up to 20kts with seas three to five ft. We were not making any headway, so I turned around and ran before the storm heading for Cedar Key. Just before dawn on the 24th, I sighted the sea buoy for the main ship channel into Cedar Key, and an hour later, I made the turn up the channel and anchored in the lee of Seahorse Key. We waited at anchor for a lull in the storm before moving the Pele to the dock at Cedar Key. Once tied to the dock, I realized that with all the wave action, it was too dangerous to stay there, so I moved the Pele away and anchored, then we went down below to take a nap as the storms raged.

It was still blowing pretty good when I woke up a couple of hours later and checked on the latest marine weather. The latest local conditions and forecast was that a stationary low-pressure area had formed over the big bend area of Florida; it looked like we were not going anywhere for a while. The weather calmed down a little later in the afternoon, and since there was no fuel dock at Cedar Key, I loaded the fuel cans in the dinghy, and we went looking for fuel. I found a gas station that had diesel fuel close to a fish dock and, after a few runs with the dinghy, filled the tank and the two fuel cans as a reserve.

Even though the weather stayed miserable with wind and rain, we ran around in the rain doing everything there was to do in Cedar Key. Nancy, on a shopping spree, bought some outdoor furniture that we loaded on the Pele to take back to Fort Walton Beach. The wind and rain never let up, and we were running out of things to do. It had been raining and blowing without letup for days; we had been there so long we were becoming part of the community. After taking part in a chicken wing eating contest, Nancy won and was invited to a city council meeting. We went to it and had a lot of fun. We were getting to know some of the local characters at this out-of-the-way hideout for artists, writers and eccentrics.

Nancy was getting nervous; she was running out of time and had to get back to Alabama for the start of school. I called and found a sailing buddy in FWB that would drive Nancy's car down to Cedar Key and help me sail the Pele the rest of the way to Fort Walton Beach,

On the afternoon of the 2nd of August, my new crew member drove in with Nancy's car. We showed him around the town in the rain and later settled in a café for drinks and some food before taking the dinghy out to the Pele. In the morning, the weather started to clear as Nancy loaded up her car to start driving to Alabama.

On the morning of the 3^{rd,} it was dead calm and not a cloud in the sky; we weighed anchor and made our way out of Cedar Keys by way of the Northwest Channel to the Gulf of Mexico. We would be running the diesel engine for as long as we were in calm conditions. The passage was pretty uneventful until 10:15 on the 4th when, after running for around 24hrs, the engine ran out of fuel. We should have had more than enough fuel, a full tank (60 gal.), to make it all the way to FWB. The cause was that the prop was fouled with seaweed that we may have picked up while leaving Cedar Key. The seaweed put an extra load on the engine, causing excessive fuel consumption. After pouring the fuel from the two five-gallon cans into the fuel tank, we were back underway and headed for Apalachicola to refuel. At the fuel dock in Apalachicola, we filled up our 60-gallon tank and figured that we had burned 2 ½ gal. per hr, twice the normal consumption rate. After refueling, we began our journey up the Apalachicola River until sundown, where we anchored for the night.

Two and a half days later, on the afternoon of the 6th of August, after an overnight stop at the No Name Bar in Panama City, we tied up to the Surfview Dock. It had been an interesting two-and-a-half-month cruise.

My parents had everything under control while I was gone and had supervised the Billy Bowlegs invasion party in June, so all was well at the Surfview. My partners in Windsong Charters kept up the search, trying to find an insurer to get us back into the charter business, but they were having no success; no one wanted to insure an old wooden boat. That didn't stop us from sailing the old Pele around the local area with our buddies.

During September, I flew out to San Diego for a reunion with the guys I flew with in C-130s while stationed at Okinawa during the Vietnam War. The reunion was held at the Hotel del Coronado. It was a lot of fun. I had a ball swapping war stories with a bunch of old trash haulers (that's what we were called by the fighter jocks).

While I was gone, my mom took my dad in for a checkup. She was concerned because he wasn't communicating and was not showing much emotion about anything. He was diagnosed with having the onset of Alzheimer's disease. This devastated the family; in just a short period of time, the disease progressed to the point where we had to watch him like a hawk, or he would just wander away. We had to install locks on the inside of the doors so he couldn't get out and disappear during the night. It was really hard on my mother; she was losing a lot of sleep worrying about her Bill. Every time I drove around town running errands, I would take my dad with me to give my mom a little break. We were trying to learn how to deal with it, but it was wearing on my mother's health, and it was obvious that we would have to do something about it.

In October, we finally found an insurer for Windsong Charters through Wooden Boat Magazine; we were back in business. The season was over, but we did pick up a charter for around the bay on the 13th of November and another on the 2nd of November. Plus, a weekend fun sail to Pensacola

in company with Fair Lady, Rick Sauter's sailboat. Our annual Thanksgiving feast went on as usual, and my dad seemed to enjoy all the activity; he still had a great appetite. During the Christmas holiday, both Michael, with his girlfriend Edithe and Jon, on leave from pilot training, came home. My girlfriend Nancy drove down from Alabama to join us all at the Surfview for Christmas dinner in my parent's apartment next door. It was a good feeling to have the boys' home again; I was seeing them less often now that they were out in the world pursuing their own destinies.

New Year was a quiet family celebration at the Surfview, just Mom, Dad and me.

1992

It became obvious that my dad was beyond our capability to take care of him. We tried taking turns watching him, but he would disappear in a second, freaking us out. He didn't know us anymore, and his wandering around the apartment at night was keeping my mother up worrying about him. He was taking a toll on us, especially on my mother. His doctor recommended that we put him in a facility that could take care of him and gave us a list of places to consider in the local area. We drove around checking them out and finally set him up at a place in Pensacola. It was close enough for my mom and me to drive over a couple of times a week and take him out to lunch; he didn't know us, but he still had a good appetite. On one occasion, when we went to

pick him up, he was walking around holding hands with a woman calling her Margaret (my mother's name); it just flat broke my mom's heart.

In February, I flew out to Arizona with my mother and uncle Eric for my son Jon's graduation from pilot training at Williams AFB, Arizona. On our arrival, Jon took us over to his house to meet his girlfriend Maura, then gave us a tour of the base and introduced us to some of his classmates and instructors. The next day we attended the graduation ceremony of class 92-07 and the pinning of his Pilot's wings. At the banquet that evening with my mom, uncle Eric, Jon and Maura, we enjoyed good food, plenty of wine and lots of conversation. I searched out Jon's flight instructor to chat with and get the lowdown on Jon as a student. He told me that Jon had great eye-hand coordination, essential for a pilot, but not so good in academics, kind of like his old man.

Jon's assignment was a banked pilot at Hurlburt Field as a finance officer, meaning that there weren't enough flying positions available for all twelve graduates. He would have to wait at that assignment until one was available, which was not all that bad since Hurlburt Field is just down the road from Fort Walton Beach. After signing in at Hurlburt, Jon moved in with his grandma, next door to his daddy. He wasn't back in town a week before he bought a sailboat, a used Catalina, 27 and tied it up to the Surfview dock.

In April, my son Michael was getting ready to compete again in the trials for the Olympics, this time on the Lechner A-390 board, to be held in Fort Pierce, Florida. I drove down to give him support. It was an exciting week of close competitive sailing, but in the end, Michael won and would be part of the U.S. Sailing Team at the Games of the XXV Olympiad to be held in Barcelona, Spain, starting on the 25th of July.

Once back at the Surfview, my mom Margaret, Jon and I started organizing a fundraiser for Michael. We ordered the T-shirts, hats, and bumper stickers, and once we had them, we handed them out to our friends to sell. The fundraiser was held the first weekend in May, a week before Michael was due to join up with the U.S.Sailing Team to attend briefings before leaving for

Europe. We had a pretty good crowd the day of the fundraiser and did raise enough cash to keep him in travel money for a while.

I drove up to Alexander City, Alabama, to visit my girlfriend Nancy during the second week of May. She took me with her to visit her professor at Auburn University; during the conversation, she wanted Nancy to go for her PhD by writing a thesis on the education systems in Europe compared to ours. Nancy wasn't too enthusiastic about doing it but told her professor she would think about it. Back at Alex City, we talked it over. I was already planning to go to Spain for the Olympics and maybe we could do both, I would be her cameraman and record her interviews for her thesis then go on to Barcelona for the Olympics plus it's good to have a travelling companion.

The more we talked about it, the more feasible it seemed, so she called her professor to accept the challenge, and we started planning. Nancy bought a video camera, airline tickets for an overnight flight to London on the 23rd of June, and Eurail passes to get around Europe. Nancy's neighbor, a retired railroad exec, had a house in Arrow, a small village northwest of London and a villa in Cala Murada, a town on the east coast of Mallorca. One of the Balearic Islands in the Mediterranean that I visited while on leave in the 60s. She chatted him up and arranged for us to stay at the house in Arrow during our first week in England and then the villa in Majorca for a week just before the start of the Olympics in Barcelona. The plan was defiantly coming together, and we were good to go. I told Nancy not to pack more than she could haul in one pass, meaning two bags and a backpack: wishful thinking on my part.

My son Jon was looking for a place to buy in town; he finally found and bought a condo located on the sound in Mary Esther close to his assignment at Hurlburt Field. The unit came with a boat slip that was just big enough for his boat. With Jon being close and while I was over in Europe, he would now be able to help around the Surfview and drive Grandma over to Pensacola to visit Grandpa while I was in Europe fooling around.

Windsong Charters managed to pick up three charters before I departed for England. Enthusiasm for operating and maintaining the Pele was waning; my partners were both married and didn't have much time to mess around with an old wooden boat. Since the Pele was in the best shape ever since we bought her, maybe it's also the best time to think about selling her.

Departing for our trip to Europe, Nancy didn't listen to me and showed up with one too many bags for our flight to England. On our arrival at Gatwick on the morning of the 24th of June, I rented a car. After getting used to driving on the wrong side of the road again, we started the 150-mile drive up the M40 looking for Arrow, a small village near Alcester in the Stratford-on-Avon district of Warwickshire. After a three-hour drive, we finally found the village, the house and our contact, who let us in and showed us around. Once we unloaded the car, I made another attempt to convince Nancy that she had way too many bags to travel around Europe on a train and needed to eliminate one of them. All to no avail; I was like talking to a brick wall. Once settled in, we went for a walk to look over the village and grocery shop. Later on, we went to the local pub for a couple of pints and some good old English pub food and to talk to the locals.

In the morning, we drove over to Stratford-upon-Avon and found their middle school, where Nancy made an after-lunch appointment for an interview. It turned out to be a good interview, considering it was our first one. Later in the afternoon, we checked out the Shakespeare Museum before driving back to Arrow. It turned out to be a long tiring day, and we were finally able to start adjusting to jet lag at the pub in Arrow with a couple of pints and English pub food.

The following day we drove over to the Cambridge, my old stomping grounds when I was stationed just up the road at RAF Alconbury thirty years earlier for her interview at Kings College. After the interview, I took Nancy punting on the Cam River and then on a little pub crawl of my old haunts. Later on, we drove up to RAF Alconbury, and to my surprise, it was still an active base; we decided to spend the night and got a room at the Guest House. At the bar in the officers club, the bartender (Rick), who I first met when I checked in at the base on the 4th of September 1960, was still there tending bar. We had a good time reminiscing the good old days. During dinner at the club, our waitress recognized me and remembered me by name, it kind of freaked me out, and as Nancy gave me a sort of cross-eyed look, I thought, uh-oh, maybe I had left some unclaimed baggage here. As it turned out, she had worked at the BX during the early 60s as a teenager and had a crush on me; I was flattered and breathed a lot easier. Alconbury was a trip down memory lane for me and a boring waste of time for Nancy.

Back at Arrow, I called up Tom's sister Jean in London to say hello, and she invited us to stay at her place in Kensington for a couple of days before we headed across the channel. We packed our bags, checked out of Arrow and headed for London. After dropping Nancy and our baggage at Jean's place in Kensington, I went and found a place to turn in the car. At dinner that evening, we had a wonderful time, Nancy and Jean hit it off, and the conversation during dinner was all about Nancy's thesis and ideas from Jean on how to do it. Jean is definitely the hostess with the mostess. After dinner, Nancy and I took a cab to the Palace Theatre in time to see Le Miserables.

Next morning, we thanked Jean for her hospitality and took a cab to St Pancras Station to catch the train to Dover for the ferry to Calais. After clearing customs in Calais and finding a cart for a bag drag, I used our Eurail passes to get seats on the train to Amsterdam. The extra baggage is a real problem; you either hire a porter or rent a cart to move it to the train platform. Once at the platform, you must check the bulletin board with the train makeup to make sure you get on the right car, or you will end up at the wrong destination.

On arrival at the Amsterdam Central Station, I checked in with the tourist aid desk to find us a hotel room close by. They found us one two blocks away on the Damrak, the main drag. Leaving Nancy sitting with our pile of bags at the train station while I walked over to the hotel with the heaviest bag and my backpack to check in, then went back to help Nancy with the rest of the bags. After settling in, we went out on the Damrak for a walkabout. We ended up at a restaurant on the Damrak for cocktails and dinner, followed by a stop at a nightclub to dance and get the tempo of the town.

When we finally got moving in the morning, Nancy found a school close by for an interview. During the interview, we learned that when they test their students during their last two years, it works as a gate to higher education. For the students who don't do well on the test, the school tries to place them in an occupation consistent with their aptitude. The school gave us an address of a restaurant that was participating in the program; Nancy called and arranged for an interview the next morning before they opened for lunch.

At the interview, the owner explained how it was supposed to work. For two days during the school week, the students are sent to work at the restaurant and hopefully learn the business. The restaurant gets free labor plus compensation for taking on the kids; the kids, in turn, get some hands-on experience in the restaurant business. Unfortunately, since drugs are legal in Amsterdam, the kids usually don't show up for work, and if they do, they're stoned and unable to work. A good program in theory, but as far as I could tell, it wasn't working.

The next day after we booked a compartment with our Eurail Pass on the overnight train to Berlin and then did some touring around Amsterdam before the train's departure. At the station, we were not at the right spot on the platform and scrambled to get on the train just before it left the station. We boarded the wrong car; the Russian Conductor informed us that his car was going to Moscow. He told us no problem and took our tickets, emptied people out of a compartment for us and assured us that the car wasn't going to be switched off for Moscow until after Berlin.

After an interesting and noisy train ride, we arrived in the morning at the Bahnhof Zoologischer Garten, the main train station in Berlin. At the station, I checked in at the tourist aid desk to find a hotel, and they found us one close to the Kurfurdtendamm, locally called the Ku'damm, Berlin's main street. Once settled in at our hotel, we went for a stroll on the Ku'damm, looking over all the shops and the remains of the bombed-out Kaiser Wilhelm WW2 Memorial Church, then took a cab to the Universitat der Kunste Berlin School of Art to set up an interview for the next morning. On the way back to our hotel, we found a beer garden where we enjoyed music, beer, and some good German food and stayed too long, having too much fun. It's surprising how much German you can understand after a couple of beers

We had a great interview with an assistant dean in the morning and had an opportunity to talk with some of the students that we met while getting a tour of the school. Afterward, at the beer garden, we took the opportunity to look over some of the interview videos before the Oompah band started to play and the beer started flowing.

The next day we walked to Checkpoint Charlie, then to the Tiergarten and on to the Brandenburg Gate, where we looked over the remains of the Berlin Wall, then continued walking through the gate to what used to be communist-controlled East Berlin.

We caught the early train in the morning for the eight-and-a-half-hour trip to our next destination, the Paris Gare du Nord train station. On arrival, tourist aid at the station found us a hotel close to the station, the Le Rocroy Hotel. By the time we got settled in our room, it was time for dinner. We found a small local restaurant called the L'Ardoise Gourmande located within a block of our hotel that was crowded, meaning they might have good food. We were the only non-French there, and everyone wanted to talk to us; even their dog came over and sat with us with his head on Nancy's lap while we ate. We had a wonderful time and enjoyed some excellent wine and French cuisine.

On the following morning, Sunday the 5th of July, we finally got moving to go sightseeing. We took the metro to the Champs-Elysees, then walked over to and up to the top of the Ach de Triomphe. For lunch, we went to the Jules Verne Restaurant on the 2nd platform of the Eiffel Tower. That afternoon we people watched from a café on the Champs-Elysees and finally ended up at the Champeaux restaurant in crowded Les Halles for a late-night dinner.

During breakfast in the morning, Nancy decided that she had enough data for her thesis and would not look for a school in Paris to interview. That revelation freed us up to see more of Paris. So as soon as we finished breakfast, we took the metro to Les Halles and walked the bridge over the Seine River to look over Notre Dame Cathedral, the center of Paris. From there, we walked up to the Basilique du Sacre-Coeur de Montmartre: the church on the highest spot in Paris. After touring the basilica, we had lunch at a little outdoor café nearby with a great view of the city. That night we went to the Crazy Horse Saloon, a cabaret on Avenue George V and enjoyed the show and expensive drinks. The following day we took the metro to the Musee du Louvre, where we spent most of the day, during which we had the opportunity to gaze upon Leonardo da Vinci's Mona Lisa and her smile. We took a break from the Louvre for a very tasty lunch at the close by Le Café Marly on the Rue de Rivoli.

In the morning, Nancy was feeling guilty about not getting an interview in Paris, so on our morning walkabout, we stopped at the Universite Paris Diderot, where she did manage to get a short interview in their admissions office. After lunch, we made our way over to check out the Musee de l'Armee, followed by a short walk over for a look at Napoleon's Tomb. That evening for dinner, we had another great meal at the little local restaurant with the dog near our hotel.

While in Paris, Nancy contacted her brother's wife's sister, Carol, who lives in Florence, Italy, who years ago had met and fallen in love with a street vendor while touring in Florence. She married him and now has two teenage kids and said she would love for us to stop by for a visit; we happily accepted the invitation. After all, our schedule was flexible.

On the morning of the 8th, after a late start, we walked over to the train station and used our Eurail Pass to book a compartment on the overnight train to Florence, then had lunch at the restaurant down the street from the hotel. After lunch, we packed up and checked out of our hotel, then took a cab to the Paris Gare de Lyon train station to catch the 19:15 train to Firenze (Florence), a fifteen-hour journey. Once the train left the station, we ordered an ice bucket for the bottle of champagne that we had brought with us. Once settled in our compartment, we headed for the dining car, where we had a nice, relaxed meal before returning to our compartment to our champagne and to watch the lights of the night pass by our window. I've been to Paris three or four times, always enjoyable, and there's always more to see; maybe next time I'll get to Versailles.

Just before noon, we pulled into the Firenze Santa Maria Novella station and were met there by Carol's husband, Philip. After a short drive, we dragged our bags up to their small three-bedroom apartment. After meeting Philip's mom and the kids, Philip and I went out shopping for dinner; he bought the groceries, and I bought the wine. He was a friendly guy, and we hit it off even though I had no Italian and he spoke only broken English, but after a little wine, I understood his every word; I volunteered to help him prepare the meal and to aid us in the process we drank some wine as we cooked. I don't know about everyone else, but we were having a good old time in the kitchen. After the meal, which turned out to be pretty good considering our condition, to accommodate Nancy and me, they were going to move their teenagers, a boy and girl, to a couch and rollaway. Nancy and I convinced them that the couch was good enough for us.

Over the next two days in Florence, we visited Michelangelo's statue of David at the Galleria dell'Accademia, the Riccardi Medici Palace, with its art museum & famous chapel and climbed up into the dome of the Cathedral of Santa Maria del Fiore. We made sure we were back every day with a couple of bottles of wine in time for the dinner feast prepared by Philip and/or his mother. Carol, Philip, their kids and Philip's mother were wonderful hosts, and we enjoyed every minute of our stay with them in Florence.

On the morning of the 12th, we flew out of Florence bound for Majorca. We landed at the Aeroport de Palma just before noon, rented a car and drove over to the California Hotel in Palma, where the tourist aid at the airport booked a reservation for us. The same hotel I stayed in thirty years earlier while on leave from RAF Alconbury. They upgraded the hotel a lot over the years; I hardly recognized the place except for the small bar that hadn't changed much.

In the morning, after breakfast at the hotel, we started our drive across Majorca to look for our contact in Cala Murada. After getting lost a couple of times, we finally found the town and our contact. He took us over to our villa that was located close to the beach, and once we moved all our baggage in, we did a walkabout town to check it out. What we observed was that there were just two bars/restaurants, a grocery store, a nightclub and a town full of Germans on holiday. Over the next four days, we hung out at the beach by our villa, where we chatted with the Germans. I can understand and speak a little German, but fortunately, they can all speak English. They gave us tips on the best restaurants in town and around the local area, and we tried them all.

I also made contact with my son Michael who was in place at the Olympic Village in Barcelona, and asked him to find us a place to stay near the sailing venue. When he called back, he told me that there were no rooms available in town and could only find for us a hotel on the outskirts of Barcelona, a half-hour drive from the venue; not good enough.

As we approached our departure date from Majorca, Nancy was getting antsy and getting hard to get along with. She had everything she came to Europe for, all the data needed to write her thesis. So maybe she was getting tired of my crap, and the romance was over, whatever the reason I told her that I was heading for Barcelona for the Olympics. She was welcome to come with me, but she needed to change her attitude or change her ticket and head back to Alabama; it was her decision to make. She finally opened up and told me that she feared going to crowded Barcelona during the Olympics, not knowing where we were going to stay. I reassured her that I would find a place on our arrival in Barcelona. I've never had a problem traveling around Europe using tourist aid at the train stations to find a place to stay at a fair price; why would Barcelona be any different. She decided to tag along, promising to be a good companion.

When we flew out of Majorca on the 17th, my plan was that once we arrived in Barcelona, take a cab to the brand new Estacion de Francia and have the tourist aid office there find us a hotel. When we arrived at the station, it was pretty much empty and no line at the tourist aid desk. Talking to the agent, I asked her to find us a room close to the Olympic Sailing Venue. After she searched around for a while, she found us a small hotel in the center of Barcelona just off La Rambla de Barcelona, the main street in Barcelona. She also warned us that it was located in the high crime part of town with a lot of pickpockets, pretty much standard for any major city in Europe.

The hotel Ingles was rated a one-star hotel, located on the Carrer de la Boqueria, an alley that's 200ft from the Rambla and 200ft away from the Basilica de Santa Maria, a Catholic Church that rang its bells during the day. The room wasn't all that bad, it did have a connecting bath, and the staff were friendly Algerians. Once settled in our room, I contacted Michael to let him know where we were located and arranged to meet him and Edithe for dinner. Edithe was over at the Olympics as a training partner for the Canadian in the female Lechner A-390 event.

Our hotel's location was perfect, a two-minute walk to the Rambla and a short 15-minute walk to the sailing venue at the Barcelona Marina. We spent the rest of the day on a walkabout town and stumbled across some of Antoni Gaudi's buildings and his renowned unfinished Sagrada Familia Basilica that he started in 1880, where we took a tour. Later on, I bought tickets for the following Sunday to the bullfights with seats on the shady side of the Plaza del Toros. That evening we met up with Edithe and Michael for dinner at a restaurant that had been recommended to them. We had a wonderful meal and conversations about life in the Olympic Village and our travels around Europe. After dinner, they headed back to the Olympic Village. Nancy and I adjourned to the Café de L'Opera just around the corner from our hotel on the Rambla for a nightcap. The café was crowded with a band playing, people dancing, and cheap drinks, my kind of place.

Over the next couple of days, we slowly adjusted to the rhythm of life in Barcelona. Once we were up and moving in the morning, we would have breakfast at a small café located on the Rambla median that was just wide enough for small cafés and vendors. After breakfast, we would wander around town until lunch, at around two in the afternoon, and go back to the hotel for a two or three-hour siesta. Then after the sun went down, we would go for a stroll and look at the sights on the Rambla until dinner at around 9 p.m. After dinner, we'd walk over to the Café de L'Opera, our now favorite hangout, and close out the evening.

On the 24th, Michael called us to come on over to the marina to pick up our passes for the opening ceremony at the Olympic Arena and passes for access to the pier at the marina to watch the Windsurfing competition. Our walk took us by the city government buildings that were flying the flags of both Spain and Catalonia. Barcelona is the capital of the Catalonian District of Spain.

They, the Catalonians, have been trying to get their independence from Spain since the Spanish revolution in 1936. When we arrived at the marina, Michael was there to meet us with our passes for the opening ceremony and then took us over to the security office to fill out the paperwork for our passes to the marina and pier. Security gave Nancy and me each two passes, one for the first day on the 27th and one for the third day on the 29th. This is the same thing that happened to me at the 1988 Olympics in Korea; not good enough. So now I have a mission to try and figure out how to get in to cheer on my son at all the races.

On the evening of Saturday the 25th, Nancy and I, to the sound of opera, started the long slow walk up the crowded stairs to the top of Sants-Montjuic and the Stadium Estadi Olimpic Lluis Companys for the opening ceremony of the XXV Olympics. The ceremony began by parading the Olympic flag around the stadium to the sound of the "Romiossine" sang by Greek messo-soprano Agnes Baltsa, followed by the raising of the Spanish and Catalan flags. After a couple of speeches, the Olympic flame cauldron was lit by a flaming arrow shot by a Paralympic archer (a spectacular moment). Followed by more speeches and operas performed by other famous singers. At the end of the ceremony was the parade of nations, where all the participating nations' athletes did a lap around the stadium. After the ceremony, Nancy and I walked back over to the Rambla and the L'Opera bar.

Sunday morning, we woke up to the sound of church bells ringing; there's no such thing as sleeping in at this hotel. After a marvelous breakfast on the Rambla, we went on our usual walk around town. In the afternoon, we walked over to the Plaza del Toros and found our seats on the shady side of the 18 000 seat bullring. There were six bulls and three Matadors. Each Matador gets to fight two bulls for up to 15 minutes each and has a crew of six assistants: two Picadores mounted on armored horses, three Banderilleros(flagmen) and a Mozo de espada (the lad of the swords).

It was a hot afternoon in the sun when the start of the bullfight was announced by a trumpet. I tried to give Nancy a heads up on what to expect. I explained to her that when a bull enters the ring, he's wearing a rosette, the colors of the estate it came from nailed to its back. The Banderilleros are next to enter the ring to entice the bull by making passes with their capes for the Matador to observe the bull's ferocity. Then two Picadores on their horses enter the ring and stab the bull's neck muscle with their lances, followed by the Banderilleros, who reenter the ring and plant their two barbed sticks decorated with paper flags into the bull's neck. This is all done to weaken the bull to the point where he can't hold up his head, restricting his vision (bulls are color blind), so he only sees the Matador's moving cape and hopefully not the Matador.

The Matador then enters the ring with a small cape (muleta) and sword. He uses the cape to attract the bull in a series of passes, getting closer and closer to the bull with each pass. Then in a final act, he thrusts the sword, called the estocada, in for a quick and clean kill by piercing the bull's heart. For an exceptional performance, the crowd can partition the president of the ring by waving their handkerchiefs to award the Matador with one or two ears and maybe even a tail. Nancy was horrified.

Our first Matador must have given a good performance. The audience waved their handkerchiefs, and he was allowed to do a lap around the ring and was given an ear. During the second fight, the Matador got gored a little just before he killed the bull; he was bleeding when he left the ring. He wasn't hurt all that bad, they patched him up fast, and he was back in the ring, good to go in time for his second bull. Nancy didn't seem to be impressed by all the pageantry of a bullfight. After it was over, we walked down to the Rambla and the Café de L'Opera for a drink.

Next morning, we walked over to the marina for the first day of racing. Our pass for the day got us in; we found Michael and gave him a pep talk, then walked out and found a good spot on the pier to watch the start of the race. We weren't really close enough to see what was going on, just a lot of sails moving around the course. Michael finished 3rd, off to a good start and after the race, we went over and talked to him about his competition. While talking to one of Michael's friends that worked for the U.S. sailing team and told me that his pass gave him unlimited access to the

marina, I asked him if there was a way for us to get more access to the marina. After talking for a while, he explained to me that every day they issue the day's spectator passes with the date written in a different way and the name of the individual with a different color marker. While talking to him, we worked out a plan whereby Nancy and I would leave our passes with him when we departed the marina. Then in the morning, he would clean our passes with a solvent and mark them the same way they were being marked for the day and meet us outside the gate with our passes. The next day, as planned, he met us outside the fence with our forged passes. It worked like a champ and for every race day thereafter.

After the third day of racing, Nancy ran out of time and packed her bags and flew back to Alabama to get ready to teach school. In a little over a month, we have seen and experienced a lot during our adventures and travels around Europe and learned a lot about each other.

Edithe, Michael's girlfriend was running out of money and would be forced to leave Barcelona before the games were over. She had an unlimited pass for the marina as a private trainer but not

the Olympic Village; she needed a place to stay. Michael had been sneaking her into the Village, but they eventually got caught. Being a good guy, I volunteered to share my hotel room with her. I had the hotel put another bed in my room and then helped Edithe lug her bags over to the hotel.

For the duration of the Windsurfing competition, my new roommate Edithe and I would walk over to the marina to watch Michael compete. After the day's competition was over, we were able to spend an hour or so with him before he went back to the Olympic Village. In the evenings, Edithe and I would go to dinner, trying different restaurants, and on the way to the hotel, after dinner, we would stop at the Café de L'Opera for a drink. At the café Edithe, being a pretty woman was always being hassled by the young bucks; to keep them at bay, she would tell them that I was her sugar daddy. It worked like a champ; they left her alone.

She's a great sport and a good dancer.

The last day of competition for Michael was the 4th of August; he was going into the race in the winning position for the gold. But after the races were over, when the committee tallied the score, Michael finished second .4 of a point behind the winner Frank David of France. The award ceremony was held shortly after the last race, where Michael was presented with the silver medal. Needless to say, Michael thought he had the coveted gold medal in the bag; well, a bag cost him the race. He snagged a plastic bag with the fin on his Lechner A-390 board that slowed him down as he headed for the finish line allowing Frank to finish ahead of him. A silver medal was also won by other members of the U. S. Sailing Team from the Panhandle of Florida, Randy Smyth and Keith Notary, competing in the Tornado event. Not bad for sailors from the Redneck Riviera!

Michael was done competing, and there were still a few days left of competition before the closing

ceremony on the 9th. Over the next couple of days, we went to the Boxing competition and to some of the events in the Track & Field competition. We did get to see Oscar De La Hoya box in the Lightweight event, where he would win a gold medal. One of the interesting pass times for people attending the Olympics was the swapping of the different country Olympic event pins. I'm guessing that the objective is that whoever collects the most pins wins.

The closing ceremony for the Games of the XXV Olympiad was held on the evening of the 9th, and during the ceremony, they announced that the 1996 XXVI Summer Olympics would be held in the United States in Atlanta, Georgia.

The games were over, and the next day Edithe and I packed up our bags, called a cab and checked out of the hotel. I dropped Edithe off at the train station on my way to the airport for my flight back to the USA. I really enjoyed her company, and she was a pleasure to be around during our stay together in Barcelona. Michael would be leaving a couple of days later, traveling with the sailing team.

Once back at the Surfview, I found that Jon and Mom had everything under control. My mom had all the apartments rented, and Jon had the grass mowed and the place looking good. Mom and I drove to Pensacola to visit Dad and were informed that they were going to perform a second operation on him for a bed sore. Mom and I looked him over and decided to get him out of there. We grabbed his stuff, loaded him in the car and drove him home to the Surfview. Sadly, when we arrived, he didn't know it was his home and didn't know who we were. Over the next couple of days, we took him to a doctor who agreed with us that he didn't need an operation and helped us find a facility in the local area for him. Mom and I had very little sleep looking after my dad until we finally found a place for him in Fort Walton Beach.

Shortly, our Olympic athletes would be back in the neighborhood, and we started planning for their arrival. As it turned out, we didn't have to plan anything; Pensacola and Fort Walton Beach Chambers of Commerce organized a reception to meet the medalists at the Pensacola Municipal Airport, followed by a motorcade through Pensacola and Fort Walton Beach.

On the 24th, a shiny new red convertible showed up, being driven by Michael's friend Jack Springfellow to take my mother Margaret, Jon and me to Pensacola to meet Michael at the airport and join the motorcade through Pensacola. When the motorcade arrived in Pensacola, we were met by a large crowd to welcome their local heroes back home from the Olympic games. After a couple of speeches by local dignitaries, Michael, Randy and Keith each gave a short speech to their fans. Then after Michael signed autographs and talked the talk with his fans, and as the crowd dispersed, Jack drove us home to the Surfview in the red convertible that was on loan for the occasion from a local Ford dealer.

On the 10th of September, the United States Olympic Sailing Team had a meeting and photo op with President Bush and First Lady Barbara, Michael's second time, at the White House. The President and the First Lady congratulated the team for their good work and then took the time to talk individually to some of his Olympians. Michael was one and had a short, enjoyable chat with them. Michael was getting all kinds of attention; he even had a photo shoot with Annie Leibowitz, the famous photographer for the cover of WindSurfer magazine.

Windsong Charters so far this year didn't have many charters, and I didn't help matters by being out of the country during the peak of the charter season. But we did pick up a couple of around the bay day charters for the Pele during the last week of September and October.

It was horrible for me to watch my father slowly waste away; then, three days before my son Michael's birthday, my father died of Alzheimer's, a terrible disease, on the 22nd of November 1992, he was 84 years old. He was born in Thalheim, Germany, on 9 October 1908 and brought to the United States on the 16th of December 1916 by his father Emil (Pop) with his mother Frieda, his brother Eric and sister Dora on the S.S. New Amsterdam. My grandfather worked in a hosiery mill in Irvington, N.J., and when my dad was old enough, he got him a job there. It was tough work on your feet all day in a dusty, noisy factory. My mom and I would stop once in a while to say hello to my dad at work, giving me an opportunity to watch my dad operating a huge knitting machine that absolutely fascinated me.

My father's funeral was on the 25th, Michael's birthday, followed by a get-together of remembrance at the Surfview for friends and relatives. Dad was a wonderful father, and I will miss his wisdom and humor. He instilled in me the concept of not buying until you had the means to pay for it. He was also blessed with the ability to fix anything mechanical or otherwise. I got that from him, but I didn't get his weird sense of humor that was inherited by his grandson Jon. I'm grateful for the fact that my parents lived next door, enabling my sons and me to spend a lot of time with them over the years.

Christmas and New Year at the Surfview were quiet and reflective events.

Chapter Eight: 1993 - 1999

In January, our insurance for the Pele was again terminated; the insurance company's excuse was that the boat was too old and made out of wood. We searched around, but no one wanted to insure an old wooden schooner, and without insurance, we were out of business. By the end of February, with no insurance and facing the reality of the situation, Windsong Charters had a meeting on board the Pele, and after much debate and a few beers, it was decided that we would put the Pele up for sale and started advertising in the local area. We were out of the charter business, but that didn't stop us from sailing the Pele around the local area loaded up with our friends. Over the next couple of months, we were having lots of fun but getting very few inquiries on the Pele. With no income from charters to pay for the ongoing maintenance, the Pele was becoming a hole in the water that we were just throwing money into. We were running out of options, sell it, sink it or give it away. We were all too cheap for the last two choices, so we had to sell it.

On the 5th of April, we had a prospective buyer come over to look over the Pele. My son Jon happened to be there at the time and suggested we take him out of a short sail. Sounded like a good idea to me, so we took him out for a short sail on the bay. It was a beautiful day, and the longer we sailed, the more interested he became. Jon and I showed him the characteristics of sailing a schooner; it helped that he had some experience sailing. Jon gave him the tour of the boat, telling him how great and how much fun he could have if he bought it. Jon was doing a great job of selling the boat. He also found out that he was a lawyer that lived in Alabama and had relatives in Panama City with a big enough dock for the Pele if he bought it.

Later that week, he called me and indicated that he wanted to buy the Pele. I called my partners to give them a heads up and arranged a date for a meeting with our prospective buyer to negotiate the sale. During the negotiations, he said that before closing the deal, he wanted to have a survey done on the Pele, we agreed, but it would be on his dime. We also agreed to deliver the Pele to Panama City after the sale was complete.

We told him to contact Jim Tucker to arrange a date to pull the Pele at his boat yard for the survey. He didn't waste any time, and later that week, he called me to take the Pele across the Sound to Tuckers for the survey. He brought in a licensed surveyor from Pensacola to do the survey; my partners and I held out breaths, we knew of a few things that were wrong with the boat, and if he found them, it could maybe queer the deal. The survey took only about a week and found only a few minor things that we promised to take care of; our buyer was satisfied, and later that day, he presented us with a check for the Pele.

Now that Windsong Charters Inc. was without a boat, our subchapter S corporation was out of business. Tom Prohaska, the president of our corporation, met with our accountant to find and file the documentation to dissolve Windsong Charters Inc. Once all the paperwork was filed, we went over to the Hogs Breath for a couple of beers to celebrate.

On the 5th of May, my mother, my son Michael and I went to my son Jon's promotion ceremony, where I had the honor to pin on his 1st Lieutenant bars. We then adjourned to the Surfview for a little promotion party.

On the morning of the 22nd of May, Tom Prohaska, Rick Sauter, Tom Stewart, and I set sail to deliver the Pele to her new owner in Panama City. Once underway, Rick headed to the galley and cooked up an elaborate breakfast for us. We had fair weather and an enjoyable sail the length of Choctawhatchee Bay. Once we entered the canal at Point Washington, we dropped the sails, started the Westerbeke diesel, and motor-sailed the rest of the way to West Bay,

where we anchored out of the channel for the night. It was a beautifully clear night, and after dinner, while enjoying a few beers on deck and talking about some of the more notable adventures we all had over the years while sailing on the Pele. It was a fun evening.

In the morning, after breakfast, we hoisted up the anchor and set sail for our final destination, the marina on the other side of the Hathaway Bridge in Panama City. The sail across West Bay was uneventful with a fair wind and clear skies, and after a four-hour sail, we tied up the Pele at the marina and handed her over to her new owners. Jack Brown was waiting with his truck to drive us back to Fort Walton Beach, marking the end of our sailing adventures on the Pele.

As the summer wound down, my ex-partners and I went about doing our own thing. I was spending a lot of time on needed maintenance at the Surfview while Jack and Tom were busy with their jobs and wives. Jack and his wife Linda lived in Niceville, a forty-minute drive to the beach, so I didn't

see much of them, especially after Jack's parents, that lived in my parent's condo at the El Matador, had passed away. Tom and his wife Donna lived on the island and would meet up with them occasionally.

For Thanksgiving, we had the usual feast at the Surfview, supervised by my mother Margaret, with the usual crowd of friends and residents in attendance. The party was a lot of fun but was cut short by the weather, it clouded over, and the wind kicked up just as the party was cranking up.

In December, Jon took some leave and went up to Boston with his girlfriend Maura to spend the Christmas holidays with her parents. My mom and I headed south, and my uncle Erik drove north from Marathon to meet up with us in Fort Pierce to be with Michael for the holidays. Michael's girlfriend Edithe flew up to Canada to be with her parents for the holidays.

Michael, a vegetarian, conjured up a great Christmas dinner with the help of his grandma, even though he endured a lot of kibitzing from Eric and me. After the meal, while having after-dinner drinks, Eric complained of having a hard time breathing. Michael and I loaded him into the car and drove him to the emergency entrance at the hospital, where they admitted him. After waiting a few hours, I asked the nurse how he was doing; she told us that he had congestive heart failure. They treated him by dehydrating his lungs, and after a couple of hours on the IV, he was good to go, and they released him. They gave him their diagnosis and told him to go see his doctor when he got back to Marathon. Driving back to the house, I asked him how long he has had congestive heart problems; he told me there was nothing wrong with his heart and that it was just indigestion. I didn't press the issue since he didn't want to talk about it.

My Mom, Eric, and I stayed on in Fort Pierce at Michael's and helped him celebrate the New Year. We went to a party that Michael knew about at a bar/restaurant in Stewart, Florida, just down the road from Fort Pierce a couple of miles. We all had a great time, and my uncle's heart problem didn't seem to slow him down any. He was in his glory flirting with all the ladies, young and old, and Eric, forever the showman, kept us all well entertained. We stayed until the crowd started to thin out. Considering that three of the four of us had some kind of heart condition, we were definitely pressing the envelope.

1994

The next morning, the 1st of January, we finally got moving. My mom and I started the six-hour drive to Fort Walton Beach; Uncle Eric headed back south to Marathon. Considering all that happened, we all had a wonderful time bringing in the new year.

The New Year started out good but didn't stay that way even though the Surfview had full occupancy, and everyone appeared to enjoy the pleasant weather. Early on the 14th of January, my mom and her girlfriend Lillian Rosas from the apartments next door drove out to Eglin AFB to catch the bus for a day trip to the Biloxi, Mississippi casinos to play the slot machines. On the way back late in the afternoon, the bus stopped halfway back for a rest stop, but when the bus arrived at Eglin, they found that my mom had died; she had a heart attack somewhere between the rest stop and Eglin AFB.

My mother was a successful businesswoman and the matriarch of the family. Born in Bloomfield, New Jersey, on March 18, 1909, into the family of Jacob and Helen Patson, the second oldest of eight children. She was a loving mother and grandmother and an inspiration in my life. Her ambition and ability to make decisions inspired me to be able to have and make my own. She was the first one in the family to go to college, taking night classes at Princeton during the war, and earn a degree in education. She also volunteered during the war as a nurse's aide at the hospital in Irvington, New Jersey. After the war, my mom used her degree to start a nursery school business, Pinewood School. After a couple of years, their preschool business expanded, and they bought an old boarding school in Lakewood, New Jersey, and opened a second school, Lakewood School. At this point, my dad started working for their businesses as a maintenance director and driver. They ran the schools until 1970, when they sold both schools and retired to DeBary, Florida.

Michael came up from Fort Pierce to join Jon and me for their grandmother's funeral, which took place on the 18th of January at St Mary's Catholic Church in Fort Walton Beach, Florida, and laid to rest at Beal Memorial Cemetery next to her husband Bill, my dad, the love of her life.

After the funeral, we had a wake at the Surfview Apartments for friends and family to reminisce on her life and the years that she supervised activities around the apartments and how much fun we had with her. It was a sad time for me and the boys, they missed their grandma, and I missed my mom. It didn't take long for me to realize that I was now the oldest person in the family and had no parents to go to for comfort and advice; it was definitely a rude awakening.

Michael headed back south to Fort Pierce after the funeral to pursue another attempt at a gold medal in the upcoming 1996 Olympics. While working at his day job in the Air Force as a finance officer at Hurlbert Field, Jon took night courses studying for an MBA at the local Troy State University. I went about doing my job managing and maintaining the Surfview, life goes on, but memories go on forever.

In late April, I went in for the annual echo cardiogram of my heart. While being scanned and chatting with the technician, he mentioned that it looked like the left ventricle of my heart had enlarged a little. The next day at my appointment with my cardiologist, he confirmed what the technician told me and prescribed getting an echo cardiogram every six months instead of every year; the wrong answer. The next day I called the Cleveland Clinic in Ohio and told them I needed an appointment to get my heart fixed. They asked who was referring me; I told them that I was. That's when they told me that they could not schedule me until they received more information, like medical records and diagnoses. Over the next week, I rounded all my medical records from the different doctors and hospitals that I went to over the years and sent them all up to the clinic. A week later, the Cleveland Clinic called and scheduled me to come up for an evaluation during the second week of June.

At the beginning of June, my Uncle Eric flew up for a visit; he is always a lot of fun to hang out with. I told him that I was going up to Cleveland to get my heart fixed in a week and asked if he wanted to go up and get evaluated with me. He thought about it for a minute or two and agreed. I called the clinic, and after I explained his heart problems, they told me to bring him along. In preparation for going to Cleveland, I got on my computer and started writing my will in case I didn't survive and asked Eric if he had a will. He didn't, so I wrote one up for him. While I worked on our wills, we talked about the disposition of our bodies. I opted to be buried in the family plot in Fort Walton, and Eric indicated he wanted to be cremated and his ashes spread on the Gulf Stream like his wife, Elfriede. We filed our wills at the courthouse and got certified copies. Over the next couple of days, we had a good old time running the bars with my friends.

The day we were scheduled to fly up to Cleveland, Eric had an attack; he could hardly breathe. I drove him to the hospital emergency room, where they admitted him with having congestive heart failure. After talking to the doctor and getting his diagnosis, I got on the phone and canceled our flight to Cleveland and our appointments at the Cleveland Clinic. I asked if we could reschedule at the clinic, and they said they only had one opening on the 1st of July; I booked it.

Checking on Eric at the hospital, his doctor told me that Eric would be in the hospital for a while. I was running out of time and told Eric about my appointment at the Cleveland Clinic in July. He really wanted to go to the Miami Heart Institute, so I called the Institute and talked to the head man there to see if I could arrange a transfer. Once I finally got the doctors to talk to each other, we got it arranged. They released him a little early so I could fly Eric to Fort Lauderdale, rent a car, drive Eric to the admitting doctor's office for a quick examination, then drove him down to Miami to be admitted to the institute. It all went as planned, Eric was admitted, and two days later, he had a triple bypass operation. The surgery was successful, and I called my son Michael to drive on down to Miami to be with him. I flew back to Fort Walton Beach with three days to spare before my appointment in Cleveland. Michael stayed with friends in Miami until Eric was discharged from the hospital, then drove him down to his home in Marathon, where Eric's friends would look after him.

The day before my appointment, I flew up to Cleveland and checked in at the Omni Hotel in the Cleveland Clinic complex, and signed in at the clinic. The next morning, they started the three-day evaluation of my heart to see if they could repair it. On the morning of the 3rd of July, the testing was over; they informed me that I was in the right place at the right time and did I want to get it done. I told them I was ready and called my boys to come up and be with their daddy.

The surgery was on the morning of the 4th of July by Dr. Delos Cosgrove to repair my Mitral valve by installing a Cosgrove ring. The surgery was successful; I know because I woke up in ICU and saw my boys. In two days, I was up and walking; in five, I was discharged and flew back to Fort Walton Beach. Two weeks later, I went to see my cardiologist in Fort Walton. I told him about the surgery, he prescribed some pills, then fired me as a patient, and I went shopping for a new cardiologist. I spent most of my time on the couch recuperating and calling my Uncle Eric every couple of days to check on how he was recovering. My tenant, Doc Enos, would take me for a walk once a day, first just around the parking lot, then eventually down the beach to the pier and back. Recovery seemed to be taking forever.

During August, I tried calling Eric on my weekly call and didn't get an answer; this went on for a couple of days. I finally got a call from his neighbor to inform me that he had died on his couch on the 11th of August. I called my Uncle Rudy, Eric's brother, who lived on Palm Coast, to give him the news about Eric's death and discuss funeral arrangements. He was in no position to do anything, I was named executor in Eric's will, so it was up to me to go down to Marathon and take care of it.

I didn't think I was strong enough yet to make the 12-to-15-hour drive, so I booked a flight to Miami and rented a car for the drive down the keys to Eric's house in Marathon, the county seat of Monroe County. After the drive, I turned in the rental at Marathon's small airport and walked the short distance to the house located in the Little Venice subdivision on the east end of Marathon.

The house was a small cement block, one bedroom with a garage on a canal to the Atlantic that Eric built his studio on top of. When his wife Elfriede died a couple of years ago, he rented out the downstairs and moved upstairs into the studio. I met his renters, and they showed me around; they were the ones that found Eric and called me. They were concerned that they would have to move. I told them not to worry; I would give them plenty of time if we decided to sell the place. I moved in upstairs and made a run in Eric's car to the grocery store; I was going to be there for a while and slowly started going through Eric's stuff.

The next day I arranged meetings with a funeral parlor and his church, the Marathon Church of God, where he had painted a mural for them. The service was planned for August 17 at 16:00, and his body was to be cremated shortly after the service. With the arrangements made, my next stop was the Monroe County Health Department, where I picked up two copies of Eric's death certificate. Then to the Monroe County Court House, where I gave them a copy of Eric's will, a copy of his death certificate, and petitioned the court for my appointment as executor of his estate. I was still recovering from surgery and was exhausted from all the running around, and I had no trouble sleeping.

Going through Eric's file cabinet, I found out that he had been commissioned by the United States Coast Guard to paint activities at their Key West Station and had Social Security and a pension from Grumman Aircraft Company. He had a little over $25,000 in the bank and a second mortgage on his house. The Toyota that he bought with some of the second mortgage funds was the extent of Eric's estate.

Eric's apartment took up half the second floor, and his studio took up about a quarter of the remaining space; a balcony that overlooked the canal and the Atlantic took up the rest. It was really a nice setup where you could watch beautiful sunrises over the Atlantic Ocean. The building was in pretty good shape except for some of the sidings on the second floor that would have to be replaced, and the apartment downstairs needed painting.

At the service on the 17th, the church was pretty much filled up, Eric was always the life of the party, and he had a lot of friends. I set up a little remembrance get-together for after the service over at Eric's house for some of his close friends and neighbors, where I learned a lot more about Eric and his many adventures in the keys.

I was pretty busy for the next couple of days going through Eric's personnel stuff. I called my Uncle Rudy and asked him if he wanted anything of Eric's. All Rudy wanted was a couple of paintings that he described to me. Eric's studio was loaded with completed and uncompleted paintings, blank canvases, many brushes and tubes of paint, and other artist supplies. After picking out the painting I liked and the ones that Rudy wanted, I called the local high school and asked them if their art department needed supplies. The art teacher from the school was on the phone in a second, I described to him what I had, and he was overjoyed. I loaded up the Toyota with all the art supplies and drove over to the school. The school's principal and art teacher were waiting for me and were very appreciative of Eric's donation. The Salvation Army got most of his clothing and other personal items, but there was still a lot of stuff to go through.

Before leaving Marathon, I called the mortgage company to find out about the second mortgage that Eric had on his house. The bank informed me that I could either buy back the second mortgage or let them take the house. They said they would give us a little time to settle Eric's affairs and make up our minds; I called up Rudy and gave him a heads up on what our options were. I figured the house was worth a lot more than what he owed. It took a lot of talking to persuade Rudy that we would have rental income from the property while our equity in it would increase. He finally agreed to get a loan and buy back the second mortgage.

Finally, after about three weeks, the Monroe County Court made me executor of Eric's estate. With the papers in my hand, I went over to Eric's bank, closed his account and transferred the balance over to our new checking account, applied for a loan, and transferred the title of the Toyota Eric left me in his will. It took another week to get the loan approved, and once we settled the second mortgage and arranged for the utilities to be paid from our account, I felt that everything was pretty much under control, and I could leave. The house was definitely a fixer-upper and needed a lot more attention; I kept finding all kinds of little things that needed repair. That meant I would be back down to Marathon in the near future

Early the next morning, I told the tenants downstairs that we were not going to sell the house in the near term and gave them my phone number in case they needed to contact me. I then loaded up the Toyota with Eric's paintings and started the drive to Rudy's place in Palm Coast. It was an all-day drive up the east coast to Palm Coast, located south of Jacksonville. Rudy built a house in a new subdivision a couple of years earlier after he retired and moved out of New Jersey. After eight hours on the road and calling Rudy for directions, I arrived at his house. Rudy and his wife Claire gave me a tour of their house, and I gave Rudy the paintings that he wanted. Over dinner that evening, we talked about what we should do with Eric's house. Rudy wanted to sell the house as soon as possible, and I wanted to take our time to fix it up to increase its value and then put it on the market. My argument was that it was producing income, so there was no rush, and maybe after a while, the housing market on Marathon would improve. We finally agreed to take our time and fix it up before putting it on the market. In the morning, after Claire fed me a great breakfast, I started my drive back to the Surfview. It was great to see my uncle Rudy and aunt Claire again; the last time I saw them was in 1982. That's when they brought my grandpa over to the Surfview, and we all went for a sail on the Pele and later at my parents' 50th wedding anniversary celebration in DeBary.

When finally back in my cave at the Surfview, I needed a rest and did nothing for a couple of days before I went back to work maintaining the place. While talking to Tom Stewart on the dock, he told me he had been hired to manage the Hog's Breath Saloon in New Orleans and invited me to come over. There was an apartment over the saloon where I could stay to recuperate. I told him I would be there as soon as I got the Surfview squared away. Doc had mowed the grass while I was out of town, but it took me a good week with Doc's help to get the place looking good. As soon as that project was finished, I drove over to New Orleans to take Tom Stewart up on his offer. I was really tired out and did nothing but eat good Cajun cuisine; people watch and sleep. I stayed for about a week before heading back to Surfview, and before I knew it, Thanksgiving was around the corner.

The Thanksgiving feast at the Surfview drew a crowd of around twenty people, mostly tenants and friends. My mom wasn't there to organize it anymore, but somehow, I got it all together and roasted a turkey for the occasion. There was none of my mom's homemade cranberry sauce, red cabbage, and holiday cakes. Nevertheless, it was a successful feast, and everyone had a great time; I just missed the fact that my family wasn't there to enjoy it.

After Thanksgiving, my tenants in Eric's house called and told me they were moving out at the end of the year. Since I needed to do some repairs on the place, this would be a good opportunity to go down there and make the repairs. I flew to Miami the day after Christmas, rented a car, and drove down the keys to Marathon. I arrived in the early afternoon, went grocery shopping, turned in the car, and after talking to my tenants who were in the process of moving out, I settled in for an extended stay.

For New Year's Eve, I had the place to myself and brought in the New Year at the local bar around the corner. It had been a sad couple of years for me losing My dad, my mom, and my uncle Eric; I forced myself to go out and take my mind off my loss. It turned out to be an interesting evening with all the local clientele from the neighborhood. I think I might have been the youngest person there and had a good old time chatting up the ladies. I got to meet people that knew my uncle, and they had stories to tell about him. Apparently, he was the darling of all the ladies in the neighborhood, and he was well known in Key West, where he spent time working for the Coast Guard and doing art shows.

1995

I decided to put my efforts into getting the apartment downstairs ready to rent. After spending a couple of days cleaning, I walked over to the hardware supply store and bought paint and rollers, and started painting. Altogether, it took about a week to finish the apartment and put a for rent sign in the window. It took another week to replace the damaged siding and get the upstairs cleaned up. I found an agent to rent the apartment, set off a couple of bug bombs, and headed back to Fort Walton. The agent called me a week later, telling me that he had found a tenant for the apartment.

I was just getting things under control at the Surfview when my son Michael called and informed me that he qualified to compete in the XII Pan American Sports Games to be held in Mar Del Plata, Argentina, from 11 to 26 March 1995, and if I wanted to go with him. The U. S. Olympic Committee would supply the airline tickets and hotel reservations at the Torres de Manantiales Hotel in Mar Del Plata. It was a sweet deal that I could not refuse, and I started packing.

I arrived at Mar Del Plata on the 10th after a long flight from Miami to Buenos Aires and then a 2-hour flight on a military C-47 transport. Michael met me at the hotel while I was checking in; he had been there training for a while and had the town pretty well checked out. That evening we went out to dinner at a restaurant close to the hotel, where I had a marvelous steak meal at a bargain price. I had noticed on the flight down from Buenos Aires that there appeared to be nothing but ranchland between the two cities, so there was plenty of beef available. Walking around town after dinner, I felt like I was in Germany; the buildings looked like something you would find in Bavaria, and the people looked like Germans. The women were blue-eyed blonds, and some of them were wearing lederhosen and knee socks. I tried approaching a couple of these beauties with my broken German, but they didn't speak German; they spoke Spanish, and my Spanish is limited. Oh well, worth a try.

Since the Sailboard competition was held in an area where there were no spectators, I was left to entertain myself while Michael competed. We would meet up after the day's competition for dinner and cocktails. I spent my days watching some of the other competitions and exploring Mar del Plata. During my explorations, I came across a well-guarded large Argentine Naval base; I found out later that it had been the home base of General Belgrano, the light cruiser the British sank during the 1982 Falklands war; it was a hand-me-down from the U.S.N. that was named the Phoenix.

The sailboard competition was all over in a week, and the results were in, Michael finished second for the silver medal, and we celebrated. The competition in other events was still going on, giving us the opportunity to be spectators at some of the tennis and wrestling competition. I really had a great time in Mar del Plata and appreciated Michael arranging for me to go.

In June, back at the Surfview, while drinking beer on a beautiful day on the dock with my sailing buddy Rick Sauter he mentioned that he wanted to get rid of his sailboat, a Choi Lee 28 that he kept at my dock and asked me if I would like to help him go find a bigger one. I had nothing pressing going on at the moment and agreed. At first, we drove around the local area, but at the time, there were very few 36-40 ft sailboats on the market, so we expanded our search. We ended up driving down the east coast of Florida, stopping at numerous marinas and looking at boats that were listed with brokers or in the Boat Trader. We ended up in Marathon and stopped in at Eric's house, giving me the opportunity to meet my new tenants. A young married couple and newcomers to Marathon, the husband's job brought him to Monroe County flying mosquito control in an old C-47 out of the airport on Marathon. We had lunch with them and then drove on down to Key West to look at more boats.

It was really hot and humid, and after a couple of days of checking the bars and marinas in and around Key West, we drove back to Marathon. We stayed a couple of days while I finished up, with Rick's help replacing some of the sidings upstairs before starting the long drive back to Fort Walton. On the way back, we crossed over to the west coast of Florida and looked at more boats as we worked our way up the coast back to Fort Walton. Our little adventure took a little over a week, and by then, I had a belly full of looking at boats. As it turned out, Rick finally found and bought his boat in Pensacola Beach, a Gulf Star 39 sloop that the bank was auctioning off after its owner fell off the boat and drowned. After closing the deal with the bank in July, I helped him sail his new boat over to join his other boat at the Surfview dock. Rick named the boat Anna Virginia, after his daughter; it was a beautiful boat with a generator, refrigerator, and air conditioning.

While I was out of town with Rick looking at boats, my son Jon finally received orders to Little Rock AFB, Arkansas, for crew training in C-130s, then on to his squadron at Dyess AFB, Texas. He had sold his Catalina 27 sailboat, put his condo on the market, and hit the road for Little Rock.

Just as I was really beginning to enjoy a beautiful end of summer on the Redneck Riviera with all the tourists gone and the kids back in school, everything changed. On the 30th of September, Tropical Storm Opal crossed over the Yucatan peninsula and entered the Bay of Campeche, and started moving NNE into the Gulf of Mexico. I got busy with my usual preparation for hurricanes, securing the area, and replenishing my supply of shingles, roofing nails, and tarpaper. I had precut plywood to board up the windows and taped up the outside of the doors as soon as my tenants evacuated. Rick was up in North Carolina, so I stripped all the sails of his boats and anchored them up in the Sound off the Surfview. By the 3rd of October, Opal was intensifying and started making a beeline for the panhandle of Florida; we were told to evacuate. Early in the morning of the 4th, Opal was 290 miles southwest of Pensacola and had strengthened to a strong category 4 hurricane with 150 mph winds that looked to be heading straight for me. It was almost impossible to get out of town; all the roads going north were in gridlock, and since I was the only one left at the Surfview, I hunkered down to ride out the storm. Opal weakened to a category 3 hurricane just before going ashore on Pensacola Beach at 5 pm on the 4th of October 1995 with 115mph sustained winds.

The Surfview apartments were located about 50 miles to the east of where Opal went ashore and experienced 80 mph with gusts to over 100mph and heavy rain. The storm surge of 7 to 10 ft came ashore, and 2 ft of it rolled over the Island. It was pretty scary with no power and all the noise of the storm. I didn't board up my bedroom window since it faced north, away from the onshore wind. I tried looking out during the night to see what was going on; I couldn't see a thing.

At first light, after a sleepless night, the wind had shifted a little to the west, and the rain had let up a bit; it was still blowing at around 30 to 40 mph. I went out to survey the damage. Rick's boats were bouncing merrily on their anchors, the Surfview lost some shingles, and that seemed to be the extent of the roof damage. After the rain and wind eased off, I went to work checking the apartments. I could see a two-foot-high waterline on the side of the building caused by the surge when it washed over my part of the Island, but when I peeled the tape off the doors and checked inside the units, I found very little water intrusion. Since there was no telling how long the power would be off, I emptied all the refrigerators, took some of the perishables and all the steaks, and threw the rest out; I put the steaks in the refrigerator on Rick's boat and started the generator.

That night with the A/C going on the boat, I had a good night's sleep, then a hearty breakfast of steak and eggs. I took the dingy ashore and went to work cleaning up the mess. Repairing the roof was first on the list, and by late afternoon the next day, I had the roof repaired and started on the next job, taking the plywood down off the windows. About this time, the Okaloosa County Sheriff showed up in his pickup truck and told me that the Island was under mandatory evacuation and to get in his truck. I explained to him that I was living on the boat and was just taking care of my property. He agreed to let me stay as long as I was on the boat by sundown and stayed on it till dawn; he was worried about looters. As soon as he drove off, I went back to work, taking the plywood down off the windows and storing them in the Conex container that I used as a workshop and storage shed.

By the 8th of September, I had the building in good shape, and all the units were ready for my tenant's return. There were still all kinds of debris lying around that would take me days to pick up and dump into a huge pile for pickup. While working, I spotted a couple of pilings floating down the Sound; I could always use a couple of spare pilings and took the dingy out to tow them ashore as salvage. I also came across all kinds of salvageable lumber lying around, some of which I recycled. Eventually, I had the apartments, and the grounds cleaned up and ready for action. The power was still out, and the Island was not accessible except for owners to assess property damage.

After a couple of weeks, they finally opened up the Island; I took a walk around the neighborhood. There was mostly roof damage and lots of sand that the storm surge washed up on the road. I walked down the Island to the El Matador to check on my apartment there, it was not damaged, but the swimming pool was filled with sand. The first-floor units that faced the beach had a lot of damage, and it looked like the roof had some damage. I walked back along what was left of the beach, where there was a lot of erosion. During my walk back, I could see that all of the condos on the beach took some sort of damage, mostly on the lower floors; it would take a while for the Island to recover. I retrieved my truck from where I had it stored on the mainland and took a drive; the further west I went, the worst it got, with Pensacola taking the biggest hit. Opal was one of the more powerful and damaging hurricanes to come ashore in the panhandle. It will take a while, but the Redneck Riviera will recover.

By the time Thanksgiving rolled around, the Island was pretty much repaired, except the roofers were still busy, and repairs at the washed-out portion of Highway 98 between Fort Walton Beach and Destin were still going on. The Surfview was back operating normally; all my people were back and ready to put on our annual Thanksgiving feast. We were all in a celebratory mood for the feast. After all, we survived Opal and had a place to live; we were the lucky ones.

With Christmas arriving, Phil and Donna DiDanato invited me over to celebrate with them, their children Derrick and Christine, and other guests. There was plenty of good food, conversation, and toys to play with. They put on a great party, and I believe everyone there had a good-fun time.

1995 ended in the usual manner by running the bars on the island; it was a lot of fun chatting with friends I hadn't seen in a while.

Not much was going on during the beginning of the year, so in March, I flew out to Abilene, Texas, to visit my son Jon stationed at Dyess AFB. After he finished crew training in the C-130 a couple of months earlier, he settled in and bought a house, and for my visit, he went on two weeks' leave.

After a day or two of driving around Abilene in Jon's red 1988 Porsche 911 that he had just bought and eating at good Mexican restaurants, we decided to take a little ski trip. All the close ski resorts were booked up, but after searching around, we found a vacancy at Ski Rio in New Mexico, just north of Santa Fe. Jon let me drive part of the way there in his Porsche; I had a blast.

Ski Rio was a relatively new ski resort, and there weren't many people there, so the lifts weren't crowded, the slopes were well groomed, and there was plenty of snow. There wasn't much in the way of nightlife, but there was enough to keep us busy. After a week of great skiing on the slopes, we headed back to Abilene. I was pretty much worn out, and after recuperating for a couple of days at Jon's house, I flew on back to Fort Walton Beach. It was good to see my boy again.

A short time later, my son Michael called and informed me that he won the sailboard trials held at Melbourne, Florida for the 1996 Atlanta Olympics.

During the games, the sailors were staying in the Olympic village in Savanna. When I drove over to cheer on Michael, I stayed nearby in a hotel on Savanna's historic waterfront, where there were plenty of restaurants and bars. The whole area was crowded with people from around the world, and I was well entertained chatting with them. The sailboard competition was held from July 22 to August 2nd, 1996, on Wassaw Sound and in the Atlantic Ocean off of Savanna, Georgia. The competitors would launch out of the Day marina, a temporary barge near the north side of Wassaw Sound at the mouth of the Wilmington River near Tybee Island.

There were spectator boats available to take people out to the races, and I volunteered to drive one mainly so I would be able to watch Michael compete. I had a lot of fun shuttling people and competitors out from Tybee Island to the Day Marina (a temporary floating dock) and spectators out to watch them compete. On one of the trips to the Day Marina, I did happen to bounce over a sand bar for some unintentional excitement.

The nine races of the sailing competition began on the 23rd and finished on the 29th. Michael finished 6th, the Gold medal going to Nikos Kaklamanakis, the Silver to Carlos EspaAnoa, and the Bronze to Gal Fridman. After a night of celebration, I started my drive in the morning to Fort Walton Beach. Michael stayed on to party with his friends before driving back to Fort Pierce. A couple of months later, he went with the team to meet President Clinton in Washington.

Back at the Surfview, I noticed that Rick's Choi Lee was no longer tied up to the dock; he had donated it to PAWS for a tax write-off. We had a big Halloween Party at the Surfview. Almost everyone had a costume; of course, it went on till way late in the evening. During the party, Rick got me aside and suggested that we take his new boat, the Anne Virginia, on a little shake-down cruise. I told Rick I was good to go but had to be back in January; I had signed on to go skiing with the local ski club with my son Jon.

In Early December, on a rainy, foggy day, we loaded up the Anna Virginia cast off from the Surfview dock and headed for Key West. We had an extra hand on board, Rick's friend Austin, a big 280-pounder from Alabama who brought plenty of scotch with him. We made it about halfway down the intercoastal to Panama City in the fog, where we tied up for the night. Two nights later, we were anchored up having some scotch inside Panama City Pass in the fog.

In the morning, we set sail in the fog that in an hour or so burned off, and by noon the wind had increased to over 20 kts out of the NE, putting us on a broad reach on a direct course to Key West. It was a beautiful but cold day, and the Anna Virginia was sailing along smartly in rough seas with a bone in her teeth. If the wind held, we would be across the big bend of Florida and abeam Clearwater in a day and a half and Key West in three. Rick's friend Austin was steady into his scotch and was bouncing around like a wrecking ball. Rick and I were both worried that he would fall overboard and there would be no way to haul him back aboard in the rough seas. We eventually talked him into staying down below, where he eventually passed out.

That night during his watch, Rick started the diesel to charge the batteries and, after an hour, noticed that the batteries were not taking charge. We spent the next morning troubleshooting the problem to no avail. Our position at noon had us around 20 miles offshore Clearwater, so the decision was made to head there and get the problem fixed. It took us five hours of motoring into the seas and headwind to get through Clearwater Pass and tie up to the marina. Austin decided that he had enough of this sea adventure and, in the morning, left for the airport.

Over the next couple of days, as the temperature dropped, Rick and I tried to figure out and fix the electrical problem. Rick finally bit the bullet and hired an electrician that was recommended by the marina to troubleshoot and fix the problem. In the meantime, it was really getting cold that had filled in behind the front we were following down the coast. We needed to find a place to get out of the electrician's way and stay warm. We solved the problem by taking the bus to the mall in Tampa, where we hung out, wandered through the stores, ate at the food concourse, and went to a movie. This went on for days until the electrician got the Anna Virginia ship shape again. We were

168

burning up time sitting there in Clearwater, and I needed to get back to the Surfview to get ready for my ski trip on January 18th.

The electrician finished the repairs just before Christmas, and on Christmas day, we sailed out of Clearwater Pass. During the sail down the coast, we tried charging the batteries to make sure the repairs worked, they charged up all right, but the way you had to do it was not that convenient. Just before sunset, we were approaching Pass-a-Grille just down the coast about 40 mi, where we anchored up just inside the pass to spend the night.

With an early start in the morning, we continued our journey on a beautiful cold day further down the coast to Fort Myers. We were not really happy with and didn't have a lot of confidence in the way we had to charge the batteries and messed with them most of the day. We anchored up in the early evening by Fort Myers Beach and went ashore for cocktails and dinner to get us prepared for the day and a half sail to Key West.

The sail to Key West, a distance of around 150 nm, was enjoyable with the boat sailing well on a reach in 15 to 20 kts of wind out of the East, plus it was warming up a little. We arrived off of Key West's NW Channel before sunrise on the 28th of December and hove to, waiting for the sunrise. While waiting, we monitored the VHF radio traffic; there was a lot of it, meaning Key West was crowded, getting ready to celebrate the New Year. We overheard a call from a boat looking for a place to tie up. During the conversation, we overheard that one might be available at the City Marina. We immediately called the marina and booked the slip; it was possibly the last slip available. When we walked into town, it was definitely crowded, but with a bit of luck, we got an outside table at Rick's, where we ate peanuts, drank beer, and looked over the people meander by.

The New Year's Eve celebration in Key West was something to behold; the town was filled to capacity with revelers. There was no way you could get into a restaurant or a bar; the place was mobbed.

1997

When we departed Key West on the 2nd of January, we sailed the Anna Virginia up the east coast to Marathon to tie her up at Eric's dock. We made it to Boot Key Harbor on the west end of Marathon and picked up a mooring from the marina before sunset in time for happy hour and dinner at a restaurant around the corner. After dinner and back on the Anna Virginia, I looked over the chart of Marathon and tried to remember where the unmarked channel into the lagoon at Eric's house. My aunt Elfriede had showed us the way on the Silent Lady with Skip and my Boys in 1980. Well, my memory wasn't that great; I couldn't remember quite exactly how we made our way to their lagoon.

After breakfast in the morning, we dropped our mooring buoy and sailed down Sister Creek to the Atlantic. After a short hour and a half sail to the east end of Marathon and up Vaca Cut to where I thought the unmarked channel cuts off, we turned and a short time later ran aground on the rocks. After a lot of aggravation and help from people ashore, we finally got her off the rocks and worked our way over to the lagoon.

Rick decided to haul his boat at the local boatyard to check the bottom for damage, get the bottom painted and try to get the boat's electrical problem fixed once and for all. He would be there in

Marathon for a while. I rented a car and headed back to Fort Walton Beach with just a couple of days to spare to get ready to leave on my trip to Tahoe, California, with the ski club.

We landed at the Reno-Tahoe International Airport on January 18th. My son Jon had flew over from Dyess AFB and was waiting for us, making a total of thirteen adventurous soles. We loaded onto the bus for the ride to the condo where we were staying. We skied the slopes at Squaw and Northstar and did a dinner cruise on the lake. Skiing with a group is a lot of fun; we had races down slalom courses and down the bumps and partied together in the evenings. We only had one incident; there was a collision between my son Jon and one of our fellow adventurers that

ended up giving him an ugly-looking black eye, all in all, it was a great two weeks. Linda Quinlan, a relator from Destin, was in our group, a sister of one of the guys I flew with in the reserves at Duke Field years ago. We kind of hit it off and started hanging out together when we got back to Florida. Jon flew back to Dyess AFB, where he was a C-130 copilot.

After being back at the Surfview for a while, I contacted Rick in Marathon to find out what was going on and if his boat was operational. He was still messing with the batteries but was eager to set sail for a cruise to the Bahamas. I told him I would be back down there as soon as possible, meaning in late April or early May before the hurricane season starts, and would help him sail over to the Bahamas but wouldn't stay.

I was back in Marathon by the end of April, and a week later, we set sail on the Anna Virginia for the Islands. We departed in the early afternoon, and by sunset, we were in the Gulf Stream, where I spread the ashes of my uncle, Eric, to join his wife Elfriede as the sun set. At the very instant the sun went down below the horizon, there was a green flash; I've always looked for it, but that was the first time I saw one; maybe it was some kind of omen.

In the morning at dawn, we were offshore Bimini, looking for the channel into the harbor. We found the channel, raised our quarantine flag, and looked for the customs dock at Alice Town.

After clearing customs and getting our cruising permit for the Anna Virginia, we moved the boat over to the city marina and took some shore leave. We had all day to wander around Alice Town, a pretty place with a bunch of little shops and brightly painted houses, followed by a pleasant evening of cocktails and dinner at one of the cafés.

In the morning, we departed Bimini and took the most direct route to Nassau; a shallow channel called the Northeast Channel across the banks. By sundown, we had successfully navigated the channel and were anchored by the buoy that marked the end of it and the beginning of deep water. The night was clear and star-filled; the reflection of the stars on the water gave the illusion that you were completely surrounded by stars; awesome. With an early start in the morning and by early afternoon, we were contacting Nassau Harbour Control for permission to enter Nassau Harbour. As we made our way down the channel past the cruise ships tied up at the Prince George Wharf, we called the marina on the eastern end of the harbor and found a place to tie up for a couple of days. Once we had the Anna Virginia secured to the dock, we headed for the marina's bar for happy hour and later to a restaurant for dinner. Over dinner, Rick and I talked over what was next on the agenda. I was flying back to Florida, and Rick, in a couple of days, had his girlfriend Pam flying in.

In the morning, I booked a flight out for the next day, and we used the rest of the day touring the harbor in the dingy. We checked out the big yachts in Hurricane Hole, then went over to walk around the casino at the Atlantis Resort on Paradise Island. After dinner, I packed my sea bag for the early flight out in the morning. It was a nice weeklong adventure on the Anna Virginia; Rick had himself a real nice comfortable boat to sail around the Islands in.

Back in Florida for a hot summer at the Surfview, there were all kinds of activities going on. The two vacant lots next to the Surfview that I've been trying to buy for years that the owner wouldn't sell to me for some reason. She sold them while I was sailing around on the Anna Virginia with Rick. I told Linda about the sale; she found out who bought the lots and somehow convinced him to sell them to me, at a profit, of course. After rounding up the money and closing on the lots, that gave me a total of 2.1 acres, a pretty good chunk of land for a developer to do something with. Not long after the closing, we had a hurricane hit the Gulf Coast, hurricane Danny a category one that spawned in the Gulf of Mexico and went ashore near Mullet Point, Alabama on July 19th. It was mainly a wind and rain event in our area that caused some local flooding.

Michael called me in September and told me that he was going to be conducting a boardsailing clinic at Lake Arenal in the northern highlands of Costa Rica and to come on down. It sounded like a good plan, and I told him I would meet him there. Rick was at the dock on his boat at the time, and when I told him I was going to Costa Rica, he wanted to go along.

The flight to Costa Rica took seven hours. On landing at San Jose, we looked around for Michael in the terminal. His flight landed just before ours, and was traveling with one of his buddies and his mother. When we found them at the car rental, they were loading up their rental car, and after tying down more of their gear on the roof of our car, we started driving to Lake Arenal. It was a slow two-hour drive on a rutted dirt road. We finally arrived at the camp and checked into our rooms. The camp was a short drive to the lake where Michael's was giving the clinic for boardsailors from many different countries.

The camp was at a remote site, and after watching them sail around on the lake for a day, we had seen enough and decided to go explore the local area. So, after breakfast the next morning, the three of us, Rick, Shirley (the mother), and I took a car and went on an exploratory expedition.

It was rough going over the dirt roads; there wasn't really much to see. We would occasionally come across a small village where we would stop to look around. Neither one of us spoke Spanish, but that didn't slow us down much when bartering with the people in the shops. On a no wind, no training day, all five of us piled into the car and drove for a little over an hour to the town of Arenal at the end of the lake close to the volcano of the same name. After having lunch in town, we drove over to the volcano to walk up it. That is until it erupted and spit out a couple of freight car-sized lumps of lava that came tumbling down toward us. Every half hour, it erupted the same way; we'd seen enough and headed back to the camp. The weeklong clinic was ending in a couple of days, and Michael told us that when it was done, he would be going to sail on Lago Cocibolca, the big lake in Nicaragua.

Instead of doing that, Rick and I checked out of the camp a day early and drove to San Jose, the capital city of Costa Rica, where we checked into a hotel. Then over the next two days, we did a walkabout town, finding some good places to eat, a couple of interesting bars, and the park of the dead dove. That's where young girls go looking for a husband by parading in front of old ex-patriots sitting on benches looking for a young bride. From San Jose, we drove to Quepos, a town on the west coast of Costa Rica that used to be a major port for exporting palm oil. We found a hotel there and went for a walk; you could see that the town had been in a decline since they moved a lot of the operations further south at Golfito. We went over to the beach that has real fine volcanic black sand that gets into everything.

After a couple of days in Quepos, we drove back to San Jose to catch our flight back to Florida.

Shirley was on our flight. During the flight, we talked a lot about our kids and Costa Rican making our flight seem shorter. Back home at the Surfview, my good buddies, Tom Prohaska, Phil DiDonato, and Bill Christie, convinced me to start running with them in 5 and 10K weekend runs again; I had stopped going after my heart surgery. There was a run just about every weekend somewhere in the local area, and we went to most of them. They were a lot of fun, giving you an opportunity to socialize around the beer that was always available after a run. Jack, Tom, and I, in the fall, started driving over to Tallahassee for the FSU football games. Jack being a member of the alumni club, had special parking and access to the games. So between going to the runs, going to FSU football games, Linda taking me as her date to network with the local movers and shakers, and working around the Surfview, I was a busy man.

A week before Halloween, Linda and I drove over to New Orleans for a weekend to shop for Halloween costumes. We had a good old time eating the wonderful food at the restaurants of New Orleans, drinking too much, and listening to New Orleans jazz until the wee hours of the morning.

During the day, we wandered around the French Quarter, shopping in the many costume shops, and finally, at a small shop, bought Dracula and Lucy costumes.

For Halloween eve, Linda had arranged with some of her friends for a limo to chauffer us around to some of the parties where we would compete in some of the costume contests, I can't remember how we did, but it was really a fun evening.

On Thanksgiving, we had our usual festivities outdoors on the picnic tables at the Surfview, which drew a crowd of around 25 friends and tenants and their friends. My contribution was a big roasted turkey, everyone else brought their favorite dish,

and we had plenty to feast on. Good weather and a lot of conversation during and after the feast kept it going till way after dark, ending when the wine ran out.

For Christmas, Linda invited me to go with her and her son and daughter, both in their twenties, to her father's house in Milton, Florida. Shortly after we arrived, her brother and his family arrived. It was a fun time meeting her father and the rest of the family and reminiscing with her brother about our flying adventures in the reserves. Linda was trying to convince her father to sell his house and move to Destin near her and his grandkids. She wasn't having much luck; he was happy living in Milton, a small nice, and quiet town.

Linda and I celebrated the New Year in Destin with our friends.

1998

It took Doc and me the first couple of months of the year to clean up the mess on the two lots that I had just bought. The area along the shoreline with the Sound was a real mess. It seemed like the storm surge funneled through there, and it took a while to clean up all the debris. By March, everything, including the dock that needed some planks replaced, was repaired. Doc was a great help in maintaining the place, and for a reduced rate on his rent, he worked with me on weekends and off days from his job at a glass company in Destin. With the apartments all squared away, I started contemplating my next project, what to do with it all. In the meantime, Linda was pressuring me to move in with her in Destin. I was happy with us living in our own separate corners. She was a very persuasive and hard-charging realtor used to getting her way. Well, I was also used to getting my way, so it was probably time to cool it some between us.

During May, while hanging around the beer locker on the dock with Tom, Jack, and Bill Liebold, Tom mentioned that he was thinking about going over to the UK to visit his sister Jean. I told him I was good to go. I figured I needed to get out of town anyway; I was still getting a lot of heat from Linda.

We booked an overnight flight on Air Canada from Atlanta to London Heathrow for Thursday, July 7th. Somehow, we ended up on the top deck of the 747, where we had what felt like our own personal Stewardess taking care of us. On arrival, we took the underground to High Street Kensington, the closest tube station to Jean's place at 11 Albert Way. On the way, while dragging our bags to her house, we passed the Goat Tavern, the closest watering hole to her house. After a short walk, we found Albert Way, a dead-end street, and a three-story row house. That we found out later from Jean was built the year Napoleon died in 1821. Jean, a psychotherapist who practices out of her house, told Tom where the key was, that she would probably be seeing clients when we arrived, and to try not to make a lot of noise going up the stairs to our rooms on the third floor. After getting settled in, we walked over to the Goat for a pint.

After a couple of pints, Jean called with an all-clear, and we made our way back over to meet her. After catching up with what was going on, she took us over to an Indian restaurant. During dinner, she told us that on Thursday the 9th, she was going on a bicycle trip to tour the Chastleton House, a 17th-century Jacobean country estate in the Cotswold, with some friends, and asked if we wanted to go. We said sure we'd go; we were ready for anything.

On Wednesday morning, we had breakfast with Jean, and just before Jean saw her first client for the day, we headed out to explore London. Taking the underground, we were all over London, and by midday, we were in the theater district by the Palace Theater. Next door was The Cambridge, where we stopped for some pub food. We sat at one of the tables outside and ordered a pint, and eventually ordered some food. It wasn't long before other people joined us at our table, and when they found out we were yanks, they started talking. For the rest of the afternoon, we sat at the table having conversations with all sorts of characters that stopped at our table for a pint or two; we learned a lot.

In the morning, after a leisurely breakfast at Jean's, we took the underground to Paddington Station

to meet Jean's friends and board the train to Morten-in-Marsh. Jean's friends turned out to be her college professor and a solicitor with his American wife. We had a pleasant conversation with them during the hour and a half ride to Morten-in-Marsh, where we rented bikes and had lunch at a nearby pub. It was a twenty-minute pedal to the Castleton House, and after spending an hour or so seeing how the upper-class lived in the 18th century, we headed back to London. During the conversation on the train ride back to Paddington Station, the solicitor told us that he and his wife were going to Africa for a couple of months with a human rights group. The wife was a little apprehensive; I could understand her unease about going since there was a lot of unrest at the time in Africa; we wished them a safe trip.

Back at Jean's house, I tried calling my son Michael; he was in Europe somewhere staying with friends while he was competing in board sailing events around Europe leading up to the 2000 Olympics in Australia. I finally made contact with him, and he was in London. Jean invited him to come over and stay at her place; he showed up in time to go with us to the Goat for food and drink. During the ensuing conversation at the Goat, we told Jean that we were going to rent a car in the morning and drive over to Ireland for a few days and asked Michael if he wanted to go. He had a couple of days off before his next competition and would go with us part of the way; we had a plan. Before leaving, Jean suggested that we should stop on the way to Aberystwyth, Wales.

In the morning, after breakfast, we rented a car. I was the designated driver since I had some experience driving on the left side of the road, and wouldn't you know it, with the first turn out of the lot, I was on the wrong side of the road.

By early afternoon we were driving past the Aberystwyth Castle, a 13th-century fortress in Aberystwyth, looking for a place to stay. We checked in at the Belle Vue Royal Hotel, located a hundred yards up the beach from the Royal Pier. After moving into our room, we walked down the beach to the upstairs bar/restaurant on the pier. The bar had music and a pool table; we ordered some beers, found a table, and looked over the young crowd. Michael got into a pool game while Tom and I watched and talked to the people around us. After a few beers while talking with one of the young guys that Michael had been shooting pool with told us his tale of woe about being married to an Irish girl and how she was dominating his life. He was pretty drunk and would lift up the skirt of any girl that happened to walk by and get a dirty look; it was quite the scene.

The next day Sunday the 12[th,] we dropped Michael at the station to catch a train back to London, and we drove down the coast to Fishguard to catch the early ferry for the three-hour crossing to Rosslare, Ireland. By the time we disembarked in Rosslare, it was past noon. We drove west out of town; we headed west out of town, and after a couple of hours, we stopped and got a room for the night at O'Farrell's B&B in the village of Castlemartyr in the county of Cork. After checking in, we went downstairs to the bar and joined the noisy crowd watching the World Cup final between France and Brazil; France won it 3-0. Later after the game ended, the crowd thinned out we got something to eat at the bar.

During breakfast at the B&B, the proprietor told us about the old Jameson distillery five miles down the road in Midleton. We arrived there just in time for the morning tour, during which I earned an Irish whiskey tasters certificate. After lunch at the distillery, we drove five hours to Dublin, arriving late in the afternoon. Luckily, shortly after arriving, we found a vacancy at the James Joyce Guesthouse with a place to park the car.

Once we checked into our room, we walked the 100 yards down the road to the Ha'penny pedestrian bridge that crossed over the River Liffey, looking for a pub to get something to eat and drink. Making our way to Essex St E and the Temple Bar, finding seats at the bar, we order some food and Guinness. While talking to the bartender and the people at the bar, the guy sitting next to Tom bought us a round of Guinness, and that started it. After a couple of rounds, some of his friends joined us. We were all having a good old time when he passed around for us to read the divorce papers he had just been served earlier in the day, then ripped them up and threw them away. After the bar closed, the party continued at an upstairs late-night club. In the wee hours of the morning, the party finally broke up. Tom and I somehow found our way back over the Ha'penny bridge to our digs.

I woke up with a terrible hangover; Tom wasn't doing much better. After a late breakfast, we tried to walk it off by wandering around Dublin. At around noon, we stopped for lunch and a bloody mary that really didn't help my condition much. Later on, in the evening, we ended up at the previous night's scene of the crime for something to eat and some hair of the dog. Even though the place had some great live music and some beautiful female clientele, it was a short evening for us.

After a hearty breakfast and the short drive to Dublin Port, we caught the early ferry for the three-hour sail across the Irish sea to Hollyhead, UK. During the crossing, we talked to a beautiful green-eyed redheaded Irish woman on her way to Wales to visit her boyfriend. I can't remember what we talked about, but she had our undivided attention. Once we disembarked from the ferry at Hollyhead, it was a four-hour drive to London, and when we arrived at Jean's, she was busy seeing a client, so we walked over to the Goat, where Jean later joined us for some pub food.

We had one full day left in London before our morning flight on the 17th out of Gatwick. We wanted to take advantage of it, so after having breakfast with Jean in the morning, we went and turned in the car, then headed out for one more walkabout London. By midday, we were in the neighborhood of the Cambridge, so we stopped for lunch and ended up spending the rest of the afternoon there. We were back in time to take Jean out to dinner and to thank her for letting us stay at her place. She is definitely the hostess with the mostess.

We were back in Florida in time to enjoy the last month or so of summer in the Redneck Riviera. A couple of weeks after my return from the UK, I got a call from my son Jon telling me that he had fulfilled his commitment to the Air Force and excepted an early out effective in September 1998. He would be living in Woodland Park, Colorado, helping a friend, Eric, whom he flew with in the Air Force, renovate his house. I asked him how long he would be there, Tom and I had booked a ski trip to Breckenridge in February, and Woodland Park was on our way up the mountain; we could stop to visit if he was still there. Jon couldn't give me an answer but said if he was still there, he would love to go skiing with us.

During the dog days of summer, I was trying to come up with a plan for the future of the Surfview Apartments. The local economy and property values were in a slump since Hurricane Opel, and over the last few years, many new apartments, condos, and hotels had been built on the island. It was overbuilt, and the developers were not looking for land to build on. I was just barely breaking even with the Surfview; good thing I had a retirement check coming in from the Air Force. I had few options, tear it down and build something new, sell it, or come up with some other option.

The Surfview was located on one side of a cul-de-sac, the Anchorage Apartments on the end, and a duplex on the other side. If I could get the owners to agree to put all these properties together into one parcel, we could all come out smelling like a rose. I arranged a meeting. Rosella, the owner of the Anchorage, was all for it, but the owner of the duplex was hesitant since he already had his property up for sale. He had inherited the property from his father, Don Elwell, a fellow survivor of the Windsong sinking who died in 1997, a couple of months before Opel hit. His son wasn't having much luck finding buyers for the place, and after thinking about my proposal for a week or so, he finally signed on. I told Linda that I had a deal and to put the word out to the local developers.

Thanksgiving that year was a little different, one of my tenants brought to the table a deep-fried turkey that he cooked on the spot in the parking lot that was absolutely delicious. As always, all the food and wine brought to the feast were by the people that lived at the Surfview and their guests. The weather was perfect, and the feast was attended by a bigger than usual crowd and carried on till late in the evening. A good time was had by all.

On Christmas day, I went to Linda's in Destin for dinner with her dad, brother, his family, and Linda's son and daughter. Linda's a good cook, and it was a marvelous meal with all the trimmings. During and after the meal, the conversation was all about Linda trying to convince her to sell his

house in Milton and to build a house on Linda's lot next door. I stayed out of it. By the end of the day, I think she had him pretty much convinced to do it, even though her brother, who lives in Milton, didn't think it was that good of an idea.

Linda and I went with Tom and his wife Donna to the Crystal Beach Inn in Destin for a Titanic black tie New Year's Eve party. The menu for dinner was the same as the last meal aboard the Titanic before it hit the iceberg and sank. There was a live band, lots of champagne, balloons, hats, horns, and streamers. The party went way on into the morning; it was a blast!

1999

Late morning on the 1st, trying to recover from the party at Linda's. We were having breakfast and talking. Linda was obsessed with getting her father to move next door so she could take care of him. I agreed with her that it was probably a good idea and tried to change the subject. When I could get a word in edgewise, I asked her if there was any interest in the parcel of land that my neighbors and I had up for sale. She told me that the developers apparently had no interest in a new project at the present time; this was not good news. Later that afternoon, I made my way back to the Surfview and bumped into Don Elwell's son and told him it would probably take some time to sell our parcel. He wanted his money and was impatient to get it. I tried to convince him to give it some time and that it would probably sell in the spring when sales pick up. I gave Rosella a call to see if she was interested in the two of us buying him out, she wasn't, and I had a bad feeling that our deal was falling apart.

Tom and I flew to Denver for our ski trip in early February, rented a car at the airport and headed up the mountain, and picked up my son Jon in Woodland Park on the way. The closer we got to Breckenridge, the worst the weather was, blowing snow and freezing cold. On arrival, we checked into our room, unloaded our gear, and headed for the closest bar to climatize. We had a couple of beers and some bar food and called it a night.

We were up bright and early in the morning to get our lift passes before the lines at the lift got long; we didn't have to worry; there weren't many people skiing. It was a beautiful clear cold day with about four inches of virgin snow; we had a blast. These perfect conditions didn't last. Later in the week, a storm blew through, and we lost a day on the slopes. The storm brought colder conditions and some new snow giving us great skiing conditions for the rest of our stay. The lifts weren't crowded, maybe because it was so cold, so every day, we were able to ski many of the different runs before the lifts closed. After our last run of the day, we stopped at the ski lodge for a little après ski before dinner. The week went fast, enjoying a lot of great skiing. I was thankful that I was able to have my son Jon join Tom and me for the trip.

The ski trip gave me plenty of time to talk to my son about what his plans were for the future. He told me that before separating from the air force at Dyess Air Force Base, he sold his house and his red Porsche and bought an old 1979 grey Dodge pickup truck. After signing out, he drove over to Colorado to help his friend Eric Hefty renovate his house. Once the house was complete, he was thinking about using the GI Bill to go back to Florida State University in Tallahassee for the fall semester. He already had an MBA but wanted to take some computer courses. Tallahassee was only three hours down the road from FWB, so I could easily visit and maybe go to some of the football games with him.

Arriving back at the Surfview from Colorado, I found out from Doc that Don's son had sold his duplex and that it was already back on the market. Apparently, the new owners bought it for a song and were trying to flip it. I called Rosella to talk about approaching the new owners to see if they would be interested in signing on to our agreement; she wasn't interested in it anymore and wanted out. I was back to square one and would have to think up a new plan.

While having lunch with Linda at the Hightide restaurant on the island, we ran into my neighbor that had a helicopter service on the island. He came over and joined us and, during the conversation, invited us to go for a short flight in his helicopter. It was a first helicopter flight for Linda, and she was scared to death. We flew all around the local area, and I got some great photos of the Surfview even though Linda had a death grip on me. After we landed, I told him my lot next to where he lived was available to rent if he needed a place for a helicopter pad. He was interested, but nothing ever came of it.

On Friday the 17th of September, Tom and I drove to Tallahassee to visit my son Jon who put us up in his apartment, and the next day went to the Florida State-North Carolina State football game. While enjoying an afternoon of drinking beer at the pool, Jon gave us an update on his exploits since skiing with us.

He told us that after we dropped him off in Woodland Park from skiing, he and Eric finished the house, and to celebrate, they took a six weeks holiday to Europe. Shortly after returning, he enrolled for the fall semester at FSU and bought a Jeep Cherokee. In July, he loaded it up with his stuff and towed it to Florida with the old Dodge truck. By the time he finished his story, it was time for dinner, and he took us to Bullwinkle's, a college bar, for some food and beer. There he told us that he had a girlfriend, Molly, whom he met shortly after arriving in Tallahassee.

Bullwinkle's was an interesting place with lots of FSU paraphernalia and a model train running around the place on a track up on the wall. After we finished eating, the music began, and it started getting crazy. Some of the girls in the noisy crowd were drinking out of cups that looked like a penis; it was a crazy scene that was something to behold.

Saturday before the game, Jon drove us around the campus and stopped to show us around his fraternity house. The place was a mess, and apparently, they couldn't afford a den mother to run the place. Leaving the car there, we walked to the stadium for the game. The stadium was filled to capacity with lots of noise, hotdogs, and beer. We had a blast, and FSU won 45 to 11. After the game, Tom and I thanked Jon for his hospitality and drove back to Fort Walton Beach.

Back in FWB, Tom, Phil, Bill Christie, and I were really getting into running, in addition to the run every weekend in the local area; on Mondays, at 17:00, we ran with the McGuire's Restaurant running team in Destin. After the run to support their team, they would feed us and give us some beer, a good deal that we never intentionally missed.

In October, I drove my truck down to Fort Pierce to support my son Michael who was competing in the US Sailing Teams Mistral class sailing trials for the 2000 Sydney Olympics. The competition was being held on Indian Harbor Beach, Florida, by the Eau Gallie Yacht Club, with a scheduled start date of October 16th. I stayed with Michael at his place in Fort Pierce during the competition and drove him up the coast every day to Indian Harbor Beach to compete. While he attended the sailors' briefing, I would, as part of his racing team, haul his board down to the beach and rig it up.

In the middle of the trials, Hurricane Irene blew by, causing a delay and the racing. The competition was restarted on October 21st and finished three days later on the 24th. When the results were tallied, Michael won and, for the fourth time, would, as a member of the US Sailing Team, compete in an Olympics. There was an awards ceremony that was noisy and outrageous where Michael was the celebrity. I had a great time at the trials being able to participate as part of my son's team.

Back in Fort Pierce, Michael and I talked about fundraising. Boardsailors don't get a lot of financial support from yacht clubs or the government to compete in the Olympics. Sponsors of the games would supply material stuff like clothing and backpacks but no cash. I would try to help fundraise by getting T-shirts made to sell around the Fort Walton Beach local area. Even though the opening ceremony for the games was almost a year away, Michael wouldn't have a lot of time to do much fundraising. In the coming months, he would be traveling to all sorts of meetings with the Olympic committee and the US Sailing Team. Then after competing in numerous international regattas, he would be sent to Colorado for the United States Olympic Teams training camp for all the US athletes competing in Sydney. The sailing team would be traveling to Sydney before the start of the games to climatize and to mainly get used to the sailing conditions there.

On November 13th Tom and I drove to Tallahassee to go to the FSU-Maryland game with Jon. They won 49 to 10 and were on a winning streak, ten in a row. After the game, we went to Bullwinkle's to get some food and drink and to observe the craziness. In the morning, while hanging around the pool, Jon mentioned that he wouldn't be there for the Surfview feast; he was going to spend Thanksgiving over at his girlfriend Molly's parent's house.

Once back at the Surfview, Thanksgiving was just over a week away, I went to work getting the Surfview ready for the feast, and as usual, I would roast a turkey while the attendees would bring their favorite dish for the table. At the feast, there was plenty of food, wine, and beer from the keg on the dock. Everyone walked away happy with a full belly, and even though it was a chilly

evening, a few others hung around the beer keg, talking until late in the evening.

For Christmas, Phil and Donna invited me over for their Christmas parties that they have every year for their family and friends. Everyone always has a wonderful time at their parties; there's always plenty of food, conversation, and even an opportunity, if you persevere, to play with Phil's trains.

To celebrate New Year's Eve, Linda and I went to the Marina Cafe in Destin for their dinner and party. Linda knew the chef who had dated her daughter, and he gave us some VIP attention. There was a big crowd with many of our friends and business associates, plenty of champagne, dancing, and lots of conversation. We all had a grand time bringing in the New Year.

Chapter Nine: 2000 – 2004

There was a lot going on during the first couple of months of the year. My son Jon finished his semester at FSU and found a job in Tallahassee at Kaiser College as an Associate Dean and was busy looking for a place to live. He was thinking of making an offer on a unit in a fourplex near the FSU campus. Oh! By the way, Molly Murphy was now his live-in girlfriend; and Jonny was doing all right in Tallahassee.

Back in Fort Walton Beach, I was trying to come up with a strategy for the Surfview. I finally decided that since all of my big plans fell through, I would just keep running the place as usual, and maybe the rental market would improve. To assist in Michael's Olympic fundraising campaign, I printed up plenty of his T-shirts and hats to sell around the local area. My friends had already bought plenty of them over the years but bought a couple more to support his campaign.

A short time later, Michael called; he had been at an Olympic team meeting with the game's sponsors. AT&T, one of the major sponsors of the 2000 Sydney Olympics, had offered as part of their support would providing round trip air travel to the games for two relatives of each competing athlete. Michael called and gave me the contact number for one of them and offered the other one to his mother. For some reason, she couldn't go and gave it to her mother, Mary.

I'd been planning to go to the games ever since Michael won the trials. Now that transportation was taken care of, I searched the internet looking for someone in Sydney to swap places with during the games. I finally made contact with someone in Manly, across the harbor from Sydney, that wanted to get out of town for the Olympics and come to Florida. After a little negotiating, we agreed to swap places for a month and a half beginning on the 15th of August. I now had a place to stay, and once I received my airline reservations, I would be good to go.

In March, Rick returned with his boat to the Surfview dock after spending five months at the A & B Marina in Key West. I don't know how he did it; I liked Key West as a port of call, but after a week of hanging around Duvall Street with all its great restaurants, bars, and entertainment, I was always ready to leave. While we talked about his sail back up to the panhandle, I mentioned that in a couple of months, I would be headed to Australia for the Olympics. I told him about the swapping arrangement, and if he was interested, I had a place for him to stay for the games. It didn't take him long to make up his mind, and he said he would meet me there before the games started.

I got a call in May from the Australian; he called to tell me that he was not coming over to Florida; he was going to Thailand to help a friend sail his new boat back to Australia. I asked him if our deal was off, he said it wasn't and gave me the contact number of his girlfriend Alice in Manly. I really came out smelling like a rose.

Later in May, my son Jon called to tell me that he asked Molly to marry him and planning to have their wedding in December. I congratulated them and wished them all the happiness; I hoped they were more successful at it than I was. It was turning out to be a very busy year.

In July, I received a message from Michael giving me the phone number of the place where he was staying in Sydney. He was staying with the sailing team in a rented house on Rushcutters Bay. I told him that I had a flight booked and would be on my way to Sydney on the 15th of August, that

I had a place to stay in Manly, and would contact him on my arrival. I love it when a plan comes together!

Just before leaving the Surfview, Monique, an old friend, gave me a contact number of a friend of hers in Australia, Andre Rog. The flight to Australia was a long and uneventful flight. Arriving at Sydney Airport, I cleared immigration, and customs collected my luggage and called my son, who

wasn't there, so I left a message that I had arrived alive. I also called my contact in Manly; she gave me directions to the flat, where the key was hidden, and would stop by after work to show me around. Leaving the airport, I hailed a cab for the short ride to Circular Quay by the Sydney Opera House to catch the Manly Ferry. While I waited for the ferry, I called Andre Rog with no success. The ferry took a half-hour to go up the length of Sydney Harbour to Manly, located on the NE end of the Harbor. The ferry trip across the bay from Sydney gives you a great photo-op of the city and the Sydney Harbour Bridge. The flat was a two-block bag drag from Manly Wharf. Finding the key to let me in, I located a bed and crashed.

Alice arrived after work, showed me how the appliances worked and gave me keys to his car and the membership guest card to his private club, The Manly 16ft Skiff Sailing Club. She suggested

we walk the short distance to the club for dinner. Over dinner, Alice was friendly, easy to talk to, and enthusiastic about having the Olympics in Australia. After dinner, we went to the bar, where she introduced me around, had a drink, then went home, leaving me in the hands of a friendly crowd. They kept buying me round after round of their local beer, Victoria Bitter, by the time I disengaged and staggered back to the flat, I was dead beat; I slept like a log.

Waking up in the morning feeling better than I should have, I went on a walkabout looking for and found a café for breakfast, then went grocery shopping. The flat was conveniently located, and

since everything I would need was within walking distance, I probably wouldn't have to use his car. Once I got my groceries squared away, I walked over to Manly Beach. I had to check it out. Supposedly, all the girls go topless there, and sure enough, there were a few. Back at the flat, I tried calling my son again and made contact. He gave me directions to the house on Rushcutters Bay and invited me over to check out the place.

From the Circular Quay in Sydney, it was just a short taxi ride, a little over a mile, to Rushcutters Bay. When I arrived at 46 New Beach Road, Michael greeted me and gave me a tour of the team's three-story house, which was conveniently located across the street from the Olympic sailing venue in Yarranabbe Park. After meeting the coach and some of the sailors, Michael took me across the street to show me around the venue from where he would be launching during the competition. From there, we looked over some of the boats at a marina on our way to the Cruising Yacht Club of Australia for dinner. During dinner, Michael gave me a heads-up on the team's training schedule. Every morning there would be a team briefing followed by physical endurance training and then sailing to familiarize themselves with the different racecourses in Sydney Harbour; for Michael, there were four different courses for the Mistal class. The training would continue until just before the start of the competition on the 17th. I probably wouldn't be seeing much of Michael before or during the games. Before I started on my way back to Manly, Michael gave me a ticket to the Olympic opening ceremony on the 15th of September, officially known as the Games of the XXVII Olympiad, to take place at the Stadium Australia in the Sydney Olympic Park.

I had a couple of weeks on my own to explore Sydney before Rick was due to show up, and I used the time walking around Manly and Sydney getting the lay of the land and staying in contact with Michael. After a couple of days, I pretty much knew my way around Manly, leaving me plenty of time to spend exploring Sydney. During my first day of wandering around in Sydney, I came across the Forbes Hotel on York Street. Their bar had tables outside on the sidewalk; the setup kind of reminded me of the Cambridge in London, where you were expected to share your table with others. Sure enough, it wasn't long after I sat down that I had company and conversation. Taking the ferry back to Manly after spending a day walking around Sydney, I would occasionally stop at the club for a couple of VB's and something to eat before heading to the flat for the night. I didn't go to the club often. Being a guest, people were always buying me a drink, and I could never get out of there without socializing and getting a belly full of VB and feeling like crap the next day.

Rick called me at the flat when he arrived on September 1st at the Sydney Airport. I told him to head for the Circular Quay, where I would meet him at the Manly Fast Ferry Wharf. During the ferry ride to Manly, he gave me the lowdown on what was happening at the Surfview. Once Rick was settled in at the flat, I took him over to the club for something to eat and to introduce him around; it was a Friday night and crowded, and we stayed at the bar socializing way too long. I told Rick as we stumbled back to the flat that he was now climatized, albeit the hard way.

In the morning, after a late breakfast, we walked over to check out Manly Beach before going grocery shopping. After returning to the flat, I tried calling Andre again, and this time, I made

contact. I identified myself as a friend of Monique; he remembered Monique from when his sister brought her along to visit a couple of years earlier. After chatting for a while, he suggested that he would like to show us around and would pick us up on Saturday the 9th.

Every day, after a leisurely breakfast, Rick and I would hop the ferry to Sydney for a walkabout the city and some of the points of interest that I found during my earlier walkabouts. During one of these walkabouts, I took him over to Rushcutters Bay to meet Michael during his lunch break and show him around the venue. We also looked over; the museum, the opera house, the Forbes Hotel Bar, the Australian National Maritime Museum, the Hog's Breath Café that we happened to stumble upon, plus numerous other points of interest. Every once in a while, we would stop in at the ATT Olympic sponsor information center in downtown Sydney to check on what was going on.

On Saturday, Andre picked us up and drove us around, showing us the sights on the west side of Sydney Harbour. He took us over to George's Head Lookout and Bradley's Head, some areas that could give us a good position to observe the Mistral race courses. When he dropped us off at the flat, he said he would be available on the 28th to take us over to the heads to watch the Mistral competition. During our conversations with Andre, he told us how his family immigrated to Australia after the Russians took over Latvia during the war and forced his family out of their home in Riga.

On the afternoon of the 15th, I made my way over to the Stadium Australia for the 7 pm opening

ceremony of the Sydney Olympics. I arrived at the stadium half an hour early, giving me

plenty of time to find my seat. A short time later, my ex-mother-in-law Mary sat down in her seat next to me. I hadn't seen her in decades, and we had a lot to talk about. We didn't have much time to chat; the ceremony started on time a 19:00 and showcased Australian heritage/history with speeches by local and international celebrities. But the best part for me came at the end of the ceremony with the Parade of Nations when the athletes of the 199 competing nations paraded around the stadium.

Michael's first race was two days later, on the 17th, and he finished in 2nd place; on the second race of the day, he finished 22nd. He was allowed to throw out his worst race so that finish was out. On the 28th, Andre picked us up and drove over to Bradley's Head to watch the races, you could see

the Mistral, but there were so many of them you really couldn't tell what was going on. On the 29th, the day before the last day of racing Michael was in 5th place, but he was sick as a dog with the flu, and at the end of the final day of racing and the points were tallied, he was in 11th place. Rick and I went over to the venue to see him after the final race; he was really in bad shape and needed to go to bed.

Rick flew back the next day on the 31st. I stayed on for the closing ceremonies on the 1st, then flew back to Florida on October 2nd. Michael stayed on in Sydney to go to all the after-Olympics parties, where he met a French girl, Barbara, who helped him recover and celebrate his retirement from the Olympic competition. Michael competed in four of the games over a period of twenty-two years; he was 34 years old.

The flight back to Florida was long and uneventful, and when I arrived at the Surfview, I found that under Doc's supervision, the apartments had survived without me during my month and a half absence. I wouldn't have much time to rest up. Thanksgiving and Jon's wedding were just around the corner. Rick beat me back to the Surfview by two days and was busy provisioning his boat, the Anna Virginia, to sail south to Key West for the winter. Before his departure, I told him that depending on what I get involved in after Thanksgiving and Jon's wedding. I might fly down to pay a visit.

As soon as I had things squared away at the Surfview, I called my son Jon and asked him if he could get Tom and me tickets to an FSU game. I wanted to meet and get to know his fiancée Molly Murphy a little before the wedding. He found us tickets to the FSU-Virginia game on October 21st and invited us to come over on Friday to stay at their flat for the night. With that taken care of, I would have plenty of time off before I would have to start thinking about getting ready for Thanksgiving.

On Friday the 20th, Tom and I hit the road for the three-hour drive to Tallahassee and found Jon's fourplex, and walked upstairs to his unit. Jon introduced us to his future bride Molly and took us on a tour of their two-bedroom flat. After a couple of beers, Molly prepared us a great meal. Then during after-dinner cocktails, she told us about some of her ideas for their upcoming wedding.

In the morning, Molly cooked us a hearty breakfast, and after a couple of hours of conversation, Tom and I drove over to the FSU stadium to find a parking spot and to meet Jack Brown for a tailgate party before the game. Being an alumnus of FSU, Jack had a reserved parking spot, and after searching around for a while, we found Jack and the party. FSU won 37 to 3, and so far, they're having another great season losing only one game to Miami. On the drive back to Fort Walton, Tom and I thought that Jon may have found a winner. After all, she could cook. It had been a couple of long tiring days, and by the time we arrived back in Fort Walton, I was beat.

Thankfully I had plenty of time to get ready for the Surfview Thanksgiving feast, and with Doc's help cleaning up the place and setting up the picnic tables, the feast went off without a hitch. The weather cooperated by giving us a beautiful day for the 20 to 25 tenants and guests that showed up with a bounty of food for the table. My contribution, as always, was a roasted turkey and a couple of bottles of wine. Everyone had a marvelous afternoon and on into the evening with conversations on the dock around the beer keg.

Shortly after Thanksgiving, I received an invitation to Jon and Molly's rehearsal dinner and wedding. The dinner was to take place on December 10th at the Tallahassee Holiday Inn, followed by the wedding on the 11th in Lafayette Park. On the 10th, I drove over to Tallahassee and checked

in at the Holiday Inn. Before going to the rehearsal, I drove over to have a beer with my uncle Rudy and aunt Clare at their hotel; they had driven over from Palm Coast for the wedding.

Once back at the Holiday Inn at the before-dinner cocktail party where Molly introduced me to her family and the rest of the wedding party. I found Molly's mother, Helen, to be very charming and that her father, Bud, worked for Bank America at their headquarters in Jacksonville.

My son Michael made it back from Australia just in time to be his brother's best man.

The next afternoon, December 11th, in Lafayette Park, Jon and Molly exchanged their wedding vows in a ceremony accompanied by a piper and serenades by Molly's brother John and his guitar. The reception was held immediately after at the park. Some of the attendees that I knew besides my uncle Rudy and Clare were; my ex, Jon's mother Gail with her mother Mary. Also attending were Jon and my friends; Tom and Donna Prohaska, Phil and Donna DiDonato with their son Derek, Bill and Marie Leibold with their son Kevin.

The reception lasted well into the evening, the food was good, and a local DJ supplied the music. I even danced with my ex, Gail, I hadn't seen or heard from her in decades, and as I found out, we really didn't have much to talk about. Everyone was having a wonderful time, and after sending Jon and Molly off on their honeymoon and with plenty of Champaign left over, the party continued. Jon and Molly had a great wedding, and I and everyone in attendance had a wonderful time. I wish them all the happiness.

I cornered Michael before he departed and quizzed him about Barbara, who he met at the Olympics. He told me that she was working for a concessionaire at the games and met her at one of the end of the Olympics parties. When he departed Sydney, he flew to India for a couple of weeks and then back to Sydney to spend more time with Barbara. From there, he flew back to the states, and she went on to Majorca in the Mediterranean. From Majorca, she flew to Miami, where Michael met her after his brother's wedding. Ah! Love, how sweet it is!

I was back home at the Surfview for only a couple of days when Jon called and told me that I was invited to my new in-laws, Bud and Helen's house in Jacksonville for Christmas. I was happy to attend and went Christmas shopping.

After a five-hour drive to Jacksonville, I found the house of my new in-laws, Bud and Helen, and joined the party. There was quite the crowd, Jon and Molly, my new in-laws, and their son John and his date. Helen took me on a tour of her beautiful house before having cocktails, conversation, exchanging gifts, and Christmas dinner. After enjoying Helen's wonderful dinner, after which I had an interesting conversation with Helen about her book that she gave me a copy of. The book was about the experiences that both she and her husband had when they were aircraft controllers on strike. Being government workers, their contract said they couldn't go on strike. They broke their contract, so Ronald Regan fired them all. They both still seemed bitter about the experience and will probably never vote for a Republican. All in all, it was an enjoyable Christmas, and I was thankful for the opportunity to get to know Molly's parents and brother a little and found the Murphy's to be wonderful hosts.

Celebrating New Year's 2001 back in Fort Walton was relatively quiet since Linda, my social director girlfriend, and I stopped dating. I stayed on Okaloosa Island to bring in the New Year at the Hog's Breath Saloon.

The year started out nice and quiet, my sons Michael and Jon were both busy with their women, and I was free of all complications. There were no vacancies at the Surfview, and I had caught up with all the maintenance. I was definitely ready for some sort of adventure. I could go down to Key West and visit Rick, but it was also ski season. I called up Tom to see if he could get a kitchen pass for a little adventure. He suggested that we talk it over at the Helen Back Saloon on the Island, where over a couple of beers, we came up with a plan. Fly over to Frankfurt, rent a car, drive on over to Switzerland, go skiing for a week, drive back to Frankfurt, turn in the car, fly to England to visit Tom's sister for a week, then fly back to Florida. It took me about a week to make the reservations, and we were ready to go.

We landed at Frankfurt Airport after an overnight flight on the morning of March 7th. After clearing immigration and customs, we picked up our baggage and rented a car. It was around noon when we started driving toward downtown Frankfurt. On the way, we came across the Zeppelin Museum, and since it was early, we decided to check it out. The door was locked, but there was someone inside, and they opened up for us. It was a small museum with all sorts of artifacts and the history of zeppelins from Count von Zeppelin's first to the crash of the Hindenburg at Lakehurst, N. J on May 6, 1937. We spent around an hour looking around and then went on our way.

In Frankfurt, we checked in at a small hotel near the Hauptbahnhof (main train station) and then went around the corner to an Irish Pub for beer and some food. We took the next day to get used to the time change by checking out the bars on Kaiserstrasse (the main street). After an early breakfast on Friday the 9th, we drove onto the autobahn and headed for Switzerland and the mountains. On the way, we called Craig, one of our running buddies from Fort Walton Beach that

was working in Germany. When we told him that we were on the autobahn just north of Heidelberg, Craig told us he had a civil service job at the U.S.Army Europe Headquarters in Heidelberg and invited us to his house for dinner and to stay for the night. We accepted his invitation, and he gave us directions to his house in Schwetzingen, a small town 4 miles SW of Heidelberg.

It was early when we arrived in Heidelberg, and since Craig was still at work, we had some time to kill, so we took a tour of Heidelberg Castle. The one thing I remember about the castle was that it had the world's largest wine barrel located below the ballroom with a hand pump in the ballroom to pump up the wine.

Craig was a Bill Clinton look-alike, back at the runners' club, we all called him mister president; he even talked like Clinton. We found his house, and after catching up over a couple of beers, his wife Lori prepared for us a lovely dinner followed by after-dinner cocktails where we solved the

world's problems. Lori insisted that we stay for another night because she wanted to prepare a German meal ala Lori for us, an offer that we just couldn't refuse.

To get us out of the house in the morning while she was cooking, she instructed Craig to go show us around town. He drove us to the Technic Museum-Speyer in Speyer on the Rhine River. It was a small museum that had on display all kinds of airplanes, boats, and military hardware. It took us quite a few hours to look it all over. After a lunch break, he drove us over to check out the 11th-century Speyer Cathedral before going back to Schwetzingen for Lori's German dinner. She had prepared the works: red cabbage, potato salad, wienerschnitzel, sauerkraut, and Rhein wine to wash it all down. The after-dinner discussion lasted well into the evening, during which Tom and I decided to forget about skiing and instead go to Normandy, where neither one of us had been before.

In the morning, we thanked Craig and Lori for their hospitality and started our estimated 8-hour drive to Normandy. Our route would take us north of Paris by way of Reims, Soissons. Compiegne, Beauvais, Rouen, then on to Questreham on the Normandy coast; we made it as far as Rouen. It was late afternoon when we drove into town and found a place to stay in a two-star hotel near the Cathedrale-Notre Dame de Rouen.

In the morning, after breakfast at our hotel, we went to look over the Cathedral and then over to the Historial Jeanne d'Arc, a history museum dedicated to Joan d'Arc. There was a lot to see, and by the time we were done, it was past noon, time for a leisurely late lunch at a nearby café. Later on, we did a walkabout town that ended up at a restaurant close to our hotel for some wonderful French cuisine for dinner.

On March 12[th,] we had miserable weather for the morning drive to Normandy; it was a dreary, overcast, rainy, and cold day. We bypassed Wuestreham and stopped instead at the

town of Arromanches les Bains on the Normandy coast. Code named Gold Beach when the British 2nd Army, 50th Infantry Division came ashore during the invasion. It was just a little past noon when we checked in at the Hotel de Normandie. From our corner room, we could see the remnants of the Mulberry Harbors, the temporary portable harbors set up during the allied invasion. Just down the street was the Musse du Deparquemeat, the commemorative museum of the D-Day landings. We walked over in the rain to check it out, but unfortunately for us, it was still closed for the winter. We were a little early for the tourist season, which was the reason why we had the place to ourselves. Almost everything was closed. We adjourned to the hotel bar for cocktails and later on to the restaurant for dinner. Maybe we should have kept to our original plan to go skiing.

The weather in the morning was still miserably cold and overcast, but the rain had stopped. We drove down the coast about three miles to the Longues-Sur-Mer battery, a fortified coastal artillery position that was part of Hitler's Atlantic Wall. We spent an hour or so checking it out and getting muddy in  the process. From there, we started driving west down the coast to the Normandy American Cemetery by Omaha Beach, where the U.S. 1st and 29 Infantry Divisions of the U.S.1st Army came ashore. We stopped on the way to the cemetery in Port en Bessin, where

we bought some bread, cheese, sausage, and wine for the road. After spending time at the cemetery walking and looking around, we drove on to La Pointe Du Hoc. That's where the U.S. 2nd Ranger Battalion scaled the cliff to attack the German battery. When they got there, the guns were gone, the Germans moved the battery inland a couple of miles, but the Rangers found and destroyed them. From there, we drove to Utah Beach, where the U.S. 4th Infantry Division of the U.S. 1st Army landed.

It was just a short drive inland from there, about 5 miles, to St Mere Eglise, where we hoped to find a place to stay. We arrived there late on the afternoon of the 13th and found a hotel. While checking in at the John Steel Hotel, the desk clerk told us that they were really still closed for the winter but would open it up for us. The hotel was named after the U.S. paratrooper of the 82nd Airborne Division that got  hung up on a spire of the Church of St Mere Eglise. He was captured by the Germans but later managed to escape and rejoined his unit. We asked the desk clerk where we could get something to eat since their restaurant was closed, and he told us that there was food at a bar down the street a couple of blocks

We found it easy enough, the only place opened on the block, and took seats at the bar. There were three other patrons there that looked like local farmers, they were looking us over, and 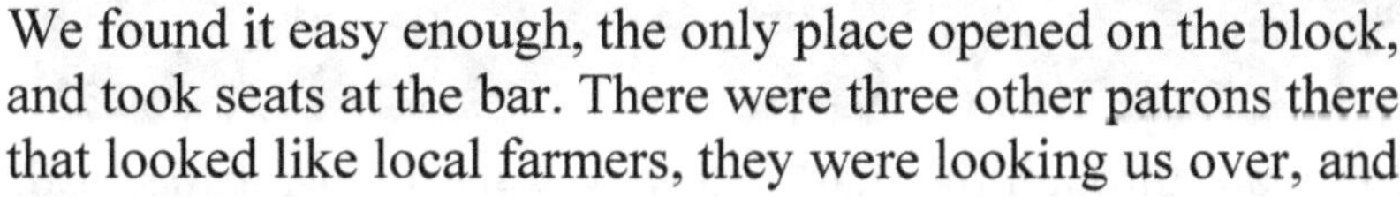 they didn't appear to be very friendly, so I ordered a round of Calvados, and all of a sudden, we were all friends. I knew about Calvados, a local brandy that's made from apples and pears, from when I was stationed in Europe 40 years earlier. We stayed until closing, playing a bar game with them that they called Skittles. It is amazing how well you can communicate after a couple of drinks. After saying farewell to our newfound friends, we headed back to our hotel through what appeared to be a deserted town.

After breakfast in the morning at a café around the corner from our hotel, we walked over to the church that had a mannequin of John Steel in his parachute and full combat gear hanging from it. Across the street was the Airborne Museum, and to our surprise, it was open. We stayed the rest of the day going over and reading everything in the museum. It also had on display WW-2 hardware, including a C-47 Gooney Bird and a Waco CG-4A Glider that the airborne divisions used. For a small museum, it had a lot of stuff.

The next morning the 15th, we started our drive back to Frankfurt. We got as far as Caen and drove toward the center of town, stopping at the first hotel we came across. After getting settled in our room, we headed to their restaurant for cocktails and dinner. On the way, we found out from the concierge that we were within walking distance of the Memorial de Caen, a D-Day Museum that was open. We decided to stay another day to check it out.

In the morning, we walked over to the museum, a twenty-minute walk. Once inside, we realized that we were going to be there all day. It was loaded with all kinds of military equipment and hardware, mostly from the British, Canadian and German armies. We just had a good old time looking at and reading all that we could. We needed another day to do it all, but we were running out of time and had to get moving. That evening we walked around the neighborhood and came

across a bar near the university. The clientele were mostly college students, and they acted just as crazy as ours. We stayed for a while watching the goings on before walking back to our hotel.

We woke up to noise from a farmers market going on outside our hotel, so before starting our

drive to Frankfurt, we took the time to walk through the market to buy some food for the road. Once on the road, we made good time, and before nightfall, we were on the ferry going across the Rhein River to Rudesheim, where we walked around town for a while. Back on the road and a half hour later, we were in Frankfurt, checking in at the hotel by the Hauptbahnhof. Once we were settled into our room, we walked around the corner to enjoy the evening at the Irish Pub.

The next morning, the 18th, we turned in the car and caught a flight to the London City Airport to visit Tom's sister Jean. It was a Sunday; Jean was home, not busy with clients, and could spend some time with us. We walked over to Hyde Park and stopped for lunch at the Italian Gardens Café by the Serpentine, the big lake in the park. Jean suggested over lunch that we go take a ride

on the London Eye, the big Ferris wheel across the Thames River from Parliament; she had wanted to go on it ever since it opened about a year earlier. It turns so slow, two revolutions per hour, that there's no need to stop it for people to get on or off. It has 32 capsules holding 25 people each and gives you a great view of London. It was well worth doing. Back in Kensington, we talked Jean into going over to the Goat for a few pints and some pub food before walking back to her home at 11 Albert Way.

We had breakfast in the morning with Jean and left the house before her first appointments; we needed to do something with the three days we had left before our flight back to Florida. We looked at our London city map and spotted the London Canal Museum, one of the few museums we hadn't been to before. It took us a while to find it, but it was well worth the effort. The museum had boats outside on a canal to look over, and inside, it told the story of the canals, boats, and the ice and ice cream trade. For a small museum, it is packed with a lot of interesting information. They stored the ice shipped in from the glaciers of Norway to a deep pit to be distributed by the canal boats and wagons. Ice cream, they claimed, was first consumed in 1671 at a feast at Windsor Castle. After spending the

morning at the museum, we adjourned to The Cambridge, one of our favorite pubs that happened to be close by, for a pint and some food. We ended up spending the afternoon there at one of the outside tables talking to people. Leaving The Cambridge at the last minute, we were back at Jean's just in time to go to dinner with her.

For the rest of our stay in London, we visited the Natural History Museum and Victoria & Albert Museum, both a short walk from Jean's and walked around London. For our last evening in town, we all went out for dinner and the theatre to see Buddy, the Buddy Holly Story; the music had people dancing in the aisles. Early the next morning, the 23rd, we took the underground to Victoria Station to catch the Gatwick Express to the Airport for our flight back to Florida. I always have a great time in London and Jean, a great hostess, is part of it. Our intended ski trip morphed into something entirely different, an awesome adventure to be remembered.

Once back at the Surfview, it took me a week or so to catch up with the apartment's bookkeeping and maintenance. I knew I had to take a trip down to Marathon to check on the house and get it ready to sell. My uncle Rudy had called informing me that his wife Claire was diagnosed with Alzheimer's and would need to sell his share of our house in Marathon. I wasn't that eager to sell it and didn't have the money to buy him out so I approached Rick to see if he was interested, he wasn't. I thought about it for a while and decided to consolidate the trip to Marathon with a visit with Rick in Key West. I called Tom to see if he was interested in going, he was all in.

On the 15th of April, we flew to Miami, rented a car, and drove down to Marathon. We would be in Marathon for just a few hours while I talked to my tenants to them that the house was going on the market and that if they were interested in buying it, I would give them a good deal. I then checked out the place to see if I had to make any repairs; it looked in good shape except for maybe a paint job. Before starting our drive to Key West, I stopped to chat with the realtor that I had phoned earlier about listing the house. He had been over earlier to inspect it and suggested a competitive asking price for the listing, I signed the contract. Now, all he needed to get was Rudy's signature.

We called Rick to tell him we were on the way, and he let us know that he had a parking place waiting for us close to the A&B Marina where his boat was tied up. Over the next four days, we dined at numerous restaurants and consumed lots of beer, mostly at Rick's on Duval St across the street for Sloppy Joe's. We always tried to corner an outside table so we could watch the crowd walk by while drinking beer and eating peanuts. On our second day there, we took the opportunity to sign up for the morning tour of Truman's Little White House, where Truman liked to rest and recuperate during his presidency. We had a good time with Rick and his fellow yachtsmen at the dock. When it was time to leave, we thanked Rick for his hospitality and hit the road; we had a flight to catch in Miami.

Back on Okaloosa Island, I was really anticipating enjoying the rest of the summer at the Surfview when I got a call from my son Jon in Tallahassee telling me that both he and Molly had lost their jobs. They were having no luck searching for jobs in Tallahassee but by searching the internet, they found there were more job opportunities in St Petersburg. When Molly found a job there with the Home Shopping Network, they decided to make the move.

It was shortly after they moved to St Petersburg that, on September 11[th,] al-Qaeda attacked the twin towers of the World Trade Center and the Pentagon, a terrorist attack that shocked the nation. Then just a couple of days later, I got a call from my son Michael telling me that he was getting married sometime in late October to Barbara in India by his guru Sai Baba at his compound in Bangalore. What next? I congratulated him and then asked about their itinerary, thinking maybe I could meet up with them somewhere along the way. After getting married, they planned on flying to London to meet Barbara's stepmother, Maria Pia, then on to Paris, where her mother, stepdad, and sisters lived. I told Michael that I would meet them in London and asked him for Maria Pia's

contact number. The next day I made flight reservations and called Jean in London to see if she would put me up for a couple of days.

I landed in the UK at Gatwick on the 6th of November and made my way to Jean's house in Kensington. Once I was settled in, I called Maria Pia to introduce myself and see if she had an arrival time for Michael and Barbara. They were arriving the next day, and Maria kindly invited me along to

meet them at the airport. Maria picked me up the next day to meet them when they cleared through immigration; from there, Maria drove us to her house where they were staying. That evening she had a party for the newlyweds. During the party, we were entertained with classical piano played by the eldest of her two daughters. It was a marvelous party, and it was late when I finally took a cab back to Jean's.

Three days later, Michael, Barbara, and I flew out of London City Airport to Paris. We were met there by Barbara's mother, Elizabeth, who drove us to her house in the Paris suburbs. After meeting Barbara's stepdad Giles and her sisters Margo and Luna, Barbara and her sisters took us on a quick tour of the neighborhood before we all went out to dinner, including the dog, to their favorite restaurant across the street.

The next day Barbara's grandfather Claude gave a party at his house located across the street from

Lafayette Park in Paris. It was quite the party Claude's wife, an artist who was a lot younger than Claude, and spoke some English, as did Claude's brother; almost everyone else spoke French. I did get into a conversation with Claude's brother about the war. He fled France to Casablanca, Morocco, when the Germans occupied France and eventually made his way from Casablanca to England to join de Gaulle's Free French forces in England. He was in the French armored division that liberated Paris. I had read that they had to fight some of the French Resistance communists for the control of Paris, I asked him about it, his recollection was that it did happen, but it wasn't much of a fight.

The next day Barbara's mother, Elizabeth, Michael, Barbara, and I took a train to grandpa Claude's farm. We were met at the station by the caretaker in an old Mercedes for the 20-minute drive to

the farm. It was really an estate with a big house, stables that were converted to guest rooms, and a swimming pool, plus a couple of other buildings; it was a big place. That evening the caretaker's wife prepared for us a wonderful meal with plenty of local wine.

In the morning, we went along with the caretaker to a farmers' market in a nearby village. We followed him around as he bartered with the vendors. We spent the morning there and had lunch before returning to the farm. With what he bought at the market, his wife prepared a grand feast for our last evening meal before our departure in the morning.

Back in Paris, Barbara took Michael and me on the Metro to the Louvre, where we spent most of

the day. There is no way you can see it all in one day, we did get to check out Mona Lisa's smile. The following day Barbara drove us out to the country to look over a 17th century estate. It was my last day in Paris, I was flying out in the morning to London. I thanked Barbara for showing me around her city and how I enjoyed meeting her family.

Back in London, I made my way to Jean's, and later that evening, after she was done seeing clients, we went out to dinner. During our meal, she mentioned that she was leaving in the morning on a business trip for a couple of days and that Maria Pia had called me. In the morning after breakfast, as she was leaving Jean told me to hold down the fort while she was gone and that her maid would be coming in to clean up the place. After Jean left, I called Maria, and after chatting for a while, she invited me to a dinner party that evening with some of her girlfriends.

Maria Pia's dinner party was a lot of fun, one of her friends was a psychologist, and the other was a schoolteacher. I knew a little about the school system in the UK and got the conversation going. The conversation was lively during before-dinner cocktails and carried on through dinner. After dinner we were serenaded for a while on the piano by Maria's daughter while we enjoyed our after-dinner drinks; it was an interesting evening.

The next morning Sunday the 18th, after making myself breakfast at Jean's, I went for a walk over to Kensington Garden, then over to Hyde Park, where there was a huge crowd down by Marble Arch and speakers' corner. They were getting organized for a demonstration against the Afghanistan war with a march to Trafalgar square. There were lots of banners and signs of the Socialist, Marxist and Communist parties mixed in with the antiwar banners. It was quite the scene. While wandering around in the crowd, I came across the London Mullah on his prayer rug praying with some of his followers. He was the one suspected of being a recruiter in London for al-Qaeda. When the march was about to start, I took the underground to

Trafalgar Square to watch the happening. When the march arrived, it was loud but peaceful. I did notice that the police were about a block away, ready to go in case the protest got out of hand.

The next morning, I flew back to Florida, departing before Jean returned from her trip. It was really nice of her to let me stay on such short notice at her lovely home in Kensington. Jean has always been a good friend and a charming hostess.

During the flight, I went over what I observed during my time with Barbara's family, it was all a little confusing, but I finally figured it out. Barbara's mother was her father's first wife, and after having Barbara they divorced. Her father then married Maria Pia and they had two girls before he died, leaving Barbara, one of the trust funds he had set up for his daughters, and leaving Maria the rest of his estate, which was probably why Maria didn't go to Paris with us. Barbara's mother married Giles and had two daughters, so Barbara was an only child with four stepsisters. Barbra's grandfather's company published all the books for the schools in Paris.

I was back at the Surfview just in time to start getting things organized for the Thanksgiving feast. I had a hard time finding a turkey for my contribution to the table but eventually found one. Luckily we had good weather for the feast, and all twenty or so guests had a wonderful time. The conversation on the dock by the beer keg went on as usual into the evening.

Christmas and New Year were just around the corner. I was worn out and needed to rest up; I stayed home for the holidays.

2002

The New Year started off slow, giving me plenty of time to manage and maintain the apartments. I planted Indian Hawthorn bushes around the perimeter of the property that sort of gave the perception of the empty lots being part of the Surfview.

A short time later, my son Michael and his bride Barbara called me; they were all excited to tell me that they had just bought a house. They were in Fort Pierce, Florida, staying at their friend Reggae's house and it just so happened that the next-door neighbor died and her family wanted to sell the property fast. Michael and Barbara were at the right place and at the right time. They made an offer that was accepted. They made a good deal buying it at a bargain basement price. I congratulated them on their buy and told them that I would be coming down in the near future to check it out.

A little over a month later, I drove down to Fort Pierce Beach to visit Michael and Barbara in their new house. It was a nice two bedroom with a garage and a small swimming pool. It needed some work, like a paint job and maybe a clean-up to spruce up the grounds. While I was there, they told me that they were going over to visit Barbara's parents for Christmas and invited me to come. I told them I didn't have anything planned for the holidays and would think it over.

It was just a short time later in March that I got a call from my son Jon telling me they were planning to move to Jacksonville to be near Molly's mother, who had just been diagnosed with breast cancer. Jon had found a job in Jacksonville with Priceline Mortgage Company and that they would be moving there at the end of the month. I told them I would drive down to St. Petersburg and help them make the move. I arrived there a couple of days early to help them finish packing and load the U-Haul, their car, and my truck. The next morning, we drove in a convoy up to their apartment in Jacksonville and helped them unload before driving back to Fort Walton Beach.

I had all my reservations for my trip to France made before the Thanksgiving Feast at the Surfview.

On the 22nd of December, I caught the flight at the Fort Walton Beach Airport for the first leg of my flight to Paris. I landed at Orly Airport in Paris the next morning, the 23rd. Michael, Barbara, and her mother, Elizabeth, were there to meet me once I cleared customs and immigration. At their house, Barbara's  teenage sisters, Margo and Luna, offered to play travel guide, and for the next day or two, they took every opportunity to show me around the neighborhood. We all exchanged gifts on Christmas eve, and on Christmas day, we had a lovely dinner at their favorite restaurant across the street.

The next day Michael, Barbara, and I took a train to Marseilles to visit a friend of theirs, Phillipe. He met us at the train station and drove us around, showing us some of the sights of Marseilles before taking us to his home. Later on that evening, he took us to a nearby restaurant where we had some fine food and wine and talked. In the morning, Phillipe took us on a little road trip up into the mountains, and we stopped at a small village for lunch, where we had a good time chatting with the locals. After lunch, we walked a short distance over to look at the ruins of a monastery before driving back to Marseilles. That evening we went out to dinner and enjoyed some really good French cuisine and conversation. We stayed in Marseilles another day as his guests before taking the train back to Paris. We had a good time with Phillipe as he was entertaining, friendly, and spoke English. We were back in Paris in time for Giles' New Year's Eve Party with his family.

The party was a small gathering, mostly family and some of their neighbors that stopped in for a drink. There was plenty of food and champagne. Most of my conversations that evening were with Michael and Barbara since everyone else spoke French. I did have fun playing some board games with Margo who spoke some English and Luna her younger sister, who only knew French.

Elizabeth kept Michael and Barbara busy shopping the New Year's sales that I had no interest in

and gave me an opportunity to spend some time at the Louvre. So, for the next couple of days, I was on my own in Paris. Every day I would take the Metro to the Louvre to spend a few hours there. On my way back, I would stop at a café for a beer and people-watch for a while. On one occasion, on my way back, I stopped in at Giles' antique shop to say hello. He wasn't there, but his employee was, and she was a fine-looking thirty-something who spoke very good English. After chatting for a while, I found her to be very inquisitive and wanting to know all about Florida and the United States. Somehow, I always seem to have a good time in Paris.

After saying my goodbyes to everyone early on the morning of the 4th of January, I took a cab to Orly Airport for my flight back to Florida. Michael and Barbara were staying in Paris with her parents for a while before coming back to the states. Michael would not be there long, he was in demand as a boardsailing coach and was hired to coach Gal Fridman the Israeli Sailboarder for the upcoming 2004 XXVIII Olympics to be held in Athens, Greece. Michael had competed against Gal in the 1996 Olympics, where Gal won a bronze medal.

Before I left France, Michael gave me something to think about on my flight back to Florida. He told me that he would be training Gal throughout the fall in Torbole, Italy, a beautiful place on Lake Garda. That I should fly on over and maybe have a couple of beers together while he was working with Gal. I didn't have to think too long or hard about it.

I was back at the Surfview from my trip to France for about four months when Tom and I flew up to Washington, DC, in June to play tourists and visit the grave of his father. We landed at Ronald

Reagan Washington National Airport, then took the Metro to Dupont Circle. From there, we dragged our bags about half a mile up Connecticut Ave to the Winsor Park Hotel. There was some sort of demonstration going on across the street, and after checking in at the hotel, we went over and talked to the demonstrators. They were all dressed in yellow and were the Falun Gong, a religious sect protesting the Chinese

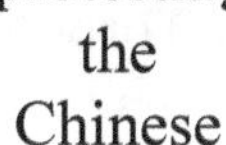

Governments persecution of their people. After chatting with them for a while, we walked down Connecticut Avenue toward Dupont Circle, looking for a place to eat and drink.

In the morning, we got on the Metro to Arlington. Tom's father was an Air Force Colonel and is buried in Arlington National Cemetery. We found the grave, and after spending some time there, we walked over to the Tomb of the Unknown Soldier. After watching the guards for a while, we walked over to Arlington House and took

the tour, and learned about its interesting history. The cemetery is on the land that was Robert E. Lee's Plantation. Lee's wife, Mary Ann, inherited the property from her father George Washington Parke Custis, who built the mansion and was the step-grandson and later adopted son of President George Washington. During the Civil War, the plantation was abandoned to the advancing union troops and became our national cemetery.

Linda Brown, the wife of Jack Brown, who was one of our partners in the Pele, was working in the Pentagon, so we gave her a call. She happened to be in town at the time and agreed to meet up with us outside the White House, where we talked for a short time before she had to go back to work. After Linda left, Tom and I walked a couple of blocks over to the Old Ebbitt Grill on 15th St, just across the street from the Treasury Department. We were a little bit early for happy hour and found seats at the bar before it got crowded. We had a good-ole time there talking to all sorts of characters, like the White House tailor for President Obama, who had a lot of stories to tell; we stayed on into the evening to enjoy the excellent food and drink at the Old Ebbitt.

Over the course of our weeklong visit to DC, we walked all over, visiting numerous memorials, monuments, and museums. We also checked out many restaurants and bars and talked to lots of people, mostly other tourists, before flying back to Florida. There is plenty to see and do in our nation's capital and, in the process, get a good dose of our country's history.

In June, I gave a heads up to Tom and Rick that I was going to Torbole, Italy, in July, and to let me know if they were interested in going along before I started making reservations. Tom said he couldn't make it, Rick said he wanted in, and I went to

work planning the trip. What I came up with were flight reservations to Verona, Italy, by way of Atlanta and Frankfurt, Germany. Arriving in Verona, we would pick up a rental car and start the hour drive to Torbole, located on the north end of Lake Garda. It would be a long travel day, but once we found our way to our hotel in Torbole, we could take a breather and maybe make contact with Michael and Gal.

The flight on July 2nd to Verona went pretty much as planned. Arriving at Verona, we picked up our car and started the 50-mile drive up the lake in heavy traffic to Torbole and finally arrived there around five in the afternoon. It had been a long day and by the time we checked into our hotel and then found something to eat we were done for the day.

In the morning, we pedaled around town using the hotel's bicycles and found my son Michael at the Circolo Surf Torbole, a sailing club on the lake. He was there with Gal and his wife Michal; she had

just flown up from Israel to stay with her husband for a couple of weeks. We had lunch with them at the club and mentioned that the next day since Gal and Michael were going to be busy training all day, we were going to take a drive to look over the area and invited Michal along for the ride.

After lunch, we continued our bike ride over to Riva del Garda, a little over a mile to the west of Torbole. It took time going around a ridge between the rivers that flow into the lake. Once we got there, we stopped for a beer and enjoyed the unbelievable scenery where the Alps dropped almost vertically to the lake. The lake, located on the south side of the Alps, is absolutely beautiful, as Michael had said. In the winter, the town is in ski country, surrounded by nine local ski areas, with Innsbruck, Austria, about 100 miles north. Back in Torbole, we dropped off our bikes at the hotel and went on foot to walk around town for a while before meeting up with Michael, Gal, and his wife for dinner.

In the morning, we picked up Michal and started driving down the west side of the lake through a series of tunnels to the town of Limone on a narrow strip of land between the sheer cliffs of the Alps and the lake. We stopped there to look at the Roman lemon orchards and walked around to some of the shops. So far, our road trip was pretty boring, driving through one long tunnel after another, so we headed up the

mountain ending up at Valvestino Dam, one of the many hydroelectric facilities around Lake Garda. After looking around and taking photos, we headed back to Torbole, stopping at a café on the way. During lunch Michal told us that she was in the Israeli Navy Reserves and that everyone in Israel has to serve one way or another, quite different from our military that's now all volunteers. We were back in Torbole a short time later; the drive was pretty much a waste of time and gas except for having some interesting conversations with Michal.

Torbole is a small town, and after a couple of days, Rick and I pretty well knew our way around and had found a few restaurants with good food and friendly staff. The proprietor of one of the restaurants was real friendly; she spent a lot of time talking to us. I thought I might get lucky, but it never happened. We also found a bar that was close to our hotel that we liked and one evening while sitting at the bar Rick and I got into a political discussion unaware that we were loud and gathering a crowd. When the bar closed and

we were leaving, the proprietor stopped us and told us about the disturbance we caused, then invited us to come back anytime; we were good for business.

The ferry between the towns on the lake stopped at Torbole every couple of hours. We found the schedule and spent a day or two taking it to some of the towns on the north end of the lake. They were short trips on the ferry and gave us some time in town to walk around and maybe stop at a café for lunch before the next ferry back to Torbole. Most of our time was spent pedaling bicycles around Torbole and Riva del Garda; there was plenty to keep up occupied.

There was a no wind day that gave Michael the day off, and he wanted to show me L'Orto ruins located on top of a high precipice. It was a short bike ride over to it and a steep climb that took a while to make it to the top, where we had a wonderful view and photo op of the river coming down the valley to Torbole and the lake. It was one of the few times I had alone with Michael, who was kept busy most of the time working with Gal, except when we all would occasionally get together for drinks or dinner.

Three days before our flight back to Florida, Rick and I said goodbye to everyone and drove down to Verona, and checked into a hotel. It was still early in the day, so we drove over to Sirmione to see the ancient castle and an archaeological site there. The 13th-century fortress Castello di Sirmione was located about half a mile from the end of the peninsula that extends out into Lake Garda. On the end of the peninsula, about half a mile from the fortress is the dig where Grotte di Catullo, the ancient ruins of a large Roman villa, was located. We wanted to check it all out but we only managed to get as far as the fortress, there was too much to see, and we ran out of time to see the ruins. We drove back in time to our hotel's small dining room for a lovely meal with wine from their vineyard.

The following day was spent in Verona at the Piazza Bra by the Arena di Verona; a Roman Amphitheater built to seat 20,000 people still in use today, hosting summer opera programs. After spending half a day at the arena, we had lunch at a café on the Piazza delle Erbe, then walked over to look at the Verona Cathedral before

202

heading back to the hotel, where we had another wonderful meal before flying out in the morning to Florida. In August, Gal went on to win a gold medal at the 2004 Olympics in Athens.

After an uneventful flight back to Florida, Rick started getting his boat ready to sail to Key West and asked if I would like to go along. He had a slip reserved in Key West starting in October for six months at the A&B Marina. I told him I would meet him there, and within days he set sail. He was eager to get to Key West in time for Fantasy Fest, a weeklong festival that ends on or near Halloween.

After taking care of business at the Surfview, I started driving to Marathon to check on the house, it had been on the market for over a year, and I needed to find out why it wasn't selling. After an uneventful drive to Marathon, where I stopped in to talk to our relator before checking in with my tenants. They were happy with the fact that the place hadn't sold, and it probably wouldn't for a while since nothing was selling in the keys at the time. I stayed in the vacant upstairs apartment

for a couple of days, cleaning, painting, and making some minor repairs. Since it was a short drive to Key West (58 miles), and that there were still four days left before the end of Fantasy Fest, I thought maybe I needed to go check it out. I gave Rick a call to see if he was there and to tell him I was on my way down to visit; he was tied up at the marina and told me where to park. On my way out of town, I stopped to talk to the realtor one more time to motivate him to try harder to sell the place.

Upon arrival in Key West, it was crowded with party goers. I found the parking lot Rick told me about by the A&B Marina where Rick's boat, the Anna Virginia, was tied up. I stowed my backpack on board and went looking for Rick and found him at Alonzo's Oyster Bar at the marina and joined him for lunch. He filled me in on his sail to Key West down the west coast of Florida. After lunch, we hung around the dock talking to some of Rick's yachting friends before walking over to Rick's Bar on Duval Street; the street was closed to vehicle traffic for the festival. We lucked into an outside table where over a beer and peanuts, we watched the crowd walk by. Rick

mentioned that every day there was a different party theme, and tonight it was Toga Party; I found a Toga.

That night there were lots of people in togas and other interesting costumes wandering around the street, trying to get into the overcrowded bars on Duval Street. In the crowd, there were many partially nude women showing off their body paint. Some of these painted ladies were in groups of two or four middle-aged friends from out of town without their spouses living out their fantasy and wanted their picture taken. As the evening progressed, the crowd grew, and by around 10 pm, it was a pretty outrageous scene. I lost track of Rick earlier in the evening, and when I finally made my back to the boat late that evening, he was in his bunk sound asleep; he was smart and quit early.

In the morning, we walked over to Pepe's Café for breakfast which was crowded but worth the wait. On the way back from Pepe's, we walked down Duval Street; all the trash from last night's toga party was all cleaned up and ready for tonight's party. Key West does a good job of managing these events. The police aren't that visible, and considering the fact that they're dealing with a bunch of drunk people. I didn't see any fights or destruction of property during my stay there. I helped Rick's party until Fantasy Fest ended on Saturday with a spectacular parade. I stayed another day on Rick's boat to recuperate before starting my drive back to Fort Walton Beach.

Back at the Surfview, I looked forward to relaxing for a couple of weeks doing nothing. I did get some time to enjoy myself before getting ready for the Surfview Thanksgiving Feast. My tenants did most of the work. I just set up the tables, roasted a turkey, and invited some old friends; they did the rest. The weather cooperated for the feast with the usual crowd of around twenty people. It was a lot of fun and gave me the opportunity to know my tenants better and be with friends. The feast always ended up with some of us on the dock by the beer locker late into the evening, solving the world's problems.

December was going to be an easy month for me; my only commitments were the 5 pm run on Mondays at McGuire's Irish Pub in Destin and driving down to Fort Pierce to spend Christmas with my son Michael and his wife, Barbara. It just didn't happen that way. On the 15th, I drove over to Destin for the run at McGuire's, and while running with Palma Jorgenson on a bike trail off the left side of the road, we were run over from behind by a hit-and-run driver. I woke up in an ambulance, and looking in the door was Bill Christie, one of my running buddies. I asked him what happened; he told me that I had been run over. I then looked down at my hand that was spurting out blood and passed out.

In the hospital, they determined that besides a bunch of cuts and bruises, I had a concussion, fractured pelvis, fractured left collarbone, and a messed up left shoulder rotator cuff. Palma was

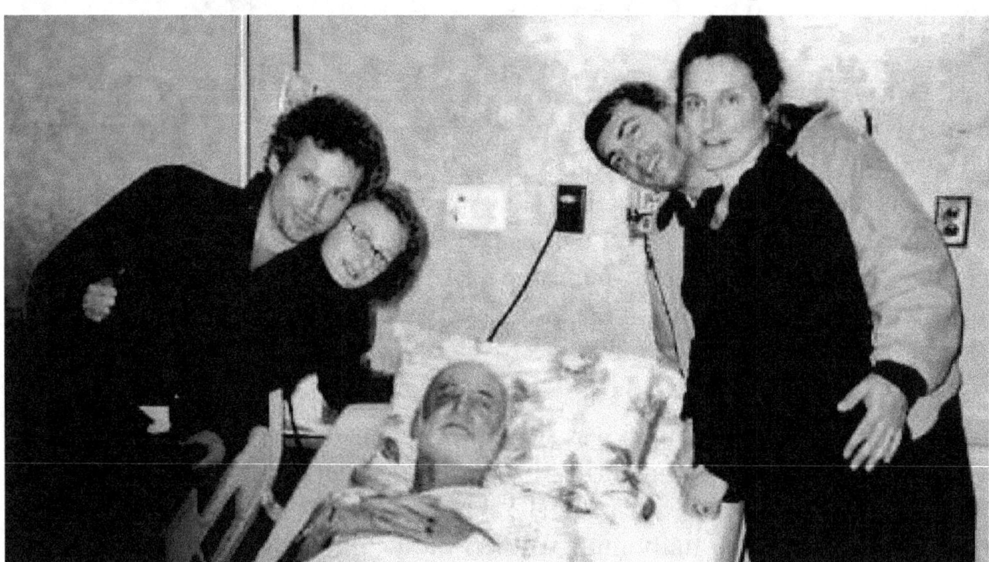

also in the hospital with a severe concussion. The next day my sons and their wives were there to visit and cheer me on. I thanked them for driving up to check up on me and told them that I would be good as new shortly. After surgery on my shoulder and putting my collarbone back together again with a metal plate, they sent me home to recuperate.

My ex-girlfriend Linda Quinlan brought me over a recliner to sit and sleep on, close to the bathroom for easy access. I had a nurse come see me every day for a while to change the bandages and had friends visit, bringing me food and telling me what they found out about us getting run over. The story they told was that a car driven by a 32-year-old woman who was hopped up on prescription drugs crossed over into the left lane and onto the bike path, hitting both Palma and me from behind. The impact threw Palma back over into the left lane of the road, where she hit the pavement headfirst. I went over the hood and smashed my head on the windshield, then was carried on the hood down the road for about 50 feet where I fell off onto the right lane hitting the road with my left shoulder. A short time later, two women driving home from shopping spotted us in the fading light of the day lying in both lanes of the road. They stopped on the road, blocking traffic, and called for help. One of the women came over to me and covered me with her jacket.

Just before Christmas, the woman that ran us over, a single mom with two small kids living with her mother-in-law, turned herself in to the police and was released on her own recognizance for the holidays until the trial. I would be spending the holidays in my cave at the Surfview recovering.

2004

During the first week of the year, I was able to walk around the parking lot and go sit out on the dock for a while; then, some good news, on the 17th of January, Elizabeth Helen Gebhardt was born, the firstborn of my son Jon and Molly, my first grandbaby. It was also the beginning of therapy, three days a week for months. The end result was that no amount of therapy was going to restore full movement to my left shoulder. It did help restore a lot of movement, maybe 80%, and that wouldn't slow me down much.

I was notified of the trial date for my hit-and-run bimbo and asked if I wanted to make a written statement. I really didn't have anything to say except how the injuries changed my life; I was knocked out the whole time except for a minute in the ambulance. I went to the trial and sat with Palma and watched the proceedings. The trial didn't take long as it was an open and shut case, and she was convicted of hit and run and numerous other crimes. The judge set a date in two weeks for the sentencing hearing. After the trial, the prosecuting attorney informed me that he was going to call both Palma and me to testify at the sentencing hearing. Outside the courtroom, I had an opportunity to talk to the women's parents, who were nice farmers from Alabama. A week after the trial, their daughter skipped bail and disappeared, leaving her kids in Destin with her mother-in-law.

A short time later, I received a call from my realtor telling me that he had a contract on the house in Marathon and hoped to close on it within a month. That was some good news, I called my uncle Rudy with the news, and during our conversation, he told me that his wife Claire was in bad shape and fading fast. A short time later, she died.

In April, Jack Brown drove me on a little road trip over to the world-class Naval Air Museum at Pensacola NAS, where we spent the day looking at airplanes. I never get tired of airplanes.

As soon as I got my arm out of the sling, I drove over to Jacksonville to see my granddaughter, Elizabeth. I hadn't been to Jon's house before; they bought it shortly after moving to Jacksonville in 2001. They showed me around the house, a nice two-bedroom in the suburbs of Jacksonville. Then Molly let me hold Elizabeth, a happy baby that wiggled a lot. Molly's father, Bud, came over, and we all had a nice chat while watching the baby. That evening after dinner I was sorry to hear from Bud that his wife Helen was in a fight for her life with breast cancer. I stayed the night, and after Molly feed me a lovely breakfast in the morning, I drove back to the Surfview. I kind of forgot how babies take over when they arrive on the scene. Unfortunately, it was just a short time later that Molly's mother, Helen lost her battle with cancer.

On the 25th of August, I drove up to Dayton, Ohio, where Wright Patterson AFB and the Air Force Museum are located, to attend a B-66 reunion with some of the people I flew with in England 40

some years ago. I checked in at the hotel, then went to the reunion welcoming party, where I signed in and looked around to see if I recognized anyone. I spotted Jerry Terhune, who was a fellow cadet in class 59-14N; we went through training together all the way to our first assignments at Alconbury. We had a lot catching up to talk about.

The next day at the museum, we gathered around the RB-66 that they opened up for us to climb around in. It happened to be one of the airplanes that belong to my squadron back at RAF Alconbury that I flew in years ago. I sat in the Nav seat for a few minutes reminiscing. At the museum, I had a great time chatting with comrades that I flew with years ago. We had another day at the museum, where they showed us around the aircraft restoration hanger before going back at the hotel for the banquet dinner that evening. The next morning there was a farewell breakfast and a business meeting that I attended before starting my drive back to Florida.

In October, I flew down to Key West to join Rick on his boat for another shot at Fantasy Fest. This time I would be there for the whole ten days; I should have known better. It was one continuous party, and after about four days, I was pretty much worn out. I brought along a doctor's costume with a stethoscope to check the heartbeats of the painted ladies. That was fun for a while, but after a couple of days and many examinations, I gave it up.

One of the costume competitions Rick and I went to was for pets; they had a little stage set up where they would parade the pets in costumes accompanied by their owner, who wore the most outrageous costumes; it was a hoot. A rescue dog with an attending nurse in a very skimpy costume won the competition. In the evenings, Rick and I would walk over to Rick's Bar to drink beer, eat peanuts, talk to people and observe the crowd in their costumes as they strolled by. By the time the festival ended with a parade on Halloween, I was pretty much worn out and needed to go home. The next morning, I thanked Rick for putting up with me and caught a flight back to Fort Walton Beach.

Back home at the Surfview, I had some time to relax before Thanksgiving and think about what to do with the apartments that needed more and more maintenance every year that I was not physically able to do anymore. It was obvious that I needed to put more effort into selling the place. I called Linda Quinlan, and she told me that we were now in a sellers' market and that she would put the word out to the developers. I had no idea what to ask for the property, so I hired a property appraiser. Just before Thanksgiving, he came back with his appraisal and told me there were no other comparable commercial properties for sale on the Island. That told me that he didn't have much to base his appraisal on, so I doubled his appraised value as my asking price. I then sent a letter to my tenants telling them that the place was up for sale.

It was a cold, windy, overcast day for what would probably be the last Thanksgiving Feast at the Surfview. We had about 15 people brave the cold weather conditions to be there. We had plenty of food and wine for everyone, and we all had a good time despite the conditions. As usual, a few of us ended up on the dock at the beer locker to close out the evening.

Shortly after Thanksgiving, I started getting calls from interested developers. I had meetings at the Surfview with a couple of them to show them around the property, and neither one of them balked at my asking price. Their reaction indicated to me that maybe I had the property priced right. Throughout December I had quite a few inquiries on the property and had one developer that seemed to be really interested. Before Christmas, I had another meeting with them over at their lawyer's office, where they made an offer for the Surfview that was a low-ball offer, and I made a counteroffer. They suggested that I put the property into the project, but I declined and told them I was too old and wanted cash. I also told them that they needed to pay Linda a finder's fee and that I would consider buying one of the units in their condo project. Finally, after a couple of hours of negotiating, I had a contract with a closing on the 31st of January. Once I had a contract, I called my tenant in unit 325 at the El Matador and told him he needed to be out by the end of January, when I would be moving in. It was all too easy. Maybe I didn't ask enough and gave it away, but after thinking about it for a while, I realized that I sold it at a fair price and was just having a case of seller's remorse.

In January 2005, I received a call from my buyers telling me they needed more time and wanted to move the closing date to the end of March. I agreed and told them that any more delays would cost them.

On the 17th, I drove over to Jacksonville for Elizabeth's first birthday party. She was no longer a little wiggling baby. I was having a fun time playing with Elizabeth when Molly complained about the way I was holding her. Maybe I was being too rough with her; I was used to having boys. All in all, it was an enjoyable visit, Jon & Molly seemed to be happy, and everything appeared to be going along good for them. Jon's job seemed secure, and he was making enough to support his family; they were living the American dream. The next day after thanking them for their hospitality, I drove back to Fort Walton Beach.

In February, my buyer for the Surfview called and wanted another extension on the closing date, I agreed to one more final closing date of the 7th of June, but the extension cost them money.

It was just a short time later in February that Jon called to inform me that he had found a new job in Colorado Springs with Countrywide Financial Corporation. He had already put their house in Jacksonville up for sale and was in the process of moving to Colorado, where they had already made an offer on a house. Oh! And by the way, Molly was pregnant.

On the 7th of June, the closing day on the Surfview, I arrived at 11:00 on time at the lawyer's office, and the buyers with their lawyers were there. We went over the closing documents, but there was a delay. Their bank in Atlanta had not released the funding yet, so we waited. They suggested postponing the closing for a couple of days. I told them if we didn't close on the 7th, the

deal would be off, and the new asking price would be higher. Finally, around one in the afternoon, after many calls, the funds were available, and we closed. They were now the new owners of the Surfview Apartments, where I lived for a little over thirty years. After paying off my loans and the IRS, I started moving my stuff out of the Surfview and had a parking lot sale, then went out and bought a new car. The new owners started tearing down the Surfview on the 1st of July.

On the 25th of August, Katrina went ashore just north of Miami as a category one hurricane and continued on into the Gulf of Mexico, where it intensified to a category four. On the 29th, it went ashore near New Orleans on the U. S. Gulf Coast, causing widespread devastation and flooding. At the El Matador on Okaloosa Island, hundreds of miles away from where Katrina went ashore, we had minimal damage with lots of wind, rain, and some flooding.

After cleaning up after Katrina, I decided to upgrade my unit at the El Matador and contracted to have new floor tiles, appliances, cabinets, and countertop put in. On the 2nd of September, when they started working on the place, I flew out to visit my son Jon and his family in Colorado Springs.

Jon picked me up at the airport and drove me over to the house that they bought in February when they moved. Molly and Elizabeth were waiting and eager to show me around the house, a nice two-story four-bedroom in a new suburb of Colorado Springs. In the afternoon, they drove me around, showing me the sights of the town, ending up at a restaurant close to their house. The next morning Jon and I drove up the mountain to Breckenridge. On the way, we stopped at Fairplay, a small town that used to be called South Park. I was looking to buy a place near a ski area, and Fairplay, with a population of 640, was about half an hour from Breckenridge. Walking around town, I stopped and talked to a relator, Brian, who drove us around to show us what was available. One listing was a newly constructed townhouse complex with two units available that seemed to be reasonably priced, and I told him I was interested before we left to continue our drive.

It took half an hour to drive over the continental divide at Hoosier Pass to Breckenridge, where we

looked at some listings before driving back to Colorado Springs. During the drive back over the pass, we stopped in Alma at the South Park Saloon for a hamburger and a beer. As we ate, Jon told me that his job at Countrywide ended two weeks after he bought the house, and found a job at Target as a manager for a couple of months. He was now employed at the AKAL Security Company as a gate guard at the Air Force Academy. He also told me he had joined the Army National Guard and that Molly was due to have the baby in October.

Over the next couple of days, using Jon's computer, I looked up all the listings in Breckenridge and Fairplay. I finally made a decision and called Brian in Fairplay to make an offer on the townhouse. The unit I wanted was an end unit, it was also the one the builder wanted, so I told Brian he had to convince him that my offer was only for the end unit. After some negotiating, the builder agreed to let me have it. The day before I flew back to Florida, Jon drove me up to Fairplay to sign the contract with a closing date in November or December. After I flew out, Jon's National Guard Unit was mobilized for Katrina disaster relief, but Jon wasn't sent because Molly was about to have a baby.

Back in Florida, in unit 325 at the El Matador, my new home was looking good. The remodeling was complete and was comfortable to live in. The only furniture in the place was what I had brought over from the Surfview. An old bedroom set that I bought in 1960, the big wooden desk that I bought years ago at an air force auction, and the round dining table from my parents. I needed more furniture and drove over to the Thomasville furniture store in Destin to order a bedroom set and some living room furniture. On the way back, I stopped in to see how the developer's project was moving along. I had thirty-some years of my life and a lot of memories there on that chunk of sand.

As soon as I got home, I called Tom and told him I had bought new bedroom furniture and that he could have my old bedroom set that was still in pretty good shape. He came over and looked it over and said he could use it and would come by and pick it up. I helped him move it to his rental unit with my truck the same day they delivered my new stuff. While we talked, I told him that I was buying a place near Breckenridge and to come up and go skiing this winter. He told me he couldn't because his wife, Donna, had somehow caught a disease that attacked her immune system, and he couldn't leave her and was on the road a lot, taking her back and forth to the Mayo Clinic in Jacksonville.

I had my 50th high school reunion coming up on the 1st of October, and I was thinking about going. While having a beer with Jack Brown, I invited him to come out to my new place in Fairplay to go skiing and found out that he was planning to drive up to Hershey, Pennsylvania, in the near future to visit his relatives. After talking for a while, we decided to kill two birds with one stone and drive up together in my new white BMW 750Li. Our plan was to drive up to Hershey, where I would drop off Jack. Then drive over to my reunion in New Jersey, stopping on the way to pick up my high school buddy Ray Rauanheimo in Philadelphia. The itinerary for the return trip was up for grabs.

On the 30th, we drove to Hershey, where I dropped Jack off as planned, then drove over to Ray's house in Philadelphia. In high school, four of us, Ray, Tom Shoemaker, Dick Shuster, and I, were sort of a rat pack that hung out together. We all joined the Army National Guard and would go to drill on Tuesday evenings at the Seagirt Armory across the bridge from Point Pleasant, New Jersey. Ray was now the curator of the small museum there, and the next morning we drove over to Seagirt, where Ray showed me around the museum. From there, we drove over to Tom Shoemaker's house across the bridge in Point Pleasant, where we would be staying during the reunion. Their house was just two blocks from the beach, so we all walked over and, like old times, strolled along the boardwalk for a while before going to the reunion.

At the reunion, we had 35 attendees out of our class of 107, mostly those that still lived in Point Pleasant. It took me a while to recognize some of them, but after mingling during cocktails before

dinner, it all came back. Toward the end of the banquet, George, one of our classmates, reminded us that part of the reunion was a cruise the next day on his fishing boat. Once the banquet was over and we were back in Tom's house, the three of us sat around boring Tom's wife, June, with stories about some of the stupid things we did as teenagers. The next day just before noon, we loaded into my car and drove over to the docks, where we joined about twenty others and started boarding the boat for the cruise that would take us on Barnegat Bay over to Seaside Heights and back. During the cruise, I went up to the pilot house and talked to George about when we both worked on the boats during high school and how I remembered him in our algebra class. Our teacher would put up an equation on the blackboard for us to solve and, after giving us time to solve it, would call on George to show us how. Then after solving it, he would show us one or two other ways to solve it. George was really something else with algebra. He was offered a math scholarship to Princeton, but he turned it down to stay in town and work on the family fishing boat.

In the morning, after breakfast Ray and I thanked Tom and June for their hospitality and drove back to Philadelphia. I dropped off Ray and then drove on over to Hershey to pick up Jack. On the road, we decided that since Gettysburg was close, we could drive over and check out the battlefield. We ended up spending the day and the next day there to take the tour. We were now close to Washington, D.C., and being that it was sort of on our way back to Florida, we felt obligated to stop and look over some of the sights.

On the way into D.C., we stopped at the Smithsonian National Air & Space Museum Steven F. Udvar-Hazy Center, which opened in 2003 by Dulles International Airport, to look at airplanes. As we were leaving, after spending hours there, while driving out of the parking lot, my car told me I had a flat tire. I got out of the car and looked at the tires, and sure enough, my right front tire had a piece of wood stuck in the sidewall. The tire didn't look totally flat, so I drove over to a

BMW dealership that happened to be close by. They replaced the tire, paid for by my tire & wheel insurance, and we went on our way. In town, we made our way to the Winsor Park Hotel, the same hotel where Tom and I stayed in 2003.

In the morning, we drove over to the Naval Academy in Annapolis. Neither one of us had been there before and walked around the busy campus. After seeing everything of interest and watching the midshipmen marching around on the parade ground, we drove over to the Washington Navy Yard, the oldest shore establishment of the U.S. Navy, built-in 1799. We arrived there just before noon and had lunch at the cafeteria by the museum. After lunch, we went aboard to tour their display ship, the destroyer USS Barry. From the Barry, we walked over to look over the WWI 14-inch railway gun that was on display in Admiral Willard Park. It was cast on-site with many others at the Navy Yard during the war. We then walked across the street to the museum, where we spent the rest of the afternoon leaving just before they closed at 5 pm.

Early in the morning, we started our 14-hour drive back down to Florida. While driving south on I-95, my son Jon called, telling me that Molly would be having the baby any day and he would need some money for the hospital since he had no health insurance. I told him I would take care of it when the hospital gave him the bill.

I was back at the El Matador for just a couple of days when on the 13th of October, Jon called to tell me that I had a new granddaughter, Emma Margaret Gebhardt. I congratulated them on the new addition to the family and sent him a check to pay off his credit card debt as a baby gift. I also told him I would be there for Christmas, driving out sometime in November or December. When Jon got the bill, he sent me a copy of it, and I called the Penrose Community Hospital and negotiated a cash price. They settled for about half what they charge insurance companies.

I started driving to Colorado in my 2002 Chevy four-wheel drive pickup loaded with my skiing gear on the 6th of December, a day after my 69th birthday. It took me two days to drive to Jon's place in Colorado Springs. Once I arrived, I took some time in Colorado Springs to go shopping before the closing of my townhouse in Fairplay on the 14th of December and to play with my granddaughters. What I ended up buying was a house full of furniture from the American Furniture Company to be delivered to my townhouse in Fairplay on the day after the closing.

I drove up to Fairplay on the 14th for the closing, and once all the paperwork was done, I had the utilities turned on, ordered a pizza, and spent the night on the floor in my sleeping bag. In the morning, the furniture arrived, and by the end of the day, the house was set up and livable. It took me a couple of days to move things around; then, I drove around town to find places like the grocery store, the hardware store, and the pharmacy. I already found the pizza place. The town's old hotel, The Fairplay Hotel, had an old western bar and good food in their dining room. The Park Bar was just a couple of blocks away and was the bar everyone went to. There was also a historical site that was the original town called South Park, but it was closed for the winter. That evening I walked over to the hotel for dinner and then went to the bar where my realtor Brian who was also a musician, was playing. When he finished his gig, we went over to the Park Bar, where he introduced me around. It had been a full day.

Once I got my house all organized and stocked with food, I drove over to Breckenridge to go skiing. I bought a season lift ticket and skied the slopes for the rest of the afternoon. Later in the week, I was back in Breckinridge to ski and took a lesson to learn some new techniques and maybe improve my skiing. Every day, weather permitting, I would drive over to go skiing and have lunch on the mountain at the Overlook Restaurant. I was really having a good-ole old time chatting with other skiers and getting familiar with all the different ski runs at Breckenridge again.

It was snowing when I drove down the mountain to be with my son and his family for Christmas. When I got there, Bud Murphy, Molly's father, was there with a friend, Emily. After chatting with everyone for a while, Jon told me I was just in time to go pick up his brother Michael who had just landed at the airport. I drove out to pick him up in what was now a snowstorm forecasted to get worse. On the way back to the house, I asked about his wife, Barbara, and he told me that she was teaching at a Montessori school and couldn't make it. I decided to stop and get a couple of bottles of champagne to help celebrate Christmas Eve. As I turned into the shopping plaza, I slid into a snow drift. Luckily, a passing snowplow with a friendly driver had a chain in the back of his truck and pulled us out.

Jon and Molly had a house full of guests, and we all were having a wonderful time. We talked, drank champagne, and played with the babies as the snowstorm raged outside. By the next day, Christmas, we were in the middle of a blizzard, and in the morning, just after we exchanged gifts, all of a sudden, some sort of argument started going on between Molly and her father. The rest of us just sat there looking at each other, wondering where it was going, when Bud announced that he was going for a walk in the blizzard. Emily and I decided to join him so he wouldn't get lost in the storm alone. While walking around in the blizzard, we came across a coffee shop that was open and went in for a cup. Bud wasn't in a very talkative mood, and maybe it wasn't a good time for me to ask, but since I knew that he was a family counselor, I asked him for some advice. I told him that ever since Molly had her babies, I've been having a hard time communicating with her and asked if he had any suggestions. His answer was that he had no advice to give me since he couldn't get along with her either.

Back at the house at around two in the afternoon, I made the mistake of asking Molly what time she was planning to have Christmas dinner. She got pissed and stomped out of the room, and Jon went after her. The rest of us sat around wondering what next; someone had to cook. After talking about it for a while, Emily and Michael went to the kitchen and started preparing Christmas Dinner. When it was ready and we sat down to eat, Jon, with an apologetic Molly, joined us. It was defiantly a Christmas to remember.

In the morning, with the roads plowed, Michael and I drove up the mountain to Fairplay. I wanted to show him my hideout in the mountains and get away from all the drama at Jon's house. When

we arrived at the townhouse, we had to shovel our way through a snow drift to the garage. After showing Michael around the house, we walked over to the hotel, and over dinner, we talked about going skiing the next day. Back at the house, Michael called a friend of his that lived near Breckenridge and agreed to meet us at the Quicksilver Super 6 chair lift in the morning with a snowboard for Michael.

With an early start in the morning, we were over Hoosier Pass, and at the chair lift shortly after, they opened and found Michael's friend waiting for us. I told them on the way up that if we got separated to meet for lunch at The Vista Restaurant on the mountain near where the ski lift dropped us off. Sure enough, on the first run, they left me way behind, and I didn't see them again until I found them at the restaurant. During lunch, Michael told me that he and his friend would be leaving to try kite snowboarding at a snow-covered lake near his friend's house and would meet up with me the next day for lunch at the Vista Haus on the mountain or at the Maggie bar at the bottom of the lifts after the last run of the day.

The next day I was there when the lift opened and skied until around noon when I stopped for lunch at the restaurant. I looked around for Michael but didn't see him or his friend in the crowd. After my last run of the day, I went into the Maggie bar by the lift and ordered a beer. Before I finished it, Michael and his friend showed up. We chatted for a while before saying goodbye to his friend, then left to start our drive to Fairplay. On the way, we stopped in Alma at the South Park Saloon, the highest saloon (10,578 ft.) in the USA, for a steak. They have really great steaks and burgers there.

For the next couple of days, Michael and I would drive over to Breckenridge in the morning to take advantage of any new snow that fell overnight and wear ourselves out on the slopes. We had a great time playing in the snow until the 29th when I drove him to the airport just in time to catch his morning flight back to Fort Pierce. During Michael's stay, when not skiing, we walked around Fairplay, finding the best places to eat and drink; there really weren't many choices.

After Michael flew home to Florida, I called Jon and invited them up to help celebrate New Year's up the mountain; he had to work on New Year's Eve and couldn't make it. I was on my own for New Year's Eve. For dinner that evening, I walked over to the hotel and stayed for a while for cocktails and enjoyed the entertainment at the bar. Before midnight I walked over to the Park Bar in the blowing snow to bring in the New Year. The bar was crowded and noisy, and the partying went on until early morning. It was a lot of fun. Finding my way home during a snowstorm in the middle of the night was a challenge.

2006

After a couple of days, I recovered and drove down the mountain to Peterson AFB, that's on the other side of the runway they share with Colorado Springs Airport. On Peterson, I drove over to Base Operations to find out if they ever had flights going to the military airfields in the Florida panhandle. I was thinking that in the future, I could leave my truck in long-term parking at Peterson and fly space available back and forth to Florida. Unfortunately, they didn't have many flights in that direction, but I found out that I could leave my truck there in long-term parking and take a cab over to the airport side of the runway to catch a commercial flight. It sounded like a good plan to me.

On my way back to Fairplay, I stopped in at Jon & Molly's to see how they were doing and play for a bit with my granddaughters. I asked Jon if he wanted to go out for a beer, where I asked him if he could get a kitchen pass to come up the mountain to go skiing for a couple of days. He didn't know; Molly was still upset and was being hard to get along with. That evening I took them out to dinner, and during the conversation, I suggested that since Jon had a couple of days off, he could go up the mountain skiing with me; Molly didn't object.

The next morning early, we drove up to Breckenridge, stopping on the way to pick up my skis and rent Jon some gear at the local ski shop. After we made a couple of runs at Breckenridge, Molly started calling. During lunch at the Vista Haus, she called Jon over and over again just to be a bitch. There was no way we could enjoy ourselves, so after lunch, we made a final run down the mountain and drove back to Colorado Springs, where I dropped Jon off and drove back up to Fairplay.

On the 17th of January, I drove down the mountain to Jon's to be there for Elizabeth's birthday party, her second. That evening we all went out to dinner, surprisingly, everyone was in good spirits, and we all had a good ol' time.

In early March, I drove down to the Colorado Springs Airport to pick up Jack Brown and Jerry Porter, who flew in to stay at my new digs and go skiing. I flew with them both in the Air Force Reserves at Duke Field years earlier, flying C-130A gunships. We had a great week of spring skiing with some beautiful sunshiny days. Both Jack and Jerry skied Breckenridge before, so there were no surprises, and took turns picking the ski runs. For a change during their stay, we skied a day at Keystone, another ski area that was close by. After a full day on the slopes,

we would occasionally stop on our way back to Fairplay at the South Park Bar in Alma for something to eat. But usually, we went on to Fairplay to one of the restaurants there for dinner, then over to the Park Bar or the hotel bar for a nightcap before calling it a night. We had a great two weeks of skiing. Just about every day, we were at the lift when they opened and skied until they closed. We had a blast!

I had been in Colorado for almost five months and needed to get back to Fort Walton Beach, so I booked a flight back to Florida on the same flight with Jack and Jerry. Leaving Fairplay, we drove down the mountain to Peterson AFB, where I parked my truck in long-term parking and called a cab. He drove us over to the airport side of the runway for our flight back to Florida. My plan for leaving the truck in Colorado worked like a champ.

I was in Fort Walton Beach for just a short time before driving down to Fort Pierce to visit my son Michael and his wife, Barbara. When I arrived, Michael was in the garage working on a surfboard, and Barbara was at work. Inside the house, the kitchen was a mess; all the cabinet doors were missing, the overhead fluorescent lights had been removed, and there was a big crack in the glass stove top. I went out back to the pool that was green, and the backyard was a jungle. Michael had planted all kinds of fruit trees that now needed to be trimmed, plus the grass needed to be cut. When I talked to him about it, he told me that he didn't like cabinet doors or fluorescent lights and he didn't need the kitchen stove because all they ate was raw food. The circulation pump for the pool had burned out, and he hadn't gotten around to replacing it or mowing the grass. He was into kiteboarding, and that was taking up a lot of his time.

During our conversation that evening, while eating Michael's raw food meal, which was actually pretty tasty, I found out that Barbara's income at her job teaching was barely enough to pay the bills. I also learned that Michael hadn't paid his taxes and was thinking about launching another Olympic campaign for the 2008 games.

To help them out over the next couple of days, I mowed the grass and installed a new circulation pump for the pool, then had a talk with them about their situation. Barbara was upset with Michael because he was sitting around playing with his kites and not making any money. Michael didn't seem to be that concerned about their financial situation because he was going to raise at least $25,000 from sponsors for his Olympic campaign, and if he didn't raise the 25K, he wouldn't go. I told him my contribution would be to try and get him square with the IRS. Since he competed in the Olympics continually for almost twenty years, all his income during those years came from contributions and was nontaxable. The 2000 Sydney Olympics was when he last competed and started working as a coach; from then on, his income would be taxable. I asked him if he kept any records; he said he did and gave me a bag of receipts, bank statements, and a spreadsheet. It took me some time to compile it all and retain a tax lawyer to give it all to.

We had a meeting with the lawyer a few days later for a talk. He explained to us that since most of his income from coaching was on cash bases and that his bank deposits didn't amount to much, he would probably get away with not filing even though he should. On his computer, he showed us the IRS file on Michael; it showed that since 2000 he hardly had any income. Before we left his office, I told the lawyer to send what was left of the retainer to Michael for his campaign. The next morning, I wished Michael and Barbara all the luck and drove back to Fort Walton Beach.

I was back out to Colorado in October for a reunion with my fellow B-66ers in Colorado Springs on the 15th. I flew out a little early to check on my place in Fairplay and to visit my son and his

family. The reunion was being held at the Antlers Hotel on the south side of town near the airport, where I had a room booked. I always have a great time at these reunions reminiscing with my old flying buddies about our interesting times at RAF Alconbury during the cold war. At the banquet dinner, this time, we had an air force colonel guest speaker who gave us an interesting update on world affairs and what was going on in the air force. These reunions are always a lot of fun, and I try to go to all of them.

After the reunion, I drove over to spend a couple of days with Jon and his family and to celebrate Emma's first birthday before driving up to Fairplay. Ski season was around the corner at Breckenridge; they already had some snow on the slopes. Jack and Jerry had contacted me about flying over in February to go skiing. The call got me thinking about the upcoming ski season, and as soon as I had an opportunity, I drove over to Breck to buy my season ticket.

During Thanksgiving at Jon's house, he told me that his National Guard unit had been notified that they were about to be activated for a year's duty in Afghanistan. Over our second beer, Jon told me that he worked with an old, retired army master sergeant at AKAL Security and told him about his guard unit being activated. The sergeant's advice was that he could solve all his problems by getting back on active duty where he belonged and to do it before his ass ended up in Afghanistan.

Jon said he thought about it for a while, then talked to an army recruiter and would probably sign up. He asked me what I thought, and I told him it was probably a good idea since he already had active-duty time in the air force, and with a few more years in the army, he could retire.

It was just days later that Jon called to tell me that he had joined the army with the rank of sergeant and had a choice of two career fields, intelligence or infantry; he chose intelligence. A few days later, he received orders and was on his way to Fort Knox for a short six-week course for prior service recruits. After he completed Fort Knox, he received orders to Fort Huachuca near Sierra Vista, Arizona, for the eight-month 35 Fox intel school; Jon's life was really getting interesting.

For Christmas, I drove down the mountain to be with Molly and the girls. I brought with me some wine for the occasion and gifts for the girls. It was a fun time watching the girls opening their gifts while we drank a little wine and chatted before going out for Christmas dinner. Molly and I had plenty of time to talk, and I think we got to know each other a little better, making for a merrier Christmas.

After playing with the girls for a while in the morning, I drove back up the mountain to Fairplay. I was able to get a couple of days skiing in before the end of the year on the crowded slopes at Breckenridge. While talking with other skiers, I found out that The South Park Saloon in Alma was putting on a big New Year's Eve party and that lots of people in Fairplay were talking about going. I thought about going but decided to stay in Fairplay. I'm too old to get a DUI, and besides, in Fairplay, the hotel and Park Bar also had parties.

It was snowing on New Year's Eve as I walked over to the hotel to get something to eat. After dinner, I headed over to the Park Bar and found a seat at the bar. It was a little before nine, and the local band was about to start playing; an hour later, the bar was packed. I was having a good time, chatting and dancing with the ladies, some of whom were skiers that were staying in town. We brought in the New Year and partied on; it was a cold walk home uphill in the blowing snow.

2007

It took me a full day to recover and another day to shovel the snow out of my driveway. On the next day, the 3rd of January, Jon showed up to go skiing; he had finished boot camp. We drove over to Breckenridge to take advantage of the new snow that fell over the last week. After a couple of days of great skiing, Jon drove back down the mountain. I was able to get in a few more days of enjoyable skiing before driving down to Colorado Springs for Elizabeth's third birthday on the 17th. Molly had a fun little party for her, and later on, in the evening, we all went out to dinner at a restaurant close by.

Two weeks later, in February, I was back down in Colorado Springs to pick up Jack and Jerry at the airport and take them up to Fairplay. During our conversation on the drive up the mountain, Jack told me that Linda's job took her to MacDill AFB and that they were now living in Tampa, close to the base. In Fairplay, on the way to the house, we stopped at the ski shop to get their skis so we would be ready to go in the morning. That night we walked over to the hotel to eat, then over to the Park Bar for a beer. On the way back to my house, it started snowing.

After an early breakfast, we were ready to go skiing, but first, we had to shovel a foot of new snow off the driveway; it was still snowing. The road to Breck was plowed, but on the other side of the pass, the temperature dropped, and it was really cold. After lunch at the Vista Haus, it started snowing pretty hard. I started to worry about driving over the pass, so we cut the day short. By the time we got to the Hoosier Pass, it was blowing up a storm, but once we got over the pass, it stopped snowing. The rest of that week, it snowed on and off, and even though it got a lot colder, we skied every day. We defiantly were having plenty of snow to play in.

The days went by fast, and before we knew it, I was driving down the mountain to the airport to drop off Jerry for his flight and to pick up Tom and his brother Jon who flew in to take his place. Before heading back up the mountain, we drove over to Peterson AFB to resupply. On the drive up to Fairplay, Tom told me that Donna's condition was stable and that she insisted he take the

trip with his brother. Arriving at Fairplay, we stopped at Prather's Market for more food, and when we arrived at the townhouse, Jack had the driveway shoveled clear of snow for us. I had a full house, four beds, and four people. We took a day to go to the ski shop to rent ski gear for Tom, and his brother, then showed them around town. For dinner, we walked over to the hotel and then later over to the Park Bar for cocktails.

The skiing conditions were about the same as the week before, cold with occasional days of snow. We skied most days with only a day or two cut short by heavy snow. We found another bar close to where we parked, The Breckenridge Brewery & Pub, to après ski before driving back to Fairplay. We mostly cooked our own meals at the house, except for lunch on the mountain at Vista Haus or stopping at the South Park Saloon for supper on the way home. I had skied with Jon before on one of our trips to Aspen years ago; he was crazy then and hadn't changed much. He complained about the CD I always played driving over the pass to Breckenridge, Blood on The Saddle by Tex Ridder. While walking around in Breckenridge, Jon bought me a Pink Floyd to play for the ride back. We all had a great time, and before we knew it, I was driving them down the mountain to catch their flight back to Florida.

In April, my son Jon called from Fort Huachuca to tell me that he had orders for Fort Shafter, Hawaii, when he completed school. In the interim, he was moving Molly and the girls to Sierra Vista, Arizona, near Fort Huachuca, and put his house on the rental market. I told him I would be in Colorado and would be available to help them pack up their stuff for the move.

Molly and the girls had already started packing when I drove down the mountain to help. Jon flew in on a Friday after work on a three-day weekend to make a move. As soon as he arrived, I drove him over to pick up a big Penske rental truck, and we started loading. In the process, they gave a lot of stuff away to their neighbors, the Salvation Army, and gave me their old computer. Just before noon on Sunday, they were all loaded up and on the road for the 10-to-12-hour drive to Sierra Vista. They couldn't waste any time; Jon had to be there at Fort Huachuca bright and early on Tuesday morning.

Days later, in Fairplay, while I was deleting files on the old computer that Jon gave me, I came across an e-mail that Molly had sent to one of her girlfriends. It describes how she was unhappy in her marriage, and in Hawaii, if she decided to divorce Jon, the army would send her back at no expense to Colorado Springs. I made a copy before I deleted it. A week later, I shut down the townhouse and flew back to Florida for the summer.

In May, I flew up to New Jersey for a family get-together at my cousin Judy's house in Glen Ridge. Most of my cousins who still lived in New Jersey were there, all from the Patson side of the family.

I hadn't seen them in years, and we had a great time reminiscing about when we were kids. My aunt Vera was also there, the last of my aunts and uncles on that side of the family, and it was great to see her again.

I stayed at Judy's for an extra day when Bob, Judy's husband, the police chief of Glen Ridge, suggested that we go on a driving tour of Manhattan in his police car. During our drive, we stopped for lunch at a café in Times Square and then drove over to see where the 9/11 attack took place. We walked around to look at the construction that was still going on and the incomplete 9/11 Memorial Plaza. I really enjoyed the drive around my old familiar stomping grounds and thanked Bob and Judy for taking me. In the morning, I thanked Judy for inviting me to the party and for letting me stay at their house and drove to Newark Airport for my flight back to Fort Walton Beach.

Manhattan was a lot cleaner than in the '50s when my friend Jackie Secor and I would drive over to the city for the hockey games at the Garden (Madison Square Garden). He was 17, a year older than me, and had a driver's license. After the game, we would drive up to the 86th street Hofbrau Bierhaus for some German beer and listen to the oomph band before driving back to New Jersey. At the time, the drinking age was 18 in N.Y. and 21 in N.J. Never once did they ID us at the Bierhaus; I guess we looked old for our age.

In July, Jon finished the 35-fox school at Fort Huachuca and flew out to his duty assignment at Fort Shafter, Hawaii. A choice assignment, and once base housing was available; he would have orders cut for his family to fly over and join him in paradise.

In late September, there was a reunion in Las Vegas for the troops that had served in the 315th Air Division during Vietnam. Since my squadron, the 817th Troop Carrier Squadron and Jack's squadron were both parts of the 315th. We decided to drive out to the reunion together in my car. Then after the reunion, we drive on to California, where Jack would meet his wife Linda, and I would check in on my son Michael who was competing in the trials for the 2008 Olympics. Linda

was out visiting her mother in Los Angeles, and Michael was staying just up the road in a house on Balboa Island for the trials.

For our route to Las Vegas, we drove west on I-10 to Phoenix, Arizona, then highway 93 into Las Vegas. It took us three days. Once we found our hotel and checked in, we picked up our agenda packet at the welcome room, where we had a beer and chatted for a while. There was nothing on the agenda for the evening, so Jack and I walked over to the strip to look over the casinos.

During the three days of the reunion, we had a tour of the Nellis AFB flight line, followed by a briefing on what was happening in the air force and the world. On the agenda for the next day was an afternoon party and buffet at a park. It gave us an opportunity to swap C-130 trash hauling stories with some old flying buddies that we haven't seen in years. The final day allowed us plenty of time to spend in the casinos before the banquet dinner; that's always a lot of fun.

During Vietnam, the C-130 crews flew missions of all types but mainly airlifting and airdropping supplies to our troops in the field. Aircraft from the different squadrons all flew missions out of the same airfields in Vietnam, and the crews knew each other. Once you were in C-130s, you knew that your next assignment would probably be to another C-130 squadron. So if you had been around for a while, you were part of the C-130 trash hauling family.

It was a short 250-mile drive from Las Vegas over to Balboa Island, where Michael was staying and where Linda would meet us. When we arrived on the Island, Linda was waiting. After talking to Linda and her mother for a while, I went up and knocked on the door. Michael wasn't there, but there were plenty of people there who told me he was out running. Jack and Linda didn't hang around and drove off to Linda's mom's house in Los Angeles. I went in to introduce myself and to wait for Michael's return. The place had the atmosphere of a commune with a massage table.

There was someone on the table being worked on, and the rest of them were just hanging out. Right off the bat, I was getting some bad vibes about what was going on.

When the guy with grey hair finished working on the table, he came over to talk to me. The first words out of his mouth were, "Well, I donated a $25,000 hyperbaric chamber for Michael to sleep in; how much did you give to his campaign?" I told him it was none of his damn business and asked him if he gave the chamber to Michael or if he was just letting him use it. The conversation went downhill from there.

By the time Michael returned from his run, I knew that my presence there would not be helpful to his campaign. After having a little lunch there, Michael and I had a chance to talk before I left to find a hotel and that I would be back to pick him up later to go out to dinner.

On the way to dinner, he showed me the sailing venue. During dinner, Michael seemed really distant when we talked and explained to me that the guy I had words with was his trainer. He wrote a book on how he could train old athletes to be competitive. I knew that if I stayed, I would be in a constant pissing contest with this guy and would be doing nothing but adding more stress to an already stressful situation. I told Michael that I would be heading back to Fort Walton in the morning and wished him good luck with his campaign. Maybe I was just being an old fool trying to protect my son even though he was a grown man and could take care of himself.

On the way back to Fort Walton Beach, I stopped in to visit my cousins Dick and Gloria Bott, who lived in a gated community in Appel Valley, California. The last time I saw them was in 1982 when the boys and I drove out to visit them in Colorado for Christmas. Gloria was one of my favorite cousins; we talked about the good times we had and about the get-together I went to at Judy's. They showed me all around their gated community that had everything: golf, tennis, a clubhouse, a restaurant, and a clinic. After spending two days with them, I thanked them for their hospitality and continued on my drive to Fort Walton Beach.

Michael came close to going to another Olympics; he finished in 2nd place at the trials behind 27 years old Ben Barger. Maybe I was wrong about his trainer. After all, Michael, an old athlete at 41, almost won. I drove down to Fort Pierce in early November to visit Michael and Barbara. When I arrived, I found that Barbara was unhappy mainly because she was struggling to pay the bills with no help from Michael. When I talked to Michael about it, he was uncommunicative and angry. I stayed a couple of days, and as I was leaving, I wrote him a check to help them out with their mortgage payment; he ripped it up; obviously, he did not want or need my help. It was just a short time later that Barbara left him, and the bank repossessed their house.

By November, Breckenridge already had plenty of snow on the mountain and was opening up for the season. I had already ordered a season pass online and was ready to get back on the mountain. So, after preparing my unit at the El Matador for me to be gone for a couple of months, I booked a flight to Colorado Springs.

After landing on the 20th of November at the Colorado Springs Airport, I took a cab over to Peterson AFB to get my truck that was parked in the long-term parking lot. I had the cab stand by while I tried to start it up. It had been sitting there for eight months, and to my amazement, it started on the first try. While I was on the base, I stopped at the commissary and loaded up with food and booze before heading up the mountain.

By the time I arrived in Fairplay and unloaded the truck at the townhouse, it was time to go to the Fairplay Hotel for something to eat. The short walk to the hotel had me huffing and puffing. The altitude change from Florida at sea level to Fairplay at 10,000ft was taking a while to get used to. For the next couple of days, I was gasping for breath. It seemed like it takes longer every year to get acclimatized.

After breakfast the next morning, I took my truck in for service and had my snow tires with rims that I bought the winter before from Tire Rack put on at the Main Street Garage. When I was finally able to breathe normally again, I drove over to Breckenridge to pick up the ski pass that was waiting for me and went skiing. It was a beautiful day, sunny and cold, with very few people skiing. I felt like I had the mountain all to myself; I knew that wouldn't last for long. I settled into a routine of skiing only on perfect days, three or four times a week. I was just having a good-ole time.

Later on, in November, I got a call from Tom and was sorry to hear that on the day after Thanksgiving, his wife, Donna, passed away. She had valiantly battled the virus that eventually killed her. She had Tom's unending support in her battle at home and in search of a cure, taking her to the best specialists around the country. She was only 57 years old. May she rest in peace.

Before I knew it, the Christmas holidays and New Years were just around the corner. I had been around town for a while and was getting to know more people, even had a cowboy hat made at the Colorado Mountain Hat shop two doors away from the Park Bar. On Christmas day, Brian and I had dinner at the Fairplay Hotel before his gig at the bar. After having a drink and listening to Brian play for a while, I headed back to the townhouse.

I drove over to Breckenridge a couple of times during the holidays to ski and catch the excitement of the crowd. The skiing wasn't that great, with long lift lines and crowded ski runs. If it became too crowded, I would, after having lunch on the mountain at the Vista Haus, ski down the mountain and call it quits for the day.

For New Year's Eve, like the year before, Fairplay was packed with holiday tourists. I ended up at the Park Bar to bring in the New Year, where I was getting to be a regular; the bar was already crowded when I got there. By the time the music started, it was packed with people trying to talk, dance, and have a good time. It was an outrageously entertaining evening that lasted way past midnight into the New Year; it was a blast.

2008

During the first month of the year, I spent most of my time enjoying the great skiing at Breckenridge. The rest of the time, I was driving around looking for places closer than Colorado Springs to shop. There was only one grocery store, hardware store, pharmacy, garage, and gas station in Fairplay, so if you needed anything else, you bought it out of town somewhere. The closest place I found was Buena Vista, about twenty minutes away.

In February, I drove down to the airport to pick up Jack and Tom, who flew in for a couple of weeks of spring skiing. I welcomed them, and while at the airport, I booked a seat on their return flight back to Fort Walton Beach. Before driving up the mountain, we stopped at Peterson AFB, where we loaded up on food and supplies that we thought we might need for the next couple of weeks. Back at Fairplay, we stayed a day at the townhouse for Jack and Tom to adjust to the altitude change before going skiing. But once we started, we were at the Quicksilver Super 6 chair lift when they opened in the morning.

It was very cold, but during the week, it started warming up, allowing us to shed some clothing and enjoy at least a week of enjoyable spring skiing. It wasn't long before we were closing down the townhouse and driving the truck down the mountain to Peterson AFB. After parking it in long-term parking, we called a cab to take us across the runway to the airport for our flight to Florida. I had a great time with my old partners from Windsong Charters. Over the years, the three of us have survived many adventures, and I look forward every year to having them come up to Fairplay to visit and go skiing with me.

On the flight back, Tom told me that he had a high school reunion in Hawaii coming up at the end of March and was thinking about going. It just so happened that I was thinking about visiting my son Jon and his family stationed at Fort Shafter, Hawaii. After talking about it for a while, we came to the conclusion that we had no choice but to plan a trip to Hawaii. A few days after landing at Fort Walton Beach, I was busy calling the Hale Koa Hotel in Fort DeRussy on Waikiki Beach, Honolulu, to reserve a room. Once that was accomplished, I called the airlines and booked our flight to Honolulu International Airport on the Island of Oahu, Hawaii.

When the beginning of April finally rolled around, we boarded our long flight to Honolulu. On our arrival, we rented a car and drove over to Fort DeRussy, an armed forces Rest & Recuperation facility, and checked in at the Hale Koa. Once settled in our room, I called my son Jon to get his address and a good time for me to visit, then called John Callahan, who I flew with during Vietnam, to set up a time and place to meet. Tom called and made contact with his high school classmates. Once that was all taken care of, we retired to the Hale Koa Barefoot Beach Bar to enjoy a Mai Tai or two while we acclimatized to the time change and observed the scene at the beach. We stayed at the bar long enough to watch a beautiful sunset on the mighty Pacific Ocean before going to the dining room for dinner.

The next day we went to meet with John Callahan at the Hickam Joint Services Base Officers Club for lunch. John retired from the U. S. Air Force to Oahu shortly after the Vietnam War was over. During the war, John flew C-130s for two years out of Naha, where I knew him. He then volunteered to fly O2s, the military version of the Cessna 337, in country Vietnam. During lunch, he told us that after retiring, he started an Island-hopping air service with a Cessna 337 and invited us to go fly with him. After lunch, we climbed aboard John's four-seat Cessna 337 and took off on an aerial tour of Oahu, then over to nearby Molokai to see the waterfall and the big cattle ranch that covers 1/3 of the island. The flight lasted around an hour, and after landing, we thanked him for the tour and chatted for a while before driving over to Fort Shafter to visit my son.

I haven't seen my son Jon or his family since I helped them pack a year ago for the move to Fort Huachuca, and I was happy to see them again. The girls had grown quite a bit, and they could not wait to show us around the house and their room. Later on, we went out to dinner at a nearby restaurant that they liked and had a lovely meal with lots of conversation, mainly with the girls. We all had a fun time, and it was late when Tom and I finally headed back to the Hale Koa.

The next day we drove out to Wahiawa, where Tom's high school is located. The town is near Wheeler AAF, where his dad was stationed. The reunion was more of a get-together for lunch with six of his high school classmates. Some of his fellow members of the football team were there to reminisce; it was a good time. After lunch, we went on a tour of Leilehua High School, where he was a student for three years. While walking around the school, Tom told me that he was one of just a few white boys there and that most of his classmates were Japanese, Samoans, or native-born Hawaiians. For a summer job, he and his friends worked in the pineapple fields for the Dole Corporation, which was miserable work in the hot sun for very little pay. It was an enjoyable afternoon listening to Tom, his classmates, and their stories before it all broke up.

We were back at Fort DeRussy in time for happy hour at the Barefoot Beach Bar, and we talked over how to spend our remaining days on Oahu. After a couple of Mai Tai's, we decided to make our first visit to the Pearl Harbor National Memorial.

In the morning, after a marvelous breakfast at the Hale Koa, we drove over to Pearl Harbor Historic Site Visitor Center. We checked out what they had at the center, then bought tickets and boarded the boat over to the memorial over the sunken hull of the Battleship Arizona. By the time we were back to the center, it was about time for lunch. We raided the vending machines and then walked over to look over the Submarine Museum and the USS Bowfin. From there, we drove over the bridge to Ford Island to tour the Battleship Missouri. After spending a good hour on board Missouri, we drove over to the Pearl Harbor Aviation Museum, also on Ford Island, where we spent another hour or so. As we were leaving, we noticed a hanger #79 about 500ft away and walked over to check it out. Walking around it, we located an open door. Inside it was a storage area for pieces of airplanes and other military equipment. We looked it all over before leaving to drive around Ford Island to see what else we could find. On the other side of the Island, we came across the USS Utah and stopped, but there was not much to see, just rusted-up remains of the capsized battleship/target ship. After looking around for a while, we decided to drive over to Wheeler Army Airfield, which was an air force base when Tom's dad was stationed there.

Once through security at the main gate, we found the house where they lived and stopped to walk around and look it over. By then, it was getting close to happy hour, and the officers club was just a short walk away, but when we got there, we found out that it was now an Army Signal Corps Headquarters. We stayed a little while longer, then drove back to Fort DeRussy, and the Barefoot Beach Bar that we knew was open. After happy hour we walked over to Kalakaua Avenue and had dinner at a Japanese noodle shop that was filled with Japanese tourists.

After another wonderful breakfast at the Hale Koa, we walked down the beach a short distance to the Hawaii Army Museum. We ended up spending most of the morning there going through all the historical information and military hardware. When we were done, we walked back to the Hale Koa and, over lunch, decided to drive over to what used to be the old fort in the crater of the Diamond Head Volcano. It was a short drive, and after going through the tunnel into the crater, we parked the car. From there, we walked up the trail up to the crest of the crater to the old fort with its great view of Honolulu. Unfortunately, the fort was closed for renovation.

That evening after dinner at the Hale Koa, we strolled down Kalakaua Avenue ending up at Duke's Waikiki, which was crowded with mostly female tourists, and had a good-ole time chatting with them. On the way back to the Hale Koa, we stopped at a titty bar to look at the girls and have a nightcap, and to our surprise, one of the girls was from Fort Walton Beach. The next morning over breakfast, we decided to take a road trip around Oahu, with our first stop being Bellows Air Force Station (Bellows Field) on the east coast of Oahu. The field was once an important airfield during World War II that's now a training and recreation area with a great beach for military personnel.

After looking over the beach and getting some sandwiches at the recreation center, we drove over to the Kalaniana'ole Hwy and later the Pali Hwy to get over the mountain ridge that runs across Oahu. Along the way, we stopped at the Nu'uanu Pali Lookout, where King Kamehameha had one of his battles to unite Hawaii. Once over the ridge, we drove up to the north shore to watch the surfers at Banzai Pipeline and Sunset Beach. On the way back to Fort DeRussy, we drove past the Dole Plantation, where Tom worked during the summer as a teenager.

The following morning, we started driving early to continue our road trip, this time to the west coast of Oahu. We drove west on the H1 to the Farrington Hwy, then followed it up the west coast to the end of the road at Ka'ena Point State Park. On the way, we drove through the towns of Maili, Makaha, and many other small beach villages. Just before getting to the state park, there was a community of campers and homeless in shacks along the beach. We stopped and walked around for a while before heading back to Honolulu. At the town of Maili, we drove inland to take a shortcut and see more of the island. The road took us to a guard shack where they checked my ID, and our little shortcut was becoming interesting. Once past the gate, we continued down the narrow road that took us by an ammunition dump, then up a winding road over a mountain ridge to Wheeler AAF. From there, we drove on to 'Fort DeRussy and retired to the Beach Bar for a Mai Tai to discuss our day's adventure and observe another beautiful sunset on the Pacific Ocean.

During our stay in Oahu, we covered a lot of territories. From John's Cessna 337, we got to see Oahu, Molokai, and a little of Maui from the air. We really enjoyed the Hale Koa; it's definitely the place to stay. They have everything you could want; I even bought a couple of Hawaiian shirts at their store before leaving. We had accomplished everything we came to Hawaii to do and then some. It definitely turned out to be an interesting adventure. Our flight back to Florida was long and uneventful.

I wasn't home a week when I got a call from my son Jon on the 18th of April telling me that Molly had filed for divorce back on the 29th of February. He didn't want to tell me about it because he, for the sake of his girls and to save his marriage, talked her into changing her mind. Molly wanting a divorce was no surprise to me; I'm sure she planned to divorce him before she ever left Colorado. The only surprise was that she waited so long to do it. I told Jon about Molly's e-mail to her girlfriend and that I could send him a copy of it if he wanted, but he said he didn't want to see it. The problem was that by the time they filed a retraction, it was too late; their final divorce decree was already in the mail. As soon as they received the decree, they hot-footed it to the courthouse to get it retracted. That's when the clerk of the court told them, "the boat has already left the harbor". So, as of the 15th of April 2008, they were divorcees whether they liked it or not, it's really what Molly wanted all along, and I hope she's happy!

The army quickly shipped Molly and the girls back to Colorado Springs and sent Jon to live in the barracks. He wasn't there long before moving off base to live in his new home, a double headsail 38' Erickson sloop that he bought and kept docked at the Ke'ehi Marine Center not far from Fort Shafter. Shortly after buying the boat, he found a fellow GI, Huey, to move on board as a boat mate to help pay for the slip fees at the Ke'ehi. Jon was no doubt miserable not having his girls. I know how he must feel. I have experience along those lines. He was just getting used to the single life in paradise when they sent him TDY for three months to Staff Sergeant School at Fort Huachuca, Arizona.

Once back in Florida, it took me a while to get caught up at the El Matador, but by late July, I was ready to go. I booked a flight to Colorado to see what goes on in Fairplay during the summer and arrived there on the 31st of July. The next morning after breakfast, I walked over to the old mining town, South Park City, and the museum on the north side of town to see if it was open. I never made it. As I approached Front Street, there were people all over the place and vendors setting up their kiosks. It was the first day of the Fairplay Burro Days, a week-long festival that was just getting underway. During which there were mock gunfights on the street in front of the Park Saloon, Llama, and pack dog races. The big event was on Friday, a Pack burro 29-mile race to the top of Mosquito Pass and back. Then on Saturday afternoon, the last day of the festival, a BBQ and barn dance at the American Legion Hall. Fairplay was packed with people for the festival, and I had a blast.

In the weeks following the festival, I finally did a walk through South Park City and the museum that was full of memorabilia of the old mining town. After spending a good part of a day there, I decided to spend some time and continue to explore the local area around Fairplay. On one of these excursions, I came across the small town of Como northeast of Fairplay, about 10 miles just off of highway 285 on Boreas Pass Road. Como, during the 1900s, was a depot for a narrow gage railroad; the roundhouse, turntable, depot, and the Como Hotel are all still standing. I stopped to look it all over and stopped for lunch at the hotel; it wasn't crowded. After lunch, I drove up Boreas Pass Road, and that followed the old railroad track bed over the pass, and down into Breckenridge, where I spent the afternoon walking around.

I was surprised when, a short time later, I received a call from Molly in Colorado Springs tearfully telling me that she had made a terrible mistake divorcing Jon. I don't know why she called me; there was nothing I could do for her. I really did not know what to tell her, only that I would come down to visit her and the girls sometime in the near future.

Over the next month or so, I drove or hiked up numerous trails that sometimes would lead to an abandoned mine, and if it was near a stream and tried to try panning for gold. One day I drove up Mosquito Pass Road over the pass to Leadville to do a walkabout town. I stopped for a beer before heading back to Fairplay at the legendary Silver Dollar Saloon that supposedly has been in business since it opened in 1879. I also did some hiking on the mountain trails around Fairplay.

In September, Rick Sauter stopped in on his drive back from a wedding in Seattle. I drove him around to show him the local area and decided to drive to Durango, the old depot for the Durango & Silverton Narrow Gage Railroad. The town had, at one time, a smelter to process the silver that the railroad brought down from the mines. The rail line is still in operation to Silverton for tourists.

It was a slow drive to Durango, getting there late in the afternoon, and after getting a room in the Durango Hotel, we did a walk around town that ended at the hotel bar. Being in the bar and the hotel was like stepping back in time a hundred years. All the helpers wore old western clothing to add to the scene. We ate dinner at the hotel and then did a short walkabout before adjourning to the bar. In the morning, we walked over to the train station to get tickets for a ride on the narrow gauge, but they were sold out. Back to the hotel, Rick told me he needed to get on the road to Florida, so we checked out of the hotel and drove back to Fairplay. Durango was definitely worth the trip.

In October, I gave Molly a call and told her that I would like to come down and visit my granddaughters for Halloween. She was okay with that and gave me their address. I drove down and found their house in a suburb close to their old neighborhood. I had a good time with the girls and went trick-or-treating with them. The next evening, I took them out for dinner, where Molly told me during the meal that she had found a job and was busy looking for a boyfriend on the internet. On the way back to Fairplay the next morning, I drove by Jon's house to see if his tenants had beat it up any; the courts gave Jon the house since they had no equity in it. That sounded familiar!

In November, just before Breckenridge opened up for the season, I got a call from Jon telling me that he was back in Hawaii. He had finished school at Fort Huachuca and got promoted to staff sergeant. He also told me that he met a woman, Emma, a veterinarian, while at school. Not that it would do much good, but I warned him about rebound affairs after a divorce. On his return to Hawaii, he found that Huey was still there and had done a good job of keeping his boat shipshape. Unfortunately for Jon, he didn't get to enjoy his boat or his life in paradise for long before being deployed to Afghanistan for a year. Once he was in place at Camp Eggers, Afghanistan, I found that we could stay in touch by using Skype.

In Colorado, there was plenty of snow on the mountains, and the skiing was great; my enthusiasm to ski was still there. I was driving over to ski Breckinridge maybe two times a week. Skiing was still enjoyable, but I noticed that I wasn't attacking the mountain as aggressively as I used to. I was turning into a defensive skier, a good thing since the crowds were getting larger. I really needed to be on my toes to dodge the snowboarders that love to cut in front of you as you shushed down the ski runs.

I drove down the mountain to visit my granddaughters for Thanksgiving and got to meet Molly's boyfriend, whom she found on the net, Brantley, an IT guy working for a contractor at Schriever

AFB. I took them out for Thanksgiving dinner at a nearby restaurant, and we all had a good time, even though Brantley did not have much to say.

I drove back down the mountain to be with the girls for Christmas Eve with their gifts and wine for Molly. I took them out for dinner; it was just the four of us. Brantley wasn't around. During our meal, the girls were all excited and talkative anticipating Santa's visit. Emma was a real chatterbox; it was a fun evening with the girls. In the morning, I was up early to watch all the excitement as the girls opened their Christmas presents. During the day, I watched and helped the girls with their gifts, and later on, while cooking dinner, Molly and I had some wine and talked. What I gathered from our conversation was that she found out that it was not that easy being divorced with two kids and was desperate to find someone. She liked Brantley, but he didn't talk much, and she didn't like his weird laugh; I just listened to her talk and poured the wine. I told Molly I wanted to continue buying swimming lessons for the girls, and she wanted to start ballet lessons for them, and I agreed to supply the funds for them both. In the morning, I said my goodbyes and drove on back up the mountain to Fairplay.

During the remainder of the holidays, I skied with the skiers and snowboarders at Breckenridge, it was crowded, but everyone was in good spirits and having a good time. On the 5th of December, I celebrated my 72nd birthday by going out for cocktails and dinner at the Fairplay Hotel. After dinner, I went to the bar, where I listened to Brian and his band play and chatted with him for a while during his break before calling it a night. The year was winding down; this would be my third year of celebrating the beginning of a New Year in Fairplay at the Park Bar.

Chapter Eleven: 2009 – 2011

During February, I drove down to Colorado Springs to pick up Tom, who flew in to do a little skiing, and while at the airport, I booked a seat on his flight back to Fort Walton Beach. The weather since the beginning of the year has been miserable and limited my trips to Breckenridge. Tom brought with him some good weather, beautiful sunshiny days with no wind to speak of, making for some great ski conditions. During the first couple of days, while Tom acclimatized to the altitude change and fitted out with ski gear at the ski shop, I drove him over to show him what I found in Como and had lunch at the hotel there.

We skied about every day, taking long lunch breaks up on the mountain at the Vista Haus Restaurant and then taking a couple of runs in the afternoon before adjourning to après ski at the Maggie, the bar/restaurant at the bottom of the Quicksilver Super 6 lift.

After having an enjoyable couple of weeks skiing Breckenridge with Tom, we shut down the townhouse and drove down to Colorado Springs to catch our flight to Florida. We stopped to say goodbye to my granddaughters on the way to Peterson AFB, where we parked the truck and caught a cab to the airport terminal. During the flight, we talked about maybe going over to London to visit his sister Jean.

In March, my son Jon called me on Skype to tell me that he had married Emma, the veterinarian he met while at Fort Huachuca. The chaplain at Camp Eggers in Afghanistan performed the ceremony online. Jon would be in Frankfurt, Germany, on R&R in June to meet up with Emma and her teenage son, Joseph. Since Tom and I were already planning to go to London, I told Jon that I would meet them in Frankfurt sometime during their stay.

As soon as we were done talking, I called Tom and gave him a heads up, and worked on finalizing an agenda for our trip to Europe. Once I had dates for Frankfurt from Jon, Tom called up Jean for a good time to visit and found that it worked best to go to Frankfurt before going to see Jean in London. We made our flight reservations for June 5th for an overnight flight to Frankfurt with a return flight from London on the 22nd, then booked a room at Jon's hotel in Frankfurt. We took with us the phone number of our German running buddies that we met in Florida to visit if we had time. We now had a plan and were good to go.

We arrived at Frankfurt Airport on the morning of June 6th after an uneventful overnight flight. After checking in at the hotel, we contacted Jon and his bride, who arrived a couple of days earlier. We went to their room, where they met us at the door wearing German lederhosen. We sat around chatting for a while with Jon, my new daughter and grandson in law then we all went out for dinner to a restaurant close by.

We had a couple of days with Emma and Joseph before they flew back to Sierra Vista, Arizona. On their last night in Frankfurt, Tom and I took them across the Rhein River to Sachsenhausen for some schweinshaxe, sauerkraut and apffelwine. We had a lot of fun even though Emma and Joseph didn't eat or drink much. You have to acquire a taste for apffelwine; Jon, Tom and I did, and we drank our fill.

On the morning of the 13th, we checked out of the hotel and drove Emma and Joseph to the airport. After seeing them off, we called our German friends, the brothers Dominic and Pascale. Making contact with Dominic, we arranged to meet at Gasthaus Ott in Villingen, their hometown about 140 miles south of Frankfurt. Tom and I had met Dominic in Fort Walton Beach when one of our

running buddies, Dave Miller, brought him to a run. He was staying with Dave while going through a three-month apprenticeship program at a local machine shop. After talking with Dominic, who was friendly and spoke English, Tom gave him his old Mercedes to drive around in during his stay.

Jon still had a week of R&R left before he had to go back to Afghanistan, so we took him with us. We arrived in Villingen on a Saturday around three in the

afternoon, and after driving around for a while, we found the Ott. Before finishing our first beer, Dominic showed up and took us over to a hotel where he had made reservations for us. On the way, he pointed out his family's machine shop, where he and his brother worked. After checking in at the Hotel inn Klosterring, we went back to the Ott, where Pascale was waiting with more beer. We had something to eat there, and since we were having such a good time, we stayed on for a while before heading back to the hotel.

After having breakfast at the hotel in the morning, the brothers picked us up for a walkabout their historic old town. After having lunch at a cafe, we walked over to the Munsterplatz (town center) to see the Munsterbrunnen, an old bronze fountain adorned with humorous portraits of characters who shaped Villingen's history. From there, we walked over to the Ott for a beer, where we stayed until the brothers took us to get some great German cuisine at the Restaurant am Pulverturmle.

After dinner, we went back to the Ott and stayed until they closed and were told to leave. We were leaving town in the morning, and the brothers had work, so out on the street in front of the Ott, we thanked them for their hospitality and for showing us around their town and auf wiedersehen (goodbye).

Early the next morning, we checked out of our hotel and started driving to our next destination,  Bastogne. We crossed over the Rhine into France at Baden Baden and, since we were in the area, went looking for the Maginot Line. By taking a side road at Haguenau that took us into the forest and driving about twenty minutes, we found part of the fortifications, The Ouvrage Schoenenbourg, a large bunker that was unfortunately closed. After we looked around for a while, Jon climbed up on top of the bunker for a better look, but there was nothing to see but trees. We drove back to Haguenau looking for a place to stay and continue our search in the morning. Having no luck, we decided to forget about it and continued on our way to Bastogne, getting as far as Luxembourg, where we checked in at the Hotel Parc Belle-Vue.

That evening after a meal at the hotel's restaurant, we went for a walk around the neighborhood. It was getting late, and it started to rain, so we ducked into a close-by café and took a table outside under a big umbrella to wait out the rain. It was while sitting there talking and listening to the rain that Jon started telling us about his close call in Afghanistan.

He was in the last vehicle riding shotgun with a long rifle for the convoy commander, a Lt. colonel, driving the up-armored Toyota in a three-car convoy halfway to Bagram from Kabul. In the first vehicle was a U.S. Army sergeant armed with a rifle driving four Afghan Intel Officers. The second vehicle had Jon's boss, a young female USAF Lieutenant Intel Officer from Hurlburt Field, Florida, driving a government intel contractor. Their vehicle was hit by an IED; the explosion tossed the Toyota in the air about 15 feet and landed upside down on the road. Running over to the Toyota, Jon saw that the blast had killed his lieutenant and wounded the contractor. While putting tourniquets on what was left of the man's legs, another convoy with an ambulance going in the opposite direction stopped to help, and their medics took over from Jon. The lead vehicle of that convoy had a Blue Force Tracker keyboard; using it, he called in a Medevac; unfortunately, the contractor died before the helicopter arrived. After directing the helicopter in to pick up the casualties, he joined in the sweep looking for the guy who set off the IED. He was already gone, escaping on a motorcycle. Later that day, Jon was told that the Afghans caught him in a nearby village and, during interrogation, admitted to setting off the IED; his target was the lead vehicle with the four Intel Officers. Jon was damn lucky; just before the convoy departed, they moved him from the second vehicle to the last because he had a rifle. They wanted the rifles in the first and last vehicles. We stayed at the café talking until they closed, then walked in the rain back to our hotel.

It was still overcast and drizzling the next morning, but that didn't stop us from walking along the Alzette River that winds its way through Luxembourg. We stopped for lunch at a café, and while we were eating, the weather cleared. Continuing our walk, we came across Scott's Pub and stopped for a pint. The bar was friendly, so we stayed for a few more beers and something to eat before walking back to our hotel.

In the morning, we continued our drive on the winding roads through the Ardennes Forest to Bastogne; wherein the center of town, we found a room for the night at the Hotel Collin. Over lunch, we realized we were running out of time. Jon's flight back to Afghanistan was leaving from Frankfurt the next day. We spent the afternoon at the 101st Airborne Museum, "The Mess", putting off touring the battlefield until we could spend at least a day or two there. The museum had a lot of interesting German WW2 vehicles, airplanes, and tanks that we could get up close to and touch.

We started the drive back to Frankfurt early the next morning and managed to get Jon to Frankfurt Airport in time for his flight back to Afghanistan. After seeing him off and wishing him luck, we turned in our rental car and caught a cab to our hotel, The Munchner Hof, by the Hauptbahnhof. After getting settled in, we walked across the street to the Hauptbahnhof and bought train tickets

for a morning departure to Brussels and the Eurostar to London St Pancras Station. Once that was all taken care of, we walked over to the Irish Pub for a pint and some food.

In the morning, we boarded the train to Brussels, where you change trains to the Eurostar for the trip through the "Chunnel" to the U.K. Having first class tickets, we took full advantage of the snacks and champagne served during our Eurostar ride under the English Channel. Once we arrived in London, we called Tom's sister, Jean, but she was out of town, so we called and got a room at the Columbia Hotel. By the time we were settled in our room, it was about time to go around the corner to the Swan for a pint and some food. We had four days to do something before our flight back to Florida. At the Swan, we decided that in the morning to head for the Imperial War Museum.

After a marvelous breakfast at the Columbia Hotel, we took the bus to the museum, we had been there before, and after a couple of hours of looking around, we were ready to leave. On the way out, we stopped at the information desk and found out that the next day, Saturday, they were running the tanks, a once-a-year event at Duxford, a branch of the museum near Cambridge. From the museum, we made our way to one of our favorite pubs in London, The Cambridge, for a pint and some food. While sitting at an outside table, we asked the people sitting with us if they had ever heard of the running of the tanks at Duxford. They didn't have a clue, so we decided to go check it out.

After a hearty English breakfast in the morning, we took the underground to Kings Cross Train Station and bought round-trip tickets to Cambridge. On our arrival, we hailed a cab for the 10-mile drive to Duxford, an old WW2 airbase. We were a little early for the running of the tanks and took the opportunity to look at an airplane sitting on the flight line. A Boeing B-17 that looked like it was ready for flight, and we took our

time getting close to it for a good look. Further down the flight line, there was a hanger full of airplanes on display and passed it by. We were really there to see tanks. Continuing, we came across the maintenance hangar where they restored tanks and other armored vehicles. Inside was a

just restored tank and a lot of parts, including a Russian 500 hp V-12 Diesel engine that's used to power most of the Russian Armor. Leaving the hangar, we walked over to the open field at the end of the runway, where the tanks were all lined up, ready to go. They started the show with WW2 armor. First out was the Russian T-34, followed by an American Sherman tank and M3 half-track. Then they stirred up the dust and made a lot of noise with numerous cold war Russian and NATO armor. It was defiantly a sight to behold. We had a grand time and stayed till the bitter end, just making our way to Cambridge in time to catch our train back to London. Arriving at London's Kings Cross Station, we took the underground to Lancaster Gate, the stop near our hotel. On the way, we stopped at the Swan to unwind, have a pint, some food, and talk about the tanks at Duxford; it had been a full day.

The next morning during a leisurely breakfast at the Columbia, Tom called his sister Jean to see if she was back in town; she was and that we would walk over to pay a visit. Taking a slow walk across Kensington Gardens to her house in Kensington just in time for lunch. During lunch, Jean mentioned that she needed our help with cleaning out one of her storage closets and some minor repairs in the kitchen. After spending the afternoon helping Jean, we adjourned to the Goat Tavern for a pint and some food before calling it a night and walking back across the park to the Columbia.

The next day, our last full day in London, we finished the repairs on Jean's kitchen and spent the rest of the day wandering around London. During our walkabout, we stopped for lunch at The

Cambridge and stayed talking to people for most of the afternoon. That evening we took Jean out to dinner at a restaurant in her neighborhood. We have a lot of fun with Jean even though she is on the other side of the political fence from Tom and me. We try to stay away from political discussions with her, but sometimes you just cannot avoid it. That night we got into it, I don't think we pissed her off too much.

During our little over two weeks in Europe, we had seen a lot and covered a lot of ground even though we really had no plan to speak of. I was thankful for being able to meet Jon's new family and for his narrow escape in Afghanistan. The trip was full of adventures that we talked about on our flight back to sunny Florida. We were back in time to enjoy the remainder of the summer's activities in the Redneck Riviera.

I hung around Fort Walton until October, then caught a flight to Colorado. A week later, after getting my townhouse up and running. I drove down the mountain to Denver Airport to pick up my son Jon who had finished his tour in Afghanistan. He was there on a delay in route on his way back to Hawaii. He was there to meet his wife, Emma, and his in-laws. They were coming there to redo their

wedding for the family. Before they arrived, Jon and I went over to Molly's to help his girls carve a pumpkin for Halloween. When his wife arrived, Jon took her over to meet his girls. She invited them to be flower girls at the wedding, but unfortunately, Molly would not let them go. The wedding was held at the Peterson Air Force Base Chapel on October 26th. I was Jon's best man. After the ceremony, we all went out to dinner, where I had the opportunity to talk for a while with my new in-laws before they left to drive back to Texas and Emma drove back to Arizona. Emma did a good job putting it all together, and it went off without a hitch.

The day they all departed, I drove Jon to the Denver Airport for his flight to Honolulu. Before going back up the mountain to Fairplay, I went back over to Colorado Springs for a couple of days to go trick or treating with the girls.

Jon had his hands full when he got back to Hawaii. What he found when he arrived at the Ke'ehi Marine Center was that his boat mate, Huey, had been reassigned, and his boat was about to sink at the dock. It would take him a while to pump it out, clean up, and make it seaworthy again.

Back in Fairplay for just a few days when an old sailing buddy, Rick Sauter, flew in to visit. I drove down to Denver to pick him up. Since there was no snow on the mountain at the time, we drove around in my truck, exploring the local area around Fairplay. On one occasion, we drove over Mosquito Pass to spend a day in Leadville, mostly at the Silver Dollar Saloon. During his last days in Fairplay, the rodeo came to town. I had never been to one before, and it was a lot of fun, defiantly something to see. On November 7th, the same day that the house passed Obamacare, I closed down the townhouse and drove Rick to the Denver Airport for his flight to St Petersburg, Florida. I drove on to Colorado Springs to visit and take Molly, her new boyfriend, and the girls out for dinner. Her new boyfriend, I cannot remember his name, worked for Apple, and even though he didn't say much, we all had a fun time. The next morning, I started my two-day drive to Fort Walton Beach, Florida.

Back in Florida, Jon called and invited me to spend Christmas with him and his new family in Hawaii. I got busy and made reservations for a round-trip flight to Hawaii, leaving on December 16th, and reservations at the Hale Koa for the 23rd for two weeks. I would be staying with Jon for a week on his boat before checking in at the Hale Koa. Emma and Joseph were flying in on the 27th and would be staying at the Hale Koa, where they had reservations for a week.

In December, Monique called to invite me to the Bay Café annual end-of-season all-you-can-eat-and-drink party. Julian, the owner, throws the party every year to get rid of his inventory before

closing the shop to go on a buying trip to France. Monique, a friend of Julian's, was able to reserve a big table and invited her friends to attend. The party on December 13th started at two in the afternoon. I was on time and joined Monique at her table outside on the deck. The whole gang was there; Tom, Phil and Donna, Neil and Norma, Bill and Marie plus Mike and Shirley with his daughter and her husband. We all just had a grand ole time drinking too much wine, making noise, and eating copious amounts of wonderful French cuisine, and when the quartet started playing, there was dancing on the deck.

Three days later, on the 16th, while still recovering from the party, I boarded my flight to Hawaii. It was a long uneventful flight to the Honolulu International Airport; Jon was there to meet me. While driving to the marina, we stopped at the Hale Koa to check on our upcoming reservations and go to the Barefoot Bar for a Mai Tai. While at the bar, Jon told me that I was there just in time to drive him to the Tripler Military Hospital in the morning for surgery to get his vasectomy reversed. Great, that sounds exciting! Bright and early the next morning, and after a short drive to the Tripler, the surgeon successfully hooked him back up. The next morning, I picked him up and helped him hobble onto his boat to recover. It didn't take long, the next day we walked over to a small restaurant two blocks away for breakfast.

Jon had a nice setup, with the marina having a coin-operated laundry and a restaurant not far away that served great meals. He has everything he needs. The problem he was facing was that his tour of duty in Hawaii was about to end, and he needed to do something with his boat. Sailing it or shipping it to the mainland was pretty much out of the question; the only good option was to find a buyer for it fast. He hated the thought of selling it, but after we talked about it for a while, he put it up for sale.

The two of us went to work and cleaned up the boat getting it ready to sell. We had a few days left before Emma, and her son arrived and took the opportunity to take it on an enjoyable short sail along the beach by Waikiki to Diamond Head and back. On the 23rd, I moved into my room at the Hale Koa, where Jon and I would celebrate Christmas.

On the 27th, we drove over to the airport to meet Emma and Joseph, who would be my roommate while in Hawaii. Once Emma and Joseph were settled in our rooms, we went down to the beach and the Barefoot Bar to talk and watch the sunset. Jon was eager to take his family out sailing on his boat, and it just so happened that while enjoying our drinks at the bar, Jon had a phone call from a prospective buyer. He wanted to look the boat over in the morning; conveniently, that's when Jon was taking his family sailing.

After dinner, Jon and Emma headed for their room. Joseph and I took a walk around the neighborhood and stopped at a bar that showed surfing videos. To get a conversation going, I asked Joseph if he was interested in surfing and if he had ever been. He was definitely interested and wanted to give it a try while in Hawaii. I told him that for his Christmas present, I would sign him up for a lesson. Before leaving, I asked the bartender where I could get lessons, he referred me to

"Animal", who gives lessons every morning just down the beach toward Diamond Head from the Hale Koa.

In the morning, after breakfast and before driving to the marina to go sailing and the appointment with the buyer, Joseph and I walked down the beach to Animal's surfing class, where I signed him up for the next morning. We watched him teach the morning class a bit, then walked back to drive out to the marina with Jon and Emma.

At the marina, Jon and I prepared the boat for inspection by the prospective buyer. He showed up at around ten. Jon showed him around the boat and invited him to go with us for the sail. He accepted the invitation and boarded the boat with us as we loaded the sub sandwiches and beer. The buyer, a just-retired army lieutenant colonel, did not know much about sailing, so we gave him the helm and taught him how and he loved it. We all had a wonderful time on a beautiful day. At the dock, Jon and the buyer talked business, telling Jon as he was leaving that he would get back with him. It had been a full day. That evening back at the Hale Koa, over dinner, we discussed where we would like to celebrate the New Year. The Hale Koa was booked, so we made reservations at the Hilton for their New Year's Eve dinner and party.

The next morning after an early breakfast, Emma and I walked Joseph to his 9 o'clock surfing class. Animal started the class with a ground training session, then took them out in the surf until around two in the afternoon. Emma and I watched a little of the ground training, then walked down the beach to a bar to watch the class out in the surf. Staying on for lunch, we talked, and when the class was over, we picked up Joseph and headed back to the Hale Koa. On the way, he excitedly

told us how much fun it was to surf and praised his instructor, Animal.

On New Year's Eve, we walked over to the Hilton for the celebration. The ballroom was crowded, and after dinner, when the band started playing, the party with all the trappings shifted to high gear. We brought in the New Year and stayed until around one in the morning, then made our way back to the Hale Koa.

2010

On Saturday, January 2nd, we checked out of the Hale Koa and drove Emma and Joseph to the airport for their flight back to Arizona, then moved back onto Jon's boat. I still had a few days before my flight back to Florida, so I called my old air force buddy John Callahan. After chatting for a while, he suggested that I go with him to fly two passengers over to the Kalaupapa Airport on Molokai. I told him I'd love to go and would meet him at his plane.

I was there in time to go with John on his preflight walk-around inspection of his Cessna 337. His

passengers arrived, and we boarded the plane for the short flight to Kalaupapa, a former leper colony located below the world's highest sea cliffs on the island's northern Kalaupapa Peninsula. Landing at the airport, John and I took a short walking tour of the town. On the flight back to Honolulu, we flew east along the north shore by the steep cliffs and the massive Olo'upena waterfall, and the remains of the 4,970 ft East Molokai Volcano. After landing in Honolulu, we drove over to the Hickam Officers Club for a beer and talked about our many Air Force flying adventures that we somehow survived. I couldn't stay long; I had to pick up Jon from work at Fort Shafter. I thanked John for taking me along on the flight and hope to see him again on my next trip to Hawaii.

On January 7th, after an action-packed three weeks in Hawaii, Jon drove me to the airport for my long flight to Florida. On the way to the airport, I wished him luck with his new family and with selling his boat.

A week after I arrived back in Florida, Jon lucked out and sold his boat to the lieutenant colonel. Two months later, he received TDY orders to Fort Rucker, Alabama, for warrant officer training. He can't say his life is boring. A short time later, I got a call from Michael, his brother, telling me that he was living in Miami and had renewed his relationship with his Canadian girlfriend, Edithe.

On March 2nd, I was getting ready to drive back out to Colorado when I got a call from Jon; he wanted me to come pick him up at Fort Rucker. The next morning the 3^{rd,} I drove over to Fort Rucker and found him as he was signing out. We loaded his gear and started driving back to Fort Walton. On the way, he told me he had only been there a couple of days, and since he had prior service as a captain, they commissioned him a CW2 (warrant officer) and gave him TDY orders to Fort Huachuca, Arizona, for another intel course. That was convenient; his wife Emma was living with her sister close to Fort Huachuca in Sierra Vista. Jon also had a two-week delay en route to pick up his car (shipped from Hawaii) in St Lois, giving him some time to visit his girls in Colorado. While closing down my place at the El Matador on Friday, before we started driving to St Lois, we went to the Chapala Mexican Restaurant to have dinner. There were about 20 old friends there that had not seen Jon in years; we just had a good old time.

After picking up his car and driving west on I-70 the next morning, just as we crossed into

Colorado, Jon, who was following, called to tell me my truck was throwing oil. We pulled off the interstate and found a gas station with a mechanic who diagnosed it as a bearing in the front differential. Luckily, he was able to find a replacement bearing, and by late afternoon we were back on the road. Late that afternoon, we arrived at Molly's, where we spent the night. In the morning, I drove up to Fairplay to get my townhouse ready for guests. Tom and his brother Jon were flying in on the 8th to visit.

On the 8th, I drove down the mountain to Colorado Springs and picked up Tom and his brother Jon at the Colorado Springs Airport. We stopped on the way to Fairplay at Peterson AFB to load up on food and booze. My son Jon followed us to spend a couple of days with us, and over the next three days, we had a blast, spring skiing at its best, with warm weather and not too slushy snow. On the 17th, Tom and I drove his brother Jon down the mountain and dropped him at the Colorado Springs Airport for his flight back to Florida.

After getting gas and a few supplies at Peterson AFB, we drove back up the mountain to Fairplay, and on the way, I told Tom about the trip Rick and I took in September to Durango. I described to him the town and the hotel and that I wanted to go back to take a ride on the Durango & Silverton R.R. and that I would be going there after he left. Back in Fairplay, I called Durango to check if the train was operating; they were back in operation after being closed down for the winter. Tom was interested in going, so the next morning, we started our drive to Durango.

On our arrival, we checked in at the hotel, then walked over to the station and bought first-class train tickets for the next day. After taking a short walk around town, we stopped at the hotel bar

for happy hour. While sitting at the bar talking to the guy next to me, I found out that he had been in the air force stationed in England a couple of years ahead of me at RAF Sculthorpe as a gunner in B-66s. By the time I got there, they were replacing the 20mm tail guns with an ECM tail cone. He was a real cowboy that bought cattle at auction and trucked them to his leased government land, where he stayed with his horse and dog for months while they grazed and fattened up for the market.

In the morning, we were at the station early and watched them get the train and the old steam engine ready. We were some of the first to board, and by the time we departed, the train was full. Because of an avalanche threat, the line was not open all the way to Silverton. Our seats had a table and were next to the small bar and bartender with food and drinks that were also available at the kiosks' where we got off the train and waited while they turned the train around for the trip back. We were back in Durango by midafternoon in time to do a tour of the roundhouse and turntable. Taking the scenic train ride through the mountains and witnessing an old steam engine in operation was well worth the trip. The next morning, we drove back to Fairplay.

We had a day left in Fairplay to sit around and talk before our flight back to Florida. I told Tom I had a reunion to go to in early September if he wanted to go along. He couldn't because he had told his sister Jean in London that he would be over to visit in September. After talking about it for a while, maybe we could do both and went to work coordinating a date with Jean. We came up with a date and booked an overnight flight to London on September 23rd with a return flight from Frankfurt on October 11th. A day later, I drove Tom to the Colorado Springs Airport for his flight back to Florida. I stayed in Fairplay a couple more weeks before shutting down the townhouse for the summer. On April 1st, I drove down the mountain, stopping for a short visit at my granddaughters on my way to catch my flight back to Florida. I found out later that before leaving Colorado Springs for the drive down to Arizona, Jon traded in his car on a used 04' Porsche Cayenne S.

I was back in Fort Walton Beach in time for the April 20th Deepwater Horizon explosion and oil spill disaster in the Gulf of Mexico; it was the summer's main event. The spill spread down the coast to the Redneck Riviera, eventually reaching Okaloosa Island, chasing away the spring breakers. We locals were on the beach helping with the cleanup that went on for weeks scooping up blobs of oil that washed up. It became a sort of social event where you get to meet your neighbors. Some say that a hurricane would have cleaned it up in a couple of days. An interesting theory, but we didn't have one to test it. In early September, Tom and I started our drive to Savanna, Georgia, for the B-66 Reunion; by then, the oil spill was history.

It was a pleasant drive to Savanna, and after checking in at the hotel on the Savanna Waterfront, we went to the bar for a drink. I had been to Savanna before during the 1996 Olympics, so I knew

some good restaurants and bars to go to. During the reunion, we signed up for the two-hour bus trip to Charleston to tour Fort Sumter. It was an all-day event but well worth the time. The banquet dinner on the last day was a gala event with an active-duty colonel guest speaker who briefed us on the latest air force programs and activities. I always enjoy these reunions and will go to them as long as I can.

Two weeks later, on September 23rd, we boarded our flight to Atlanta to connect with our overnight flight to visit Tom's sister Jean in London. Arriving at London-Gatwick Airport before noon on Friday the 24th, then took the Gatwick Express to Liverpool station and the underground to Kensington High Street. From there, we walked to Jean's house; she was busy with patients, so we dropped our luggage and made our way to the Cambridge, one of our favorite pubs in London, for lunch. While at the Cambridge, we talked about our agenda. We knew that we were going out to dinner with Jean and maybe to the theater over the weekend and taking the Eurostar train to Frankfurt sometime shortly thereafter. That left us with a couple of free days during the week to do something before leaving London. Over a pint of bitters, we talked about the Bovington Tank Museum that we heard about during the running of the tanks at Duxford the year before. We decided that we needed to go check it out and looked for it on our map and found that the museum was in Bovington Camp near the town of Wool. That evening at dinner with Jean at her favorite nearby restaurant, we told her our plan. She laughed and called us warmongers; she's probably right.

We spent all the next day with Jean, then on Sunday we took the underground to Liverpool station and bought a ticket to Wool. It turned out to be an over three-hour train ride, and when we stepped off the train onto the small train platform at Wool, we were the only ones. With no hotels or taxis in sight, we started walking and finally found a taxi and asked the driver to take us to a hotel near the museum. He told us there were no hotels in town and only one B&B, the East Burton House. When we arrived there, he waited while we checked to see if there was a room available. We lucked out they had a room; the cabbie suggested that we could still get in a half day at the museum. On the way there, he told us that it was the Museum of the Royal Tank Regiment and Royal Armoured Corps. When he dropped us at the museum, we asked him to come pick us up when they closed.

The museum is something to behold; it has almost 300 vehicles from 26 countries and is the third

largest collection of armored vehicles and the largest collection of tanks in the world. The collection traces the history of the tank, starting with the WWI British Mark I tank. We were in our glory and had barely scratched the surface when the museum closed for the day. When we walked out of the museum, our cab was waiting and when he dropped us off at the B&B asked him to come back in the morning. The cab was there to pick us up in the morning for the short ride to the museum. On the way, we saw a tank stopped on an open field in front of the museum; our driver told us it was a Leopard. We told him to stop and let us out for a closer look. There was a fence around the field with a gate that wasn't locked, so we let ourselves in and headed across the field toward the tank. We didn't get very far before the two people standing by the tank were telling us to go back.

As we turned to leave, I asked them if it was a Leopard; they said it was and, to our surprise, waved us on in. The two people there were the museum's curator, who had waved us on, and a mechanic who was test-driving the tank. We chatted for a while, and they invited us to crawl around on the tank, then asked if we wanted to go for a ride on it over to the maintenance building. It was an exceptionally good start for a day at the museum. We found out in the museum that the 62-ton Leopard 2 was developed in the '70s by Krauss-Mallei for the West German Army and that the different versions of it over the years were still being used as a main battle tank by 32 countries.

The museum is unbelievable; there was a lot to see, including the main attraction, Tiger 131, the only known working German Tiger 1 tank from WW2 that was later used in the movie Fury with Brad Pitt. When they shooed us out the door at closing, our cab was waiting. Arriving back at the B&B, we thanked him for taking care of us with a big tip. After all, if it wasn't for his knowledge about tanks, we would never have had a ride on the Leopard.

The next day we caught our train back to London, arriving there in the early afternoon. After dropping our bags off at Jean's, who was busy with patients, we walked over to the Goat for a pint and talk over our next move. Since Jean was busy with patients all day and that evening was seeing patients for the National Healthcare, we decided to spend one more day in London to take Jean out to dinner and the theater before leaving for Frankfurt.

In the morning, over breakfast, we asked Jean to pick a place to eat and a show as she hurried off to see her first patient for the day. We decided to catch a bus to the Imperial War Museum to see if they had anything new; there wasn't, so we didn't stay long. We had lunch at a pub by the museum, then took the underground to Trafalgar Square and the National Gallery, where we stayed until it was time to head back to Kensington for our date with Jean.

Next morning at breakfast, we thanked Jean for her hospitality and then took the underground to the St Pancras Train Station to catch the Eurostar to Brussels and the train to Frankfurt. On arrival at the Frankfurt Hauptbahnhof, we walked across the street to get a room in our favorite one-star hotel, The Munchner Hof. Once that was taken care of, we walked around the corner to O'Reillys Irish Pub to talk over what we wanted to do during our remaining 11 days in Europe. We didn't decide much except to go sign up for a day cruise on the Rhine River.

During the cruise, we met two Italian women who spoke fairly good English and a Chinese couple who were a lot of fun. The boat stopped on the way back to Frankfurt at Rudesheim for a typical German dinner. The cruise was informative about the points of interest on the Rhine and well worth the money. During the cruise, someone mentioned Budapest; that's where my Grandpa Patson was a policeman before immigrating to the U.S. in the early 1900s. Since neither Tom nor I had ever been to Budapest, we needed to go check it out. The next day we bought tickets on the overnight train to Budapest, Hungary.

On arrival at the Budapest-Nyugati train station we went to the tourist aid counter, where they found us a room at the two-star Avenue Hostel Hotel. Once checked into our room, we walked over to the House of Terror Museum and Memorial to Political Victims just up Andrassy Street from our hotel. The museum is in the old Russian KGB building. Going through it and seeing the torture chambers firsthand, you can understand why the Hungarians hate the Russians.

In the morning, after breakfast at our hotel and a short walk around the neighborhood, we took a cab to the Buda Castle and palace complex on the west side of the Danube River in the Buda District of Budapest and took the tour. There was a lot to see, and we ended up spending the day there.

On our last day in Budapest, we walked down Andrassy Street outside our hotel toward the center of town. We got as far as Memento Park, where we stopped at a café for lunch and looked over our map. After lunch, while still in the park, two young women started talking to us in English and suggested we go get a coffee. We headed back toward the café where we had lunch, but the girls wanted to go somewhere else. I had a bad feeling about it, but we agreed, and they took us to a bar close by. As we entered the bar, I noticed that the place was empty except for a woman working over some poor guy in a booth. Sitting down at a table, we ordered drinks and the fact that the girls did not want me to take their picture set off my warning bells ringing loudly, and I took the picture anyway. I told Tom that we needed to buy them one drink and get out of there,

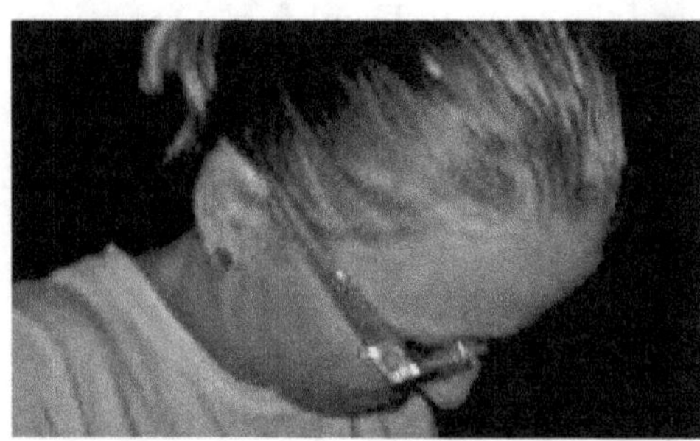

but he wanted to stay and mess with them s'more. I had been in these situations before and knew we had to get out of there ASAP before it cost us an arm and a leg. The girls drank their watered-down drinks and wanted to order more, that's when I called for our check, and we left. Tom wasn't too happy about it, but I feel that we escaped relatively unscathed. The girls had obviously targeted us old farts as being easy marks, but then again, they were pretty girls.

In the morning, we boarded the train to Vienna, Austria, to spend a couple of days there before our flight out of Frankfurt back to Florida on October 11th. Arriving at the Wein Hauptbahnhof in the Favoriten district of Vienna, where tourist aid found us accommodations at a nearby three-star hotel. Once checked into our room, we took a walk around town and came across the Leopold Museum of Modern Art, where we spent the afternoon. The next and our last day in Vienna, we spent walking around town, stopping for lunch at a café outdoor table, where we stayed most of the afternoon chatting with the people around us.

In the morning, at the Hauptbahnhof, we bought first-class tickets on the

high-speed ICE train to Frankfurt. It was an interesting six-and-a-half-hour ride; our seats were right behind the engineer, separated by a transparent screen that he would occasionally make opaque. On arrival in Frankfurt, we walked across the street and checked in at our favorite hotel, the Munchner Hof, then walked the Eiserner Stag footbridge across the Rhein to Sachsenhausen for a beer.

It was early, and no one was around, so we didn't stay long and walked back across the bridge to Romerberg Market Square. At the square, we found a table in front of the old Romer Town Hall and, from a kiosk, bought some bratwurst and beer and talked about our morning flight back to Florida. I had heard somewhere that if you called the airline 12 hours before your flight, you could upgrade to first class for a minimal fee. To check it out, Tom called our friend Jan Nye an airline agent in N.Y. She told us it was true, but you had to call exactly 12 hours before the flight and gave us the number to call. Our flight was in a little over 13 hours away, so we waited at the square and had another beer. At exactly 12 hours before our flight, we called the airline, and sure enough, for a couple of hundred dollars, we upgraded to first class. It was a very enjoyable flight back to Florida; first class is definitely the way to go if you can afford it.

Back in Florida for just two days when I got a call from Michael inviting me to Canada for Thanksgiving at Edithe's house in St. Anicet, a suburb of Montreal. Michael had moved in after getting back together with her earlier in the year. I told him I would be there and went about booking a flight for November 23rd. Just before I left town, Jon called to tell me that he had finished up at Fort Huachuca in May and had moved with his wife Emma to his PCS assignment, Fort Riley, Kansas, and bought a fifth-wheel camper to live in parked at the Mill Creek Campground near Fort Riley. He also informed me that he had orders to Iraq, leaving on November 1st for a year, and by the way, Emma's pregnant! Shortly after Jon departed for Iraq, Emma towed the 5th wheel with her Chevy 250 to Casa Grande, Arizona, and moved in with her sister.

Toward the end of October, Tom and I decided to go visit Jack and Linda Brown in Tampa and go see the Tampa Bay Devil Rays play and maybe a Buccaneers football game. It would also give me a chance to check on The Towers, a condominium completed in 2007 that I looked at in 2008 when the market was down but still priced too high for me. I had been looking for a couple of years for a place in a bigger town than Fort Walton, where getting around would be a lot easier without a car. I liked the Towers because a trolley went by the front door that took you downtown and to Ybor City. That Friday, before going to a Ray's game, we went to Hooters for lunch across the street from the Towers. After lunch, we went over to see if the price had come down any since the last time I checked a year ago. There were a lot of people milling around, and I spotted a relator that I knew and asked her what was going on. She told us that they had gone

bankrupt and were selling the units at half price; I asked her to show us a couple of units. She had an appointment shortly and only had time to show us a three and a two-bedroom on the 12th floor. The two-bedroom faced S.E. and overlooked the Port of Tampa. It was what I was looking for, and I asked her how much they were asking. I could afford it and told her I wanted it. Once she realized that I was serious, she canceled her appointment. In the closing room, I signed a contract and put down the deposit, and as we were leaving, she asked Tom if he wanted one. He told her he would get back with her, and we left to go to the ballgame. The next day, just down the street from the towers, we went to see the Tampa Bay Lightning Hockey team play. It turned out to be an interesting four-event weekend, three sporting events, baseball, Hockey, Football, and buying a condo. About two weeks later, Tom bought the two-bedroom unit right below mine on the 11th floor.

When my flight arrived in Montreal on the 23rd, Michael was there to meet me, and we drove over to pick up Edithe at her office in the Merrill Lynch building in downtown Montreal. Parking in her reserved spot, we took the private elevator to the top floor, where her secretary let us into her office. She was sitting there behind a big desk, and after chatting for a while, she showed us around her office. Being one of their top analysts, she had a corner office overlooking the city. Edithe had come a long way since last seeing her years ago at the 92' Olympics in Barcelona. On the way to her home near St. Anicet, we stopped in Montreal for dinner and had an opportunity to catch up.

It was a short drive that crossed over the St Laurence River to just east of St Anicet and turned onto her driveway. Driving up a long driveway that went by a small house before reaching her house on the river that she had built to her specks about a year earlier. As we approached her house, I noticed a garage/apartment near the house and a lot of cut-up trees lying around. After parking my bags in a downstairs bedroom, Edithe gave me a tour of the house, her office, bedroom, a large

kitchen/living room, and a balcony that were all upstairs facing the river. Downstairs there was a two-car garage, three bedrooms, and a laundry room.

Getting up in the morning, I had breakfast with Edithe before she left for work. Michael was still asleep, so I went for a walk down to the river, where there was a short dock. After looking out over the river, I walked over to the garage. Inside was a John Deere Tractor with a front-end loader, and in the other half a workshop; the apartment upstairs didn't appear to be occupied. From there, I walked past a small chicken coop and a shack, then up the driveway through the maple trees to the small house that was occupied; Edithe had quite a setup.

By the time I got back to the house, Michael was on his laptop and didn't want to talk, so I went back outside and walked around in the maple trees and noticed that most of them were tapped. When Edithe came home from work, and I asked her about the shack, it was her sugar shack. We walked over to it, and she showed me the big pot where she boiled down the sap from her trees into maple syrup. From there, we walked over to the garage, and on the way, I asked her what she was going to do with all the cut-up trees lying around. She intended to barrow a splitter and turn it all into firewood; I volunteered to help if she found the splitter. At the garage, she started up the tractor, and we drove it around for a while, showing me how to operate it. Back in the garage, we looked over the workshop before we went upstairs to show me the unfurnished one-bedroom with a nice view of the river.

Next morning the 25th, Thanksgiving and Michael's 45th birthday that we celebrated with a champagne breakfast. That evening we were invited to Thanksgiving dinner with Edithe's friends at their house and had a marvelous Thanksgiving with cocktails and lots of conversation during and after dinner. The party didn't break up until late in the evening; it had snowed during the party, making the drive home interesting.

Shortly after having breakfast with Edithe and just before leaving for work, her friend showed up with the splitter and showed me how to use it. I cranked up the tractor and loaded the front-end loader with a couple of the two-foot pieces of maple to take over to the splitter. I had been at it for about an hour when Michael showed up to help; it didn't take us long to develop a routine. Over the remaining days before my flight back to Florida on December 1st, Michael and I split and stacked all the wood. It was still snowing when Michael drove me to the airport. I thanked him for a really enjoyable visit with them at Edithe's lovely home in St. Anicet.

Back in Fort Walton Beach, I celebrated my 74th birthday and stayed on to join my friends at the Bay Café's party on the 12th. The next day with a hangover, I flew out to Colorado to go skiing and spend Christmas with my granddaughters. I wouldn't be able to stay long in Colorado; I had to be back in Tampa in January for the closing on unit #1205 at the Towers. Once I was settled in at Fairplay and adjusted to the altitude change, I ventured over to Breckenridge to go skiing. It was good skiing that day.

Two days later, I drove down to Colorado Springs to take Molly and the girls out for dinner on Christmas Eve and to watch the girls open presents on Christmas Day. Molly cooked up a marvelous meal on Christmas Day, and with the wine I picked up on the way down the mountain, we just had a good ol' time. In the morning, I parked my truck at Peterson AFB long-term parking and flew back to Fort Walton Beach.

I celebrated New Year in Fort Walton Beach at Neil and Norma Christianson's party in their house on Okaloosa Island. It was a wonderful party with the same group of friends that I have known for at least twenty or thirty years.

2011

I stayed for a while in Fort Walton, deciding what to take with me in my BMW to Tampa for the closing on my Towers condo. I started driving early to get there in time; that night in Tampa, I slept on the floor on an air mattress in my new digs in unit #1205. In the following days, I was busy ordering furniture, getting the power turned on, and exploring the neighborhood. I took the streetcar to Ybor City to look around and came across Bernini's bar/restaurant in the old Bank of Ybor building. I sat at the bar and had a happy hour martini and a good meal; the bartenders, staff, and clientele were friendly. Then on January 12[th,] just after my furniture arrived, Tom showed up for his closing. It was the same day that Tampa was invaded by Pirates, the beginning of the annual Gasparilla Pirate Festival that goes on for over a month. We both stayed in Tampa for a while, getting our apartments tricked out.

On Fridays, we would take the streetcar to Ybor City and walk over to Bernini's for happy hour, hopefully getting there early enough to get one of the four sidewalk tables. If we snagged one, we would sit there, drink martinis, smoke a cigar, watch the girls walk by, and converse with the people at the tables near us. Then before seven, to take advantage of happy hour prices, order dinner. Later in the evening, we would catch the streetcar back to the Towers before they shut down for the night.

One day while walking around the neighborhood, I came across Cars, Inc., two blocks away from the Towers. The owner, Jud, sells high-end used cars that he buys at auction and has a mechanic (Jossie) who services them; I started taking my BMW there for serving. Baseball season opened, and Tom and I started going to see the Tampa Bay Rays play at the Tropicana ballpark in St Petersburg. During one of the games, I told Tom that I was heading back to Colorado to get in some skiing before the season ended and if he wanted to go.

On March 7th Tom and I flew out to Colorado Springs, arriving in one piece. We picked up my truck at Peterson AFB and loaded up on supplies. We stopped in to visit Molly, and the girls for a bit, then headed up the mountain to Fairplay. After acclimatizing to the altitude for a couple of days, we drove over to Breckenridge to ski. Just as Tom and I were getting off at the top of the Quicksilver lift for our first run of the day, I received a call from my son Michael inviting me to his wedding the next day, on the 12th, to marry Edithe in the Bahamas. I told him I was in Colorado skiing and that there was no way I could make it with such short notice. I wished them all the

happiness and skied down to the lift for another run. Tom and I had five days of really having a good old time skiing and needed a day of rest. Since Mosquito Pass was open, we used our day off to drive over the pass to Leadville. We did a walkabout town and stopped at the old Silver Dollar Saloon for lunch and a beer before heading back. We stayed in Fairplay a while longer to ski another day or two before shutting down the townhouse and driving down the mountain to fly back to Tampa.

On our arrival in Tampa, I went back to work on my apartment, driving around looking for odds and ends to finish my attempt at decorating. When the Tampa Bay Rays were in town, Tom and I would drive over to Tropicana Ballpark in St Petersburg to watch them play. On the way over to a game, I would call Rick Sauter in St. Petersburg to come join us for a beer before the game at Ferg's Sport's Bar, near the ballpark. After I sold the Surfview, Rick had to find a new home for his boat and found one, the St. Petersburg Yacht Club, and bought an apartment in a co-op close by.

Rick never went to a game with us, but he would meet us at Ferg's for a beer. He offered us a place to stay any time we drank too much at the ballgame, either on his boat or in his apartment. On the first Friday of the month, St Petersburg closes a portion of Central Ave for a street party, and if there happened to be a ballgame, we would sometimes take up Rick's offer to kill two birds with one stone.

In May, my son Jon Skyped me from Iraq to let me know he would be coming to Colorado on R&R for the first two weeks of June. He wanted to be there for his daughters' Ballet Recital on the 4th in Colorado Springs and for Emma giving birth to their baby in Arizona. I figured that maybe I ought to be there and went about getting an airline reservation.

On May 28th, I took an Uber to Tampa International Airport for a flight to Colorado Springs. After landing, I took a cab over to Peterson AFB to retrieve my truck, then stopped on my way up to Fairplay to visit Molly and the girls. The girls excitedly talked about their upcoming recital, and I told them I would be there to watch them perform. On the 29[th,] Jon called, giving me his estimated arrival date of June 2nd at the Denver International Airport; I told him I would be there to meet him.

On the 2[nd,] I shut down the townhouse and drove down the mountain to the airport and picked up Jon, then drove to Colorado Springs to see his girls. After playing with the girls for a while, Molly was kind enough to invite us to stay until after the recital. That night we all went out to dinner and had a good time. After the recital, we had a little party for the girls, who

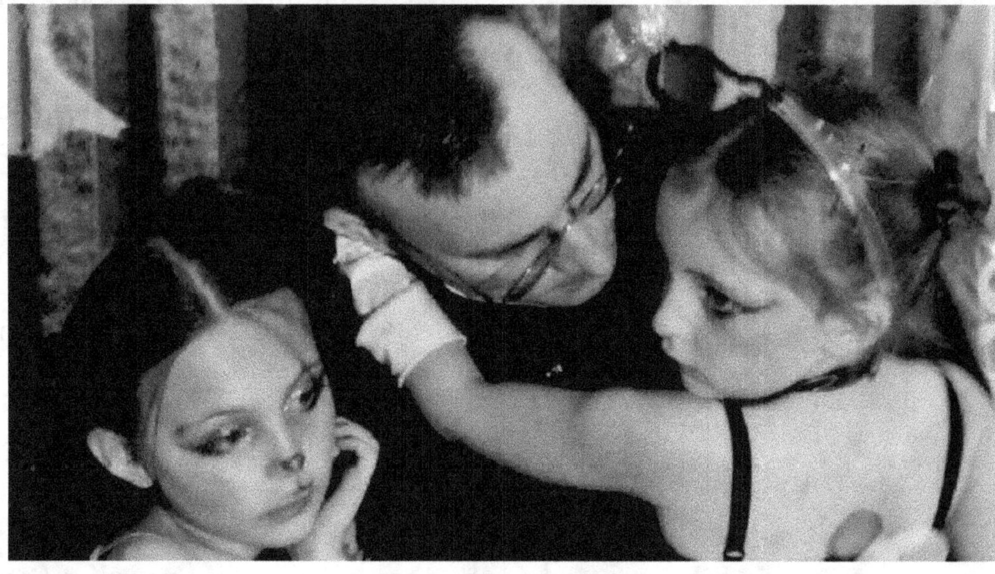

were all fired up after the performance. The next morning Jon and I were up early, and after saying goodbye to the girls, we started our estimated twelve-hour drive to Casa Grande, Arizona.

We made good time and arrived at Casa Grande in time to join everyone for something to eat at the Golden Corral Buffet & Grill. We had quite a crowd; besides Jon and me, there was Jon's wife Emma, her sister Jennifer, her sister's husband Carlton, and her mother, Ann. After eating way too much, I stopped in to chat for a while at their house before checking in at a motel. The first thing I noticed was that there were three little Chihuahua dogs running around making noise and a sick cat in the house; go figure, Emma's a veterinarian.

In the morning, after a leisurely breakfast at a Waffle House near the motel, I drove over to Emma's sisters to get to know my in-laws better. Emma was very pregnant, close to giving birth, miserable, and relentlessly bitching at Jon. The rest of her family were big people (obese) who just sat there watching a veterinarian channel on the T.V. I finally got a conversation going with Emma's brother-in-law, Carlton, a professor at a local college and global warming advocate. He started lecturing me on how global warming caused by humans was killing the polar bears. I pulled up the latest government polar bear count on my phone, showing that the polar bear population was actually growing. I presented him with the data; he started ranting and raving, getting red in the face, sweating, and hyperventilating. I thought he was about to have a heart attack. I guess by being a

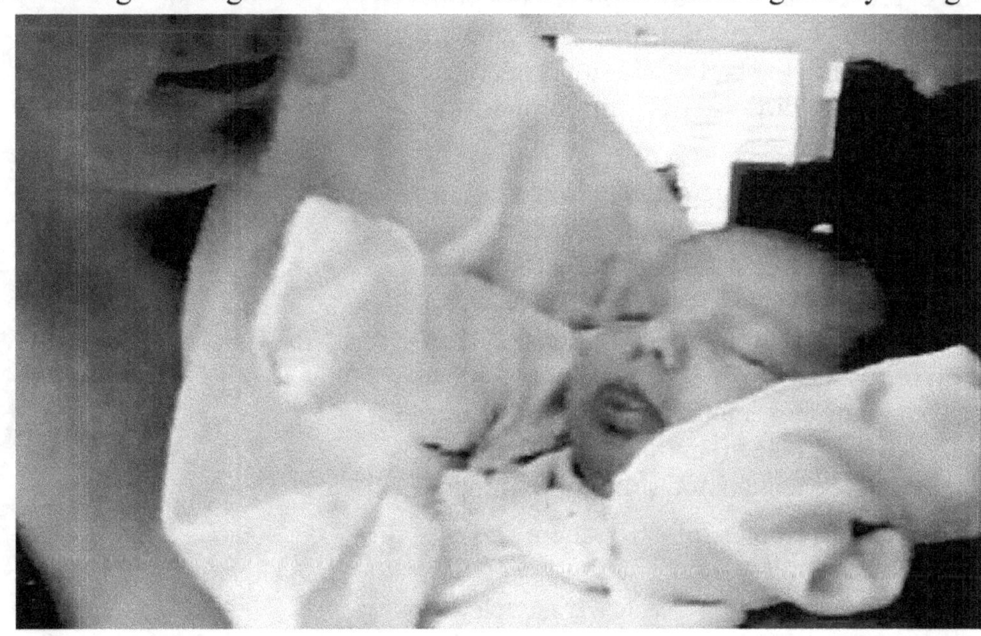

professor, no one ever challenged him before. Well, so much for making a hit with my in-laws.

The next morning, I stopped by on my way out of town to say goodbye and started driving east on I-10 bound for Fort Walton Beach, Florida. Days later, Jon was on his way back to Iraq, just missing Emma giving birth to a baby girl, Amelia Abigail Gebhardt, on June 16th.

During the long drive to Florida, I had a lot of time to think about the townhouse in Fairplay. Now that I had a place in Tampa where I was spending a lot of time, I needed to sell either the townhouse in Fairplay or my apartment in the El Matador. I really liked both places, one on the beach and the other in the mountains. I decided to wait a while and see how much time I spent at them before making a decision.

Back on Okaloosa Island for a month or so, paying bills and enjoying the beach before driving my truck down to Tampa, where my car was parked. That evening Tom and I took the streetcar to Ybor City for dinner. While having a martini and a cigar at Bernini's before dinner, we talked about the Civil War. We both had read many books on the Civil War and decided to take a road trip in my car to tour the battlefield at Gettysburg. I had been there before with Jack Brown years ago for a short one-day visit and needed to go back. Over the next month or so, the planned road trip expanded to include a stop on our way back to Florida in Washington, D.C. Before leaving on August 7th, I did some research on the internet and found the West Point walking guide for Gettysburg and printed it out to take with us.

When we arrived late in the afternoon, we found accommodations in the middle of town at the Gettysburg Hotel and, later, at their restaurant, enjoyed cocktails and a good meal. In the morning, we walked over to the Battlefield Museum, where we spent the morning then started out touring the battlefield. We spent a better part of four days walking the battlefield using our guide and came away with a good understanding of the three-day battle. During our stay, we had an interesting lunch with Bill Rosenbach, a fellow navigator who I served with in the 817th TCS on Okinawa during Vietnam. He told us that since retiring as a history professor from Gettysburg College that he now has a business using the battlefield in his business seminars that draws CEO from around the world.

It was a short drive in my car to Washington, where we took a room at the Windsor Park Hotel, where we had stayed before. We walked the National Mall, around downtown Washington, bought tickets on the Hop-On-Hop-Off bus, and visited most of our national monuments. After three days, we had seen about everything we needed to see and started driving to Tampa.

Back in Tampa on October 9th, there was the Tampa Red Bull Flugtag, a fun event that drew 125,000 fans to downtown Tampa. Of

the 40 teams that competed with their flying machines, most failed and just nose-dived into the water. The winning team, Willy Wonka's Amazing Flying Adventure, was the first team with consecutive wins. None of the teams came close to beating the record flight of 207 ft.

Later on in October, Tom and I rented a car and drove down to visit Rick in Key West for Fantasy Fest, arriving in time for the last five days of the fest. We found Rick and his girlfriend Colleen at the A&B Marina, and after loading our gear on his boat, the Anna Virginia, we joined them for a drink at Alfonso's Oyster Bar. Colleen was a flight nurse during Vietnam and wore hearing aids like me; just about everyone that flew around in C-130s wears them. The festival was in full swing, with people running around half naked all over the place. We did our usual thing, corner an outside table at Rick's Bar, eat peanuts, drink beer and watch

the crowd walk by; some of the costumes were really outrageous. Tom and I did take time to go to the Key West Shipwreck Museum and take a tour of Hemingway's House. The thrill of peanuts, beer, and watching costumed people acting crazy wears off after a while. When Fantasy Fest ended on the 30th with the big parade, I was worn out and ready to head back to Tampa. I guess I'm not much of a party animal anymore.

Back in Tampa, there were three cruise ships in port; neither Tom nor I had ever been on a cruise, so we signed up for one: A short four-day cruise on the Royal Caribbean ship, Liberty of the Seas,

to the Bahamas, Jamaica, and Cozumel. We had a cabin with a balcony and were underway by four in the afternoon for the overnight sail to Nassau in the Bahamas. The food was good, the crap table was cold, and you don't get a lot of time at our ports-of-call to look around. In Cozumel, we rented a taxi to take us around the island with a lunch stop at a tequila distillery. He dropped us off at a bar close to the dock, where we were descended upon by the bar girls wanting us to buy them drinks. We didn't have a lot of time to play with them before boarding our ship for the last leg of the cruise back to Tampa.

On November 29th, Mitt Romney, a Republican running for president, gave a speech at the Aquarium two streets over from the Towers. Tom went over to listen to him; he was there warming up for the RNC National Convention to be held in Tampa next August. Before leaving Tampa, I took a day and went aboard the S.S. American Victory that's tied up by the aquarium, one of four operational ships from WW2. While onboard the historical ship, I found out that every once in a while, they start it up, load it up with people and sail it around Tampa Bay.

In November, Jon finished his tour in Iraq and took leave to retrieve his family in Arizona and move them to Kansas. During which everything went to hell-in-a-handbasket ending with Jon filing for a divorce. Emma and Amelia stayed in Arizona, living with her sister, and Jon took the fifth wheel back to Kansas and parked it at the Owl's Nest Campground in Junction City, close to Fort Riley, Kansas, where he's stationed.

I drove my truck up to Fort Walton Beach to be there in time for the annual party at the Bay Café this year on December 11th. Monique had reserved a big table for us, and we all had a good old time eating, drinking, talking, and dancing until they shooed us out the door. The parties are always a big success and a great opportunity to catch up with old friends. I hung around town until after Christmas and talked Tom into driving with me out to Colorado in my truck for another go at skiing.

We stopped on the way to visit my granddaughters in Colorado Springs before going up the mountain. On the way, we made a stop at Cripple Creek to shoot some craps arriving in Fairplay just before the New Year. We celebrated the event by going to the Fairplay Hotel for dinner and then to the Park Bar New Year's Eve party.

The bar was crowded with a fun crowd of revelers, where we had a wonderful time chatting and dancing with the ladies. The stagger back up the hill to the townhouse in the middle of the night was a challenge.

Chapter Twelve: 2012 – 2014

Tom and I had two weeks of good skiing at Breckenridge before closing up the townhouse and starting our drive to Florida.

I decided to sell the townhouse but would wait another year before putting it on the market, I was not using it enough to justify owning it and didn't need the expense of maintaining three houses, but I loved the place. On the way to Florida, we stopped to visit Jon in Kansas and give him some divorce support. While there, Jon and I swapped cars; I bought his '04 Porsche Cayenne S for what he owed on it and gave him my '02 Chevy Truck.

Back in Tampa, Jack, Tom, and I started running with the Four Green Field's Irish Pub runners, the pubs about a twenty-minute walk from the Towers. They sponsor a run every Wednesday down Bayshore Drive with free beer and food after the run. On March 17th, St. Patrick's Day, we went to their party and had a good ol' time dancing to the music and enjoying some good Irish whiskey and stew. We also drove over to the Fantasy of Flight, a privately owned airfield with a collection of all sorts of flyable airplanes and equipment.

Later in the month, Jon flew in from Kansas on leave for a few days. He arrived just in time to go with us on the 24th for a day cruise around the bay on the WWII freighter, S.S. American Victory. There was a good crowd of a couple of hundred people that showed up for the cruise. The tickets included a boxed lunch that they gave to you when you boarded. All the crew's uniforms and music were from the 1940s; there was also a bar and snack bar set up on deck. We were able to walk all over the ship, including the engine room. About halfway through

the day, there was a simulated torpedo attack by a WW2 aircraft (AT-6). It was an enjoyable day on the old ship and well worth the money.

Driving around the next day, we found a private museum with a MIG 21 setting outside and inside a lot of WW2 military hardware. We also took Jon to a Ray's game at the Tropicana ballpark in St. Petersburg and to Ybor City for martinis, cigars, and dinner at Bernini's. While at Bernini's, he told us about Donna, a woman that he was dating in Junction City. A few days after, Jon flew back to Kansas.

Royal Caribbean notified us about a repositioning cruise to England for $1000 that sounded like a good deal. Tom and I decided to go and booked a cabin with a balcony on the Jewel of the Seas, leaving from Miami on May 3rd. It was to be a 13-day transatlantic voyage to the International Port of Harwich in the U.K., with stops at the Portuguese Island of Sao Miguel in the Azores and two more stops in France at the Ports at Brest and Cherbourg.

Early on the 3rd, we drove a rental down to Miami, where we turned in the car and boarded the

Jewel of the Seas. It took us a while to clear through customs and immigration and find our cabin, which was toward the stern of the ship on the port side. Once we got our gear stowed, there was a lifeboat drill, after which the Jewel of the Seas set sail. We did a walkabout the ship to get familiar with it and to find out where the buffet was located. The ship had numerous restaurants, cocktail lounges, entertainment, shops, and a casino. A day into our voyage, I came down with the green apple quick step and went to the clinic, where they gave me some drugs and quarantined me to my cabin for a day. The clinic was staffed with four friendly young beautiful blonds from different countries around Europe. During the cruise, we fraternized with them every chance we got; they were interesting and a lot of fun. En route to the Azores, we were kept busy on board going to the gym, eating way too much, shooting craps at the casino, drinking at the cocktail lounges, going to the floor shows, and taking full advantage of all the onboard activities.

After seven and a half days at sea, we arrived in the Azores on the morning of the 10th at Ponta Delgada, the capital city on the Island of Sao Miguel, the largest Island of the Azores. We had a good seven hours of shore leave, and during our walkabout, we toured the historic Church of the Jesuit College (Igreja of Colegio dos Jesuetes de Ponta Delgada) that they started building in 1592. On our way back to the ship, we stopped at the Restaurant Mercado do Peixi, where we had a marvelous late lunch.

Three days later, on the morning of May 13th, we arrived at Port de Brest, France, and tied up to what looked like a dry dock. Onshore during our walkabout, we came across a big old fort that turned out to be the Brest Naval Museum, but unfortunately, it was closed. On our walk back to the ship, we stopped for some lunch at a sidewalk café, and people watched. Brest is a big city, and we really didn't have enough time ashore to do much. As the ship left the port, we sailed past some interesting old Nazi sub-pens that looked like they might still be in use by the French.

The next morning, we arrived at Cherbourg, where the Titanic had made its last stop to pick up passengers before it hit an iceberg and sank on April 14th, 1912. We had a day of shore leave during which we visited the museum Notre Dames de Queens, and the French decommissioned 420ft nuclear submarine Le Redoutable. By the time we were finally done looking at everything, it was late afternoon. While walking around town, we came across Kileeggan's Irish Pub, where we stopped for a pint of Guinness before making our way back to the ship. That night, our last night aboard the Jewel of the Seas, there was a farewell party that lasted well into the evening. On the morning of May 15th, we reached our destinations at Harwich in the UK. For the duration of this adventure, I was on drugs to keep my bowels under control and would have to get it looked at as soon as I got back to Florida.

It was a two-hour train ride to Kings Cross Station in London, where we hailed a cab to take us to Jean's in Kensington. We had a week before our flight back to Florida to enjoy London, during which we went to see Danny DeVito in the

Sunshine Boys at the Savoy. Jean was busy during the week, but on the weekend, she was available to play. On Saturday, we took her out to dinner and to the theater to see What the Butler Saw, a Joe Orton Play at the Vaudeville Theater. The rest of our time in London was spent in museums, our favorite pubs and walking around town. On Tuesday, May 21st, we took a Taxi to Gatwick to catch a flight back to Florida.

Shortly after landing in Tampa, I drove up to Fort Walton Beach and made an appointment with my gastroenterologist, who, after checking me out, scheduled me for a colonoscopy. After the procedure, his diagnosis was that I had collagenous colitis, and he prescribed me a drug to control it. It seems like the older you get; the more shit happens to your body.

In August, the Republican National Convention was held in Tampa; there was a lot of apprehension about possible destructive demonstrations. In response, there was a noticeable increase in the amount of police on the streets, and a secure area was set up around the Tampa Bay Times Forum, the site of the convention. It just so happened that when the convention began, Tampa was in a hurricane warning that scared away the demonstrators. Romney and Ryan came out of the convention as the Republican presidential candidates.

In the 2012 election, President Obama and Vice President Biden were reelected for a second term in the White House. Before the election, Tom and I had signed up for a National Review Post Election Cruise on the Holland American ship Nieuw Amsterdam departing from Port Everglades, Florida.

On November 11th, we rented a car from Hertz and drove to Fort Lauderdale, turned it in, and took their shuttle to Port Everglades and the Nieuw Amsterdam. The ship's first port of call was at a

private island in the Bahamas, followed by stops at the Cayman Islands and their resort in Jamaica and Honduras. We had a busy schedule and didn't spend a lot of time ashore; on board, there were daily seminars, and we went to all of them. Every day we had private dinners with National Review writers and guest speakers. On our last day at sea, there was a National Review farewell cocktail party with the National Review people and their guest speakers. It was an interesting, informative experience meeting and talking with people that I have only read

about or seen on T.V.

Back in Tampa when on December 3rd, I got a call from Maureen Shuster, the wife of Dick Shuster, my high school buddy, telling me that he had died. I drove down to Marco Island for his funeral. Dick was an Army helicopter pilot during Vietnam and stayed in contact over the years. The last time I saw Dick was in 1967 when I bumped into him at a Bob Hope Show at Pleiku-Holloway Army Airfield in Vietnam. A few days after the funeral, I drove up to Fort Walton for the Bay Café annual party on the 12th; then, on the 23rd, I flew out to Colorado to spend Christmas with my granddaughters and go skiing.

Jon picked me up at the airport and drove to the Academy Hotel, where we had connecting rooms. From the hotel, we drove over to Molly's to take the girls out for a Christmas Eve dinner, and again on Christmas day, we drove over to watch the girls open presents. On the 26th, Jon's fiancée, Donna, drove in from Kansas with her son Wyatt to meet us at the hotel. That evening Jon picked up his girls, and we all met up with Molly at a restaurant where Molly had made a reservation. It was an interesting meal with Jon, his x-wife Molly with their two girls, and his fiancée Donna and her son; it was all very amicable. Elizabeth, Emma, and Wyatt were immediate friends; they were all about the same age and spent most of the time in the hotel's big indoor swimming pool. Over cocktails that evening with Jon and Donna, I suggested that we all go up to Fairplay and over to Breckenridge, where I would buy ski lessons for the kids.

The next day we drove up the mountain in a two-car convoy to my townhouse in Fairplay and spent a day there walking around the neighborhood. The next day we drove over to Breckenridge and signed the kids up for ski school. The six-hour class included a box lunch for on the mountain. While they were learning how to ski, Jon, Donna, and I waited for their return at the Maggie

bar/restaurant by the lift, which gave me an opportunity to get acquainted with Donna, Jon's future bride.

It was around three in the afternoon when the kids skied down from their class and turned in their skis. On our drive back to Fairplay, they excitedly told us about their ski lesson. After driving through Alma on the way to Fairplay, we encountered a detour around an accident that knocked down a power pole. Arriving at the townhouse, we found that there was no electrical power, so we packed up and drove back down the mountain to our rooms at the Academy Hotel. Molly picked up the girls on the 30th, and the rest of us stayed on to celebrate the arrival of the New Year at the hotel's party.

2013

It was decision time for what to do with my townhouse in Fairplay. During the past year, I only stayed there for maybe a week or so; it was obvious that I needed to sell it. I walked over to Snowshoe Realty and talked to Margaret about what it was worth, and signed a contract to sell it. I flew back to Fort Walton Beach on January 3rd.

Back in Fort Walton for just a few days when my son Jon called and told me that on their drive back to Kansas, they decided to get married. They exchanged vows on January 4th at the Fort Riley Main Post Chapel.

On the 5th, my son Michael drove in to visit while on his way back to Canada from Miami. I was glad to see him and catch up on what he and his bride, Edithe, have been doing since they married in 2011. I told him that his

brother had just gotten married again for the third time and was sorry to hear from him that Edithe had suffered a miscarriage. The next day while he was slicing up vegetables for a salad, he sliced off the tip of his left index finger. After we stopped the bleeding, I took him over to my old friend, little Mary, a nurse who patched him up.

The Friday before he departed on his drive to Canada, Michael and I were able to join my old friends that meet every Friday for dinner at the Chapala Authentic Mexican Restaurant.

Shortly after Michael departed, I drove down to Tampa in time for the start of the Gasparilla Pirate Festival on the 13th. My cousins Carol and Virgie came over to stay for the weekend of the festival's big parade down Bayshore Drive. Tom was in Tampa at the time, and the four of us had a lot of fun mingling in the crowd during the parade and later at Bernini's for martinis and something to eat.

I was back in Fort Walton Beach in April for a 919th AFRES reunion at the Air Force Armament Museum. There was a big crowd to enjoy the buffet, beer, and some speeches. They also had aircraft 129, a C-130 gunship, open for us to crawl around in. I flew in it many times and was the first C-130 delivered to the air force in the 50s. I could not help but notice that there were not many old timers like me there. One person I did recognize was General Don Haugen; he recruited me into the 919th when it was first activated in the '70s. After the reunion, I stayed in Fort Walton for

just a week or so before driving down to Tampa for the start of the baseball season on April 1st.

While having martinis with Tom at Bernini's in Ybor City, he suggested that in the near future, we needed to go visit his sister in London; I told him I was good to go anytime. Within a week, we booked reservations for June 6th on British Air's nonstop overnight flight from Tampa-TPA to London-Gatwick Airport (LGW).

In May, I received a call from my son Jon telling me that he had orders to the Marine Corps Base Quantico in Virginia. They were in the process of moving their 5th wheel from Kansas to Brady's Hill mobile home Park in Triangle, Virginia, just outside the main gate at Quantico. A month after completing the move, Donna flew back to Kansas for her parents' 50th wedding anniversary and decided to have her baby there.

Back in Tampa on June 6th, Tom and I took Uber out the Tampa-TPA for our flight on the 6th to the U.K. Arriving at Gatwick, Tom called his sister Jean who told him that

she had house guests and would get with him after they left. From the airport, we took the Gatwick Express to Victoria Station, then the underground to Lancaster Gate, the stop close to the Columbia Hotel. After checking in, we walked around the corner to the Swan for a pint and some lunch, where we talked over our agenda for the next couple of weeks. We decided to go to Frankfurt, Germany, for a start and decided where to go from there.

After early morning breakfast at the Columbia Hotel, we walked across Kensington Gardens to a travel agency in Kensington and bought Eurail Passes and used them to book 1st class seats the next day on the Eurostar to Frankfurt. After stopping for lunch at the Goat Tavern, we walked over to spend the rest of the day at the Victoria and Albert Museum.

Arriving in Frankfurt, we checked in at the hotel Munchner Hof across the street from the Hauptbahnhof. After getting everything squared away at the hotel, we walked across the street to the Irish Pub for some food and to contemplate our next move. Back at Bernini's in Ybor City, we had talked to a person who raved about his hometown Krakow, Poland. During lunch, we decided that Krakow would be an interesting destination. After finishing lunch, we walked over to the Hauptbahnhof and used our Eurail passes for tickets on the overnight train to Warsaw, where we would change trains for Krakow.

Late in the afternoon of June 10th, we boarded the train, and the conductor showed us our compartment. That evening we had a nice dinner in the dining car and then relaxed to enjoy the ride. Then, around midnight the train stopped and they shooed us off the train onto a small station platform somewhere near Dortmund, Germany. As we were getting off the train, the conductor told us that the rails were flooded ahead and that another train would be by to pick us up.

About an hour later, when the train arrived, there was a lot of scurrying around. In the confusion, we cornered a conductor and showed her our tickets; she studied them for a while, then took us to a compartment telling us on the way that we would like our female roommate. Entering our compartment, we were greeted by a Russian woman in her early '30s. She was attractive, spoke particularly good English, and told us that she had boarded the train in Switzerland. She lived there with

her husband and was on her way to visit her parents in Moscow. We talked for an hour or so, telling stories before I finally left the conversation and crawled into an upper bunk to get some sleep.

In Warsaw, we left our Russian friend and went looking for the train to Krakow. Wandering around the station, we located the schedule board with the time and track number of the next train to Krakow. The train was a commuter and crowded, with no seats available. We ended up standing with our bags and four or five other people by the toilet. A fellow passenger standing with us broke out a bottle of vodka and offered us some. He didn't speak English, and we didn't speak Polish, but after a couple of hits of vodka, it didn't matter; we had no trouble communicating. We were just having a good old time when the conductor showed up to check our tickets. I gave him a hand full of our first-class tickets that he looked over and moved people out of seats for us to sit for the duration of the trip to Krakow.

The train station in Krakow was in a shopping complex that took us a while to find our way out off. We dragged our bags to the closest hotel, the Polonia, a grand old hotel with big rooms, high ceilings, huge windows, and no a/c. After resting for a while in our room with the windows open, we found our way to the lounge and ordered a couple of martinis. The young bartender brought us Martini Vermouth on the rocks; I took the drinks back, and after a little tutoring, we got our

martinis to celebrate arriving in one piece from an interesting overnight train adventure.

In the morning, the concierge told us the hotel was located just across the street from Old Town Krakow and gave us some tour pamphlets. At breakfast, we looked them over and signed up for a tour on the 14th of the Nazi Auschwitz-Birkenau concentration camps.

Leaving the hotel, we walked crossed the street to Old Town Krakow and

the Rynek Glowny, the 13th-century town square with its 14th-century Saint Mary's Basilica. Walking around the square, we came across a bronze sculpture by Ihor Mitory, The Eros Bendato, a big head laying on its side, a symbol of such passionate love from which people lose their heads. Around the square, there were many shops, cafés, and restaurants. We stopped at a café for lunch and to people watch. We noticed that there were very few fat people and many beautiful tall, slender, predominately blond women of all ages. We speculated that maybe the reason why was that there were lots of people on bicycles or walking to get around town. After lunch, we walked over to the Suki Ennice Market Hall, looking for the History Museum in the middle of the square. We walked through the market just before they closed, but there was no museum. We stopped for cocktails and dinner at one of the restaurants in the square before heading back to the hotel, where we had a nightcap and talked about the missing museum.

In the morning, we went over to the market hall on the square and walked around the outside of it, and came across a side door opposite Saint Mary's Basilica. Inside and to the right was another door with museum printed on it; going down the stairs we found the Rynek Underground Museum located four meters under the town square. In 2009 the architectural excavation started and cost 38 million zloty to complete. The dig uncovered an area of over 6,000 square meters of medieval streets, burnt-out settlements, and reconstructed merchants' stalls, waterworks, and a lot more. It opened to the public on September 24th, 2010; an extraordinary place where you could get the feel of how people lived 700 years ago; we spent most of the day there. We had dinner on the town square again, this time at an Italian restaurant with tables out on the square. We had a wonderful meal there and stayed for a while watching the activities on the square before calling it a night.

On the morning of June 14th, we boarded the tour bus for the 20-mile drive to Auschwitz-Birkenau Concentration/Extermination Camp. Just before we arrived, Prime Minister Netanyahu of Israel, in his motorcade, went by us going the opposite direction; he had been there to dedicate a new memorial at the international monument for the victims of fascism. I had seen photos and had read about the Holocaust, but nothing prepared me for being there; it was truly eye-opening. It was an unbelievably large-scale horrific operation that the Nazis had set up. Those arriving by train and

strong enough to work were separated from the rest, who were sent to die in the gas chamber and cremated.

From the railhead, we walked to Auschwitz-Birkenau Museum, then went through a barracks to see the terrible living conditions and into the rooms with piles of shoes, hair, and luggage. It was an all-day tour, and on the bus back to Krakow, nobody said a word.

The next day while walking around the square, we noticed some electric carts lined up advertising tours of the city.

We went over to talk to one of the drivers, a pretty blond, and after talking to her for a while, we signed up for the tour. While she was driving on the bridge over the Vistula River on our way to tour the historic Schindler's factory, she was stopped by the police and given a ticket, probably because we had distracted her with all our questions. The factory was owned by Oscar Schindler, a German businessman and a member of the Nazi party. He

employed workers for his enamel works from the nearby Jewish ghetto and was credited with saving 1200 Jews from the Holocaust. After a short lunch stop, she drove us over to Plac Bohaterow Getta, a public square in the center of what was the Jewish Ghetto. The square is next to a train station where they loaded Jews on trains going to the extermination camps at Auschwitz -Birkenau. Another historical site is on the S.W. corner of the square, the Eagle Pharmacy (Apteka Pod Orlem). That's where the Polish proprietor helped the Jews by giving them free drugs and a place to meet. Our surrey tour driver was not only beautiful, but she was also informative about the interesting places to see around Krakow. The tour was well worth the money, and we gave her a big tip plus enough to cover the ticket. It was late in the afternoon when she dropped us off. The square was crowded and had a carnival atmosphere, and joined in to enjoy the jugglers, mimes, and music. We stayed at the square for cocktails and dinner at one of the restaurants. On our way back to the hotel, we came across the Jazz Club u Muniaka and stopped for a nightcap. Walking downstairs to the underground club, we found seats at the bar and chatted with the women sitting there. They were young, in their 20s, spoke some English, and were interesting to talk to. The bartender, who was about to leave, tried to talk us into going with him to his second job in a gentlemen's club, it was tempting, but we didn't go and stayed at the bar to talk to the girls.

On Sunday, after a leisurely breakfast at our hotel, we walked over to the square where they were having a full day of activities. As soon as the church services at the basilica ended, the school bands marched around the square, followed by afternoon bike races. After spending most of the day sitting at a café watching the action at the square, we walked back to our hotel. On the way, two chunky middle-aged Russian hookers latched on to us. We bantered with them until they tried to follow us into our hotel; we were saved by the doorman who shooed them away.

On our last day in Krakow, we walked up Wawel Hill by the Vistula River to tour the 14th-century Wawel Royal Castle and the 11th-century Wawel Cathedral next to it. After spending most of the day there, we walked back to our hotel for dinner and to get ready for the long train ride back to the U.K. In the morning, Tom called his sister Jean before we boarded the train to tell her we were on our way back to London. During the conversation, she invited us to stay at her place in Kensington. In Warsaw, we transferred to the overnight train to Frankfurt, where we were able to get tickets on the Eurostar to the U.K.

We arrived at the St. Pancras station in London on Tuesday, June 18th, and took the underground to High Street Kensington and walked down High Street dragging our bags. It was early, and knowing that Jean would be busy with patients, we stopped at the Goat Tavern for a pint. That evening we took Jean out to dinner at the little India Restaurant a couple of blocks away on Gloucester Road. Over dinner, we told her all about our adventures in Poland.

In the morning, at breakfast, before Jean's first patient, we asked her when she would be available for dinner and the theater. She told us that Saturday would be good for her and suggested we go see The Women in Black playing at the Fortune Theatre and would get the tickets. With that settled, we had a few free days to continue our exploration of London. We started by taking the underground to the Imperial War Museum. When we got there, we found that it had closed for

renovation back in January for six months and that it would close again for the first six months of 2014 to complete the job. We went to a pub around the corner for lunch and talked about our next move. After lunch, we did a little walkabout, then hopped a bus to Kensington and the Goat Tavern for a pint. We were getting good at taking the double-decker buses, it's slower, but you get to see more of London than taking the underground. On Saturday, while sitting at one of the Cambridge Pub's sidewalk tables having lunch and killing time before our date with Jean. We witnessed, for our amusement, the annual Dyke March as it passed by in front of us on Charing Cross Road. There were two hundred or more women in the march wearing costumes, waving banners, some on roller skates, and making a lot of noise.

We were back in Kensington in time for our date with Jean, who drove us over to our dinner reservation at the Ritz, a high-end French restaurant. We had a good but expensive meal there before going to see The Women in Black, followed by cocktails at a close-by bar. Later that evening, back at Jean's, Tom had a bellyache; we figured it was an inflamed Gall Bladder from eating foie gras at the

Ritz. He hurt in the same area where I hurt before I had my Gall Bladder removed a year earlier and told him he would probably have to get it cut out. He survived a painful night and had a day or two to recover before we were saying goodbye to Jean. On June 25th, we took a taxi to London-LGW and, with a little luck, were able to upgrade our tickets to first class for our flight to Tampa-TPA. Tom eventually had his Gall Bladder removed when it fired up again on him in Fort Walton Beach.

I did not stay long in Tampa. A few days after arriving back in town, Molly called me and invited me to join her and the girls at Disneyland. I told her that I would love to and drove over to Orlando early the next day. We met with Molly and the girls, her father Bud, and a friend of Molly's, who worked at Disney who and had free tickets for us in the Disney parking lot. We all had a wonderful time and I was thankful for the opportunity to spend a day with my granddaughters.

In Kansas, at 11:54 p.m. on August 21st at the Fort Riley Irwin Army Hospital, my son Jon's wife Donna gave birth to a 6lb 9oz baby girl, Macie Marie Gebhardt. I now have four beautiful granddaughters.

By the end of July, I was back in my apartment at the El Matador in Fort Walton Beach for some R&R at the beach and pay bills. On September 12th, I joined old friends at the Capala Mexican Restaurant to celebrate birthdays. A short time later, I drove back to Tampa, where while having dinner with Tom at Bernini's, we talked about a road trip to see some Civil War Battlefields. My suggestion was to go up to D.C to the battlefields in Virginia and, while we were there, visit my son Jon who was batching it in Triangle.

On October 30th, we drove up to Triangle, Virginia, and found Brady's Hill mobile home Park, where Jon

welcomed us. After chewing the fat for a while, we went out to a restaurant for cocktails and something to eat. That night we stayed in Jon's 5th wheel; it was cold and miserable. The next day when Jon went to work, we checked in at a hotel, The Ambassador Suites, near the mobile home park, then drove over to spend the day at the Chancellorsville battlefield.

The battle (May 1863), where Gen. Lee was outnumbered 2-1 by Gen. Hookers Union Army, split his army and outflanked Hooker. It was Lee's greatest victory, but in the battle, he lost his gifted tactical commander, "Stonewall" Jackson, to friendly fire. Driving back to Triangle, we picked up Jon after work at his 5th wheel and went out to dinner, where we talked about civil war battlefields; there are a lot of them in Virginia.

On Saturday, the three of us drove over to the close by Fredericksburg battlefield (Dec. 1862), which was a Union loss to Lee and his Army of Northern Virginia. Union General Burnside's army was repulsed, trying to cross the Rappahannock River by the entrenched Confederates on Marye's Heights. We spent most of the morning walking around the battlefield, then joined the street party that was going on in Fredericksburg.

On Sunday afternoon, while having a beer at his 5ᵗʰ wheel, Jon showed us the AR-15 rifle he was building up from parts that he had bought online and told me he would send it to me when he finished. Before going to dinner, I called my second cousin Brian Hucker who lived in Fredericksburg, and invited him to join us. The last time we met was in 1992 when my mother and I went to his wedding in New Jersey. He works as a government contractor and has two teenage

daughters and a wife that was about to divorce him. My son and Brian are both government contractors and had a lot to talk about. During the weekend, we hung out with Brian, and on Monday morning, before Tom and I left, Brian stopped on his way to work to join us at our hotel for breakfast. After checking out, Jon drove to work while Tom and I drove over to Alexandria and got a room at the Ramada Inn on King's Street.

Once settled in our room, we took the Metro into D.C. to tour the National Monuments. The first thing I noticed when we got off the Metro was that the Washington Monument had scaffolding on it to repair damage from the August 23ʳᵈ, 2011 earthquake. When we got to the Mall, it was roped off. President Obama had ordered the closure of all the national parks, monuments, and battlefields late Sunday; he was having a funding dispute with Congress. Closing it all down was obviously nothing but political theater to put pressure on Congress to get more money to spend. Great. We walked over to the WW2 Memorial, which was closed and crowded with WW2 Veterans. Most of them had just flown in on Freedom Flights for a one-time visit to see their monument. We joined the crowd that eventually forced its way in past the National Park Service guards, who only put in a token effort to stop us. It was quite a scene; the media was there as well as a couple of Republican Congressmen were in the crowd to support the veterans. That evening we walked over to Theismann's Restaurant just up the street from our hotel in Alexandria for cocktails and dinner at the bar.

We went back to the WW2 Memorial the next day, it was still closed, but the guards were letting the old vets slip in. We found out from one of the NPS guards that the one place that was still open to the public was Mount Vernon, which is privately owned and operated by the Mount Vernon Ladies Assoc. Leaving the memorial, we walked over toward the White House and stopped at a small café across the street from the Ford Theater. After lunch, we walked over and got on the Hop-On-Hop-Off Tour Bus. On our last day in Virginia, we drove over to Mount Vernon and took the tour, spending most of the day there. We were back in Alexandria and Theismann's in time for happy hour and later dinner at the bar. They get a good after-work crowd of mostly government workers: we were able to get into some interesting conversations with some of them about working in D.C.

Tom and I started driving back to Tampa the next day, November 5th. On the way, we decided to spend the night in Charleston, South Carolina. Arriving in town on a cold afternoon and found there were no rooms available at the Frances Marion Hotel, where we had stayed before. They sent us across the street to the old Citadel, now a hotel and where our partner in the Windsong Bubba Bost went to school.

In the morning, in front of the hotel on what used to be the Citadel's parade ground, there were information booths and enclosures set up with all sorts of live animals on display. The elephant and a couple of camels didn't look very happy standing out in the cold: when it started to snow, they packed up everything, including the animals, in trucks and left.

That evening while we were having dinner at the hotel, the snowfall continued. After dinner, we went to the bar, where there was what appeared to be panic over the snow that was now coming down heavily. By morning, the snow had stopped and started to melt into a slushy mess. After a leisurely breakfast, we continued our drive south.

Shortly after arriving back in Tampa, Jon traded up to a bigger 5th wheel, and Donna flew out from Kansas to Virginia with Macie to join Jon on Brady's Hill.

About a week after arriving back in Tampa, I drove up to Fort Walton Beach. I had plenty to do, doctor appointments, paying bills, and contacting a lawyer to establish a trust. I also met with my old friends on Fridays at the Chapala Mexican Restaurant and with another group called the Lobster Heads in Destin that Tom introduced me, that met for dinner on Wednesdays. While Tom and I were both in town, we drove over to the Naval Air Museum on Pensacola NAS. On the base

to see if they added anything since our last visit. Once on the base, we stopped to look over Fort Barrancas. Built in 1844, it was one of the three forts to defend Pensacola.

On November 23rd, I flew back to Virginia for Macie's baptism at the St Francis of Assisi Catholic Church in Triangle. My x-wife, Gail, and my son Michael were there for the ceremony. We all stayed on to celebrate Thanksgiving and Michael's birthday with Jon and his family at their 5th wheel.

On the 30th, Michael and I flew back to Fort Walton Beach and stayed long enough to go to a Friday night Mexican dinner at Chapala's with our old friends. The next morning, we left early enough for a quick walk through the Naval Air Museum at Pensacola NAS before his flight to Canada. I stayed in Fort Walton Beach for the Bay Café's Annual Party on December 15th, then flew out to Colorado to visit my grandchildren for Christmas.

Brantley English, Molly's on-again-off-again boyfriend, picked me up at the Colorado Springs Airport. It was good to see the girls again, and we had a wonderful Christmas together. On the 28th, Jon drove over to pick us up (his daughters and me) to meet up with Donna, Macie, Joshua, and Wyatt at the Academy Hotel. He had reservations for us through New Year's, just like last year. That evening Molly joined us after work at a nearby restaurant, where we had a fun time and an enjoyable dinner. Donna's boys and Jon's girls got along great together and spent most of their time in the hotel's pool. On the day of the party, they wore themselves out at the pool and were in bed way before the New Year. The next morning Molly picked up the girls, and Jon dropped me off at the airport on their way back to Kansas.

While I was in Colorado Springs, I called Margaret, my realtor in Fairplay, to find out if she had any offers on the townhouse. There were no offers; she suggested that I lower the price a little and get rid of the furniture. I agreed to lower the price and told her I would think about the furniture.

2014

Just two days after getting back to Tampa, my son Michael and his wife Edithe stopped in to visit.

That evening we took the streetcar over to Ybor City for cocktails and dinner at Bernini's and had a good talk. The next day Edithe flew on to Canada to go to work, and Michael stayed to go with me to my uncle Rudy's 90th birthday party on the 4th in Palm Coast on the east coast of Florida.

The party was in a VFW hall; his stepson Eddie was the D.J. and supplied the entertainment for the party. Rudy danced with all the women just like his father, my grandpa, did on his 100th birthday. Rudy's other stepson and his family were also there. They lived with Rudy in his house and took care of him. At the party, there was plenty of food and beer; we had a good time with Rudy, who was enjoying himself and seemed spry. We stayed until the party ended. Michael stayed with me at the Towers for a few more days before flying on to Canada.

A week later, the month-long Gasparilla Pirate Festival started, and my cousins Carol and Virgie came over to stay with me for the big parade weekend. Tom was in town and let one of my cousins stay with him. It was mobbed as usual, and the four of us had a lot of fun mingling with the crowd. We always have a good time with my cousins when they come over to visit.

In March, I drove up to Fort Walton Beach to start working on my taxes. All the information I needed from my broker wasn't there yet, and I probably wouldn't get it until the end of the month. I had some time to kill and called Tom to see if he was interested in a road trip. We decided to go to the National WWII Museum in New Orleans. Our friend Bill Leibold told us they had a display there of the USS Tang, the submarine that his father, William Leibold, a Chief boatswain's mate, served on during the war as the chief of the boat (COB).

We made a reservation at the Holiday Inn Express-St Charles on Lee Circle, close to the museum, and the next morning hit the road. Once checked in at the hotel, we took the streetcar to the French Quarter for an evening of entertainment and food.

Before leaving our hotel in the morning, we made a dinner reservation at Emeril's Delmonico Creole Restaurant and then walked over to the museum just two blocks away. When you first walk in the door of the museum, you see the famous Higgins boat, an amphibious landing craft (LCVP) built by Higgins Industries in New Orleans, used in the D-Day invasion and during the Pacific campaign. They also had some German hardware like the infamous 88mm AAA cannon, our military hardware, and found the display of the USS Tang (SS-306) final mission.

The display, with a hands-on simulation of the final mission where one of their own torpedoes aimed at a Jap troopship, turned back and sank their sub. Bill's dad, Capt. Richard O'Kane plus three other crewmen were picked up and spent the rest of the war in a Japanese prison camp. Most of the day was spent looking at and reading the material on display. Later that evening, we walked the three blocks down St Charles Ave to Emeril's Delmonico Restaurant, where we enjoyed a wonderful creole dinner. In the morning, we finished up at the museum and went next door, where they were restoring PT305, originally built by Higgins Industries. We couldn't get into the building, but we could see PT305 through the windows. From there, we took the streetcar to the French Quarter, where we stayed till late in the evening.

In the morning, we were off to our next destination, the National Museum of the Pacific War, in Admiral Nimitz's hometown of Fredericksburg, Texas. On the way, we stopped and checked into a motel just short of Huston and drove over to see the WWI battleship Texas where we spent the rest of the day. The next day we made another stop for about an hour at the Confederate Air Force Wing at the San Marcos Airport. We found their hangar at the airport, but no one was around, so we went into the hangar to look over their collection of airplanes. While we were looking, someone showed up and gave us a short tour before continuing on to Fredericksburg. Arriving in Fredericksburg, we checked in at the Sunday House Inn and did a walkabout town, and stopped in at the Auslander Beer Garden for a beer and some German cuisine before calling it a night.

After breakfast in the morning at the Inn, we walked over to the museum, a block away. We were

there all day; it was much bigger and had a lot more for us to absorb than we expected. The museum comprehensively covered all phases of the war in the Pacific with documentation, videos, and weapons. They had on display U.S military and Japanese armor, vehicles, aircraft, and a Japanese mini-sub. We were no-way near done seeing it all when they closed for the day. Walking back to the Inn, we passed by the Nimitz Museum; we put it on our to-do list to see before leaving town.

The next day we finished up inside the museum and walked a short distance to look at the Pacific Combat Zone. A field

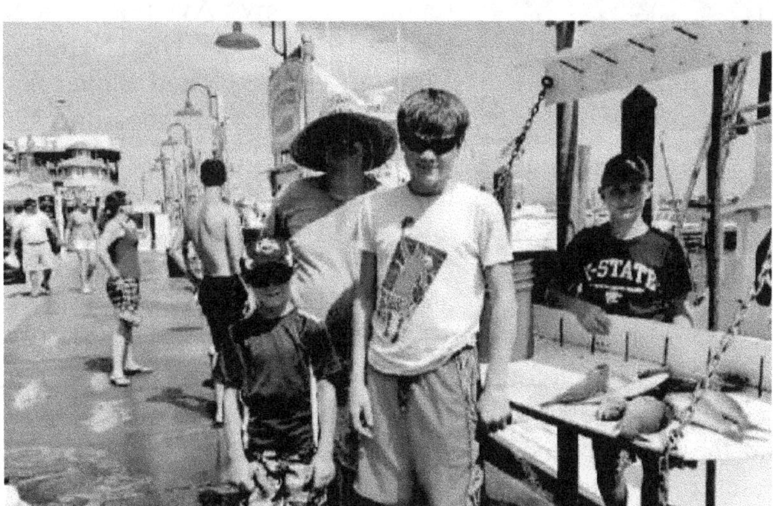

with bunkers, foxholes, a Sherman tank, and an Armored Personal Carrier was used in demonstrations of how battles were fought on the islands in the South Pacific. Unfortunately, we would not be in town long enough to witness one of the mock battles. We were there in the morning when the Nimitz Museum opened to go through it before leaving town to drive back to Florida.

We got as far as the Texas state capital, Austin, and stayed a couple of days. While we were in town, we toured the capital building, went to see the bats under the Congress Avenue Bridge that spanned the Colorado River, and took a boat tour of Lake Travis.

We found the Tex-Mex food and nightlife in Austin to be interesting.

Late in the afternoon of March 24th, after an eight-hour drive from Austin, we arrived back in Fort Walton Beach. I didn't stay long; all the crazy college kids were in town for spring break making noise. After paying off the IRS, I drove down to Tamp and went to a Ray game at the Tropicana.

I stayed in Tampa until June, when I drove up to Fort Walton Beach to get my apartment at the El Matador Condominium ready for company. Jon and his family were coming over to visit for a week at the beach. Jon flew in on Friday after work; Donna flew to Kansas with Macie, rented a van, and picked up her boys (Kameron, Joshua, and Wyatt) for the two-day drive to Florida. I had no idea where they were all going to sleep in my one-bedroom apartment, but they managed. Thankfully, Tom let me stay in his guest room at his condo, Emerald Isle, just down the road. While they were there, Jon chartered a fish ing boat in Destin to take the boys fishing in the Gulf; they had a good catch, and that evening, we feasted on grilled fish. On the Friday before they left, I took them over to the Chapala Authentic Mexican Restaurant to have Mexican food with Jon and my old friends that meet there on Fridays. We had a crowd of over twenty people at one long table; they hadn't seen Jon in years and were eager to meet his family; we all just had a wonderful time.

I drove back down to Tampa a week later, where I stayed until August, when Tom went with me on another road trip. This time to a reunion of my Aviation Cadet Class 59-14N at The National Museum of the United States Air Force on Wright Patterson Air Force Base in Dayton, Ohio. Tom's dad was stationed at Wright-Pat and went to high school in Fairborn, a small town next to the airbase. He went to school there until his dad was assigned to Wheeler Air Force Base, Hawaii, and went along to see his old stomping grounds. The reunion was a one-day affair, a tour of the museum followed by dinner at the Hotel. After the museum tour in the morning, we drove over to where Tom lived on base. We looked at the house and walked around the neighborhood, then over to the Officer's Club; it was closed. That evening there were only seven of my classmates with their wives at the dinner, but it was good to see them and swap cadet tales. Tom and I stayed on to spend another day at the museum; there was a lot more to see. I wanted to go back and see the C-130A gunship added since my B-66 reunion in 2004. It was open to walk around in, and the RB-66 that they painted

and hung from the ceiling. While I was in the air force, they were the two types of airplanes I spent

most of my time flying around in. It's a big museum, three huge hangers filled with all sorts of aircraft, and a courtyard with aircraft memorials for the crews that flew in them, one of them for the B-66. From there, we drove over to Fairborn and drove by the high school, then went to a bar/restaurant for some food before calling it a night. That was my second visit to the museum, and there is still plenty for me to see.

Tom went with me to another B-66 reunion on the 16th in Bronson, Missouri. Once checked in at

the Bronson Hotel and signed in at the reunion. One of the activities we signed up for was a rodeo that was most memorable; they even served us a chicken meal with all the trimmings as we watched the show. Another activity we signed up for was a riverboat, where we were fed and entertained. At the reunion, there were over a hundred people but just three people that I flew with in the B-66. At the banquet on our last night in Bronson, there was a guest speaker that briefed us on the latest challenges for the air force.

Back at Fort Walton Beach, I voted early in the 2014 Mid-Term Election, then drove down to Tampa on April 29th. I was running out of time, and I had things to do. Months before the election, Tom and I had signed up for the National Review Post Election seven-day Cruise on the Royal Caribbean ship, Allure of the Seas. Our second N.R. cruise, with ports of call at Phillipsburg on St. Maarten, the Dutch half of the island, and Nassau in the Bahamas. The next day I walked over to Hertz in the Marriott and made car reservations for November 9th to drive to Fort Lauderdale and another reservation for the drive back to Tampa when we returned. Once that was accomplished, we were good to go.

On the morning of November 9th, we walked over to Hertz, picked up our car, and drove to Fort Lauderdale. We turned in the car at a Hertz near Port Everglades and confirmed our reservation for the car to drive back to Tampa on our return on the 16th. We were early, so we walked around the corner to a Cuban Café for a little lunch before taking the Hertz shuttle to our ship. It took us a while to clear onto the ship, and we succeeded in smuggling onboard some Crown Royal in our mouthwash bottles. Once settled in our cabin, we called the steward for some ice for cocktails on our balcony for a cocktail before the lifeboat drill.

Once the Allure of the Seas cleared out of Fort Lauderdale's Port Everglades, we checked in with the National Review and picked up our packet with the events schedule, and made our way aft to the National Review welcome party. There was a lot of champagne and the opportunity to meet and talk to the editor-in-chief, Richard Lowry, and N.R. correspondents, Jay Nordlinger, Jim Geraghty, Jonah Goldberg, Charley Cooke, and contributing editor Andrew McCarthy. We had met all of them before, on our last National Review cruise. The big topics of conversation were Obama's second term and the non-politician Republican candidate for president, Donald Trump, a billionaire developer from New York. They didn't know what to make of this rude, crude, obnoxious, egotistical New Yorker with a campaign slogan, Make America Great Again. They didn't seem to like him very much and didn't give him much chance of winning the primary. I didn't like Trump's personality, just another loudmouth New Yorker. I liked his policies, his patriotic zeal, and the fact that he was a successful businessman who put his own money into his campaign and not at a politician that's in someone's back pocket.

Every day there were seminars, and every evening we put on a coat and tie and made our way to N.R. dining room Adagio at 8:30p.m to get a table assignment and join four or six others plus an N.R. writer or guest speaker for dinner. This mix of different people every night made for interesting and sometimes lively conversations during our meals. After dinner, Tom and I would usually go to the casino to check out the action at the crap table and if the table was dead, go check out the other entertainment available that night.

In the morning, after going to a seminar on board the ship, we went on shore leave in Nassau. Just off the dock, there's a big market full of tourist junk; the town has changed a lot since the cruise ships started stopping there. Nassau seemed deserted with all the action over the bridge on Paradise Island. We weren't interested in going there and walked around the town for a short while before returning to the ship.

We arrived at Phillipsburg on St. Maarten Island on the morning of the 13th and, after breakfast, went ashore. After walking around for a while, we rented a cab to take us on a tour of the island. Our cabbie talked about how he enjoyed working at the U.S. Airbase and radar site during the cold war while showing us everything there was to see on the Dutch half of the island. We never made it over to St Martin on the French side; we just ran out of time.

During the two-day sail back to Port Everglades, we were kept busy going to seminars, National Review cocktail parties, and shooting craps at night in the casino. We had a lot of fun at the cocktail parties picking out which N.R. personality or guest speaker to go pick on. On our last night at sea, they had a grand farewell party with cognac and cigars that lasted way late into the evening. These National Review Cruises give you an opportunity to meet some interesting people and go to informative seminars that are lots of fun. I'm looking forward to going on the National Review's post-2016 Presidential election cruise.

In December, two of the Lobsterheads, Bob and Debora, drove down to visit and go to the Fleetwood Mac concert at the Amelie Arena on the 20th. Years ago, Bob Nagy and Tom worked for the same contractor at Eglin AFB. That evening we took them to Ybor City on the streetcar for martinis and dinner at Bernini's. The next day for breakfast, we walked over to Zelda's, and for lunch, we took the streetcar to the brewery in Ybor City. While waiting for a table at the bar talking to people, Bob invited the woman he was talking to (Laura) to join us for lunch. During a conversation over lunch, we learned that she lived in our neighborhood (Channelside) with her boyfriend and invited her over for afternoon cocktails at the Towers. Tom and Bob hosted the cocktails in Tom's apartment where Bob was staying; when Laura showed up, Bob was all over her and wanted to take her home to FWB. After cocktails, Bob, Debora, and Tom left to walk over to the concert, Laura and I walked over to see a play at the Stageworks, just down the street.

After a late breakfast in the morning at Zelda's, Bob and Debora drove back to Fort Walton Beach. I followed them to Fort Walton Beach a few days later to go to the annual party at the Bay Café on the 13th. Monique had a big table outside on the deck reserved for the gang. We had a great time and, as usual, ate and drank too much. I stayed in town a few days recuperating before driving back down to Tampa to go to the Christmas party at the Towers. During the drive, I got a transmission warning light. The party was given by a dentist in his penthouse and was quite the event. There was plenty of food, drink, and an opportunity to meet other residents of the Towers. This party was followed by the Towers New Year's Eve bash at the pool party house, which got a little crazy.

Chapter Thirteen: 2015 – 2016

In January, my cousins Carol and Virgie came over to join Tom and me for a fun weekend at the Tampa Bay Gasparilla Pirate Festival. The festival goes on for months with all sorts of events and gets bigger every year. After they left, Tom and I signed up for the March 24th start of the five-day Gasparilla Film Festival

In early March, Tom and I flew up to Virginia-Ronald Reagan Washington National Airport (DCA) to pay my son Jon a visit. See more of the capital and maybe even go to a battlefield. Jon, Donna, and Macie met us at the airport and drove us over to get a room at the Embassy Suites near where they live. At Brady's Hill, Jon had a fire pit going by his 5th wheel. Donna fed us while Macie entertained. Later while sitting around the fire pit drinking wine, we talked about battlefields and decided to go check out the Bull Run battlefield. The next morning, Sunday, Jon picked us up at the hotel, and we drove over to Bull Run, where we spent most of the day.

On his way to work on Monday, Jon picked us up at the hotel and drove us to the Franconia Springfield

Metro station, where we took the Metro to the Alexandria High Street stop. From there, we walked down High Street and checked in at the Hampton Inn. Once settled, we did a walkabout Alexandria and ended up at the Theismann's Restaurant across the street from the Metro Station for happy hour and food.

At Theismann's, owned by Joe Theismann, the pro football player who broke his leg during a game, we found seats at the bar just before the bar became crowded with government employees on their way home from work. After a couple of pints of Broken Leg beer and some interesting conversations, we stayed on after happy hour for a delicious meal at the bar.

Over the next four days, we did a walkabout in D.C., going to the Smithsonian National Museum of American History, National Building Museum that used to be the U.S. Pension Bureau built in1887, the Naval Heritage Center by the FBI building, and the National Gallery of Art. Every day we would have lunch at the museum or at a close-by café and try to make it back to Alexandria in time for happy hour at Theismann's. They were busy days at the museums where we barely scratched the surface. The evening before our flight back to Florida, Jon and his family drove over to Alexandria to join Tom and me for dinner at Theismann's. The trip to D.C. gave me the opportunity to visit with my son and his family and find out more about our nation's capital.

On the 20th of March, we flew back to Tampa-TPA then on the 24th went to the opening night of the film festival at the historic Tampa Theatre in downtown Tampa. Over the next four days, we overdosed on three to four movies a day at the Channelside Cinemas 10 across the street from the Towers.

After recovering from movie overload on the 6th of April, Tom and I drove over to The Tropicana in St. Pete to watch the Rays' first game of the season. On the way, we called Rick to meet us at Fergie's for a beer before the game, but he was still in the process of sailing back up the coast from Key West. The Rays lost to the Baltimore Orioles 2 to 6. Two days later, we went to another Orioles game, where the Rays won 2 to 0.

I drove back to Fort Walton at the end of the month to get my place at the El Matador ready for company and moved over to Tom's futon in his spare room. On Saturday, the 16th of May, I drove over to Pensacola and picked up Jon at the airport. Two days later after flying to Kansas with Macie, Donna drove in from Junction City, Kansas, with the kids. The weather was perfect, and you couldn't keep the kids off the beach.

During the week, Jon took the boys, Kameron, Joshua, and Wyatt, deep sea fishing for a day on a charter boat out of Destin, and that night we all feasted on their catch. On Friday, before they left to go home, I took them over to eat with Jon and my old friends at the Chapala Authentic Mexican Restaurant. We had a fun time. They hadn't seen his family since their last visit a year ago. The day after Donna and the kids left on their drive back to Kansas, Tom and I drove Jon to the Naval Air Museum located at Pensacola Naval Air Station, where we spent a couple of hours before his flight back to Virginia.

I stayed at my place at the El Matador, enjoying the beach for a while before heading back to Tampa. On the drive back to Tampa in my BMW, I got a transmission warning light. The next day I took it over to get it checked out by Jossie at Car's Inc. When I went to pick it up a couple of days later, he told me the reason for the warning light was that the hydraulic pump in the transmission was getting weak, causing the transmission to overheat on long drives. Great!

On a Friday, over martinis at Bernini's with Tom, talking about going to a Rays' game and ended up deciding to take another trip to London to see his sister Jean. Tom called his sister to find a convenient time for a visit, then booked an overnight flight for the 3rd of September from Tampa International (TPA) to London-Gatwick (LGW).

On the 5th of August, my son Jon called and told me he would be retiring soon from the army and took advantage of the no down payment V.A. loan only available to active-duty troops to buy a house in Junction City, Kansas.

On the 7th of August, Tom and I drove over to St. Pete to go to the first Friday party on Central Ave. and to the Rays' game the next day at the Tropicana. We called Rick on the way for a place to stay and a place to park for the night. When we arrived at Rick's, he gave us a choice of either his boat or his one-bedroom apartment. We chose to stay on his boat just two blocks away.

The street party was a lot of fun; there was music, dancing, beer, and food. Later on in the afternoon, when the crowd started to thin out, we walked down Central Ave. to Ceviche Tapas Bar and Restaurant for dinner, then downstairs to the cellar bar, where we closed out the evening.

At the game the next day, the Rays beat the NY Mets 4 to 3.

Jon called me on September 2nd while he and Donna were driving to Kansas to close on their house in Junction City. I asked him if he needed furniture for it. They did, so I told them there was a house full in Fairplay that they could have. They didn't waste any time and rented a U-Haul, drove out to Colorado on the 5th, and hired a couple of locals in Fairplay to help clean out my townhouse. I called my realtor Margaret in Fairplay and told her that the townhouse was now unfurnished and hopefully making it easier to sell. She told me that she had some inquiries about the place, so maybe it will sell soon.

On the afternoon of the 10th of September, Tom and I took Uber to the airport to catch our British Air overnight flight to Gatwick-London (LGW). The next morning after clearing customs and immigration at Gatwick, we took the Gatwick Express to Liverpool Station, then the underground to Kensington High Street, and dragged our bags over to Jean's. It was a Friday, and she was busy with patients, so we dropped our bags there and walked over to the Goat Tavern for a pint and something to eat. During lunch, we talked about where we might want to go. I suggested Tallinn, where my son Michael competed in 1986 at the Goodwill Games in Russian-occupied Estonia. The occupation ended in 1990, and it might be interesting to go there. After lunch, we walked down High Street to a travel agency and made reservations. That evening we took Jean out to dinner, where she told us she was leaving in the morning for a week and for Tom and me to hold down the fort with her housekeeper, who would be in to clean three times a week. We told her we were also leaving on Thursday for Estonia and would see her when we got back. We still have five full days in London before our flight to mess around town. We started at the Imperial War Museum to check out what was added since the 2013 and 2014 renovations; there were quite a few new displays that took a couple of hours to look over.

Over the next couple of days, we spent time at the British Museum and Trafalgar Square, where we bought tickets for our last day in town to see, The Commitment at the Palace Theatre next door to one of our favorite pubs, the Cambridge.

On the morning of the 16th, we boarded a Ryanair flight out of London-Stansted Airport (STN) for Tallinn Airport (TLL), Estonia. On arrival, we took a cab to the Meriton Old Town Hotel, where we had reservations. The hotel is in the old walled section of Tallinn, the capital city of Estonia, located on the Gulf of Finland in the Baltic Sea that first appeared on the map in 1154. We checked

in at our hotel, located at the north end of Old Town and a block away from St. Olaf's, a 12th-century church. After spending some time at St. Olaf's,

which has a 405 ft tower, a good landmark to find our hotel with, we walked over to the town square with the 13th century St. Nicholas Church and town hall. Around the square, there were many restaurants, café, shops, and bars; we stopped at one of the cafés for a beer and to observe the action. So far, everyone we met spoke English; asking our waitress about it, she said she learned English as a second language in school.

The next day, while walking around the town square, we met an interesting couple. Tim Pugh who was recently discharged from the British Army with his girlfriend Ania Berka, we joined them for a beer at the Pepper Shack Bar. After a couple of beers, we found out that Ania was headed back to London the next day, where she was a schoolteacher, and Tim was about to drive his motorcycle across Russia and maybe around the world. We wished him luck

and told Ania we would give her a call when we got back to London.

During our week in Tallinn, we visited the Tallinn Maritime Museum, the Estonian Museum of Natural History, and the Alexander Nevsky Cathedral, a Russian Orthodox Church built in 1900 when Estonia was part of Czarist Russia. During our stay, we patronized Hell Hunt, a bar just down the street from our hotel with friendly female bartenders that spoke excellent English. It was our preferred happy hour stop before finding a restaurant for dinner and on our way back to our hotel for a nightcap.

On the 23rd, we took the ferry on a two-and-a-half-hour passage across the Bay of Finland to Helsinki, where we took a Hop-on-Hop-off bus tour of the city. Walking around after getting off the bus, we stopped at the Aino Restaurant just down the street from the capital building for something to eat before boarding the ferry back to Tallinn.

On our last day in Estonia, while walking around Old Town Tallinn, we came across the Brotherhood of Blackheads building, an association of local unmarried merchants and ship owners that originated in the mid-14th century. The association was still active, was open to the public, and had lots of historic memorabilia on display. We flew back to London-Stansted Airport (STN) on the 25th. Tallinn, the birthplace of Skype and Estonia, with its interesting history, was definitely worth the trip.

Back in London, we made our way back to Kensington, on the way to Jean's, we made a stop at

the Goat for a pint and something to eat. Arriving at the house, we found that Jean wasn't back yet. The next day, Saturday, we called Ania and invited her to join us for dinner at the Brasserie Zedel, a French restaurant on Piccadilly Circus. Over dinner, Ania told us that she planned to fly out to join Tim wherever he was during her Christmas holiday. Two days later, we flew back to Tampa International (TPA). Jean never made it back to town before we left.

I stayed in Tampa for about a month before driving up to Fort Walton Beach for a 919th reunion at the Air Force Armament Museum. They had a big turnout of mostly the younger troops, but there were a few I recognized from back in the 70s when I was in the 919th. We had a fun time talking about our exploits while serving in the raggedy-ass militia. On the drive back to Tampa, my car went into limp-home mode. Jossie, the mechanic at Car's Inc., had warned me about the transmission overheating. I stopped for a while to let it cool down, then continued on my way.

In October, I drove over for a weekend at my cousin Carol's condo in Tarpon Springs for a mini cousins reunion. Carol's sister Helen, who I had not seen in twenty years or more, flew in from New Jersey and Virgie drove over from Vero Beach. After Carol showed us around her place, we went out to dinner at a restaurant on the city wharf just a short walk away. We just had a wonderful time telling stories of when we were kids growing up. All our families lived close to each other and would get together on

weekends. Carol tried to talk her sister into moving to Florida, where there is no state income tax. It was a very enjoyable weekend.

I had been driving the BMW back and forth to Fort Walton Beach and the Porsche around Tampa, they both had over a hundred thousand miles on them, and it was probably time to get rid of them both. I went over and talked to Judd, the owner of Car's Inc., about cars. He told me that he was going to a Christmas car auction on the weekend of the 19th of December, and if I wanted a car, he would pick one up for me. We went into his office and looked over the cars for auction on the auction website. I have never owned a Mercedes, so I chose three S 550's to bid on; my first choice was a grey 2013 company car with 12,000 miles. It would be a cash deal; Judd would buy my two cars, and I would pay the difference. On the 22nd, Judd called to tell me he got the car I wanted and was ready for pickup. I walked over to Car's Inc. and looked over my new car, the grey 2013 Mercedes S 550, and closed the deal.

The next day I flew up to Virginia to spend Christmas with Jon and his family. Jon picked me up at the airport and drove me over to Embassy Suites for a room, then over to Brady's Hill. We sat around the fire pit drinking wine, watching Macie run around in the lederhosen that I bought in Germany for her father in 1969 and the sweeter I sent her for Christmas from Tallinn. Donna somehow put together a delicious Christmas dinner for us in the 5th wheel. The next day we drove into D.C. to look at the Christmas

decorations; it was a fun Christmas on Brady's Hill. I flew back to Tampa on the 27th to be there for the New Year.

2016

Joe and Stacy Myrda, my neighbors in the Tower, came down from their apartment on the 16th floor to help me bring in the New Year with some champagne and to watch the fireworks in the harbor from my balcony.

On the 2nd of January, my cousin Carol drove over for a visit from Tarpon Springs. On her arrival, we caught the trolly to Ybor City for martinis at Bernini's. Later we cornered an outside table for dinner and enjoyed an evening of catching up and people-watching; there's always something of interest walking by our table on Ybor City's East 7th Ave.

A couple of weeks later, Tom came down from Fort Walton Beach, and Carol came back over for the Gasparilla Pirates Parade. The crowd gets bigger and noisier every year and was quite the scene with kids and grownups alike begging for beads and trinkets. Later that evening, we went to Ybor City for something to eat and watch the craziness.

On the 2nd of February, Tom and I rented a car and drove to Key West to visit Rick on his boat,

the Anna Virginia. Arriving in Key West after a seven-hour drive that took us through the Everglades and the Keys, we parked in the lot by the A&B Marina. We found Rick sitting at Alonzo's Oyster Bar, and after chewing the fat for a while, we loaded our gear onto the Anne Virginia and walked over to Rick's Bar for a beer. There were no cruise ships or festivals going on, so the town wasn't that crowded enabling us to enjoy a couple of days of the laid-back ambiance of Key West. While in Key West, I got a call from my realtor, Margaret, in Fairplay, telling me she had a contract on my townhouse with a closing date of 8 April; it took three years to sell, and getting rid of the furniture was the charm.

On the drive back to Tampa, we drove up the Keys to Homestead, then took highway 997 to 27, which took us through the farmland and orange groves in the interior of Florida, then to the cattle ranches around Lake Okeechobee. Highway 27 eventually took us to Lake Wales and highway 60 to Tampa; it was an interesting drive that took a little over eight hours to complete. I stayed in Tampa for the Valentine's Day costume party at the Towers party room by the pool, which was a blast, before driving up to Fort Walton Beach.

The 3rd of March was Jon's last workday, and he would be on leave until he officially retired from the Army on the 1st of May. During that time, he found a job with BEA Systems as a contractor at the DIA, starting on the 28th of March.

Donna drove down to Florida from Kansas and arrived on the 21st of May at the El Matador for a visit with Macie and her sons Joshua, Wyatt, Kameron, and his friend Dalton. Jon didn't come along; he was busy with his new job at the DIA. Donna and I celebrated his retirement from the army without him. They were all crowded into my one-bedroom apartment at the El Matador while I stayed at Tom's place in Emerald Isle. They had a good week; the weather at the beach was perfect, and I was able to spend some time with my granddaughter Macie. The boys charted a boat in Destin to go fishing, and that evening we all had a feast on their catch. On Friday, before they left, I took them over to the Chapala Authentic Mexican Restaurant to have dinner with my old friends that have known Jon since he was a kid. The next day Danna and her crew started their two-day drive back to Kansas, then flew back to Virginia with Macie.

A short time later, Jon called and asked me if I could escort his daughter Amelia from Italy to Virginia for her monthly visitation with her father. He couldn't get off from work to do it. Amelia, my five-year-old granddaughter, was living with her mother, an army veterinarian stationed at Camp Ederle, a U.S. military complex in Vicenza, Italy. I told Jon to get the paperwork together, and I would think about it. I called Tom to see if he was interested in going to Venice, Italy, with a stop on the way back at close-by Vicenza to pick up my granddaughter.

I told Tom that I was a little apprehensive about the exchange because Amelia and I have only talked on the phone and never personally met. Tom was ok with that, so I called Jon and told him I would do it with Tom as a chaperone. Jon called me back with a pickup date of 25 June at Vicenza, and I got busy making reservations. A couple of days later, we had a plan.; on July 14th fly to Ronald Reagan Washington National Airport (DCA), spend a couple of days in Alexandria and get the paperwork from Jon, and on the 18th, board the overnight flight to Venice-Marco Polo

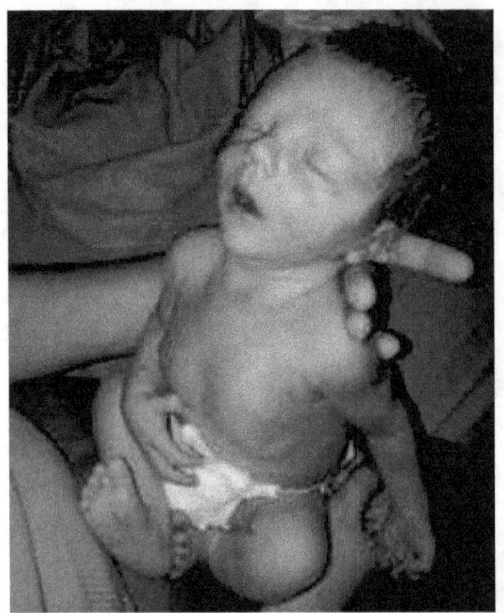

Airport (VCE), Italy, on the 24th take the train to Vicenza and pick up Amelia, take the train to Vicenza Airport (VCE) on the morning of the 25th for our flight to New York, at JFK clear Customs and Immigration and fly to DCA to hand over Amelia to her Daddy. With the mission complete, at our conveyance, rent a car and drive back to Florida.

In Cabarete, Dominican Republic, on June the 4th, my son Michael and his fiancé Ashley Howell had a baby boy, Zen Alexander William Gebhardt, my first grandson. I now have five grandchildren, one boy, and four girls.

On the 11th of June, Donald Trump had a rally at the Tampa Convention Center, Tom and I decided to go. We walked over to the convention center arriving about an hour early, and just managed to get in. It was standing room only, and after waiting for a while, the rally got underway with warm-

up speakers. When Trump took the podium and started talking; about cutting taxes, securing our southern border, getting rid of outdated regulations, getting out of Afghanistan, dumping the Iran agreement, making NATO pay their fair share for defense, and getting out of the climate accords, it all sounded good to me. I especially like his proposed corporate tax cut to 15% to entice our companies that left when President Obama imposed a 38% corporate tax to come back to the USA. I also liked the fact that

Trump was a get-things-done billionaire businessman indebted to no one instead of a politician who owed payback favors. I liked his policies. The only thing about Trump that I was hesitant about was his caustic New Yorker personality.

At the rally, Trump put on a good show laying out his agenda to an enthusiastic crowd that I noticed was predominantly young people. This indicated to me that maybe Trump would be able to beat Hillary Clinton and her big social government agenda in the upcoming November Presidential election. Trump did bash the press by calling them fake news and calling out Hillary for her actions in Benghazi while she was Secretary of State for the Obama administration. By the time the rally was over, and we walked back to the Towers, I was exhausted.

On the 14th of June, Tom and I took an Uber to the Tampa International Airport (TPA) and boarded our flight to Ronald Reagan Washington National Airport (DCA). Arriving at DCA, we took the Metro to Alexandria and checked in at the Hampton Inn on High Street just in time to walk over for a happy hour at Theismann's.

We had three days before our overnight flight to Venice and spent most of it in Alexandria, although we did take the Metro into D.C. for a day. In the evening before our flight to Venice, Jon, Donna, Macie, Donna's sister Sheri and her daughter Megan with her daughter Lacie joined Tom and me for dinner at Theismann's. It was a fun dinner party with good food, conversation, and entertainment by the two three-year old's, Macie and Lacie.

The next day we boarded our flight to Venice-Marco Polo Airport (VCE), arriving late in the morning of the 19th of June, and caught the ferry to the Venice San Marco ferry terminal on the Grand Canal by St. Mark's Square. From there, we dragged our bags into the piazza (square) past the two tall granite entrance columns in front of the Doge's Palace that are topped by the two patron saints of Venice. On one is St. Theodore, the patron saint before St. Mark, who holds a spear with a crocodile to represent the

dragon he supposedly killed. The second column holds a winged lion of Venice, the symbol of St. Mark. We then passed by St. Mark's Basilica with the four bronze horses, replicas of the ones taken from the Hippodrome during the sack of Constantinople during the Fourth Crusade in 1204 by the Venetian Crusaders; the originals are inside the Basilica.

It took us a while to find our hotel; the Ca del Duca on 93 Per S. Marco St. The hotel was just a

door on the street that we walked by a couple of times. Once we found it, they buzzed it open for us, then up a flight of stairs to a window where we signed in and were shown our small room. Two beds, a small bathroom with a shower, T.V., and breakfast that they brought up to our room every morning. Once settled in our room we walked back over to Piazza San Marcos (St. Mark's Square). It was late in the afternoon and was packed with Japanese tourists. We walked around the piazza for a while, listening to the quartet's play, then went back to explore the neighborhood around our hotel. At a trattoria close to our hotel, we stopped for something to eat and a beer before turning in for the night; it had been an exhausting day.

In the morning, we went back to Piazza St. Marcos during our walkabout and took the tour of the Museum of Venetian art & antiquities at the other end of the square from St. Marks Basilica. That evening we had a wonderful meal at Trattoria Vini Da'Arturo.

Over the next couple of days, we walked all over Venice, went to the Museo Storico Navale di

Venezia (naval & maritime museum), and did the tour of the Doge's Palace (Palazzo Ducale), a Gothic-style palace and museum. During the tour of the palace, we learned some of Venice's history. When Napoleon took over Venice in 1797, he had the horses removed from the basilica and taken to Paris, where they were used in the design of the Arch de Triumph. In 1804 Napoleon conquered

the rest of Italy and Venice became part of Napoleon's Kingdom of Italy. After Napoleon's defeat at Waterloo in 1815, Northern Italy was returned to Austrian rule, and the horses were returned to the basilica in Venice. We wanted to take the tour of St. Marks Basilica, but the lines were way too long, and we ran out of time.

On the morning of the 25th, we took the shuttle boat on the Grand Canal to Stazione di Venezia Santa Lucia (the train station) to catch a train to Vicenza. On our arrival in Vincenza, I called Emma and arranged a meeting at our hotel. Finally, meeting my granddaughter Amelia for the first time, who ran over and gave me a big hug. Emma gave me Amelia's travel documents, and we all went to lunch, where we met Emma's boyfriend, Bill, a major in the army; to my relief, it was all very amicable. After lunch, we chatted for a while before Amelia, Tom, and I went to our hotel. The next day we took the train to (VCE) for our morning nonstop flight to John F. Kennedy International Airport (JFK).

We arrived early in the afternoon at JFK for our connecting flight to Ronald Reagan International Airport (DCA). It took us a good hour to get through immigration at JFK, and we almost missed

our flight to DCA. When we arrived, Jon, Donna, and Macie were there to meet us. Back at Jon's place, Donna made us dinner. Then after watching the girls play for a while, Jon drove us over to the close by Embassy Suites for a room. In the morning, Jon, Donna, and the girls came over to the hotel to join us for breakfast and swim in the pool and drive me over to Hertz for a car. The girls were just having a good old time at the pool. Later that evening, we all went out for dinner at a local restaurant.

The next day Tom and I started driving back to Florida. We got as far as Richmond, where we stopped for an hour or so to look over the ruins of the Tredegar Ironworks, one of the largest Confederate munitions plants during the Civil War. From Tredegar, we drove down to the Petersburg battlefield. That's where Ulysses S. Grant's assault on Robert E. Lee's armies failed to

capture the Confederacy's vital supply center there. The result was a nine-month siege that ultimately cost the South the war. After spending most of the day there, we drove the short drive over to downtown Norfolk and checked into a hotel close to the Nauticus Museum and Iowa class Battleship Wisconsin (BB-64); it had been a busy day.

We were at the museum in the morning when they opened and stayed until early afternoon, trying to see and absorb everything in the museum and on the battleship. Later in the afternoon, we took a boat tour of Norfolk Harbor and Naval Station Norfolk, a major base for the U.S. Atlantic Fleet. The two-hour tour gave us a close-up look at the aircraft carriers, frigates, destroyers, and other navy ships in port at the time.

With an early departure in the morning, we headed South toward our next destination Fort Pulaski National Monument on Cockspur Island at the mouth of the Savannah River between Savannah and Tybee Island, Georgia. It was late in the afternoon when we checked in at a motel close to the fort on Tybee Island.

In the morning, we drove over to take a tour of the fort. During the tour, we were told that the fort was completed in 1847 before the Civil War and was thought to be impregnable because of its 11 ft thick walls and being on an island out of range of the smooth-bore cannons at the time. On the morning of April 10, 1862, Union forces asked for the surrender of the Fort. The Confederate commander rejected the offer, and the Union troops began a bombardment of the Fort from Tybee Island with their new James rifled cannons and Parrott rifles with longer range. Within 30 hours, the new rifled cannons breached one of the fort's corner walls threatening the main powder magazine, and the garrison reluctantly surrendered. The park rangers, as part of the tour, demonstrated how a gun crew loaded and fired one of the cannons. They gave a good tour and were very

informative, answering all our questions. It was a short drive to Tampa in the morning, ending an action-packed two-week adventure.

I did not stay long in Tampa; I drove up to Fort Walton for Tom's brother Jon Prohaska's July 9th wedding to Malissa on the Okaloosa Island beach. There was a small group of Jon and Melissa's friends at the beach for the wedding. Tom was the best man for his brother, and after the ceremony, we all went to the Fubar Bar on the island,

where there was plenty of champagne to celebrate the occasion.

During the rest of July and most of August, I stayed at the El Matador enjoying the beach, going on Fridays to meet my friends at the Chapala Mexican Restaurant, and on Wednesdays going out to eat with the Lobsterheads in Destin.

I had another B-66 reunion coming up on the 27th of August in Charleston, South Carolina, and I asked Tom if he was interested in going along, and he was.

With an early start on the 27^{th,} we arrived at Charleston and checked in at the Francis Marion Hotel for the reunion. After picking up our agenda packet on the way up to our room, we walked over to the renovated Embassy Suites, where we had stayed three years earlier during a November snowstorm. We had signed up for another visit to Fort Sumpter and a bus trip to Shaw AFB in Sumpter, S.C., where we had a look at a B-66 on display at the main gate. After a tour of the base, we got a briefing on the F-16 Wild Weasel mission and what was in the future for the mission.

On our last day before the banquet that evening, I called Barbara, my son Michael's x-wife who lives in Mount Pleasant just across the Cooper River from Charleston, to visit and go to lunch. In the morning, before driving over to meet Barbara, we took a two-hour bus tour of the city. During lunch, Barbara told us that she was thinking of moving to Denver. She looked good, seemed to be in good spirits, and was excited about moving. She is really a pleasant woman with a charming French accent. After lunch, Tom and I drove over to and went aboard the Aircraft Carrier Yorktown CV-10 at the Patriots Point Naval Museum on the same side of the river, not far from where we had lunch. The ship was built in 1943 to replace the original Yorktown CV-5 that was sunk during the battle of Midway. There was a lot of material to look over on the ship, and we spent most of the afternoon there. That night at the banquet, Tom and I sat with Frank Doyle and Bob Gazolla. Ike Espie, another squadron member from Alconbury who is usually at the reunions, couldn't make it. He had a death in the family, his wife, Edie, passed away. The speeches were long and boring, but the reunion events were always interesting and informative.

As we started our drive back to Fort Walton Beach, the panhandle of Florida was on watch for hurricane Hermine in the Gulf of Mexico. We diverted to Kennesaw, in northwest Georgia, to wait and see where Hermine was going to come ashore. Kennesaw is also the home of the Southern

Museum of Civil War & Locomotive History. On display at the museum, they have the "General", the Confederate steam locomotive used in the Great Locomotive Chase in 1862. Where Union volunteers commandeered the "General" and took it north toward Chattanooga, Tennessee, doing as much damage as they could to the line, they were chased by Confederate forces in other locomotives, including the "Texas" for 87 miles. The raiders were eventually caught and executed as spies. We spent a day at the museum while Hermine came ashore at Apalachicola as a category one and blew itself out, heading inland toward the northeast.

Back in Fort Walton Beach, I got a call from my son Jon on the 21st of September, telling me that he had changed jobs and was now working for Mission Essential, a government contractor. That he was moving his family back to Kansas with the Army moving his 5th wheel there for him on the 23rd. His new job was sending him back to Afghanistan in November as a counter-intelligence analyst for the army for Hamid Karzai International Airport in Kabul for a year.

I stayed in Fort Walton Beach long enough to cast my early vote in the Presidential Election before heading to Tampa to get ready for the National Review Post Election Cruise on the 13th of November. Donald Trump won the election to become our 45 President, to the chagrin of the Democrats who thought they had the election in the bag.

Early in the morning of the 13th, Tom and I drove down to Ft. Lauderdale in a Hertz rental and boarded the Holland America Line's Nieuw Amsterdam. We again smuggled aboard some Crown Royal in our mouthwash bottles for cocktails on our balcony after the lifeboat drill while the New Amsterdam got underway, leaving Port Everglades. Our cruise was bound for the Caribbean ports of Grand Cayman, Cozumel, Key West, and Half Moon Bay. Most of the guest speakers and National Review writers on the cruise we had met and talked to before. At the cocktail party that evening, I thought everyone would be overjoyed that Trump won the election. Especially since the Democrats already want to impeach him, and he hadn't even been sworn in yet. To my surprise, when I talked with some of the National Review people, they were hesitant with their support for Trump; it was like they did not think he was conservative enough to be a Republican. Needless to say, Tom and I had some interesting conversations with them.

The seminars with guest speakers like Bing West, who laid out the terrorist and military threats, and Andrew McCarthy, the legal complications facing the new administration, were fascinating. The seminars are always interesting, and even though I didn't agree with all the speakers, we tried to go to all of them. Once in a while, at dinner, we were seated with one of the guest speakers giving us the opportunity to engage him or her in some good one-on-one conversation.

The cruise took us to Cozumel, where we went ashore at San Miguel de Cozumel, the one major city on the Island. Once ashore, we hired a cabbie to show us around; he took us to Playa Chen Rio, the beach on the other side of the Island, then to a distillery for lunch and tequila. When we arrived back in town, we had an hour left before we sailed, so we had our cabbie drop us off for a beer at a bar close to Terminal Maritima, where Nieuw Amsterdam was tied up. We sat at a table, and the bar girls descended on us; we played with them for a while, then walked over to the ship. There's not much outside of San Miguel de Cozumel, which has 77,000 of the island's total population of 100,000.

When we stopped at Key West, we walked over to the A&B Marina and paid a short visit to Rick and his girlfriend, Diane. We went over to the Schooner Wharf for a couple of beers. Her friend from Poland had just finished delivering a boat to Fort Lauderdale from Europe. She drove down to visit Diane and to see if she wanted to go with her to deliver a catamaran to the Dominican Republic. She was quite the character, and I enjoyed listening to her sea stories before Tom and I headed back to our ship. The cigars and cognac party on our last night at sea was a grand event where Tom and I had our last shot at the guest speakers and the National Review crew that we stayed at to the end. These cruises are a lot of fun and very informative about what's going on in our country and around the world; I hope to be fortunate enough to go on their next Post Election Cruise in 2018.

I didn't stay long in Tampa before driving up to Fort Walton Beach to go to the annual Christmas parties with my old buddies. The first was on the 10th of December with the Lobsterheads in Destin, then the annual party at the Bay Café. Unfortunately, Monique didn't get a reservation early enough, so we didn't get to go. A couple of days later, I drove back to Tampa to get ready for Christmas.

On the 22nd, I flew to Junction City, Kansas, to join Donna and her children, Kameron, Joshua, Wyatt, and my granddaughter, Macie, for Christmas. Michael, Ashley, and Zen flew in on the 23rd from the Dominican Republic to join us in their big house. The only one missing was Jon in Afghanistan. We had a marvelous time; Macie, a three-year-old, finally met her six-month-old cousin Zen; the two of them kept us well-entertained opening presents on Christmas Day

On the 27th, I flew over to Colorado Springs to visit

my teenage granddaughters, Elizabeth and Emma. Brantley picked me up at the airport and drove me over to their apartment. I was able to spend time with the girls during the day while Molly and Brantley were at work. The girls seemed to be standoffish with me;

they just didn't seem to be my same happy, smiling granddaughters from a year ago. While I was there, Molly informed me that she was getting married to Brantley later on in January.

I flew back to Tampa on the 31st, where I brought in the new year at the Towers with my neighbors, Joe and Stacy.

Chapter Fourteen: 2017 – 2020

By the middle of January, Tampa was all geared up for The Gasparilla Pirates Festival, and the town was crowded with people ready to party. On January 22, the Destin Lobsterhead crew called

Tom and invited us to meet at JoJo's new house and have lunch in Orlando, giving Tom and me a good excuse to get out of town for a day. After a short drive to Orlando on the 22nd, we meet Scott, Betsy, Debora, and Ann at JoJo's new place. After spending some time looking over her new digs, we went out for lunch at a nearby restaurant. After lunch, while the girls shopped, Scott, Tom, and I chatted for a while before Scott headed back to St. Augustine, and we headed back to Tampa.

On their way back to Destin the next day, Betsy, Debora, and Ann stopped in Tampa to spend the night and gave us a call. That evening we met them in Ybor City at Bernini's for dinner, then walked over to the Bad Monkey Bar for drinks, where we ran into Joe and Stacy. It turned into a party to celebrate Trump's Inauguration as our 45th President.

A day later, I got a Skype call from my son Jon in Afghanistan telling me he would be going on R&R the last two weeks of April and asked if I had any recommendations for a good place to meet Donna and Macie. I recommended the Columbia Hotel in London or maybe the beautiful Lake Garda in Italy, where I had been years earlier. A week later, Jon called, telling me he had made reservations for a week at the Columbia Hotel, London, and a week at the Hotel Sole on Lake Garda in Riva Del Garda, Italy. I told him I would meet them in London and called Tom to see if he was ready for a little adventure and got busy making reservations.

At Tampa International (TPA) on April 13, Tom and I boarded our nonstop overnight flight to London-Gatwick (LGW), we had first-class tickets on a British Air flight, and they were worth every penny. Before leaving, Tom checked in with his sister Jean and found out that she had a buyer for her rowhouse in Kensington and probably would not be available for a visit; she was busy shopping for some new digs.

When we arrived at the Columbia Hotel, Jon and his family were there to meet us. They had checked in a few days earlier. Later on, in the afternoon, after getting settled in at the Columbia, we walked around the corner to the Swan for a pint and some food, where Jon told us about all his adventures in Afghanistan.

The next morning after a great English breakfast at the Columbia, we walked across the street to Lancaster Gate for a slow walk across Kensington Gardens. We stopped at Round Pond by Kensington Palace for Macie to mess with the swans and ducks before having lunch at the Palace Café, followed by a tour of the Palace. Later on, we crossed over High Street Kensington to the Goat Tavern, where we lucked out in getting window seats to watch the street traffic. We stayed for pub food and a pint or two before walking back across the park to the Columbia Hotel bar, where we closed out the evening.

For the next couple of days, we traveled around London by bus to Buckingham Palace, Speakers Corner at Marble Arch, Parliament, and to shop. On one occasion, we had lunch at the Red Lion across the street from the Palace of Westminster, the seat of the British Parliament. That's where on March 22, just around the corner from the Red Lion on the Westminster Bridge, a Muslim terrorist ran over pedestrians, killing six and hospitalizing fifty before crashing into the gate outside Parliament. Then armed with a knife, he killed an unarmed police officer and ran toward Parliament, where he was shot and killed by the police. London had a rash of terrorist attacks that summer.

The day before Tom and I left for Italy, we all bought tickets on the Hop-on Hop-off combination bus and Thames River boat tour that took most of the day and came with lunch. The boat made stops at the WW2 cruiser Belfast, Greenwich, and the Tower of London. I always enjoy visiting London and was overjoyed to have the opportunity to show Jon, Donna, and my granddaughter Macie around town.

On April 20, Tom and I made our way to Gatwick for our flight to Italy-Verona Airport (VRN). On arrival, we were greeted at the airport by the driver we had booked for the thirty-minute drive

to the Hotel Sole in Riva del Garda on the northwest corner of the lake at the foot of the Alps. Once settled in our hotel, we did a little walk around the Piazza Catena in front of our hotel with its 13th-century clock tower, hotels, restaurants, a dock for the ferry, and a hydroelectric plant. The rest of the afternoon, we spent walking about the town and found the Bar Pasticceria Copat with a friendly crowd on the Vale Dante Alighieri for happy hour. That evening Tom and I had dinner at the Hotel Centrale restaurant next door to our hotel, which had entertaining waiters and good food. From our table, we could see what looked like ruins of a castle up the mountain, with what looked like a switchback road going up to it, something to put on our to-do list.

In the morning, we walked over to Torbole, about 3 miles to the east along the north shore of the lake. I was there in 2003 with my sailing buddy Rick to meet up with my son Michael who was there training Gal Fridman, the Israeli Olympic sailboarder for the 2004 Olympics in Athens, where he won the gold medal. Walking around, it appeared that Torbole hadn't changed much since my last visit. Walking back along the lake, stopping at the Bar dei pini for lunch. Later in the afternoon, we took the ferry to Limone, where the Romans had lemon orchards. We looked them over, then walked over to check out the nearby shops for a while before catching the next ferry back to Riva del Garda.

The next day Tom and I walked up to what we thought was a castle that turned out to be the remains of a tower. We thoroughly looked it over, then walked to the Bastione restaurant by the tower for lunch. Talking to our waitress, we found out the tower, Bastione, was a fortified tower built by the Venetians between 1507 & 1508. She also told us that she was a college student in Florida at FSU. and that the restaurant was a family business. In the Fall, they close the restaurant to spend the other half the year in the Florida panhandle at Destin, small world.

On the 23rd, over breakfast, Tom and I figured we had enough time to take the morning tour of the Ponale Hydroelectric Power Plant before Jon, Donna, and Macie, who were flying in later that day, arrived at the hotel. We walked the short distance to the plant and signed up for what turned out to be an informative and interesting tour of the plant that was built in the 1920s and overhauled in 1998. Our tour guide explained how the water from the Lake Ledo

Dam on the River Ponale is ducted several kilometers to a point almost directly over the power station at Riva del Garda. From there, it falls through tunnels on a gradient of 3:1 to the turbines that have an output capability of 76MW. Built as a pumped storage plant, it uses the excess power generated by the turbines to pump water back up to the lake to be used again.

On the way back from the tour, we spotted Jon, Donna, and Macie at the hotel, standing out on the balcony of their room; we waved at them and got their attention. That evening we took them to the

restaurant at the Hotel Centrale for an excellent Italian meal. The next day we took the ferry over to Malcesine, where we had lunch and walked around the town for a while before catching the ferry back to Riva del Garda.

For the rest of our time in Riva del Garda, we stayed by our hotel, walking around the neighborhood of the Piazza Catena with Jon, Donna, and my granddaughter Macie.

Early on April 27, our driver was waiting at our hotel to drive Tom and me to the Verona Airport for our flight to London-Gatwick. Arriving at Gatwick, we took a room for the night at the Airport Hotel to rest up for our early flight back to Tampa the next day.

I didn't stay long in Tampa. After about a week of getting used to the time change, I drove up to Fort Walton Beach to take care of business, catch up with old friends and spend some time at the beach. By late June, I was back on the road driving back down to Tampa to go to a ballgame or two. I stayed for a month before driving up to Fort Walton Beach to get ready for a visit from Donna and her children driving down from Junction City, Kansas.

On July 17, Donna arrived with Joshua, Wyatt, Macie, and Kameron with his friend Dalton to

spend a week at the beach. I moved over to Tom's guest room, having no idea where all six of them slept in my one-bedroom apartment. The next morning Tom and I took Kameron, Joshua, and Dalton to our gym on guest passes, where they signed up for a week. Every morning we would meet them at the gym, and later on, in the afternoon, I would join them at the beach. In the evening, we would invite Tom to join us for dinner ala Donna or barbecue on the outdoor grill. We Skyped Jon in Afghanistan about every day to keep him

informed of the activities at the beach; he would be coming home in October. On Friday, before they drove back to Kansas, Tom and I took them to dinner at Chapala's Mexican Restaurant with all our old friends. It's always a good time when they come to visit. I stayed on at the El Matador in Fort Walton Beach until the middle of September, then drove down to Tampa.

On October 10, Jon completed his contract in Afghanistan and flew back to Kansas. He didn't waste any time finding a new job with the F.B.I. as a contract intel analyst and moved his family on October 31 to Alexandria, Virginia. He rented an apartment close to the Metro to commute to his job in the F.B.I. Building in D.C., where he started work on November 6.

While having martinis on a Friday evening in Ybor City at Bernini's, Tom and I decide to take a trip up to visit Washington D.C. and Jon with his family in their new home in Alexandria. The next day we made reservations on American Airlines and at the Hampton Inn on King Street in Alexandria, Virginia.

On the morning of November 11, we arrived at Ronald Regan Washington National Airport (DCA) and took the Metro to the High Street station in Alexandria. After checking in at the Hampton Inn, we walked over to Jon and Donna's apartment for a little visit. They were busy getting the apartment organized. We didn't stay long before leaving, we invited them to join us for dinner at our favorite restaurant in Alexandria, Theismann's. Tom and I then walked over to Theismann's to reserve a table for dinner and found seats at the bar for happy hour. The after-work crowd arrived, and the conversations we had with the government workers were boisterous and enlightening. Over dinner with Jon and his family, we decided, since they were busy during the

week, to meet up again during the weekend. Giving Tom and me the opportunity to spend a day at the Air & Space Museum by Dulles International Airport and maybe go talk to our Congressman Matt Gaetz.

Getting to the museum the next day took a while, the Metro to Dulles wasn't complete, and we had to take the bus from the last stop to the museum. Since my last visit in 2004, they added more airplanes, including the amazing German twin jet engine flying wing fighter built by the Horton Brothers during WW2; we spent most of the day there. When we arrived back in Alexandria, it was time for happy hour and dinner at Theismann's.

We spent the next couple of days at the Mall going to the Smithsonian Museum and the Museum of Natural History and eventually found Matt Gaetz's office in the Longworth House Office Building, he wasn't there, but his secretary showed us around and gave us a quest pass to a session of Congress. The rest of our time in town was spent around the Mall being tourists. When Jon got off work on Friday, we met for dinner again at Theismann's. On Saturday, we all took the Metro into D.C. to spend the day on the Mall and the Smithsonian Museum. It was a good week; being able to spend time with my son Jon and his family in Alexandria and our nation's capital, was a gift.

I flew back up to DCA for a family Christmas with Jon, Donna, their three-year-old Macie, and Amelia, that Jon was also able to get from his x-wife Emma for Christmas. Jon's brother Michael flew in for the occasion with Ashley and their one-and-a-half-year-old son Zen and were staying at the Hampton Inn. We had a wonderful Christmas together, playing and opening presents with Macie, Amelia, and Zen, my grandchildren. For Christmas dinner, we all walked over to Theismann's, where we had a feist. Altogether, I think we all had a wonderful Christmas.

I was back in Fort Walton Beach in time to celebrate the New Year with the Lobsterheads in Destin at the Crystal Beach Inn.

2018

Shortly after the beginning of the year, I drove back down to Tampa just in time to go to a party at Joe & Stacy's, my neighbors at the Towers. Followed a few days later by the Gasparilla Pirate Festival. My cousin Carol drove over from Tarpon Springs to join Tom and I for the weekend pirates parade. We walked our way around in the larger-than-ever crowd at the parade to beg with them for beads and trinkets from the pirates. After being tussled around in the crowd for a few hours, we adjourned to the close-by Irish Pub to listen to the music and have some food and Guinness; it was a fun weekend.

A short time later, while in Tampa, Tom suggested that we make another trip to London to visit his sister Jean and maybe find a new place to explore in Europe. Tom called his sister for a good time to visit and went to work making reservations. Shopping around, we found and booked reasonably priced roundtrip business class tickets on a Norwegian Air Boeing 787 to London-Gatwick (LGW) for May 13. We also made reservations in London at the Columbia Hotel.

On January 27, Tom and I flew down to Key West to visit Rick for a week. Stepping off the plane in Key West, it was hot and humid, and not a cloud in the sky, and since there were no festivals

going on, we anticipated an enjoyably low-keyed stay. We found Rick at the A&B Marina in Alonzo's Oyster Bar, where we joined him for lunch before stowing our gear on his boat, the Anna Virginia.

The town wasn't crowded, making it easy getting around to our favorite restaurants and bars. In the morning, we walked over to Pepe's Restaurant for breakfast, followed by a walk around the docks looking at boats. After lunch at Alonzo's, we walked over to Duval Street and Rick's Bar to while away the afternoon eating peanuts, drinking beer, and people watch. That was pretty much our routine for the week, except occasionally spending the afternoon on the A&B dock talking to the other sailors. On the 4th, we found a bar with good seats to watch Super Bowl LII, where the Philadelphia Eagles upset the New England Patriots 41-33. On our last day in Key West, while drinking beer at Rick's Bar, Rick mentioned that he was thinking about selling his boat; he was the last holdout of friends with sailboats.

Late in the afternoon of May 13 at Tampa International Airport (TPA), we boarded our overnight flight to London-Gatwick (LGW). Arriving the next morning, we checked in at the Columbia Hotel and, after getting settled in our room, walked across Kensington Gardens to the Goat Tavern for

lunch. During lunch, we tried to decide on a destination to explore and couldn't, so after lunch, we walked over to a travel agency on High Street. At the Trailfinders Agency, with help from a pretty agent, we finally decided on a few days in Athens, Greece, and made a reservation.

To celebrate, we went back to the Goat, where we stayed for a pint, some food and made contact with Jean, who invited us to come stay at her new home in Primrose Hill. It was late in the evening when we left the Goat and walked back across the park to the Columbia Hotel. Luckily when we arrived at the Lancaster Gate by our hotel, it wasn't locked up for the night.

After having breakfast and checking out of the Columbia Hotel in the morning, we made our way over to Primrose Hill near Regent's Park and found Jean's place in a three-story rowhouse on Rothwell Street. It was Tuesday, and Jean was busy with patients, so we dropped our bags and did a walkabout Primrose Hill. Just around the corner was Regent's Park Road, the main street with cafés, restaurants, and two pubs, The Queens and The Pembroke Castle, where we stopped for some food. It was crowded, but after a pint at the bar, we found a table on the patio and had some good pub food. After lunch, we walked across the R.R. Bridge by the pub to the neighboring village of Chalk Farm and walked around for a bit before heading back to Jean's.

As Jean was showing us around her new home, she mentioned that shortly before she bought it, the previous owners had a total interior rebuild and renovation done; they did a beautiful job. Over dinner that evening, Jean told us that she would be busy during the week and wouldn't be able to play until the weekend. We suggested to Jean that we go then to dinner and the theatre. It sounded like a plan, and made reservations for dinner at the Brasserie Zedel on Piccadilly Circus for Saturday and,

after looking over the reviews, bought tickets to see Chicago with Billy Flynn later that evening at the Phoenix Theatre.

Tom and I only saw Jean in passing during the week. We found The Ripe Kitchen, a café around the corner on Regent's Park Road that served a great breakfast where we eat just about every morning, then spend the rest of the day walking around the neighborhood. On one occasion, we walked across the R.R. Bridge to Chalk Farm and down Chalk Farm Road to Camden Town, where the famous Camden Market is located by the Regent's Canal. We spent most of the day there walking around the huge market that had everything, including nightclubs, an old-school pub, and cafés.

On Saturday morning, Jean drove us in her new battery-powered BMW to tour a historic estate and garden where we had lunch. That evening Jean somehow found a place to park by the Brasserie Zedel for dinner. Tom and I had dined there three years earlier with Ania Berka, who we met in Tallinn, Estonia. The Zedel is a grand Parisian brasserie best known for serving traditional French food at a good value; we had a marvelous meal. After dinner, Jean again found a place to park by The Cambridge, one of our favorite pubs just down the street from the Phoenix Theatre. After the show, we walked back to the Cambridge for drinks before heading home; it had been a full day.

The following day we took Jean to a late breakfast at the Ripe Kitchen. On the way, we noticed that Regent's Park Road was crowded with people; they were setting up for a street party. The Ripe Kitchen was crowded, but we were able to get served after a short wait. By the time we finished breakfast, the street party was underway; we joined the crowd. Later on in the afternoon, we

stopped at the Pembroke Castle for a pint or two.

The next morning Tom and I took the train to London Stansted Airport (STN) for our flight to Athens International Airport (ATH). On arrival, we took a cab and checked in at our hotel, the Divani Palace Acropolis, that's located just a short walk from the Acropolis. That evening we had cocktails at the hotel bar before dinner on the terrace with a view of the Acropolis, awesome. On my last visit to Athens in 1962, the Acropolis was mostly rubble laying around the ruins of the Parthenon and other temples on the Acropolis, with workmen putting pieces together in a restoration effort.

The next morning after a hearty breakfast at our hotel, we set out on the short walk to the Acropolis.

Once we completed the steep climb up to the Beule Gate, then by the Temple of Athena Nike, whose restoration was completed in 2010, and the Propylaea, the gateway to the Acropolis where the Parthenon, the temple of Athena, dominated. We spent the day looking over the Sanctuary of Zeus, Erechtheum, Alter of Athena, and the Arrephorion, plus most of the other temples and structures on and around the Acropolis. While we were there, the Odeon of Herodes Atticus, one of the amphitheaters around the Acropolis, was being prepared for a performance. The Acropolis is an amazing place, there was a restoration in process on many of the structures, and it appeared that there was a major restoration effort underway on the Parthenon. They've come a long way in the sixty years since my last visit. The view of Athens from the Acropolis is spectacular.

Our hotel was also close to the new Acropolis Museum, a world-class museum that opened to the public on June 20, 2009. Its main focus is on one archaeological site, the Acropolis, and the surrounding slopes, and is full of artifacts from the Greek Bronze Age to Roman and Byzantine Greece. We walked over to it and spent the day there; it's a big modern building with a lot of artifacts and information to absorb; we didn't get to see it all. On the way back to our hotel, we stopped for dinner at a small café, where we were welcomed with open arms.

We flew back to London on the 24th and would be flying from there back to Tampa on the 26th.

On our last evening in London, Jean walked us over to and along the Regent's Canal to the Feng Shang Princess Chinese floating Restaurant for dinner. During dinner, we thanked Jean for putting us up in her beautiful new home and told her all about our adventures in Athens. Jean has always been the most gracious hostess, and I look forward to coming back to London to visit again.

The flight back to Tampa on Norwegian Air was pleasant and uneventful. It seems to take me longer to adjust to the time change heading west than it is going east for some reason. Tampa in the summer is hot and humid and enjoyably slow-paced. A good time to go see the Tampa Bay Rays play at the airconditioned Tropicana. When Tom and I go to see the Rays play, we call Rick to meet us at Ferg's before the game. At the bar, Rick mentioned that he listed his boat, the Anne Virginia, with a broker, so he was serious about selling the boat he had owned for over twenty years.

I drove up to Fort Walton Beach in July to get my apartment in the El Matador ready for a visit from my son Jon and his family; besides Jon, there was his wife Donna and their daughter Macie,

Donna's sons Joshua, Wyatt, Kameron and his friend Dalton. They arrived in a rental van on Saturday the 21st for a week at the beach, and I moved into Tom's guest room at the Emerald Isle.

The weather was good, making for a great week at the beach. Everything was going good until the van took a hit at the Waffle House, where Kameron and Dalton stopped on their way back from at night at the Okaloosa Island Pier. After looking over the damage and the fact that they didn't get insurance when it was rented it, we found a shop to repair it before they left. On Friday, before they started their drive back to Kansas, I took them out to dinner at Chapala's Mexican Restaurant with all my old friends.

I had a B-66 reunion coming up in October in Las Vegas. I approached Tom to see if he was interested in going, and he was, so I signed up for it for the reunion and two of the side trips. One to Creech Air Force Base, where they train drone pilots, and the other a tour of Hover Dam.

We flew out to Las Vegas on September 30 and checked in at the Gold Coast Hotel/Casino. At the reunion welcome room, we picked up our agenda packets and had a couple of beers with some of my old flying buddies. After getting settled in our room, we went to check out the casino bar for happy hour and looked over their crap tables on the way to dinner.

In the morning, the bus left early for the half-hour drive to Creech AFB On aur arrival, we were met by anti-war demonstrators that were gathered outside the main gate. After being cleared onto the base, we received a briefing on drone operations and then a tour of the base. What I found most interesting was the room with ground control stations from where the pilots fly the General Atomic MQ-9 Reaper / Predator B on armed UAV missions in the Middle East. Each UAV has a crew of two, a pilot, and a sensor operator. A pilot in the Middle East flies the UAV off from an airfield

there and then hands over control to the crew at Creech who fly the mission; then, when the mission is complete, hands control back to him for landing to refuel and rearm. Quite an amazing operation. That evening after dinner Tom and I strolled the neighborhood and stopped at t nearby casino to check out their crap tables before heading back to our hotel.

We had an early departure in the morning to tour Hover Dam in Boulder City, Colorado. The tour started with a boat cruise with lunch on Lake Mead, followed by a guided tour of the dam. It was an interesting tour that took up most of the day.

The next day we were on our own to wander around the casinos until the reunion banquet that evening, the reunion's big event. Tom and I sat at a table with Bob Gazzola, a fellow squadron member from the 1st TRS at RAF Alconbury in the early '60s. We had a lot of war stories to tell. The reunions are always a lot of fun seeing and talking to guys I flew and partied with almost 60 years ago in Egland.

In the morning, before checking out of our hotel, there was a farewell breakfast and a business meeting where we decided on the location of the next and last reunion to be held in San Antonio, Texas.

Back in Tampa for just a short time before driving up to Fort Walton Beach to take care of business at the El Matador. I stayed in town long enough to go out for Thanksgiving dinner with Tom, his brother Jon and his wife Malissa before driving back down to Tampa.

On December 1, Tom and I drove a rental car to Fort Lauderdale and boarded the Holland America ship M.S. Oosterdam for the mid-term National Review Post Election Cruise. During the election, the Republicans kept their majority in the Senate but lost it in the House of Representatives. Meaning that not much would get done during President Trump's remaining two years unless he gets reelected for another term.

Our first port-o-call, Key West. We arrived the next day and went ashore for four hours of shore leave, just enough time to walk over to Rick's Bar on Duval Street for some beer and peanuts. From there, we sailed to Nassau in the Bahamas for another short visit, where we walked around the shops for a short while before heading back to the ship. The next leg of the cruise was a day and a half at sea to Puerta Plata in the Dominican Republic. I called my son Michael who lives just up the road from Puerta Plata in Cabarete, to come to meet us on our arrival at the port.

It was a short drive to his apartment that he had just rented, and he showed Tom and me around. He was in the process of moving in, and it was a mess. Ashley and Zen were in Canada, and Michael was trying to get the move done before they came back. The apartment was at a beautiful location on the beach in the small town of Cabarete, located on the north coast of the Dominican

Republic. We walked down the beach a short way to a bar and had a beer before heading back to Puerto Plata to our ship. On the way, we stopped at Michael's place of business, the Body Temple, where he does stretch therapy on his clients. He had found himself a place in a third-world paradise to live and work.

During the cruise, most of the talk at the seminars was about the result of the election. Where the Republicans maintained control of the Senate and the Democrats won the majority in the House of Representatives. The conversations at the dinners and cocktail parties were about what could be done before the upcoming presidential election in 2020. I think I can speak for both Tom and I that these cruises with National Review have always been interesting and well worth the money.

Back in Tampa, Tom drove up to Fort Walton Beach. I followed a short time later to my condo in the El Matador. I joined Tom, his brother Jon and his wife Melissa for Thanksgiving dinner at the Seland Restaurant before driving back down to Tampa. A short time later, I flew out to Kansas for a Christmas visit with my son Jon and his family. Michacl, Ashlcy, and their son Zen flew in from

the Dominican Republic to join the family at Jon's big house in Junction City. It was a fun time with all the kids, Kameron, Joshua, Wyatt, Macie, and Zen. Donna put on a big feed for Christmas dinner that everyone enjoyed. All in all, it was a successful and Merry Christmas for all.

I celebrated New Year at a party in the Towers, my condo in Tampa. The years seem to go by faster the older I get.

2019

Shortly after New Year, my cousin Carol drove over from Tarpon Springs to visit me in Tampa for the Gasparilla Pirates Festival parade weekend. We walked around in the crowd of revelers and watched the parade for a while, then took the streetcar to Ybor City to have dinner at Bernini's. It was a fun weekend with my Cuz.

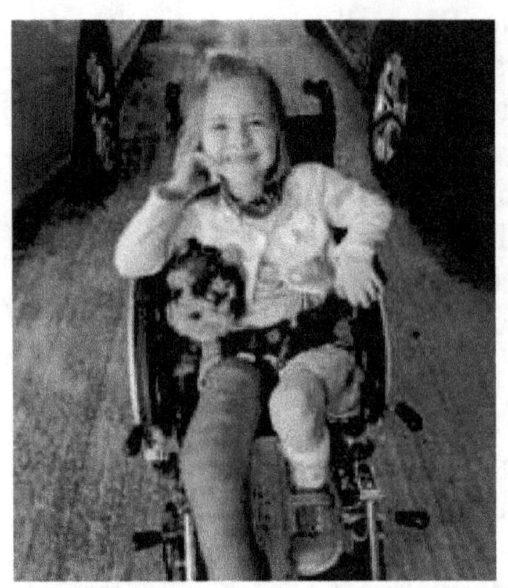

In later February, my granddaughter Macie in Alexandria, Virginia, fractured her leg and was in a cast. At about the same time, I fell while getting a cup of coffee, hit my head on the coffee table, and ended up with three stitches over my right eye. Not a good start for the year.

Back in Tampa on March 19, Tom and I went to a party at the Tampa Theater to celebrate the opening night of the Gasparilla Film Festival. It was a gala event with plenty of champagne at the historic old movie theater. For the next five days, we went to see numerous movies; some were good, and some not so good. After each of the films, we were given the opportunity to talk to the people that directed and produced them. After five days, we had movie overload, but the film festival is something we look forward to doing every year.

On May 25, Jon, Donna, Wyatt, and Macie flew into Tampa International (TPA) from Virginia to visit and spend a couple of days with me in my condo at the Towers before driving up to Fort Walton Beach with me for some time at the beach. Tom was in Tampa at the time and helped me show them around the neighborhood and Ybor City. We took them on the streetcar to Ybor City and to dinner at Bernini's.

After a couple of fun days around Tampa, we drove up to Fort Walton, where they spent the rest of the week at the El Matador and the beach before flying back to Virginia.

In July, after talking for a while about taking another trip to London to visit Tom's sister Jean, we finally booked seats on a Norwegian Air overnight flight to London-Gatwick (LGW) that departed from Tampa International (TPA) on September 8. We also made reservations at the Columbia Hotel, our favorite hotel in London.

In late July, my son Jon was laid off from his job at the F.B.I. and, within a week or two, found another analyst job back over in Afghanistan at Bagram Air Base.

On the afternoon of September 8, Tom and I took UBER to Tampa International and boarded our Norwegian Air flight that landed at Gatwick a little before noon on the 9th. It took us another hour

and a half to get to the Columbia Hotel using the Gatwick Express and underground. Once we were checked into our room, we took a walk across Kensington Gardens to one of our favorite pubs, the Goat Tavern in Kensington, for a pint, some food, and call Tom's sister Jean. She invited us to her daughter Linsey's art show on the evening of the 17th.

From the Goat, we walked down King Street a couple of blocks to a travel agency to see what kind of travel deals they had going on. After chatting with the pretty agent for a while, we signed up for a bus tour of Stonehenge and the Roman Baths on the 19th.

After three days of enjoying ourselves in London, spending a lot of time at the British Museum, which happens to be close to the Cambridge, another one of our favorite pubs. Our reservation at the Columbia Hotel ran out, so we moved around the corner to the newly renovated Best Western Mornington Hotel. It was a lot smaller than the Columbia, but it was comfortable and served a nice breakfast buffet.

On the afternoon of September 17, Tom and I made our way to the Meiner Gallery for the art show, where we met up with Tom's sister and his niece Linsey. On display at the gallery were the works of many artists, including Lindsey's. After a few hours, Tom, Jean, and I went across the street to a bar and ordered a pizza. We had a

nice chat with Jean and arranged to meet again before Lindsey left town for dinner at the Ivy, Jean's favorite restaurant, for dinner on the 20th.

After a great breakfast at the Mornington on the 19th, Tom and I took the underground to Victoria Station and wandered around looking for the bus terminal. We finally gave up and hailed a cab to take us there in time to catch the bus for the hour or so drive to Stonehenge. I had been to Stonehenge once before, in 1961, while stationed at RAF Alconbury, where I heard about it and drove over to it in my bug-eyed Sprite to check it out. What I found then were some big rocks in a circle on a deserted open field. Times have changed; the place is now a big tourist attraction crowded with tour buses and kiosks selling food and trinkets to hundreds of tourists. We joined the crowd to walk around and look at the rocks. It looked like some of the rocks had been repositioned since the last time I was there.

Our next stop on the tour was the Roman Baths at the natural hot springs in the town of Bath. The baths, built-in 60-70 A.D., were used as a public baths until Roman rule ended in the 5th century. After touring the Baths and the Museum, we walked around town and stopped at a sandwich shop close to the Bath Abbey for lunch before boarding the bus back to London.

On the afternoon of the 20th, Tom and I made our way to an outside table at the Cambridge Pub to people-watch for a while before meeting up with Jean and Lindsey at the Ivy Restaurant for dinner. We had been there before with Jean and knew they had a wonderful menu. Over dinner, we talked about our bus tour, Linsey's art show at the Meiner, and politics. During the conversation, we found that Jean didn't like Trump that much and that Lindsley was a real adamant Trump hater. Tom and I tried to point out some of Trump's achievements, but they didn't want to hear about them; it was an interesting evening.

As Jean and Lindsley drove away in Jean's electric BMW, as we walked over to the Cambridge for a nightcap. We noticed that across the street at the St Martin's Theater, Agatha Christie's The Mousetrap was playing Over a pint, we talked about maybe going to see The Mousetrap before leaving the country.

We were down to our last couple of days in London, and while walking around Trafalgar Square, we stopped at a ticket agent to buy theatre tickets to The Mousetrap. We lucked out and were able to get tickets for the 24th, the day before our flight back to Tampa.

We had arranged for a driver to pick us up at our hotel and take us to Gatwick on the morning of September 25. Our driver was there on time the next morning, and by that afternoon, we were getting off our Norwegian Air 787 at Tampa International (TPA).

I didn't stay long in Tampa; I had an appointment with my cardiologist in Fort Walton Beach, who had scheduled M.R.I. to check the size of my Aorta. What the M.R.I. showed was that the Aorta hadn't grown any, but it revealed that I had a 3cm tumor on my left kidney. He made an appointment for me to see a Urologist. She told me that the tumor was cancerous and needed to be cut out, probably taking the whole kidney. That didn't sound like a good prognosis to me, so I called Moffitt Cancer Center in Tampa and made an appointment.

My son Jon was back in Virginia after being in Afghanistan for only four months. His company closed down its operations ending Jon's job at Bagram Air Base, and sent him home. Arriving back in Virginia and needing a job, it didn't take him long to find one at Fort Reilly, Kansas, near his house in Junction City. By early November, they completed the move to Kansas in time for Thanksgiving.

I drove down to Tampa for my appointment at Moffitt Cancer Center with all my medical records and a DVD copy of the M.R.I. After more testing in early December, their diagnosis confirmed that the tumor was cancerous and needed to be removed. They scheduled me for surgery on January 7.

I flew out to Kansas on December 23 to spend Christmas with my family. Everyone was there Jon, Donna, Macie, Wyatt, Joshua, Kameron, Michael, Ashley, and Zen. The only ones not there were Elizabeth and Emma, granddaughters that I hadn't seen or heard from in three years. It was wonderful Christmas watching Macie and Zen chase each other around and feasting on Donna's Christmas dinner. I believe everyone enjoyed themselves.

I was back in Tampa on the 26th and spent a quiet New Year's at the Towers getting ready for a date with my surgeon, Dr. Manley, at Moffitt Cancer Center.

2020

In the early morning of January 7, Tom drove me over to the Moffitt Cancer Center. The surgery successfully removed the tumor from my left kidney. After two days, they released me to

309

recuperate in my apartment at the Towers with an appointment for a follow-up C.T. scan in three months.

In late January, my son Michael flew in from the Dominican Republic to check up on his daddy. He stayed for a week and did the cooking while I laid around doing nothing. He had a cold, but toward the end of his stay, he was on the road to recovery. Just before he departed, we took the streetcar to Ybor City, where they were still celebrating the Gasparilla Pirates Festival, and had dinner at Bernini's on an outside table to people-watch.

The China Covid 19 virus invaded the United States about this time, and I had a cold. I probably caught it from Michael, I thought I had the virus, so I stayed in my cave watching Netflix and recovered except for a persistent cough.

At my follow-up appointment at Moffitt, they found no signs of cancer. I told them about my cough, and they sent me to Toratix's to see a Pulmonologist. They did more testing and diagnosed me of having a .05cm nodule in my left lung and some COPD. They put me on the drug "Trelegy".

St Petersburg, Florida.

In March, I drove up to Fort Walton Beach to get my taxes done. While in town, I had the opportunity to see my old friends for dinner at Chapala Authentic Mexican Restaurant. We had a good crowd of around 28 people.

In May, Kamoren graduated from Kansas State University with an Architectural Engineering degree and found a job with a firm in

I was spending a good part of the year in doctor's offices and hiding in my cave from the virus. The only highlight of the year was that Michael and Ashley had their second child in the Dominican Republic. Ashley gave birth to my sixth grandchild, Samadhi Rae Francis Gebhardt, on July 30.

President Trump fast-tracked the development of a vaccine to fight the virus. When it became available in November, I called the V.A. in Tampa to put me on the list to get the shot. Trump lost the 2020 Presidential Election to the Democrat Joe Biden. The Democrats also maintained a majority in the House of Representatives, and the Senate split 50/50. Later on, in November, I joined Tom and his brother Jon with his wife Malissa at the Sealand Restaurant in Fort Walton Beach for Thanksgiving dinner.

In December, I drove down to my apartment at the Towers in Tampa for Christmas and the New Year. It had been a bummer of a year with the China virus hanging over us, causing everyone to hunker down in their homes.

Chapter Fifteen: 2021 - 2022

On January 27, the V.A. called me in to get the Pfizer Covid 19 shot and again on February 17 for the second dose. It looks like another year of the China virus and, for me, seeing doctors. It looks like I'm not going to do a lot of traveling again this year.

In March, I drove up to Fort Walton Beach to get my taxes ready for the I.R.S. While in town, I met up with the Lobsterheads at The Wine Bar in Destin for dinner.

Later on, in May, I drove back down to Tampa and Joined Tom for dinner at Bernini's in Ybor City. Kameron drove over from St Pete to join us at Bernini's and gave us an update on his job. Baseball season started, and the Rays were in town, and we decided to go to a game. On the way to the game, we would pick Kamoren up at his apartment on the way.

On June 27, Tom and I drove over to his apartment in St Pete. After Kameron showed us around, we drove over to Ferg's for beer and food before the game. At the game, the Rays lost to the L. A. Angels 6-4.

In May, I drove up to Fort Walton Beach to get my apartment ready for a visit from Jon and his family from Kansas. Jon, Donna, Wyatt, and Macie arrived at the El Matador on July 31, ready for a week at the beach. Joshua, who was working, wasn't with them this year. The next day Donna and Wyatt drove down to St Petersburg to visit Kameron for a couple of days, leaving Jon and Macie at the beach. Over the next couple of days, before Donna and Wyatt came back, Macie, with

a little help from her daddy, caught her first wave and became an enthusiastic surfer girl. The rest of the week, they took advantage of perfect weather and spent most of their remaining days in town at the beach. The afternoon before leaving to drive back to Kansas, I took them to A.J's Oyster Shanty just down the street on Okaloosa Island for some seafood.

Shortly after Jon and his family left Fort Walton Beach, I drove down to Tampa for a follow-up appointment at Moffitt Cancer Center. They found no reoccurrence of cancer, that my lungs were stable, and scheduled me for a backup appointment in a year. Good news, but I was still coughing up a storm and didn't feel like I was getting any better.

It seems like I'm spending a lot of my time driving back and forth between Tampa and Fort Walton Beach to doctor appointments and less traveling around for pleasure. Now there's a new variant of the China virus going around the country to further slow things down and stop me from traveling out of the country even if I wanted to.

For the rest of the time during the summer, I was laying low in Tampa, going to St. Pete for a Rays baseball game once in a while and going to Ybor City for dinner on Fridays with Tom when he was in town.

In October, I went to the Tampa October Fest with Tom, where they had some good German beer, food, and music. It was a friendly crowd; we spent the afternoon there people-watching and listening to the oom-pah band.

Nothing of interest happened until I flew out to Kansas to spend Christmas at Jon's place in Junction City with my family. I sent airline tickets to Michael in the Dominican Republic, so he and his family to join us. Unfortunately, they didn't have their antivirus shot and were not allowed on the plane. I was hoping to see their daughter Samadhi who is almost a year and a half-year-old, my granddaughter, for the first time.

Christmas in Junction City was a lot of fun with Jon, Donna, Joshua, Kameron, Wyatt, Mancy, and their dog Saber. We were also joined by Jon's daughter and my granddaughter Amelia who

flew in from New Mexico. Donna cooked up a turkey for dinner on Christmas Day. While I was there, I sort of helped Jon shore up his carriage house and play with his still that he bought online to make some booze that everyone was afraid to drink. All in all, I believe everyone had a wonderful time.

I flew back to Tampa on the 26th and brought in the New Year in my apartment at the Towers. While sitting on my balcony watching the fireworks, I realized that over the last two years, I really hadn't done much except visit family, friends, and doctors. The China virus and my health have brought an end to my international travels.

For over eight decades of my life, I have been on a grand adventure. I have no idea what the future holds; maybe I will get the opportunity to experience new adventures; then again, nothing goes on forever!

www.ingramcontent.com/pod-product-compliance
Lightning Source LLC
Chambersburg PA
CBHW080344030726
47598CB00009B/2624